Harmony in Haydn and Mozart

Integrating Schenkerian tools and an innovative approach to harmony, David Damschroder provides numerous penetrating analyses of works by Haydn and Mozart. A series of introductory chapters assist readers in developing their analytical capacity. Beginning with short excerpts from string quartets, the study proceeds by assessing the inner workings of twelve expositions from Haydn piano sonatas, six arias in G Minor from Mozart operas, and three rondos in D Major from piano concertos by Haydn and Mozart. In the Masterworks section that follows, Damschroder presents detailed analyses of six movements from symphonies, chamber music, and opera by Haydn and Mozart, and compares his outcomes with those of other analysts, including V. Kofi Agawu, Robert O. Gjerdingen, James Hepokoski and Warren Darcy, Carl Schachter, and James Webster. The book represents an important contribution to modern analytical discourse on a treasured body of music, and an assessment of recent accomplishments within that realm.

DAVID DAMSCHRODER is Professor of Music Theory at the University of Minnesota. His current research focuses on harmony in tonal music, a project that began with a careful examination of historical analytical practices, the basis for his *Thinking About Harmony: Historical Perspectives on Analysis* (Cambridge, 2008). The project continues with focused studies on selected repertoires: *Harmony in Schubert* (Cambridge, 2010), and the present volume. Damschroder is the co-author of *Music Theory from Zarlino to Schenker* (1990), and his articles and reviews have appeared in many publications including *Music Theory Spectrum*, *The Journal of Music Theory*, and *Music Theory Online*.

Harmony in Haydn and Mozart

DAVID DAMSCHRODER

The University of Minnesota

CAMBRIDGE UNIVERSITY PRESS
Cambridge, New York, Melbourne, Madrid, Cape Town,
Singapore, São Paulo, Delhi, Mexico City

Cambridge University Press
The Edinburgh Building, Cambridge CB2 8RU, UK

Published in the United States of America by Cambridge University Press, New York

www.cambridge.org
Information on this title: www.cambridge.org/9781107025349

© David Damschroder 2012

This publication is in copyright. Subject to statutory exception
and to the provisions of relevant collective licensing agreements,
no reproduction of any part may take place without the written
permission of Cambridge University Press.

First published 2012

Printed and bound in the United Kingdom by the MPG Books Group

A catalogue record for this publication is available from the British Library

Library of Congress Cataloguing in Publication data
Damschroder, David.
Harmony in Haydn and Mozart / David Damschroder.
　p.　cm.
Includes bibliographical references and index.
ISBN 978-1-107-02534-9
1. Haydn, Joseph, 1732–1809 – Criticism and interpretation.　2. Mozart, Wolfgang Amadeus, 1756–1791 – Criticism and interpretation.　3. Music – 18th century – History and criticism.　4. Music – 18th century – Analysis, appreciation.　5. Harmony.　I. Title.
ML195.D36　2012
780.92′2–dc23

2012000795

ISBN 978-1-107-02534-9 Hardback

Cambridge University Press has no responsibility for the persistence or
accuracy of URLs for external or third-party internet websites referred to
in this publication, and does not guarantee that any content on such
websites is, or will remain, accurate or appropriate.

Contents

Preface [*page* vii]

PART ONE METHODOLOGICAL ORIENTATION

1 Harmonic practice in the late eighteenth century: twelve excerpts from string quartets by Haydn and Mozart [3]

2 Anatomy of the I–II♯–V two-part exposition: twelve keyboard sonatas by Haydn [41]

3 Composition in a minor key: six arias in G Minor from operas by Mozart [89]

4 The happy ending: three sonata-rondos in D Major from piano concertos by Haydn and Mozart [120]

PART TWO MASTERPIECES

5 Haydn: Symphony No. 45 in F♯ Minor ("Farewell"), movement 2 [153]
in response to James Webster

6 Haydn: String Quartet in G Minor (op. 20, no. 3), movement 3 [166]
in response to Robert O. Gjerdingen

7 Mozart: String Quintet in C Major (K. 515), movement 1 [183]
in response to V. Kofi Agawu and Michael Spitzer

8 Mozart: *Don Giovanni* (K. 527), Act I, Scene 13: Donna Anna's recitative and aria [205]
in response to Carl Schachter

9 Mozart: Symphony No. 40 in G Minor (K. 550), movement 3, Trio [221]
in response to Leonard B. Meyer

10 Haydn: Symphony No. 96 in D Major ("Miracle"),
movement 1   [232]
in response to Warren Darcy, James Hepokoski, and Lauri Suurpää

Notes   [247]
List of references to music examples   [283]
Select bibliography   [284]
Index of Haydn's works   [294]
Index of Mozart's works   [295]
Index of names and concepts   [296]

Preface

Within the bewilderingly diverse array of musical repertoires at our disposal, the music of Haydn and Mozart holds a special place. To take pleasure in and to be moved by their works is to celebrate the human condition in a unique and wondrous way and to become part of an unbroken chain of enthusiasts extending back over two hundred years. For many musicians and aficionados, this repertoire remains the core of a revered tradition. Such favor makes it especially worthy of our attention, as does its extraordinary impact upon later generations of composers. By presenting in-depth analyses of a carefully chosen assemblage of works by Haydn and Mozart, with emphasis on harmony, I offer guidance to serious listeners and performers who seek to develop fresh ways of thinking about this music, thereby deepening their understanding of how it is structured and enhancing their capacity to bring it to life in performance.

This volume is part of a broader project that began with a consideration of how harmonic analysis emerged as a field of musical inquiry: *Thinking About Harmony: Historical Perspectives on Analysis* (Cambridge University Press, 2008; hereafter abbreviated as *TAH*). I then developed my own distinctive approach to harmonic analysis, integrating various historical notions, the Schenkerian perspective, and my own speculations in the context of music by Franz Schubert: *Harmony in Schubert* (Cambridge University Press, 2010; hereafter abbreviated as *Schubert*). Currently I am testing and refining those ideas in the context of music by other composers. *Harmony in Haydn and Mozart* is in some ways a more foundational book than is *Schubert*, and readers may prefer to start here. (Eventually other volumes may appear as well. Avid readers may choose to proceed chronologically, or in the order of publication, or according to which composers interest them the most.) As I did also in *Schubert*, I provide a foundation for my perspective in an introductory Methodological Orientation – here encompassing the first four chapters – that explores twelve excerpts from Haydn and Mozart string quartets, twelve Haydn piano sonata expositions in major keys, six Mozart opera arias in the key of G Minor, and three sonata-rondos from Haydn and Mozart piano concertos. I assume a prior exposure to Roman-numeral harmonic analysis and to the Schenkerian perspective, especially that presented in Schenker's *Der freie Satz* (Vienna: Universal Edition, 1935; translation of Oswald Jonas's 1956 edition by Ernst Oster as *Free Composition*, New York: Longman, 1979; hereafter abbreviated as *FC*). Though nowadays analytical work is being pursued from a wide range of perspectives, to the extent that some (for example, Joseph Kerman and Robert O. Gjerdingen) question the utility of the Schenkerian approach, I hope to demonstrate through my project not only that it offers extraordinary insights, but also that it may serve as a foundation for potent new developments in analytical thinking. Consequently my discussion of harmony takes place in the context of an exploration of a work's underlying voice-leading structure. Whereas in *Schubert* the relationship between harmony and narrative often came to the fore, in *Harmony in Haydn and Mozart* issues of form – especially the various manifestations of sonata form – often intersect my harmonic investigation.

My original intent when writing *Schubert* was to offer a thorough exposition of my own views on harmony, tracing their development out of the analytical practices I had explored in *TAH*. At the urging of a colleague and through the coincidental alignment of repertoire by Schubert that I wanted to address and the published analyses of several other authors, I expanded my purview by integrating my analytical presentations with assessments of alternative approaches to the same works, a practice that not only made for a more varied and engaging commentary but also led me in directions I likely would not have pursued without the prodding of those other authors. By both seeing how my analyses unfold and also coming to understand why I do not proceed in certain other ways, readers attain a more thorough and penetrating comprehension of the analytical perspective that I espouse. I have elected to continue the practice of presenting analyses in conjunction with those of other authors in this volume. Though this is a somewhat dangerous undertaking, in that I have not invested the many thousands of hours pursuing each alternative methodology as I have my own and thus might inadvertently have taken some wrong turns, I accept that risk as healthier for the field than the alternative: that only committed advocates of a system, who indeed have spent those thousands of hours attaining expertise, be permitted to offer criticism. The heart of the book, following the Methodological Orientation, is a Masterpieces section consisting of six chapters that juxtapose my interpretations of movements by Haydn or Mozart with critical commentary on analyses of the same works by others, set off from the flow of my analyses via shading. (Readers may choose to skip over these sections without disturbing the continuity of my analytical discussion.) The alternative analyses appear in journals and books that should be available at any music research library (and in some cases also on the Internet), allowing committed readers to maximize their exposure to the issues at hand. From Chapter 2 onwards, readers will need to obtain scores for the works discussed. Though the Methodological Orientation should be read first and in the order presented, the chapters of the Masterpieces section, which is arranged chronologically, may be read selectively or out of order.

My work stems from the premise that one will succeed best in listening to and performing music by coming to understand the logic through which the composer has set down a composition's pitches. (That exploration may complement the pursuit of various other worthwhile perspectives, such as music/text relationships or the semiotic study of musical topics.) Though ultimately an analytical fluency will develop, in the initial stages one needs to proceed slowly and methodically in working through the substance of a composition. My project is designed to help committed aspirants make progress in developing that insight. Since many approaches to analysis are available, I offer readers the opportunity to compare a range of procedures and their outcomes. Though I will show a preference for some analytical practices over others, ultimately readers must decide for themselves which path(s) to pursue as they progress in their artistic developments.

I appreciate the feedback on drafts of this work that I have received from various quarters. I also acknowledge the support of a single-semester leave and an Imagine Fund award from the University of Minnesota, which have allowed me to bring this work to fruition sooner than I had anticipated and to have access to a wide range of materials. Pete Smucker has provided expert setting of the music examples.

Conventions regarding note relations, chords, keys, and Roman numerals

Pitch simultaneities (such as C-E-G) are indicated using hyphens (-), while pitch successions (such as C–E–G) are indicated using dashes (–). Direction may be indicated in melodic succession: ascending as C<E<G, descending as G>E>C. A black arrow may be used to indicate a descending-fifth relationship that is or emulates a $V^{(7)}$–I succession, whereas an outline arrow may be used to indicate a succession from a chord of the augmented-sixth type: for example, C→F–D→G→C; C–A♭–D⇒G→C.

Keys and chords are distinguished as follows: C Major (with a capital M) is the key of C Major; C major (with a small m) is a C major chord.

Unless another analyst's methodology is being discussed, Roman numerals are presented in capital letters regardless of a chord's quality, modified by one or more accidentals if the chord is altered. Thus C Major: I II V I and not I ii V I; and C Minor: I II V♯ I♮ (closing on a major tonic), not i ii° V I. An accidental to the left of the numeral corresponds to the chord's root, to the right corresponds to its third. If the chordal fifth, seventh, or ninth is altered, the analytical symbol will incorporate the corresponding Arabic numeral, as in C Minor: II$_{♯}^{5♮}$. (Arrow notation – here II→ – offers an attractive, though less precise, alternative to the complete analytical symbol.) The bullet symbol (•) indicates an absent root. For example, B-D-F in C Major will be analyzed as V$_{•}^{7}$ (or, with less precision, as V→).

Likewise a progression of chordal roots generally is presented in capital letters (C–D–G–C), though on occasions when quality is a factor in the discussion a capital letter may refer to major quality, a small letter to minor quality, and a small letter followed by a degree circle (°) to diminished quality: for example, C–a–F–d–b°–G–e–C.

A bracket is used to connect the analytical notation for two musical events that normally would follow one another but that in the context under discussion occur at the same moment: for example, C ⌐F♯ B⌐ E when an F♯-A♯-C♯ chord sounds with, rather than before, root B in a descending circle of fifths.

Parentheses around a pitch in an analytical example indicate that it is not actually present in the score, though it is understood. Parentheses around analytical notation may refer to the expansion of a deeper-level harmony (for example, when I is expanded by I IV V I) or to the harmonic assertion of a voice-leading phenomenon (for example, when the 6 phase of a I$^{5-6}$, as in C-E-G to C-E-A, asserts the harmonic role of VI). Open parentheses designate a voice-leading transition between two harmonies. For example, I ( ) IV indicates that the chords between I and IV (perhaps a circular, parallel, or sequential progression) do not themselves participate in the harmonic progression, but instead serve to connect the harmonies I and IV.

When a score's chordal spellings do not coincide with the structurally appropriate spellings (for example, the substitution of easier-to-read F♯-A-C♯ for cumbersome G♭-B♭♭-D♭), I generally will use the structurally appropriate spellings in my examples and commentaries, often placing the enharmonic spellings within square brackets to assist readers in locating the pitches in question within the score.

I pay very close attention to hierarchies among pitches and chords. To alert readers to various hierarchical relationships I often will underline some pitch names to indicate their hierarchical prominence. For example, C<E D>B C above bass C–G–C conveys the relationship between two unfolded strands: a more prominent outer strand E>D>C, and a subordinate inner strand C>B<C.

Because diverse musical contexts are analyzed using graphs, it is difficult to pin down precise guidelines for how their notation should be crafted and read. Many styles of "Schenkerian" notation have appeared since the publication of *FC* (which itself does not present a single normative style). I regard the creation of a reductive graph as an art, endeavoring to use notation that is as clear and informative as possible. In general, open noteheads in my graphs represent deeper structural or harmonic events than filled-in noteheads, while notes at the endpoints of beams or slurs are deeper than internal notes. Notes connected to a beam by a stem are more integral to the structure than those that are not. Especially in the early chapters I offer abundant commentary, which will give readers the opportunity to develop facility in interpreting my notation. Occasional annotations using abbreviations indicate functions of individual pitches or formal events, as follows:

ant.	anticipation
C	closing zone
CP	chromatic passing note
EEC	essential expositional closure
ESC	essential structural closure
HC	half cadence
IAC	imperfect authentic cadence
IN	incomplete neighboring note
MC	medial caesura
N	neighboring note
P	an individual pitch: passing note
P	form: primary-theme zone
PAC	perfect authentic cadence
P^{rf}	primary-theme zone (refrain) in a sonata-rondo
prg.	progression
S	secondary-theme zone
susp.	suspension
TR	transition
W	wobble

Of course, the graphs often will incorporate Roman-numeral harmonic analyses, and in this regard I often depart from Schenker's practice. Because it is innovative, I document my Roman-numeral usage very carefully as the chapters unfold.

Because measure numbers are a pervasive feature in my close analyses, I have developed an abbreviated style of reference, in the form measure$_{\text{beat}}$. For example, the symbol 2_3 indicates the third beat of measure 2. Generally the word "measure" will not precede the number. I regard measures in $\frac{2}{2}$ and $\frac{6}{8}$ as containing two beats. A measure designation such as 14/16 means that a given chord is prolonged from measure 14 through measure 16, with contrasting content occurring between statements of the chord, whereas the designation 14–16 indicates a continuous prolongation of a single chord without significant internal contrast. The symbol 15|16 indicates measure 16 along with its upbeat.

PART ONE

Methodological Orientation

1 | Harmonic practice in the late eighteenth century: twelve excerpts from string quartets by Haydn and Mozart

Phrases and periods offer an ideal starting point for an exploration of harmony in Haydn and Mozart. What occurs in these small-scale contexts often will translate into how broader musical expanses develop. The twelve excerpts presented in this chapter exemplify many of the hallmark features of the style. Our close attention to the details of their construction and careful consideration of how to convey our insights using analytical notation will prepare us for the study of more extended and complex works in subsequent chapters.

The analytical graphs in this chapter display each excerpt's deepest level as background structure. Though this practice artificially widens the range of analytical notation, a useful clarity results. Readers should keep in mind that, if these graphs were incorporated within analyses of the complete movements, what appear to be background events would in most cases become middleground events, and many of the open noteheads consequently would become filled-in noteheads.

Haydn: String Quartet in D Major (op. 76, no. 5), movement 1, measures 0|1–8

To establish a key one engages the three members of its tonic chord in prominent and meaningful ways. In the opening measures of Haydn's Quartet in D Major [1.1a], those pitches form a dynamic ascending arpeggiation (A<D<F♯), with passing note E connecting the tonic's root and third [1.1b].[1] In this case $\hat{3}$ (F♯) serves as the *Kopfton* (literally "head-tone"), the pitch from which the excerpt's deep structural descent – the ultimate tonic-confirming event – will emanate. The melody also presents an inner strand – D>C♯<D – that coordinates with the D<E<F♯ third above it in the manner of first-species counterpoint. (The $\frac{E}{C\sharp}$ and $\frac{F\sharp}{D}$ thirds are *unfolded* – that is, presented successively rather than simultaneously.) With the cello's concurrent pedal point on D, tonic D Major is firmly grounded. Yet the arpeggiation of the tonic triad's pitches generally is not sufficient for

establishing the key. (Perhaps Haydn is here arpeggiating the V harmony in the key of G Major.) A chord progression forms a more secure foundation, and thus the very tonic harmony that is being established must be left and then later cadentially confirmed. In a major key such a progression generally will proceed from I through II or IV to V, which may serve as the cadential goal (HC) or lead within the phrase to the restored tonic (either IAC or PAC).[2] Though I–II or I–IV may transpire directly, Haydn and Mozart often pursue a more nuanced connection: when I proceeds to II, I-space often will be extended via a *5–6 shift* (to be discussed later); when I proceeds to IV, the tonic harmony often will evolve via *dominant emulation*. Whereas D-F♯-A in Haydn's quartet is a neutral entity without a specific harmonic tendency, the evolved state D-F♯-A-C♮ during 2_1 points vigorously towards IV. Haydn inserts C♮ at the exact moment when the ascending tonic arpeggiation peaks. The augmented-fourth dissonance, prominently positioned at the edges of the texture, propels the progression forward, exiting I-space. The subdominant arrival (in first inversion) is made more emphatic through a *forzando*.

The model in **1.1c** displays the first violin's G as an *incomplete* neighbor, despite the fact that an F♯ sounds immediately thereafter. Though the pitches D, F♯, and A often assert themselves as the tonic harmony in D Major, they may sound together in other contexts as well. Here they play a connective role within IV^{5-6} (G-B-D to G-B-E, in which the 5-phase chord of the 5–6 shift is inverted). The F♯ that follows G is not a restoration of the *Kopfton*, but instead a local passing note leading to E (= $\hat{2}$). Determining the hierarchical relationships among chords is one of the most challenging aspects of harmonic analysis. Here I propose that the G major subdominant is the principal connector between the opening tonic and the cadential dominant of measure 4. (The 6-phase G-B-E extends IV-space, introducing the dominant's $\hat{2}$ in the manner of an anticipation.) An alternative hypothesis would propose that I-space extends through the end of measure 2 and that the following E minor supertonic is the principal connector. I reject that hypothesis due to the prominence of the G major arrival (dissonance resolution, melodic peak, *forzando*, octave leap in the cello line) and the placement of the potential second-inversion tonic harmony within a voice exchange ($^G_B X^B_G$ in the second violin and cello), a common context for a passing chord.

The harmonic analysis in **1.1c** differs from the current conventional practice in several ways. Capital Roman numerals track the progression of roots within the specified key. Arabic numbers and accidentals account for all substantial additions and adjustments to the diatonic triadic pitch

Harmonic practice in the late eighteenth century 5

Example 1.1 Haydn: String Quartet in D Major (op. 76, no. 5), mvmt. 1 (a) Score of mm. 0|1–8; (b) Analysis of mm. 0|1–2; (c) Analysis of mm. 1–3; (d) Analysis of mm. 0|1–4.

content, here documenting the addition of a minor seventh within I-space (7♮) and the 5–6 shift that extends IV-space. Note that these numbers are calculated in terms of the chords in their root positions: in the quartet the evolved tonic occurs in $^4_2$ position, whereas the subdominant occurs in $^6_3$ position. (Readers who would like to acknowledge inversions may add

Example 1.1 (cont.)

(c)

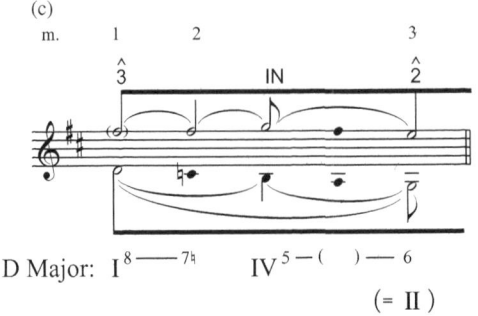

D Major: $\text{I}^{8\text{---}7\natural}$ $\text{IV}^{5-(\quad)-6}$
$\phantom{\text{D Major: I}^{8\text{---}7\natural}\text{ IV}^{5-(\quad)}}(=\text{II})$

(d)

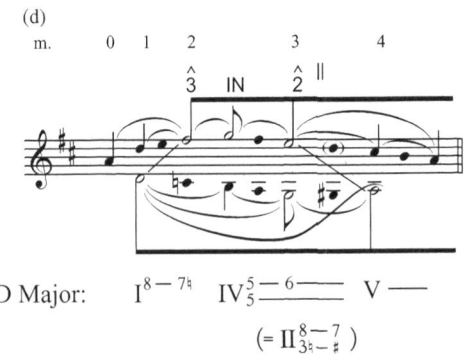

D Major: $\text{I}^{8-7\natural}$ IV^{5-6}_{5} ——— V ———
$\phantom{\text{D Major: I}^{8-7\natural}\text{ }}(=\text{II}^{8-7}_{3\natural-\sharp})$

those figured-bass numbers in a separate row *above* the Roman numerals, avoiding conflicts with the root-oriented Arabic numbers placed *to the right of* the Roman numerals.) When a chord is extended via its 6 phase, the 6 might function as no more than an anticipation of the following chord's fifth (here the dominant's E). Yet often this 6-phase chord will evolve in a way that causes us to interpret the 6 as an asserted chordal root. When that occurs the root function is acknowledged via a Roman numeral placed within parentheses below the Arabic 6. (Because **1.1c** does not extend beyond the downbeat of measure 3, the evolved state E-G♯-B-(D) is not displayed. It is this latter chord, shown in **1.1d**, that confirms E's role as an asserted root.)

Neither the C♮ of measure 2 nor the G♯ of measure 3 induces a shift of tonal center. (See **1.1d**.) The chords in which they reside are not dominants in the keys of G Major and A Major, as the conventional symbols V/IV and V/V propose, but instead retain their roles as I and II, respectively, within D Major. Through chordal evolution the fifth-relationships between I and IV and between II and V *emulate* that which occurs between V and I. (Dominant-emulating relationships may be displayed using a solid arrow, here as I➔ IV and II➔ V.) These moments are surges in which the inherent potentiality for a descending-fifth harmonic succession is enhanced through chromatic and dissonant accretions. Not two individual harmonies – for example, I followed by V^7/IV – but instead two phases of a single harmonic initiative.

Whereas the *Kopfton* F♯ arrives as the I-space expansion concludes, its successor E sounds even before the onset of V-space. (Note the diagonal lines connecting background $\frac{F\sharp}{D}$ and $\frac{E}{A}$ in **1.1d**.) By the time soprano F♯ sounds, the bass has begun its trajectory downwards to the subdominant root G; by the time the subdominant root G sounds, IV has proceeded to its 6 phase; by the time the dominant root A sounds, the descent from E to A has reached C♯.[3] The upward leap to B in the first violin line at 3_2 may seem to be an inconsequential diversion from the melody's central thrust, yet its repetition during the consequent phrase is extended to a high D, placing the passing note that fills in the E>C♯ third in the spotlight. This D forms a dissonant diminished fifth against the cello's G♯, dynamically propelling the surge towards V and justifying the placement of D within measure 3 during the antecedent phrase.[4]

Though concluding the phrase with a half cadence (HC) is sufficient for establishing D Major as the tonic, often such an antecedent will be followed by a consequent phrase that closes more decisively, restoring the tonic harmony in the context of a PAC, as is the case here. The $\hat{2}$ left dangling at the end of **1.1d** will, after a repetition of the $\hat{3}>\hat{2}$ span, achieve $\hat{1}$ at the close of the consequent phrase. (The *interruption* of the $\hat{3}$–$\hat{2}$–$\hat{1}$ descent at $\hat{2}$, indicated by the two vertical lines to the right of the number $\hat{2}$ in **1.1d**, results in the creation of a binary period.) In measure 7 the evolution of II extends further than that in measure 3. The transformation of E-G-B into E-G♯-B-D (measure 3) is sufficient to provide a surge, with diminished fifth $\frac{D}{G\sharp}$ targeting the dominant's root and third. In measure 7 Haydn instead writes G♯-B-D-E♯, which I interpret as G♯-B-D-F♮ (II with absent root, raised third, and added seventh and minor ninth, whose complete analytical symbol would appear as II$^{9\natural}_{7}_{\sharp}$, the bullet indicating the absent root). Why did Haydn write E♯, rather than F♮? In that the dominant during 8_1 is embellished by a $^6_4$, a detour to F♯ precedes the resolution to E. Thus instead of a direct F♮>E connection, Haydn steers the motion in the upward direction with the spelling E♯. Against this F♯ the first violin D at 8_1 restores the obligatory register after the brief upward excursion. Once these pitches descend into the dominant chord members E and C♯, the broad descent from $\hat{3}$ concludes with $\hat{1}$ at 8_2, forming a PAC.[5]

Haydn: String Quartet in D Minor (op. 42), movement 3, measures 1–12

The analysis of an excerpt from Haydn's Quartet in D Minor [**1.2a**] brings to the fore the question of exactly what constitutes harmonic progression. I doubt whether a precise border between the realms of melodic embellishment and harmony can in all cases be determined. Consider the models assembled in **1.2b**. Can one state with certainty whether the internal chords result from two melodic neighboring notes, or from a shift of root by a fifth (B♭–F–B♭, B♭–E♭–B♭, etc.)? How might context or duration affect our perception of melodic versus harmonic activity?[6] In my view Roman numeral labels (I–V–I, I–IV–I, etc.) too often are applied indiscriminately. As a remedy I propose the notion of *assertion*: because a combination of pitches might or might not convey a harmonic intent, the analyst must decide that a chord asserts itself as a harmony before proceeding to label it with a Roman numeral. If such a chord does not warrant a harmonic interpretation, it might be referred to as an *embellishing chord*. Note how both Models 1 and 2 correspond to initiatives within the quartet movement's first two measures (the first with an added E♭, the second with the $^6_4$ chord *unfurled* into $^6_3$ position and the restored tonic also sounding in $^6_3$ position). I suggest that neither of the internal chords asserts itself as a harmony.[7] Likewise F-A-C is prolonged during measure 5 and most of measure 6. The B♭-D-F chord that sounds during 5_2 is an embellishing chord (unfurled from $^6_4$ into $^5_3$ position), corresponding to Model 4. (Model 3 does not occur in this excerpt, but does appear – transposed up a major third – in **1.1a**, measure 4.)

This twelve-measure excerpt projects the ternary form a_1–b–a_2, with four measures devoted to each component. The initial tonic, prolonged for two measures, leads directly to IV. This harmonic succession is aided by chordal inversion: the tonic's bass D during 2_2 ascends by step to E♭. The B♭<D third in the cello (realized as a descending sixth) is paralleled by D<F in the first violin, which in turn motivates a G>E♭ third during IV$^{5-6}$ (measures 3 and 4). Such activity above the structural line emanating from the *Kopfton*, displayed using filled-in noteheads in my analytical graph [**1.2c**], is very common in tonal music.

Example 1.2 Haydn: String Quartet in D Minor (op. 42), mvmt. 3 (a) Score of mm. 1–12; (b) Four models for auxiliary chords; (c) Analysis of mm. 1–12.

Example 1.2 (cont.)

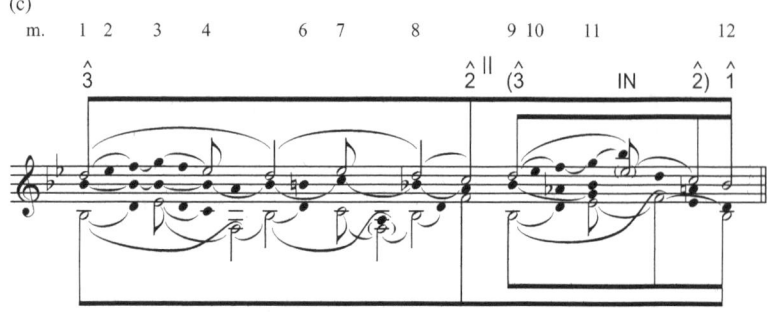

A comparison of the score and my reading of IV$^{5-6}$ in **1.2c** reveals that the score's first violin line lags: the pitch F "belongs" at the end of measure 3, while the pitch E♭ "belongs" at the downbeat of measure 4.[8] The proposed foundational structure, in which E♭>D>C and G>F>E♭ lines descend in parallel tenths, corresponds (switching the positions of the two lines) to a passage from the String Quartet in D Major discussed above (see **1.1c**), where the B>A>G and G>F♯>E lines descend in parallel sixths during the transition from IV's 5 to 6 phase. (I refer to the soprano line as presented in **1.2c**, which Haydn subjects to rhythmic displacements.) In both cases a passing chord containing the pitches – but not projecting the function – of the tonic comes between these two more foundational chords.[9] Note that in this case the 6-phase chord does not assert itself as II. (That is, the pitch C at 4_1 is an anticipation of the dominant's fifth without also taking over from E♭ the office of *generating* the other chord members that sound concurrently.) The phrase proceeds from this IV$^{5-6}$ to its expected successor, V^7, and concludes with an IAC at 4_2.

The b section opens with an F major chord. Granted, the b section's goal (at 8_2) likewise is an F major chord. Yet these four measures do not project a large-scale extension of V-space. The earlier chord, emanating from the cadence in measure 4, resides within an expansion of I-space, a common occurrence in an internal phrase that leads ultimately to V. Just as the third (sixth) from B♭ to D is conveyed in the cello during measures 1 and 2, the B♭

of measure 4 leads to D (also with *forzando*) at the end of measure 6. In this case the tonic harmony shifts from its 5 phase to its 6 phase during the prolongation. Whereas the diatonic 6-phase chord would sound as B♭-D-G, here G is asserted as a root, from which the evolved chord (G)-B♮-D-F emanates. (Note that the 6 phase's eponymous 6 – G – is absent from the chord as presented by Haydn. This is a common occurrence.[10]) In my view F-A-C in measures 5 and 6 is an embellishing chord functioning like the middle chord of **1.2b**, Model 1, though with the restored tonic displaced by its 6 phase. (That is, the chord's 5-phase restoration is elided.) Because this F-A-C chord is itself extended in the manner of Model 4, one might reasonably propose that it asserts itself as V within a local I–V–I^6 progression (where the ^{6} denotes the 6 phase, *not* inversion). Nevertheless it does not appear in **1.2c**. That graph omits this and other foreground features, focusing instead on the role of E♭ in measure 7 as upper neighbor to the *Kopfton* D (= $\hat{3}$). Observe that Haydn's melody extends above the graph's structural line, in foreground decoration. The chief difference between the theme's a_1 and b sections is that the first prolongs $\hat{3}$ by means of a tonic-expanding harmonic progression, whereas the second does that again (employing II rather than IV) and then continues onward to $\hat{2}$, supported by V at the HC. The melodic line's interrupted $\hat{2}$ will proceed to $\hat{1}$ after the repeat of $\hat{3}$ and $\hat{2}$ during the theme's concluding a_2 section.

The a_2 section differs from a_1 in two principal respects. First, the succession from I to IV is intensified by a surge at the end of measure 10: A♭ joins the diatonic pitches of I, in an instance of dominant emulation. (Thus I→IV occurs instead of I IV.) Then, to provide a definitive close, the phrase's third measure is revised so that the tonic can arrive on the final downbeat, where it is embellished by three suspensions before the emergence of soprano $\hat{1}$. Whereas IV in measure 3 was luxuriantly extended, with its 6-phase chord sounding at 4_1, it is important for the dominant to arrive during the a_2 phrase's third measure. Haydn is able to reprise the melody's excursion up to B♭ during measure 11 (just barely: B♭ is a thirty-second note!), yet he omits the structurally deeper E♭ neighbor to the *Kopfton* D that sounded during 4_1. My graph [**1.2c**] clarifies the foundational structure by imaginatively reinstating the omitted E♭ within parentheses below the high B♭. In confirmation, the melody's D and C during 11_2 proceed as if E♭ indeed had sounded after all. That descent continues to B♭ for the PAC in measure 12. This B♭ completes the broad descending third emanating from the *Kopfton*, as displayed by the connection of D, C, and B♭ via the upper beam in **1.2c**. Though the interruption results in the reinstatement of $\hat{3}$ after the structural dominant of measure 8, ultimately the line does descend to its goal pitch, B♭.

The notion of harmonic assertion is important both for analytical decision-making and for interpretive choices in performance. The pitches B♭, D, and F sound together twelve times during the twelve measures of **1.2a** (including at 12_2, where F is understood but not stated), projecting a variety of structural meanings, as follows:

- *Stability*: A root-position I harmony occurs at 1_1, 2_1, 4_2, 9_1, 10_1, and 12_2. When the soprano pitch is B♭ (at 2_1, 10_1, and 12_2), the maximum degree of stability is attained. Because the tonic of 12_2 serves as the goal of the broad descent from the *Kopfton* (as displayed in **1.2c**), it is the most stable of all.
- *Ready for upward bass motion*: Both of the first-inversion I harmonies (at 2_2 and 8_1) proceed upwards in the bass, to E♭ or to F. The destabilization caused by inversion is subtle, yet, given that the trajectory of the harmonic progression is B♭<F, D is a useful internal point along that path in the bass. This notion retains its potency even when registral shifts occur. Note in the score how the B♭<F trajectory is presented as B♭>D<E♭>F during measures 1 through 4.
- *Upward bass motion in the context of a surge*: When inversion and dissonance combine, the tendency for bass D in a first-inversion I harmony to proceed to E♭ (root of IV) is enhanced. During 10_2 the diminished fifth formed by D and A♭ dynamically propels the lines forward to the E♭ and G of IV.
- *Rhythmic displacement*: In **1.2c** measure 11 is represented as $\frac{\text{E♭}>\text{D}>\text{C}}{\text{E♭}<\text{F}\text{——}}$, where passing note D occurs in an accented position. This usage is a variant of a more foundational structure derived from the second species of counterpoint: $\frac{\text{E♭}>\text{D}>\text{C}}{\text{E♭}\text{——}<\text{F}}$, corresponding to IV$^{8-7}$ V. The cadential $^6_4$ chord at 11_2 comes about through the coordinated sounding of this accented passing note along with a B♭ suspension in the second violin. Both pitches are lingering elements of the preceding harmony that extend into the domain of the dominant, which is announced by the viola and cello F. Though the symbol I$^6_4$ (which in an alternative methodology stands for tonic in second inversion) once was a common label for this chord, nowadays most analysts concur that B♭ does not assert itself as a root. My deployment of Arabic numbers to indicate intervals above the root (rather than to indicate inversion) allows me to juxtapose the Roman numeral V and the stacked 6 and 4 (as in **1.2c**) without ambiguity: that symbol will never be used for a second-inversion dominant harmony in my system.

- *Neighboring embellishment*: Just as E♭ serves as a neighbor to D during the tonic prolongation between 1_1 and 2_1, D serves as a neighbor to C in the first violin line between measures 5_1 and 6_1. (Both the E♭ and the D neighbors arrive after the beat, due to embellishment by an appoggiatura.) Since B♭ concurrently plays a neighboring role in the second violin during 5_2, the pitches of the tonic harmony all sound together. Yet here, as in the cadential $^6_4$, the B♭ does not assert itself as a root. Even the added prominence of B♭ sounding in the cello (resulting from chordal unfurling) does not transform B♭-D-F into a harmony.
- *Connective passing motion*: Just as the pitches of the tonic harmony may sound together as a result of concurrent neighboring motions, they also may unite during concurrent passing motions, as during 3_2. (I refer to the foundational version of this passage, as presented in **1.2c**, where the score's displacements have been rectified.) Here the linear connection of IV's 5 and 6 phases on successive downbeats forms the context for a passing chord, which does not assert itself as I.

Procedures for harmonic analysis fall into two basic categories, which I call literalist and imaginative. From a literalist perspective, creating a Roman numeral analysis tends to be a mechanical process. Successive groups of notes are rearranged into stacks of thirds, whose lowest notes are interpreted as the roots from which Roman numerals are derived.[11] I instead advocate an imaginative approach, in which context plays a decisive role in determining how a chord is interpreted. Many chords play an embellishing or a connective – rather than a harmonic – role. This perspective generally results in a less harmony-intensive interpretation. For example, whereas around thirty chords occur within **1.2a**, only thirteen Roman numerals are employed in **1.2c**.

Mozart: String Quartet in D Minor (K. 421), movement 1, measures 83|84–88

In **1.2a** (graphed in **1.2c**), Haydn extends I-space for over seven measures before proceeding to the dominant. His means of prolongation is itself harmonic: local I–IV–V–I and I–II–V–I progressions. Mozart undertakes a similar tonic prolongation in an excerpt from his Quartet in D Minor [**1.3a**]. In this case his procedure broadly corresponds to an ascending parallel progression of $^6_3$ chords, with

Example 1.3 Mozart: String Quartet in D Minor (K. 421), mvmt. 1 (a) Score of mm. 83| 84–88; (b) Analysis of mm. 84–87; (c) Analysis of mm. 87–88.

(a)

(b)
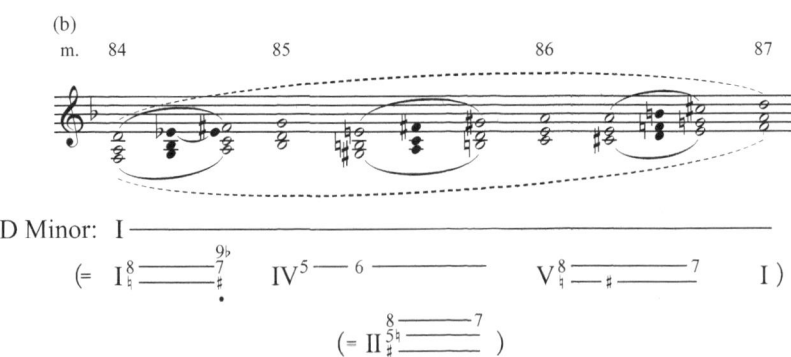

Example 1.3 (cont.)

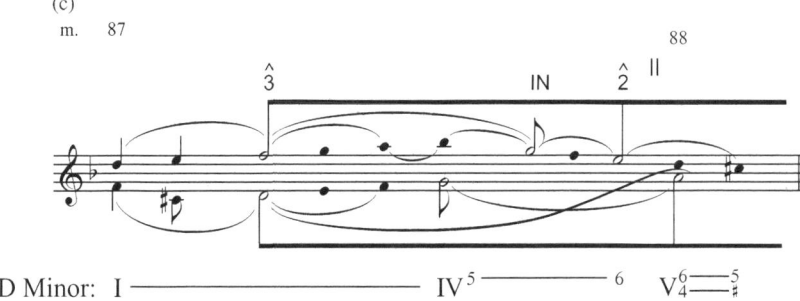

first-inversion tonic chords at both endpoints [**1.3b**]. Whereas no harmonic progression would be discernable within a diatonic parallel progression of eight stepwise-ascending $^6_3$ chords,[12] Mozart here modifies the internal chords with abundant chromaticism and repeats one segment of the ascent in a modified form (measure 85), thereby shaping these chords into a I→IV$^{5-6}$–V→I progression. The chordal evolution required to generate I→ in a minor key involves raising the tonic's third, in addition to adding the minor seventh. (Minor ninth E♭ sounds as well.) The IV^6 requires a more extensive transformation to become dominant emulating (as an asserted II→): from diminished E-G-B♭ into major E-G♯-B♮, here with dissonant seventh D and, at the outset of measure 86, minor ninth F as well. This conception coheres only if one interprets some of the chords as connectors of hierarchically deeper chords. The three chords notated with filled-in noteheads in **1.3b** are not asserted as harmonies. There are several things one might say about the E♭ in the first violin line at 84$_3$: it is a chromatic displacement of the more normative diatonic E♮; it anticipates the E♭ at 84$_4$, which is the minor ninth of the I→ harmony; and the augmented second that it forms with F♯ helps propel the motion to IV. But one thing that one should not say about it is that it is asserted as the root of ♭II (the so-called "Neapolitan" chord). In this context G-B♭-E♭ performs a connective – not a harmonic – role.[13]

Through this extended prolongation the tonic that arrives at 87$_1$ will be etched deeply within the attentive listener's consciousness. Mozart persists with its expansion for two additional beats, during which *Kopfton* F is attained, before proceeding to IV and then V♯. The model of **1.3c** shares many features with Haydn's tonic-to-dominant connections displayed in

1.1d and **1.2c** (measures 9 through 11). The surge in Haydn's tonic chords, created by the addition of a minor seventh to a major triad (thus I→ IV), is absent in Mozart's rendition, which proceeds from a minor tonic to a minor subdominant. Note that $\hat{2}$ arrives during the subdominant's 6 phase in **1.1d** and **1.3c**, whereas it is delayed until after dominant root F arrives in measure 11 in **1.2c**.

Haydn: String Quartet in A Major (op. 55, no. 1), movement 1, measures 145|146–164

An excerpt from Haydn's Quartet in A Major [**1.4a**] offers a surprise in measure 153. Though an expanse of eight measures often is sufficient for presenting a complete musical idea, here Haydn fails to attain closure: an IAC occurs where a PAC is expected. The definitive close is postponed until measure 164.[14] Though the structure of the initial four measures, graphed in **1.4b**, conventionally traverses the melodic span $\hat{5}>\hat{4}>\hat{3}$, the arrival of $\hat{3}$ (supported by the tonic) is premature: it "should" occur at the downbeat of measure 149. Concurrently Haydn inverts the melodic descending third that has extended each member of the structural line (E>C♯, D>B) into an ascending sixth (C♯<A). A melodic event of this nature is provocative, suggesting that a registral shift is in progress. That would require that a high C♯ supersede the A. As **1.4c** shows, those expectations are disappointed, for the initial register is restored and maintained through the IAC. Yet this hoped-for registral shift may have been sufficient reason for Haydn to postpone the PAC, since during the continuation he does achieve a high C♯ (during measure 159).

My analysis [**1.4d**] of that second try (during which the span from $\hat{3}$ to $\hat{1}$ is successfully traversed) proposes that this high C♯ is supported by a tonic chord in second inversion. Two arpeggiations proceed concurrently: the ascending line C♯<(E)<A<C♯ in the first violin (extending the C♯<E<A of measures 148 and 149) and the descending line A>E>C♯ in the cello. This reading is especially speculative in its suggestion that the cello pitch C♯ "should" sound at the end of measure 161. In the score C♯ is delayed until 162_1, by which point the upper strings have proceeded to supertonic pitches.[15] The chords of measure 158 are not asserted as harmonies. Instead, multiple lines proceed in an expanding wedge shape, all connecting members of the tonic harmony (A<C♯, C♯<E, A>E).[16] The excitement of the registral transfer is intensified through the dramatic lowering of the C♯ by two octaves in the first violin line of measures 159 through 161 (a line that

Example 1.4 Haydn: String Quartet in A Major (op. 55, no. 1), mvmt. 1 (a) Score of mm. 145|146–164; (b) Analysis of mm. 145–149; (c) Analysis of mm. 148–153; (d) Analysis of mm. 153–164; (e) Analysis of mm. 153–158.

Example 1.4 (cont.)

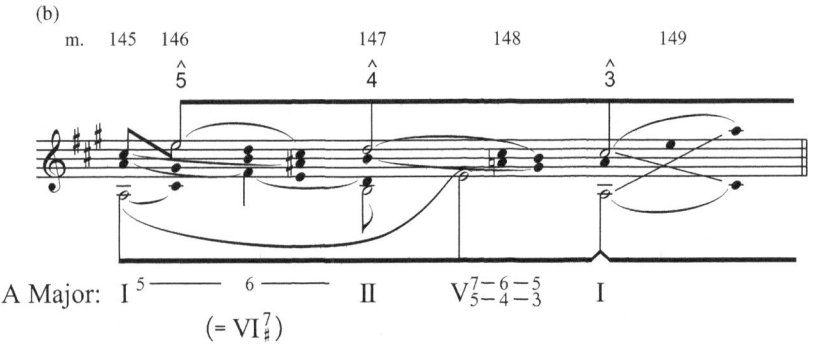

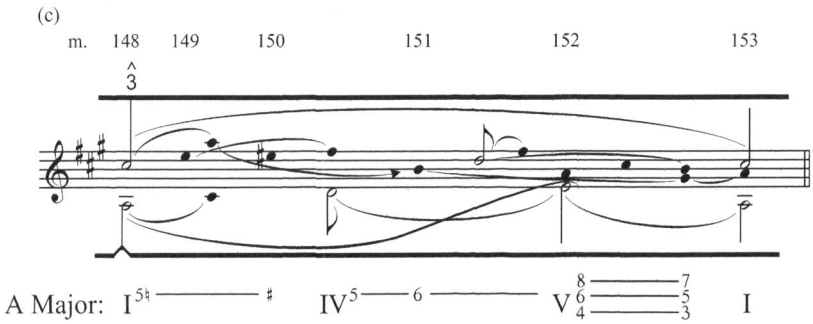

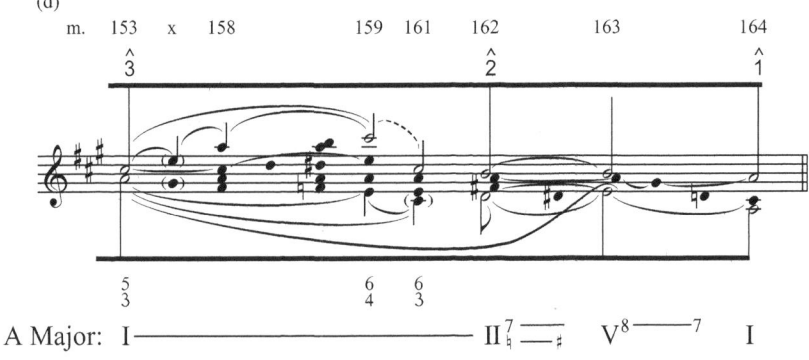

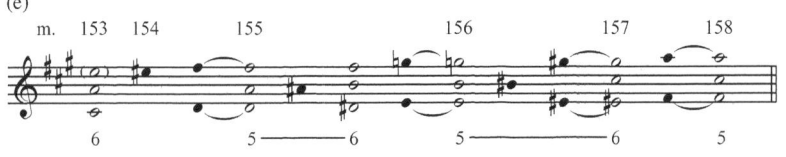

includes an extension to upper-third E before the lowering), so that the final measures of the excerpt transpire an octave *lower* than the initial register. (The single-staff graph in **1.4d** does not convey the full force of this transfer.)

Whereas **1.4d** displays a standard linear perspective during the path between measures 153 and 158, Haydn ambitiously connects the initiating A major and internal F♯ minor chords via an idiosyncratic ascending 5–6 sequence, displayed in **1.4e**.[17] (The open noteheads correspond to the essential pitches of the sequence, whereas the filled-in noteheads are either chromatic passing notes or – if tied to open noteheads – anticipations.) This sequential initiative induces a reorientation of the phrase's harmonic path. In measure 150 D-F♯-A is asserted as IV, whereas in measures 154 and 155 these same pitches reside within the sequence. The II in measure 162 serves as the connector between an extended I-space and the dominant. The concluding II→V–I cadential progression supports $\hat{2}>\hat{1}$, achieving the elusive PAC.

Mozart: String Quartet in D Minor (K. 421), movement 3, measures 0|1–10

In the workings of harmony, the path between the tonic root and the subdominant root or supertonic third (e.g., bass D to G in D Minor) often is negotiated by transforming the tonic into first inversion (D through F to G). We have encountered that shift both as an ascending third [**1.2c**, **1.3c**, **1.4c**] and as a descending sixth [**1.4d**]. The latter trajectory prevails in an excerpt from Mozart's Quartet in D Minor [**1.5a**]. (Note the $^F_D X^D_F$ voice exchange in the outer voices between 1_3 and 8_3.) The luxuriant span of a sixth allows for further compositional development: the D>A>F bass arpeggiation [**1.5b**] coordinates with a local I–V♯–I harmonic progression (contrasting the strategy Haydn employs in **1.4a/1.4d**).

The expansion and mutation of the conventional I^{5-6}–II–V♯ progression that transpires during the excerpt's opening eight measures is especially creative. (See **1.5c**.) I propose that the B♭-D-F-G♯ chord at 7_1, which often is classified in relation to the interval of an augmented sixth and given the nickname "German," is in fact a highly evolved supertonic harmony.[18] When the fourth scale degree occurs in the bass, either as the subdominant root or as the supertonic third (perhaps when the supertonic asserts itself during the 6 phase of IV^{5-6}), a chromatic approach to the dominant root is a

Example 1.5 Mozart: String Quartet in D Minor (K. 421), mvmt. 3 (a) Score of mm. 0|1–10; (b) Analysis of mm. 1–10; (c) Analysis of mm. 1–8.

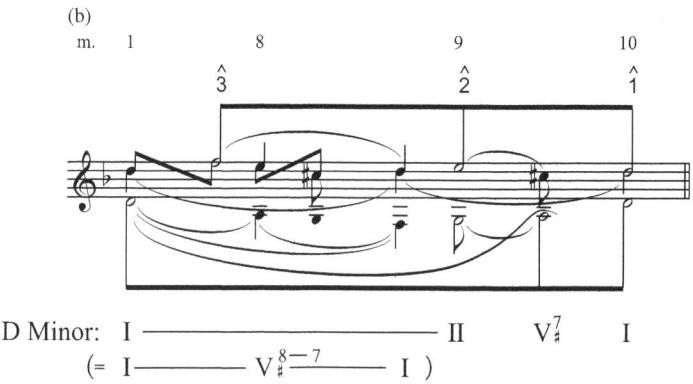

Example 1.5 (cont.)

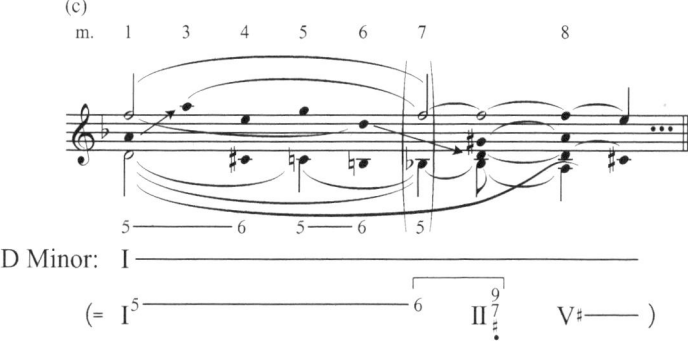

common continuation. (We have encountered that event in a major-key context in **1.1d** and **1.4d**.) Can this chromatic shift transpire in the context of a minor key as well, and in an inversion in which the sixth scale degree resides in the bass? Certainly! Though the simultaneous sounding of the raised fourth and diatonic sixth scale degrees (G♯ and B♭ in D Minor) produces a powerful and most useful drive towards the dominant, their concurrence is something of an embarrassment for analysts who attempt to explain chromatic activity in a diatonic context (e.g., E-G♯-B-D in D Major as V^7/V rather than as II$^7_{\sharp}$). The label "German" both masks the breakdown of the "all chords are diatonic in one key or another" approach to harmonic analysis and conceals the derivation from the minor-key supertonic harmony (accessible in major as well through modal mixture). I suggest instead that through the chromatic raising of the fourth scale degree D Minor's diatonic E-G-B♭-D supertonic may be represented by E-G♯-B♭-D (the source of both the so-called "French" and "Italian" augmented sixth chords), and that, as is also often the case with the major supertonic with minor seventh, when the ninth is added the root is omitted: G♯-B♭-D-F (the "German" augmented sixth chord). One may indicate this construct either by providing an inventory of the chordal content (as in **1.5c**, which acknowledges II's absent root, raised third, and added seventh and ninth) or by the shorthand symbol of an outline arrow: II⇛ V. (In D Minor, E-G♯-B♮-D and G♯-B♮-D-F are instances of II→, whereas E-G♯-B♭-D and G♯-B♭-D-F are instances of II⇛.)

Though the tonic's 5- and 6-phase chords often occur in direct succession, various means of connection are possible.[19] In this excerpt a sequence to the unfurled 6-phase chord proceeds obstinately from D through C to B♭, as displayed in **1.5c**. (For the sake of clarity the arrival of the B♭-D-F 6-phase chord and the addition of G♯ are displayed as distinct events. In Mozart's score they collide, as indicated by the horizontal bracket above the analytical symbols.) The internal chords of the sequence are not asserted as harmonies. Three filled-in descending thirds are traversed concurrently: F>D, A>F, and D>B♭, each connected by a slur in the graph. The endpoints of these motions correspond to the tonic's 5- and 6-phase chords. The interior is guided by voice leading, not by harmonic thinking.

Mozart: String Quartet in E♭ Major (K. 428), movement 1, measures 40–48

The very notion of authentic and half cadences emphasizes the fact that the tonic key may be projected not only via the traversal of a closed harmonic progression (beginning and ending on the tonic, with an internal dominant), but also via a progression that extends only as far as the dominant. What follows that dominant may serve as the initial tonic's reinstatement or successor rather than as a continuation from the dominant. Only in a hierarchical analytical perspective will this subtle set of interrelationships be conveyed appropriately.

An excerpt from Mozart's Quartet in E♭ Major [**1.6a**] proceeds from tonicized B♭ to its dominant in measures 40 through 44. The Roman numerals that annotate my graph [**1.6b**] present that motion as subordinate to a broader I–II–V–I progression extending through the entire excerpt. A comparison with **1.5b** is instructive. There the unfolded thirds D<F and E>C♯ in measures 1 and 8 (which correspond to the B♭<D and C>A♮ thirds of **1.6b**) continue onward to a resolution on unison D, supported by the tonic. In **1.6b** those lines are left dangling. Though the C is picked up for the supertonic unfolding, the deeper connection is that between the initial B♭<C<D third and the supertonic's C<D<E♭ third.

Two analytical decisions within **1.6b** may cause confusion or protest. First, I propose that when one hears a I$^{5-6}$, the supertonic – rather than the dominant – is the most likely successor. Consequently I interpret the A♮-C-F chord at 43_1 as an unfurled $^6_4$ embellishment of II♮. My graph displays bass C for the entire measure, with the A♮ appearing in its "rightful" position as an internal chord element. Second, I regard bass B♭ at 47_1 as an upper neighbor to the leading tone, and not as its resolution. It is common for a dominant to be prolonged via a combination of passing and neighboring motions. Here the dominant

Harmonic practice in the late eighteenth century 23

Example 1.6 Mozart: String Quartet in E♭ Major (K. 428), mvmt. 1 (a) Score of mm. 40–48; (b) Analysis of mm. 40–48.

(a)

(b)
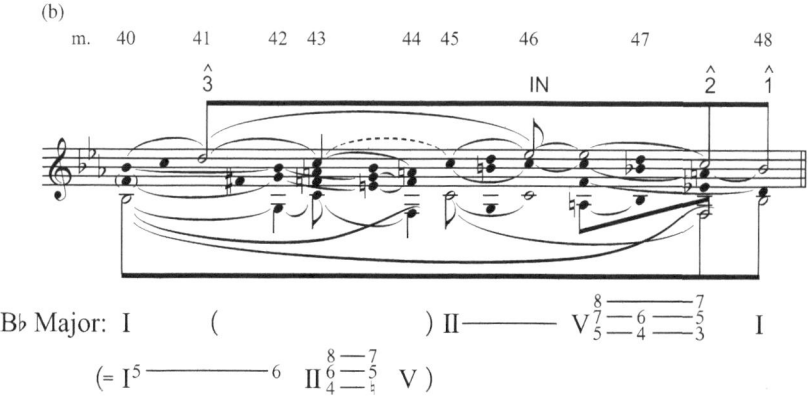

appears first in $^6_5$ position, while the interior passing chord (labeled as a $^6_4$ in **1.6b**) appears in $^5_3$ position. The parallel descents in the two violin lines (E♭>D>C and C>B♭>A♮) encourage the interpretation of D and B♭ as accented passing notes, in a construction similar to the dominant prolongation displayed in **1.2b**, Model 4. (Likewise the supertonic harmony in measures 45 and 46 is extended via an embellishing chord, in the manner of Model 1.)

Through unfolding, non-adjacent pitches are connected in meaningful ways. For example, the unfolded B♭<D in measures 40 and 41 is answered by C>A♮ in measures 43 and 44. Though the inner-strand pitches B♭ and A♮ are separated by over three measures, they are directly linked in this broader perspective. A more local set of unfoldings transpires during measures 42 through 44. (To enhance clarity, these unfoldings are presented as simultaneities in **1.6b**.) I propose that the first violin line unfolds four successive thirds: $\genfrac{}{}{0pt}{}{D>C\ >B♭>A♮}{B♭>A♮>G\ >F}$. Instead of a conventional alternation between inner and outer strands, in this case the following arrangement prevails:

$$\genfrac{}{}{0pt}{}{D>C>B♭>\ \ \ \ \ \ \ \ A♮}{B♭>\ \ \ \ \ \ \ \ \ \ A♮>G>\ \ F}.^{20}$$

Mozart: String Quartet in E♭ Major (K. 428), movement 1, measures 12–24

In an excerpt from Mozart's Quartet in E♭ Major [**1.7a**], the tonic harmony is stated at five points – 12_1, 13_2, 18_1, 20_1, and 22_1 – during a prolongation of I-space before the definitive progression through II to V occurs. The first linking passage begins as a conventional I^{5-6} (measure 12). The 6 (pitch C) might be an anticipation (of the fifth of II, for example), a passing note, or a neighboring note. When A♮ and F♯ join C at 13_1, we come to understand that Mozart is here deploying what often is called a "common-tone diminished seventh" chord, with the tonic root E♭ serving as the common tone. Consequently the C is a neighboring note. The model of **1.7b** may take its place beside the first two models in **1.2b** as an option for tonic expansion achieved via concurrent neighboring motions. Just as I refrain from labeling the embellishing chords in **1.2b** as V and IV, respectively, I refrain from formulating a Roman-numeral label for that in **1.7b**. It instead is a dissonant internal moment within I-space. It may be unfurled so that any of its members reside in the soprano and bass.

Example 1.7 Mozart: String Quartet in E♭ Major (K. 428), mvmt. 1 (a) Score of mm. 12–24; (b) Analysis of mm. 12–13; (c) Analysis of mm. 13–15; (d) Analysis of mm. 12–18; (e) Analysis of mm. 12–18; (f) Analysis of mm. 12–20; (g) Analysis of mm. 20–24; (h) Analysis of mm. 22–23.

Such an unfurling here places F♯ in the bass, and so the tonic that is restored during 13_2 is in first inversion, an ideal starting point for a shortcut version of the ascending 5–6 sequence connecting the tonic's 5- and 6-phase chords. Because the first and sixth chords in the full sequence (E♭^{5} and G^6) contain the same pitch classes, the progression

Example 1.7 (cont.)

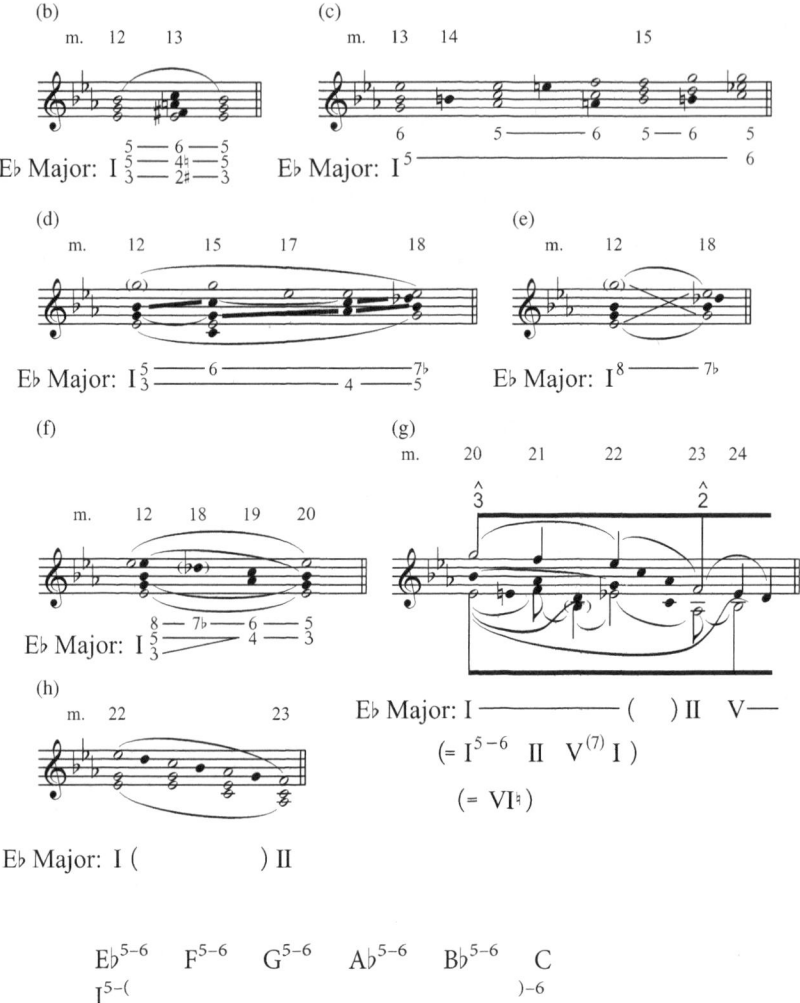

may be presented in an abbreviated form, as

$$G^6 \quad A\flat^{5-6} \quad B\flat^{5-6} \quad C$$

This progression is shown in **1.7c**. The various chromatic pitches that Mozart employs are displayed as filled-in noteheads. In the quartet several chords evolve even further. For example, in the penultimate chord diatonic B♭-D-G evolves beyond chromatic B♮-D-G to dissonant B♮-D-F-A♭. (Though A♭ sounds in place of G, the chord still serves as the 6 phase of B♭-D-F.)

This connection via sequential ascent, from E♭-G-B♭ to E♭-G-C, turns out to be just the first phase in a tonic expansion, the essence of which is displayed in **1.7d**. Two melodic thirds within $\mathrm{I}^{8-7\flat}$ are traversed: that from third to fifth (G<A♭<B♭) and that from fifth to minor seventh (B♭<C<D♭). The net result is displayed in **1.7e**.[21] Though often this structure would lead to the subdominant (I→ IV), the continuation in measures 19 and 20 suggests instead a linear connection within I-space. Compare this tonic prolongation, graphed in **1.7f**, and the dominant prolongation in **1.6b**, measures 46 and 47.[22] Just as I proposed that no tonic harmony is asserted during measure 47 in **1.6b**, I likewise propose that no subdominant harmony is asserted during measure 19 in **1.7f**. A♭ is a neighbor to the tonic's third (G), and not a harmonic root.[23] One may regard **1.7f** as a variant of **1.2b**, Model 2.

The harmonic progression that transpires from 20_1 through 22_1 is more conventional than the prolongational expansions that have preceded it [**1.7g**].[24] A local I^{5-6}–II–V–I progression supports the descending third G>F>E♭, which is answered an octave lower by F>E♭>D during the II–V continuation in measures 23 and 24.[25] The most interesting aspect of this progression is how Mozart connects the tonic and supertonic harmonies during measures 22 and 23. The model displayed in **1.7h** reveals that this structure traverses a segment of the descending circle of thirds. (Mozart's accented passing notes have been restored to their normative unaccented positions in my model.)

Haydn: String Quartet in B Minor (op. 33, no. 1), movement 1, measures 0|1–12

Though in most cases a movement will begin with the sounding of its tonic harmony, an especially compelling strategy for initiating an engagement with the listener results from withholding the tonic for several measures. Sometimes a composer may even raise false expectations regarding what pitch will serve as the tonic. Likely the meek D and F♯ that open Haydn's Quartet in B Minor [**1.8a**] will be interpreted by listeners as an inverted D major chord. The next two chords support the hypothesis that the movement is in the key of D Major: a major tonic in first inversion often proceeds to IV (G major), and that IV may be extended via its 6 phase [**1.8b**]. That presumption is challenged during the second half of measure 2, where Haydn proceeds not to an A major dominant, but instead to a 6–5

Example 1.8 Haydn: String Quartet in B Minor (op. 33, no. 1), mvmt. 1 (a) Score of mm. 0|1–12; (b) Analysis of mm. 1–2; (c) Analysis of mm. 2–6; (d) Analysis of mm. 2–12.

Example 1.8 (cont.)

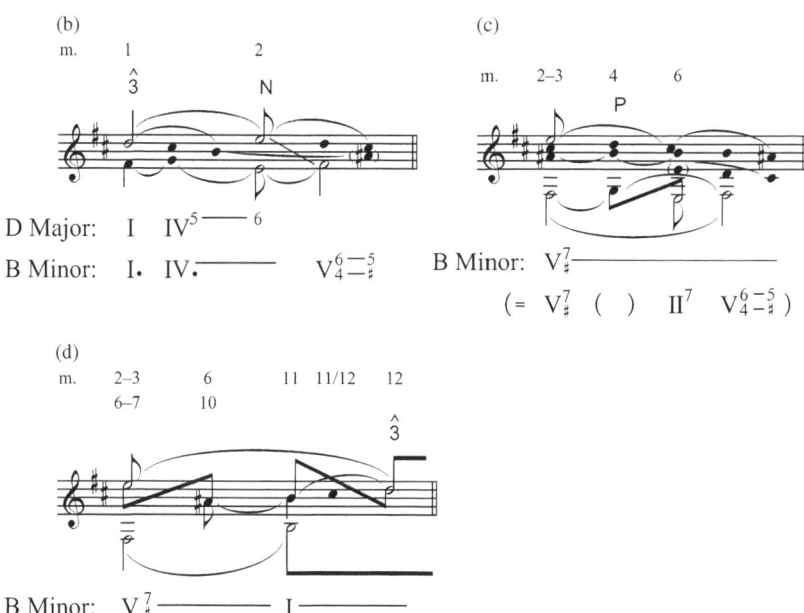

embellishment of F♯ major (representing $^{6-5}_{4-3♯}$), suggesting that the movement is in B Minor. This F♯ dominant is prolonged through measure 10, after which B Minor's tonic role is confirmed. In retrospect one may understand the initial D<G root succession as an upper-third substitution for B<E, with a restoration of the E during measure 2.[26] Haydn's contrivance requires that the B tonic pitch be withheld during the initial measure. In **1.8b** I go so far as to label $^{D}_{F♯}$ as I• in B Minor, proposing that retrospectively the listener may comprehend a tonic function in the nebulous opening.

The minor third $^{G}_{E}$ sounds in a number of guises during these introductory measures. It is stated melodically by the first and second violins during measure 2. In measure 3 the first violin offers a slower presentation, while in the cello G and E seem more embellishing in nature.[27] In all, the $^{G}_{E}$ third sounds within four different harmonic contexts: IV (measure 2), V→ (measures 3–4 and 7–8), II^7 (measures 4 through 6, successively in the cello and simultaneously between the cello and the viola), and ♮II (measures 8 through 10, likewise both successively and simultaneously).

Contexts for a succession from the dominant to the submediant vary widely. At 4_4 I interpret that moment not as a resolution of the dominant to a 6-phase tonic (I^6), but instead as a connector between the structurally deeper $V^7_\sharp$ and II^7 harmonies that surround it, within a prolongation of the dominant [**1.8c**]. (Bass G>E, which occurs in both **1.8b** and **1.8c**, is a unifying force throughout the excerpt.) The unfolding of the diminished fifth E>A♯ in the first violin line is a most significant aspect of this dominant prolongation. That unfolding is repeated during the modified repetition in measures 7 through 10, where ♮II substitutes for II^7. (One may interpret the C♮ as a temporary *wobble* of the diatonic C♯, which is restored in the viola line at the end of measure 10. A wobble is defined as a chromatic shift from one to another version of the same scale degree, generally with an eventual restoration of the original state: here C♯>C♮<C♯.) The resolution is more than a mere succession from the dominant to the tonic. As **1.8d** shows, Haydn responds to the E>A♯ unfolding during V^7 by unfolding its resolution B<D during $I.^{28}$ Within that broad B<C♯<D ascending line in the first violin, Haydn inserts a traversal of an F♯>D>B fifth (measure 11), notably with upper neighbor G embellishing the F♯. Though in an altered harmonic context, this gesture reprises the descending line of measure 1.

Haydn: String Quartet in F Minor (op. 55, no. 2), movement 1, measures 17–26

The excerpt from Haydn's Quartet in F Minor presented in **1.9a** is ten measures in length, two measures longer than the normative eight-measure phrase that begins the movement. (Measures 1 through 26 present the theme, cast in an |: a_1 :|: b a_2 :| form, for a set of variations.) The extra measures are 21 and 22, which extend the *forzando* ♭II harmony of measure 20. Measures 17 through 23 project the opening tonic within the broader I–IV–V–I progression displayed in **1.9b**. That harmonic progression is straightforward, with some special flair only during the IV chord's 6 phase, at which point diatonic B♭-D♭-G is displaced by its evolved state B♮-D♭-F-A♭ (= II⇛). The hierarchical relationships among the melodic pitches are less straightforward. In particular, my assertion of a deep $\hat{3}>\hat{2}>\hat{1}$ structural descent (incorporating a downward register transfer and with the B♭>A♭>G segment of the soprano line during measures 24 and 25 performed by the viola, an octave lower) may seem to be an egregious case of struggling to conform to a Schenkerian template. Yet the first violin's

Example 1.9 Haydn: String Quartet in F Minor (op. 55, no. 2), mvmt. 1 (a) Score of mm. 17–26; (b) Analysis of mm. 17–26; (c) Analysis of mm. 17–23.

B♮ at the end of measure 24 depends upon the B♭ that I project as $\hat{3}$'s incomplete neighbor. Just as the upper-third D♭ supersedes the *Kopfton*'s neighbor B♭ at 20_1, it covers an assumed B♭ at 24_1.

The connection between root-position and first-inversion tonic chords that transpires during measures 17 through 23 (displayed in **1.9c**) is similar

Example 1.9 (cont.)

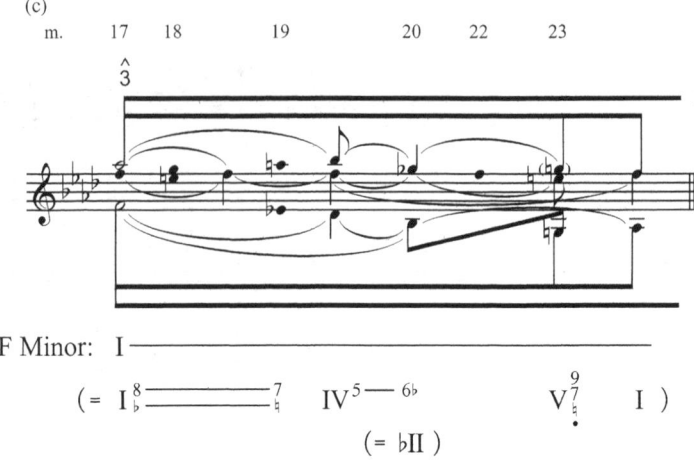

to a passage we analyzed above [**1.1d**]. Because this quartet movement is in a minor key, the tonic third A♭ must be raised to A♮ to form an augmented fourth against bass E♭ (measure 19) during the surge to the local IV. In both excerpts that IV sounds in first inversion, and by the time the bass has descended to the subdominant root the IV has shifted to its 6 phase. In **1.1d** that 6-phase chord begins diatonically and then evolves, resulting in II➔ leading to V. In **1.9c** a different scenario, one that is especially appropriate in a minor key, is pursued: the 6 of IV$^{5-6}$ is lowered chromatically, so that B♭-D♭-G is replaced by B♭-D♭-G♭, which here asserts itself as ♭II. During the evolved dominant harmony that follows, the wobbly note G♭ yields to diatonic G♮ in the bass.

Because the ♭II chord incorporates a wobbly note, its participation within some conventional unfolding is unconventional. In **1.1d**, the tonic's D<E<F♯ third is complemented by E>D>C♯, which transpires during the succession from the asserted II to V. The $^{E}_{C\sharp}$ third is a meaningful interval within the goal dominant chord. In **1.9c**, A♭>G>F is complemented by G♭>F>E♮, the traversal of a diminished third! The $^{G\flat}_{E\natural}$ interval is meaningful neither within the asserted ♭II nor within the V♮ to which it leads. As a wobble, G♭ fills the slot that "should" be occupied by G♮. The wayward G♭ reverts to G♮ during the dominant chord, so that belatedly the deeper tonal sense is restored. Similarly in measure 24 a curious interval is traversed: D♭>C>B♮. In this instance an elision occurs: a voice exchange between the first violin and cello seems to be swapping D♭ and B♭, and yet the goal B♭ is

Harmonic practice in the late eighteenth century 33

elided, with chromatic passing note B♮ sounding in its place. (The elided B♭ is displayed in **1.9b**, within parentheses.)

Haydn: String Quartet in E♭ Major (op. 71, no. 3), movement 2, measures 0|1–16

The excerpt presented in **1.10a** serves as the theme for a set of variations, which Haydn offers as the second movement of his Quartet in E♭ Major. The tonic is arpeggiated in two distinct stages at the outset, first peaking on D and then on the *Kopfton* F [**1.10b**].[29] The D/F dichotomy is maintained in the continuation: D reigns from measure 5 through the middle of measure 10, including a bold, full-octave D-to-D descent before the double bar; and F's upper neighbor G emerges above D in measure 10 and is prolonged until F is restored around the beginning of measure 14. The structural descent occurs during the final three measures [**1.10c**]. Its $\hat{4}>\hat{3}>\hat{2}$ segment corresponds to a span that often occurs when a $\hat{3}>\hat{2}$ connection is embellished by an incomplete upper neighbor.[30] (Compare **1.10c** with **1.1c** and **1.3c**.)

Though I think it is reasonable to propose, as I do in **1.10c**, that the tonic fifth $^F_{B\flat}$ of measure 3 is prolonged through measure 14, where it takes on dominant-emulating characteristics, the internal content of these measures nearly obliterates the reinstatement of the tonic. The progression in measures 9 through 14 builds up an enormous forward momentum: G→C→F→B♭→E♭ [**1.10d**]. I suggest that the restoration of the B♭, D, and F pitch classes and the return of *Kopfton* F in the soprano at 14_1 (after an upper-neighbor excursion) are sufficient to project the sense of tonic. If that indeed is the case, then these chords represent a highly evolved version of the local tonic-prolonging harmonic progression I^6 II V I, followed by IV.

How the D minor chord of measure 8 fits into its broader context is shown in **1.10d**. A I$^{5-6}$ expansion transpires during measures 3 through 9. The D-F-A chord's A (sounded at 7_1 and extended into measure 8 via the filled-in fifth A̱>D) functions as a passing note within that expansion. Haydn goes about this in an unusual way. Until 7_2 it seems that the phrase is heading for a close on B♭'s F major dominant, attained via a I$^{5-6}$–II$^7_4$–V progression leading into 7_1. (The bass of measures 7 and 8 would in that case have proceeded as F B♭ C C | F C F.) For the expanse of the first nine measures, large-scale B♭–F–G and B♭–D–G connections of the tonic's 5- and 6-phase chords are equally viable. (For example, B♭–F–G occurs in **1.2a**, 4_2 through 6_2; B♭–D–G occurs in a more local context earlier in this

Example 1.10 Haydn: String Quartet in E♭ Major (op. 71, no. 3), mvmt. 2 (a) Score of mm. 0|1–16; (b) Analysis of mm. 0|1–3; (c) Analysis of mm. 3–16; (d) Analysis of mm. 3–14.

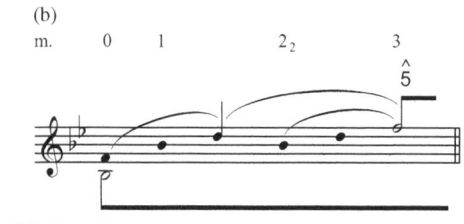

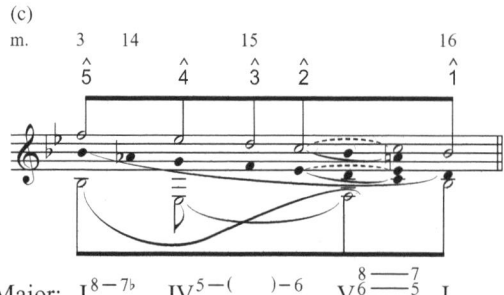

Example 1.10 (cont.)

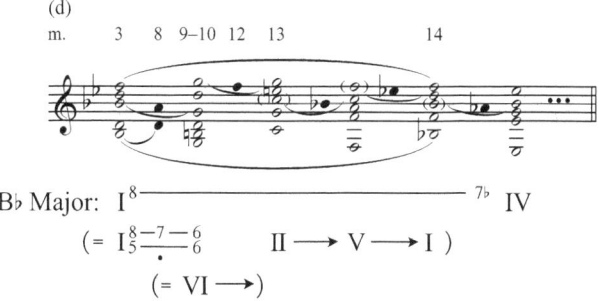

excerpt: 5_1 through 6_1.) Haydn gives listeners a jolt by shifting from the former to the latter trajectory just before the cadence of measure 8.

Haydn: String Quartet in D Major (op. 71, no. 2), movement 1, measures 33–38

In an excerpt from his Quartet in D Major [**1.11a**], Haydn allows himself to back up and proceed through a passage a second time. The two traversals (measures 35–36 and 37–38) employ differing harmonic strategies to reach the dominant goal, thereby highlighting the variety of means available to the composer, in this case juxtaposing chromatic variants of the tonic's lower- and upper-third chords.

The frenzy of sixteenth-note activity within measures 33 and 34 places emphasis upon the on-the-beat chords, which alternate between the tonic A-C♯-E (beats 1 through 3) and an embellishing chord G♯-B-E or G♯-B-D-E (beat 4). (Compare with **1.2b**, Model 1.) Especially in measure 34 the concurrent linear motions create some spectacular simultaneities that do *not* register as harmonies.[31] The embellishing chord continues into measure 35, where the sixteenth-note motion abruptly ceases. Though the resolution to a first-inversion tonic chord might be expected, the tonic is here represented by its evolved 6 phase (A♯-C♯-E-G), a common connector between I and II.

The tonic-to-supertonic connection warrants careful consideration. The direct succession from I to II is presented in **1.11b**. Because these chords are in root position the voice leading into the supertonic's fifth (F♯) must be by leap: stepwise E<F♯ would create parallel fifths with the bass, a situation that

Example 1.11 Haydn: String Quartet in D Major (op. 71, no. 2), mvmt. 1 (a) Score of mm. 33–38; (b) Succession from I to II; (c) Succession from I to II; (d) Succession from I to II; (e) Succession from I to II; (f) Succession from I to II$^{5\natural}$; (g) Analysis of mm. 33–38.

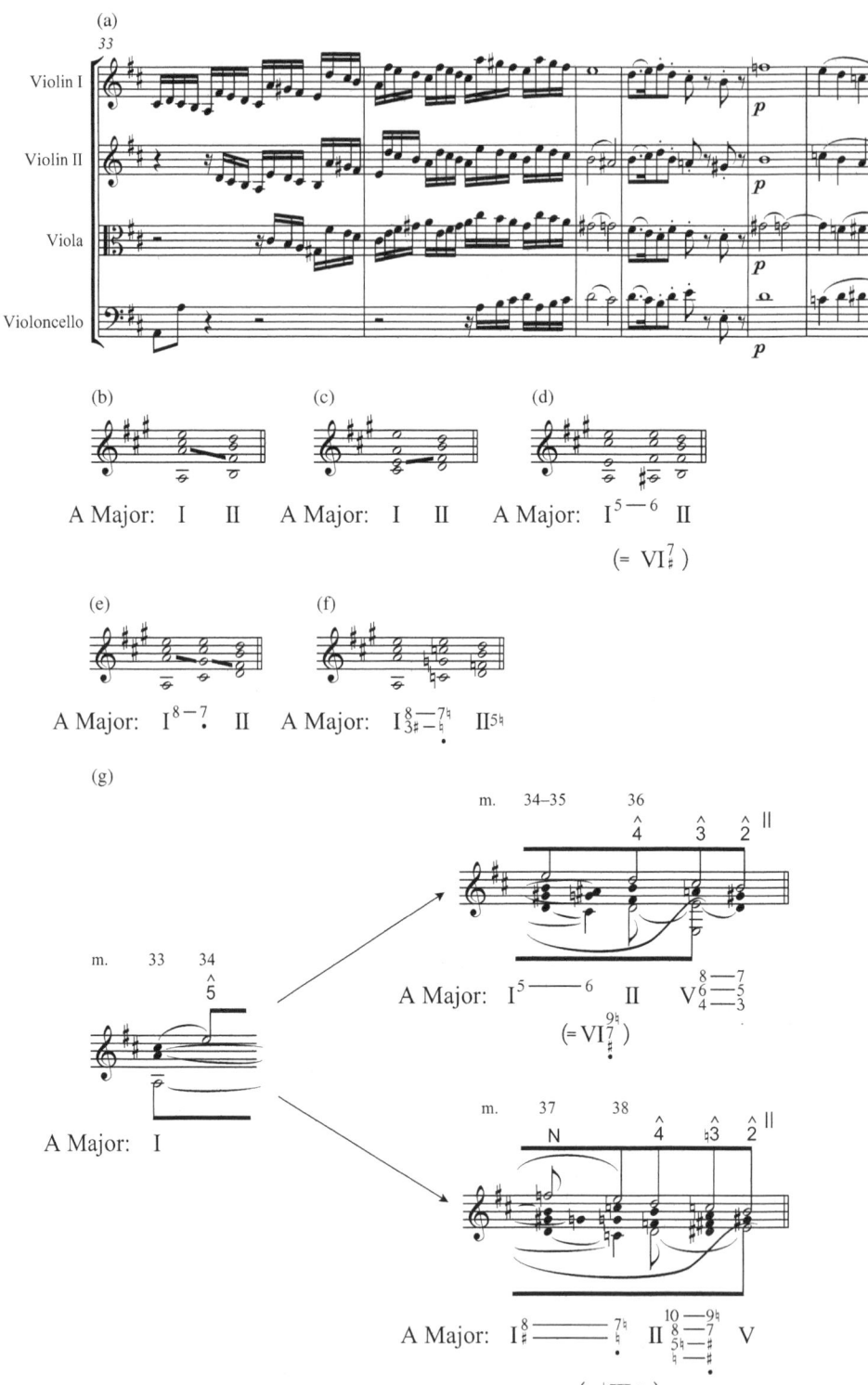

encourages the deployment of the 5–6 shift in this context. (That concern is not a factor when these chords are in first inversion [**1.11c**].) A chromaticized version of I$^{5-6}$ II appears in **1.11d**. By retaining the fifth E along with sixth F♯ and by raising the A to A♯, Haydn creates a dynamic surge incorporating a diminished fifth that propels the progression onward to II. The same tendencies prevail in other inversions as well, as in measures 35 and 36 of the quartet, where ninth G♮ displaces root F♯.

The tonic's upper-third chord offers an alternative approach to the supertonic, as shown in **1.11e**. Observe that the A>F♯ third from **1.11b** has been filled in by step and that the tonic root is suppressed during this passing motion. In this context the chord – which I label as I^{7} – does not assert itself as III. This motion is replicated in **1.11f**, with one significant change: modal mixture temporarily infuses the passage with an A Minor character. This is the version that Haydn employs during measure 38.[32]

Two contrasting routes by which the initial tonic expansion of measures 33 and 34 may lead to the dominant are displayed in **1.11g**. In the first routing the G♯-B-D-E embellishing chord's resolution is diverted to the tonic's 6-phase chord (in the evolved state A♯-C♯-E-G♮), which leads – as expected – to diatonic II and then V. Then, unexpectedly, the listener is pulled back to the moment of 35$_1$ again. One slight yet significant shift occurs in this restatement: F♮ displaces E during 37$_1$. Whereas G♯-B-D-E is directed towards tonic A (or, in this case, its 6-phase extension), G♯-B-D-F♮ is open to numerous possibilities. By lowering G♯ to G♮ during measure 37, Haydn focuses his harmonic aim not on an A or an F♯ chord, but instead upon C♮-E-G♮. (The second branch of **1.11g** pursues this trajectory, which corresponds to **1.11f**.) The modal mixture that emerges at this point comes about because diminished seventh chords are good at bringing about shifts of a minor third (here from tonic A to *lowered* upper-third C♮).[33] The minor-hued supertonic chord that follows evolves into II→ (supporting ♭3̂) on the path towards V.

The very institution of the string quartet is a reminder that four individual wills can be joined together in the pursuit of a higher unity. During this excerpt Haydn playfully experiments with just how far the juxtaposition of these wills may go without having the enterprise fall to pieces. As **1.11b** through **1.11f** remind us, in most cases the connection between two adjacent harmonies engages small intervals: seconds and thirds will predominate. During 34$_3$ to 35$_1$ Haydn instead purposefully employs spans of a fourth in the connection between tonic A-C♯-E and its G♯-B-D-E embellishing chord. The first violin traverses A>E, the second violin E>B, the viola C♯>G♯, and the cello A<D. So far, so good! His next instruction is astonishing: he asks each of

the four instruments to fill in the assigned fourth with two diatonic passing notes. Imagine how the first performers of this quartet must have responded to what they heard at their rehearsal. Each part presents what appears to be a reasonable line, and yet the combination of the four lines makes for an unprecedented progression of simultaneities that still astounds us today. The interior chords fall into place as they will, a reminder to listeners that not all associations in life are comfortable or conventional.

Haydn: String Quartet in G Major (op. 54, no. 1), movement 2, measures 34–52

The tonal system harbors an inherent tension between key-based pitch hierarchies and equal subdivisions of the octave. In a tonal context the twelve half steps of the octave divide not into six plus six, but instead into seven plus five. G – not F♯ – is the C tonic's staunchest ally. The octave naturally subdivides into C–E–G–C (based on the 3:2 and 5:4 ratios), not into C–E–G♯[A♭]–C or C–E♭–F♯[G♭]–A–C. As the nineteenth century progressed, segmentations of the octave into 4+4+4, 3+3+3+3, and 2+2+2+2+2+2 became more common. In my view such passages transpire during a suspension of normative tonal practice, which is reinstated once the modulo 12 progression has reached its goal.[34]

In an excerpt from Haydn's Quartet in G Major [**1.12a**], a circular progression of descending perfect fifths leads from tonicized G Major eventually to its antipode, D♭ Major.[35] The progression is structured as two equivalent minor-third ascents: G→C→F→B♭ followed by B♭→E♭→A♭→D♭ [**1.12b**]. (This structure could be conceptualized within modulo 12 as 0+3+3. Each +3 comes about through the succession 0-7-7-7, or -21, which is +3 from the -24 double-octave equivalent.) Each ascending minor third is a convincing and trouble-free event. It is the juxtaposition of two such events that leads into the abyss.[36]

The diminished seventh chord has a special relationship with the 5–6 shift and the dominant-emulating 8–7♭. We have observed, in the context of **1.11g**, that a diminished seventh chord can, through enharmonic reinterpretation, reorient its resolutional tendency by a minor third. Consider now what happens in measures 36 through 38 of **1.12a**. Given that the phrase began in G Major, likely the C major chord will be interpreted as IV, at least initially; and given how harmonic progressions tend to go, we may expect that soon V will emerge. In that IV V is a whole-step relationship, a IV$^{5-6}$ expansion is in order, and

Example 1.12 Haydn: String Quartet in G Major (op. 54, no. 1), mvmt. 2 (a) Score of mm. 34–52; (b) Analysis of mm. 34–52; (c) Analysis of mm. 46–51.

Example 1.12 (cont.)

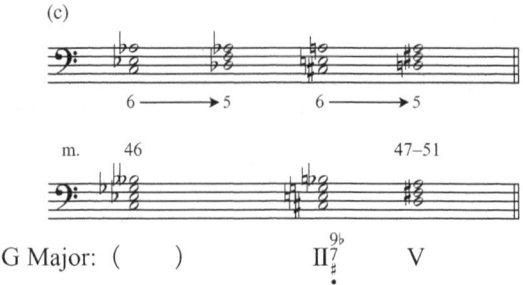

indeed the C♯-E-G-B♭ chord at 37₂ – a dominant-emulating evolved state of IV's 6-phase C-E-A – appears to suit that bill. Yet this chord does not resolve to dominant D. Instead, Haydn proceeds to F major. Note that I have spelled C♯-E-G-B♭ as E-G-B♭-D♭ in **1.12b**. That spelling corresponds to the resolution to F that Haydn pursues. Amazingly, the same diminished seventh sonority can represent *either* C-E-G's 6 phase (C♯-E-G-B♭) *or* its dominant-emulating $\overset{9\flat}{\underset{\bullet}{7\flat}}$ extension (E-G-B♭-D♭). What initially may have seemed to be the onset of a *harmonic* progression (G C$^{5-6}$ D G) turns out instead to be a *circular* progression (G C F B♭).

Getting to the antipode is not difficult: the domain of modulo 12 offers routings – both ascending and descending – either via three major seconds (2+2+2) or, as here, two minor thirds (3+3). Getting back on track within the prevailing tonality is more challenging. The two models of **1.12c** may assist us in making sense of how Haydn accomplishes this in his quartet. The first progression is a segment of an obstinate 5–6 sequence, ascending in half steps. Observe that the 6-phase chords are dominant-emulating. The successive 5-phase chords correspond to tonic G's antipode D♭ and the arrival of dominant D. The second progression displays the essence of what transpires after antipode D♭ is attained in measure 44. It seems at first that a local progression will serve to prolong D♭ major, with the diminished seventh chord at 46₁ poised to resolve back to D♭-F-A♭. Instead, that diminished seventh chord is hoisted upwards by a half step, to a diminished seventh chord that will resolve to G Major's dominant D-F♯-A, thereby restoring the influence of the original tonality. One might interpret this turn of events either as an outgrowth of the 6–5–6–5 progression displayed in **1.12c**, in which the D♭ 5-phase chord has been elided,[37] or as what I call *seismic* composition – an unexpected and mysterious force that repositions a chord at a higher or lower point, from which it behaves as it was set to behave before the shift.[38]

2 | Anatomy of the I–II♯–V two-part exposition: twelve keyboard sonatas by Haydn

As a means of organizing tonal space, the two-part sonata exposition is a wondrous invention. Though the tonic key is presented as the movement's controlling tonal center, it is juxtaposed with a closely allied key in the exposition's second part. In a major-key movement by Haydn or Mozart, one may expect that the tonic zone will be followed by another zone in which the dominant is tonicized. Both zones will include memorable thematic and motivic content. (Especially with Haydn the two zones may share similar content.) This tonal contrast offers a suitable tension: the exposition hangs together because these keys are closely related, yet it is not a self-sufficient entity because it concludes away from the home tonic. That tension will not be resolved until the second half of the recapitulation.

The twelve expositions by Haydn that we explore in this chapter all pursue a particular course in departing the tonic key and announcing the dominant key. First the tonic is destabilized via a 5–6 shift. This leads to a dominant-emulating supertonic, followed by a pause (medial caesura) awaiting the onset of the tonicized dominant.[1] Sometimes the medial caesura is emphasized by means of a literal halt – silence in all parts – though in other cases some motivic/rhythmic content persists during that juncture.

My structural and harmonic observations will be placed within the formal framework set forth by James Hepokoski and Warren Darcy in their *Elements of Sonata Theory*.[2] In what they call the two-part exposition, the tonic is presented in the opening primary-theme zone (P), after which the transition (TR) culminates in a medial caesura (MC) to close the first part. The secondary-theme zone (S) is the principal component of the second part, culminating in the essential expositional closure (EEC) and a closing zone (C). Though my analyses place greater emphasis on the traversal of linear progressions (emphasizing their repetition, fragmentation, and interruption) than do those of Hepokoski and Darcy, to a large extent my presentation is compatible with their perspective.

Of the twelve sonatas by Haydn that we shall explore, nine were written within the period from 1766 through 1779, with the final three coming later, between 1789 and 1796. These sonatas will be referred to via the

Arabic portions of their Hoboken numbers, enclosed within boxes. Though in many cases their dates of composition are impossible to determine with precision, their chronological order is approximately as follows:

45	Sonata in E♭ Major, H. XVI: 45
46	Sonata in A♭ Major, H. XVI: 46
23	Sonata in F Major, H. XVI: 23
25	Sonata in E♭ Major, H. XVI: 25
28	Sonata in E♭ Major, H. XVI: 28
29	Sonata in F Major, H. XVI: 29
30	Sonata in A Major, H. XVI: 30
31	Sonata in E Major, H. XVI: 31
35	Sonata in C Major, H. XVI: 35
49	Sonata in E♭ Major, H. XVI: 49
52	Sonata in E♭ Major, H. XVI: 52
51	Sonata in D Major, H. XVI: 51

To facilitate comprehension of the structural content and to maximize sensitivity to the range of alternatives that Haydn pursued, the ensuing discussion proceeds region by region: that is, first I explore P in all twelve expositions, then TR in all twelve, and so on. To encourage comparison among the expositions, a C Major transposition is provided for the basic structural models. Haydn's harmonic vocabulary here falls within a remarkably narrow range, with diatonic I, II, IV, and V, as well as dominant-emulating I→, II→, and VI→ shaping most of his progressions. His writing is wondrously sophisticated nevertheless, especially in the interplay between foundational progressions and embellishing figuration. Consequently I have found the Schenkerian perspective to be indispensable. This chapter's concentrated Schenkerian focus, which I integrate with my distinctive style of harmonic analysis, gives readers the opportunity both to enhance their understanding of how that methodology may be applied in the context of an important element of musical form and to develop a facility in analyzing passages that may seem resistant to a cogent interpretation using those tools.[3]

This chapter's arrangement facilitates the careful study of each exposition component in turn. The perspective attained through this process will be called upon frequently in later chapters. Readers are encouraged to take a second pass through the chapter, putting the twelve expositions back together again by reassembling the P–TR–S–C thread for each.

The primary-theme zone (P)

Without exception Haydn's primary themes in these sonatas employ a limited range of mostly diatonic harmonies, along with arpeggiation, registral shifts, and the stepwise filling-in of chordal thirds and fourths (such as $\hat{3}>\hat{1}$, $\hat{5}>\hat{3}$ and $5<\hat{8}$), all working in concord to establish the tonic key – that is, to instill hierarchical relationships such that the movement's seven diatonic pitch classes are distinguished from the remaining chromatic ones, and such that the three tonic-triad pitch classes are distinguished from the remaining diatonic ones. Two crucial structural lines give shape to the basic harmonic progression within this opening tonic region: a bass that ascends from $\hat{1}$ to $\hat{5}$, often filled in by internal scale degrees, such as $\hat{3}$ for the tonic's first inversion and $\hat{4}$ for IV or for II in first inversion;[4] and a middleground melodic line that descends either from $\hat{3}$ or from $\hat{5}$. Though $\hat{2}$ supported by the dominant may serve as a cadential goal (HC), usually – sometimes on a second attempt – the progression will lead onward to the tonic (PAC). In 46 and 49 P traverses the span from $\hat{5}$ to $\hat{3}$ (IAC), which I interpret as a segment of the movement's background descent, since without exception $\hat{2}$ prevails during S.

The basic structures that Haydn employs during P for the sonatas under consideration are displayed in C Major in **2.1**. Transpositions of these models, incorporating measure numbers, accompany the discussion below. When Haydn omits or makes a substitution for a structural pitch, the corresponding measure number will be placed within parentheses. The stated arrival points are determined without regard to a suspension or other tactic that may delay the timely sounding of a structural pitch. I recommend that readers mark up their scores: find and then circle the soprano and bass pitches indicated and add the Roman numerals as you proceed through the following commentary.

Regarding **2.1a** (transposed in **2.2**):

29 Brevity and harmonic restraint characterize P in 29. The only substantive contrast to the tonic chord occurs during 3_4, where soprano pitch G serves as a link between the tonic's A and F, as shown in **2.2**. (The theme is repeated in a truncated form beginning at 4_1, where the first statement's PAC dovetails with the onset of the modified second statement.) This interpretation proposes that G should be regarded as hierarchically distinct from the neighboring notes (also embellished by grace notes) in measure 2. How can this be so? The theme's three-note motive expands and contracts: C–C–C (measure 1), C<D>C (measure 2, introducing rhythmic augmentation

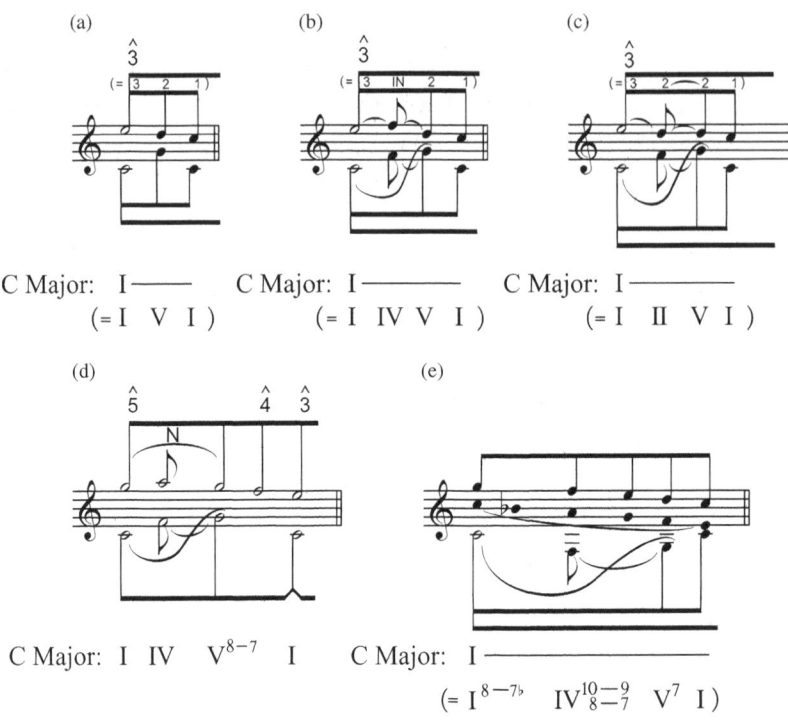

Example 2.1 Five models for the primary-theme zone (P) within Haydn's expositions.

and a neighboring note), A<B♭>A (measures 2–3, with neighboring note and truncated rhythm), F–F–F (measure 3, rescinding the neighboring note), returning to a foundational A–A–A (bass clef of measure 4, restoring the original rhythm within the second statement of the theme). The G of 3_4 falls outside that motivic trajectory, and consequently its grace note (A, following after a conspicuous cessation of rhythmic activity) may be interpreted as a reinstatement – as a suspension – of *Kopfton* A, which was introduced during 2_4–3_1 and extended during a tonic-prolonging ^A_FX^F_A voice exchange. The *Kopfton* is preceded by its upper third, C (at 2_{1-3}). That third is featured during TR as well: C>A, the first and ninth sixteenth notes of measures 7 and 9; and A<C>A, incorporating a descending register transfer, during measures 13 and 14.

Regarding **2.1b** (transposed in **2.3**):

45 The ascending arpeggiation of a sixth helps shape the initial I-space in 45 . The B♭ at 1_1, though emphasized by metrical placement and through repetition, ultimately proves to be internal to a G<B♭<E♭

Example 2.2 Analysis of Haydn: Piano Sonata in F Major (H. XVI: 29), mvmt. 1, mm. 2–6.

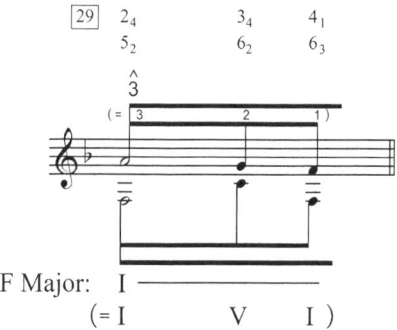

Example 2.3 Analysis of Haydn: (a) Piano Sonata in E♭ Major (H. XVI: 45), mvmt. 1, mm. 0|1–11; Piano Sonata in E♭ Major (H. XVI: 25), mvmt. 1, mm. 3–8; (b) Piano Sonata in F Major (H. XVI: 23), mvmt. 1, mm. 1–12; (c) Piano Sonata in A Major (H. XVI: 30), mvmt. 1, mm. 1–8; (d) Piano Sonata in D Major (H. XVI: 51), mvmt. 1, mm. 2–20.

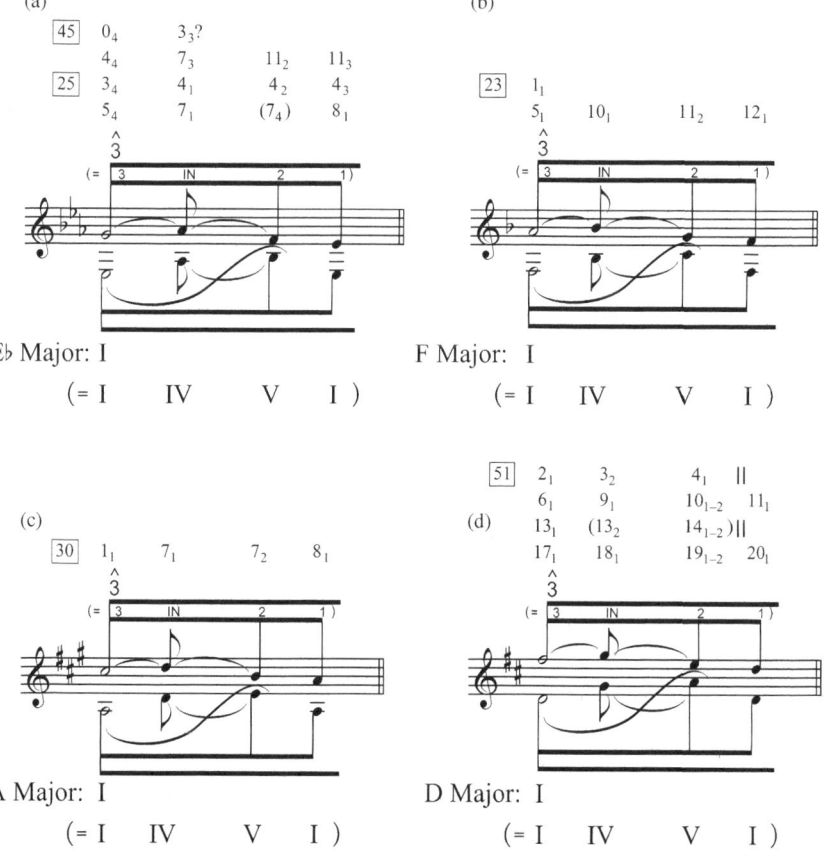

Example 2.4 Analysis of Haydn: Piano Sonata in E♭ Major (H. XVI: 45), mvmt. 1, mm. 3–4.

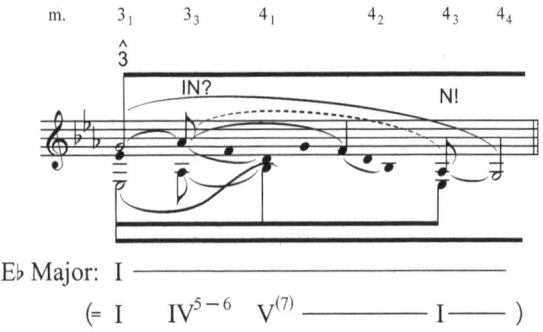

tonic arpeggiation that is fully realized only on the fifth try (during 2_{2-3}). G is restated in the downbeat position at 3_1, now with the perimeter pitches of the sixth inverted to form a conventional E♭<G unfolding to the *Kopfton*. (During TR the melody will ascend a third above the higher E♭ to G.) IV serves as the intermediary between I-space and the arrival of V at 4_1. Usually IV supports $\hat{3}$'s incomplete upper neighbor (as shown in **2.3**). Although A♭ "belongs" at 3_3, it does not sound in the soprano until the middle of the following beat, by which point the IV harmony has undergone a 5–6 shift: A♭-C-(E♭) to A♭-C-F.

In the structure that Haydn here subverts [**2.3**] the neighbor is labeled as "incomplete" because the line proceeds downwards to $\hat{2}$ without reestablishing $\hat{3}$. (A passing note often connects the incomplete neighbor and $\hat{2}$.) Through 4_2 Haydn pursues this conventional course [**2.4**], likely causing attentive listeners to expect a PAC at 4_3. Yet this time he fools us: A♭ is restored in the melody (an octave lower) just in time for the cadence. Consequently an IAC substitutes for the anticipated PAC. The progression has not advanced beyond a prolongation of the initial tonic (supporting $\hat{3}$). The phrase must be repeated – with suitable revisions – to achieve full closure.

Haydn's second phrase is more extensively revamped than the situation requires. IV-space is extended to nearly four measures, middleground $\hat{2}$ is firmly established during IV's 6 phase [**2.5a**], and chordal support is provided for the passing note (G) that connects the incomplete neighbor and $\hat{2}$ [**2.5b**]. Yet Haydn goes even further: likely inspired by the opening G<B♭ third, upper thirds

Anatomy of the I–II♯–V two-part exposition   47

Example 2.5 Analysis of Haydn: Piano Sonata in E♭ Major (H. XVI: 45), mvmt. 1, mm. 4–11.

(a)
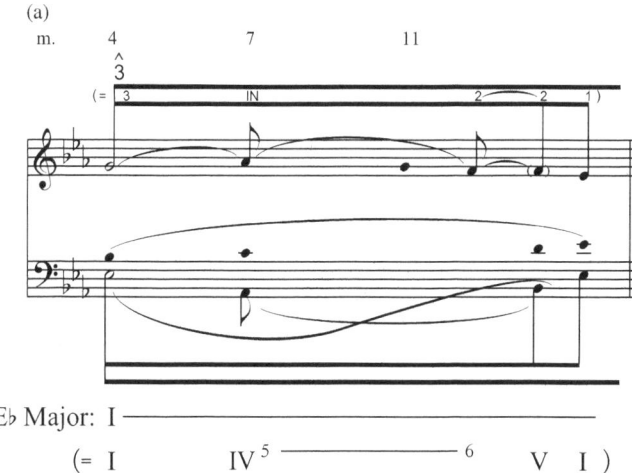

(b)
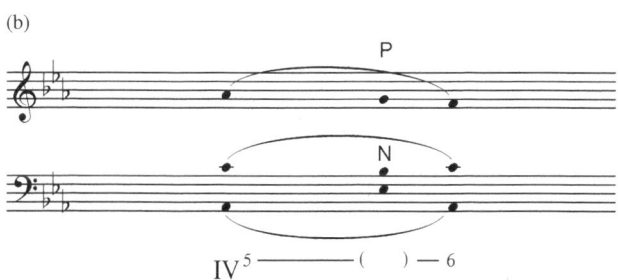

(c)
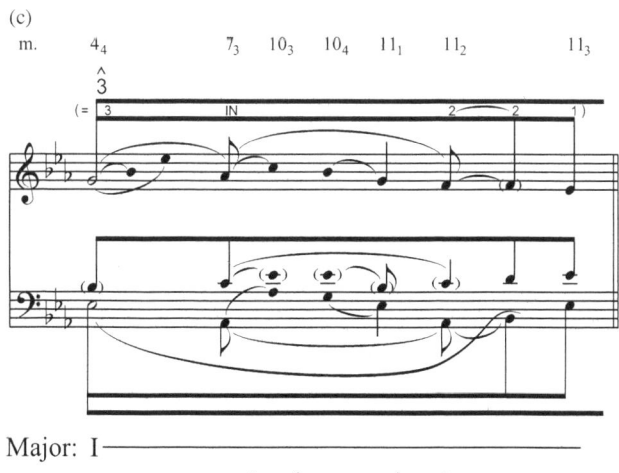

enhance both the incomplete neighbor A♭ and the following passing note G [**2.5c**]. The first of these is filled in via a sequential ascent – A♭$^{5-6}$ B♭$^{5-6}$ C$^{5-6}$ – that extends for over three measures.[5] This glorious phrase reaches a PAC at 11_3.

|23| My analysis of |45| revealed how two phrases may coordinate so that the second completes a structure left unfinished in the first. The two phrases that constitute P in |23| relate in this manner as well. Whereas the first concludes with an IAC in measure 4, Haydn takes pains to extend the second by moving the bass to D at 8_2, rather than to F.[6] Consequently that phrase must continue, in this case for eight measures, at the end of which a PAC is achieved. My contrasting interpretations of the chords at 3_2 and 7_2–8_1 may seem curious. Because I accept the span of music concluding at 4_2 as a phrase, the convergence of C, (E), G, and B♭ during measure 3 functions as an asserted V^7 harmony. Yet in the context of the extended phrase of measures 4|5 through 12, those same pitches in measures 7 and 8 instead reside within the initial I-space, where they form an embellishing chord. The phrase's V does not occur until measure 11, as displayed in **2.3**.

A local connection from *Kopfton* A to F is traversed between 1_1 and 2_1. Immediately thereafter the line shoots upwards, touching upon C, F, and finally a high A (reinforcing the *Kopfton*), before the lower A is restored at the end of the phrase. Neighboring notes abound: B♭>A, D>C, and G>F. (That the B♭ at 3_2 is a neighbor to A rather than a passing note from C is more clearly discernable during the restatement in measure 7. I interpret trilled $^C/_{B\flat}$ as the convergence of the C resolution of upper neighbor D and the B♭ upper neighbor to the *Kopfton* A.) It turns out that bass D at 8_2 is a neighbor as well, part of a 5-6-5 expansion of I-space. At 9_1 the restored tonic takes on dominant-emulating characteristics. Though no F sounds during measure 10, clearly IV – B♭-D-(F) – is implied, with F♯ leading from the imagined F to the 6-phase G (thus IV$^{5-6}$). The ascending D<B♭ sixth outlined in the melody of measure 10 resolves the A>E♭ augmented fourth of measures 8 and 9. This B♭ is the incomplete neighbor displayed in **2.3**. The line then descends through A to G. All three of these pitches are embellished by their upper thirds (thus B♭<D, C>A, B♭>G between 10_2 and 11_2).[7] Embellished by suspensions, the PAC arrives as expected in measure 12.

25 The local harmonic progression I$^{5-6}$ II$^7_4$ V$^{8-7}$ I, with an expansion of the internal V between 2_3 and 3_3, establishes I-space and supports the melody's E♭<F<G ascent during the opening three measures of **25**. *Kopfton* G is presented as a mere thirty-second note at the end of 3_4. (In measure 6, which contains an insertion to the restatement of that passage, Haydn compensates by making a huge fuss over G, traversing both descending and ascending stepwise G–G octaves.) Though bass A♭ sounds after rather than with soprano G during 4_1, those pitches form a unity that imposes upon G the role of dissonant suspension, here with upward resolution to A♭, G's incomplete upper neighbor, as shown in **2.3**. (Note that soprano G and bass G at the end of measure 3 both ultimately lead to A♭. Bald parallel octaves are prevented through the bass descent G>A♭, instead of G<A♭, and through the nonsynchronous arrival of the two A♭s.[8]) The dominant's quick F>D third (during 4_2) complements the broad E♭<G third of the preceding I-space. The cadence is embellished by suspensions at 4_3. The latter portion of the phrase is repeated in an expanded form, ending in a more decisive PAC (at 8_1, which coincides with the onset of a P-codetta that continues through 12_1). Haydn employs upper thirds freely: B♭ above G in measure 6, C above A♭ during the first half of measure 7, and B♭ above the G that passes between incomplete neighbor A♭ and (absent) F during the second half of measure 7.[9]

The complete and truncated statements of the P theme occur in separate registers. Whereas the upper and lower Gs are connected during measure 6, ultimately the cadence of 8_1 transpires in the upper register, which will prevail during the TR and S sections as well. The P-codetta offers a temporary restoration of the lower register, via a stepwise-descending E♭>E♭ octave. This descent is undertaken amidst considerable resistance. Though E♭>D>D♭>C>B♭ transpires without a hitch in measures 8 and 9, the B♭ soars back into the upper register at both 9_4 and 10_4. The A♭, G, and F of the octave descent occur in that upper register, among the sixty-fourth and thirty-second notes of measure 11, followed by a restoration of the lower register prior to the cadence on E♭ during 12_1.[10]

30 The exposition's first part (P and TR) is set as an a_1 b a_2 ternary form in **30**: a_1 establishes the tonic (with a PAC at 8_1), b leads to the dominant (which supports a middleground $\hat{2}$ at 14_1, extended through 16_1), and then a_2 reinstates the tonic material. Since it serves as the venue for the journey away from the tonic, a_2 falls outside of P. It fulfills the role of TR, concluding the exposition's first part.

A local harmonic progression (I IV$^{5-6}_{5-}$ V$^{8-7}$ I) establishes I-space during the first six measures, with $\hat{3}$ serving as the *Kopfton*. In measures 6 and 7 a descending seventh (C♯>A>F♯>D) substitutes for the conventional ascending-second approach to the *Kopfton*'s incomplete neighbor. The PAC (coinciding with $\hat{2}>\hat{1}$) transpires in this lower register, as does the following b section. The a_2 section pursues a registral shift in the opposite direction, attaining C♯ in the upper register during 19_2.

Registral shifts are a common occurrence within Haydn's P sections. In this movement the opening statement of the tonic (a_1) exudes a sense of failure, for Haydn sets up the initial stages of an upward shift by positioning the F♯ of 3_1 up an octave during 4_2 and the B of 4_1 up an octave during 5_1, only to return at 6_2 to the C♯ that was introduced at the outset. The downward cascade from 5_1 through 6_2 proves to be unstoppable: instead of holding firm at the register of the restored C♯, the downward momentum continues, so that the A of the PAC is a tenth, rather than a third, below the initial C♯.[11] Haydn overcomes that defeat during a_2, where the elusive high C♯ finally is attained (during 19_2).

|51| As in |45|, Haydn juxtaposes the inversion-related third and sixth formed by the tonic root and third during the opening tonic statement in |51| (D<F♯ followed by D>F♯). Pitches above the structural line pervade P: incomplete neighbor G at 3_2 is followed by upper-third B, and the E at the HC is followed by a stepwise ascent to G. In the consequent phrase this device is taken to greater heights: F♯<A in measure 8 (by which point *Kopfton* $\hat{3}$ has risen to the upper register), followed by G<B, and A>F♯. (This F♯ is a passing note between incomplete neighbor G and the E at the end of measure 10, by which point the upward register transfer has been rescinded.) D at the PAC initiates a varied restatement of the entire theme, extending P to 20_1. (See **2.3**.[12])

Regarding **2.1c** (transposed in **2.6**):

|31| Though the P in |31| utilizes II rather than IV as the intermediary harmony between I- and V-spaces, it shares many features with

Example 2.6 Analysis of Haydn: (a) Piano Sonata in E Major (H. XVI: 31), mvmt. 1, mm. 1–8; (b) Piano Sonata in C Major (H. XVI: 35), mvmt. 1, mm. 0|1–16; (c) Piano Sonata in E♭ Major (H. XVI: 52), mvmt. 1, mm. 1–8.

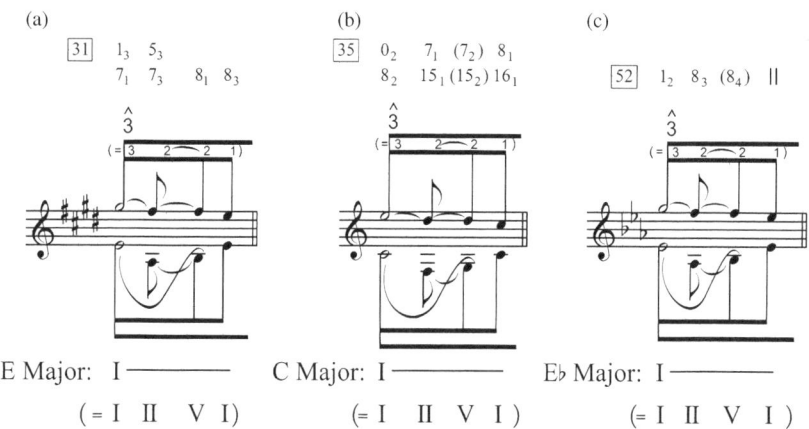

various P sections that incorporate IV, explored above. The initial B>A>G♯ descent to the *Kopfton* in measure 1 resembles how 30 opens; the local harmonic progression that grounds the initial tonic between 1_1 and 2_1 is akin to that in 25 ; the inversional third and sixth that occur here (G♯>E between 2_2 and 2_3, G♯<E between 4_2 and 5_1) echo those in 45 and 51 ; and, as was the case in 45 , $\hat{1}$ (the expected successor of $\hat{2}$, at 5_3), which "should" coordinate with the attainment of harmonic goal I to form a PAC during the second half of measure 6, is absent, a state of affairs that here motivates a modified repetition of the latter portion of the phrase. Even on the second try the cadence is somewhat diffuse: instead of a forceful F♯>E melodic close, F♯<A to G♯>E places the goal $\hat{1}$ off the beat during 8_3. Yet such upper-third play is ideally suited to a theme that began with an upper third: B>G♯.[13]

35 The P of 35 is built from two similar phrases, both ending in a PAC. The chief difference between them is that in the first the tonic is restored at the endpoint of a local E>D>C melodic descent (through 6_2), whereas in the second that C is supported by the tonic's unfurled 6-phase chord, A-C-E (at 14_2). In the model of P's structure in **2.7**, the second phrase is favored in the region where they differ.

The initial presentation of the *Kopfton* resembles that in 45 , where a G<E♭ sixth and an E♭<G third are juxtaposed (separated by a rest) and where the fifth scale degree (internal to the G<E♭ sixth)

Example 2.7 Analysis of Haydn: Piano Sonata in C Major (H. XVI: 35), mvmt. 1, mm. 0|1–16.

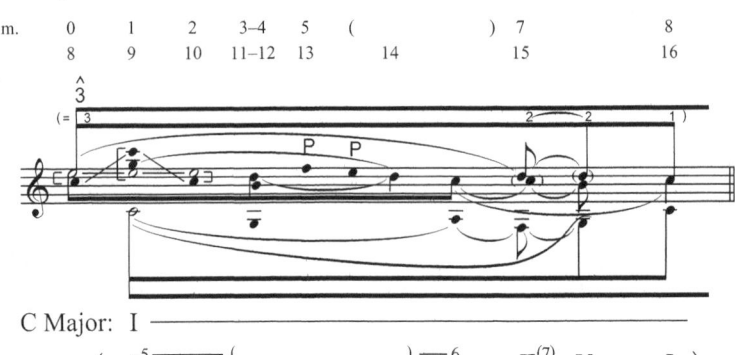

sounds on the first downbeat. In ⟦35⟧ no rests separate *two* thirds and *two* sixths: that is, third C<E interlocks with sixth E<C, which interlocks with sixth C>E, which interlocks with third E>C. The prominent B<D third in measures 3 and 4 helps the ear to recognize retrospectively the importance of the ^E_C third in the preceding measures. (A look ahead to the opening of TR, measures 16 through 23, where ^E_C and ^F_B occur in alternation, confirms the preeminence of E. Note especially measure 18, which reprises the contour of measures 0 through 2 and supports the choice of E – not G – as the *Kopfton*: G is even omitted from the C>E descending sixth.[14]) The G within the initial E<C sixth serves as the initiation point for local descents: G>F>E to restate the *Kopfton* (at 5_2) during the first phrase, and G>F>E>D to restate the D within the E>C third (at 14_1) during the second phrase.

⟦52⟧ The opening eight-measure antecedent phrase within ⟦52⟧ is devoted almost exclusively to launching the initial I-space; the concluding II–V HC occupies a mere half measure. The consequent phrase resides outside of P: since it initiates the move away from the tonic, it serves as TR.

Haydn deploys two separate initiatives during the tonic expansion. The first emanates from a straightforward neighboring embellishment in two voices. The tonic root (E♭) and third (*Kopfton* G) may both be displaced by half-step neighbors forming an embellishing chord, a notion that Haydn here fleshes out with more overt harmonic support. (See **2.8**.) The second tonic-prolonging initiative's

Example 2.8 Analysis of Haydn: Piano Sonata in E♭ Major (H. XVI: 52), mvmt. 1, mm. 1–2.

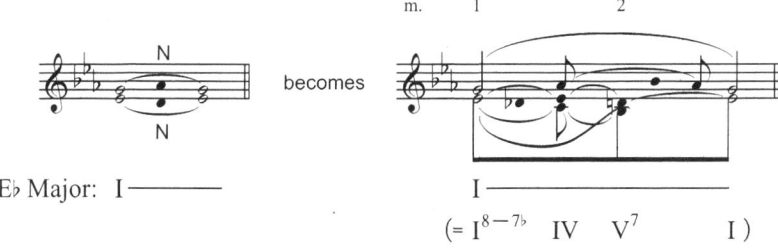

E♭ Major: I —————— I ——————————————
              (= I$^{8-7♭}$ IV   V^7 I)

Example 2.9 Analysis of Haydn: Piano Sonata in E♭ Major (H. XVI: 52), mvmt. 1, mm. 1–8.

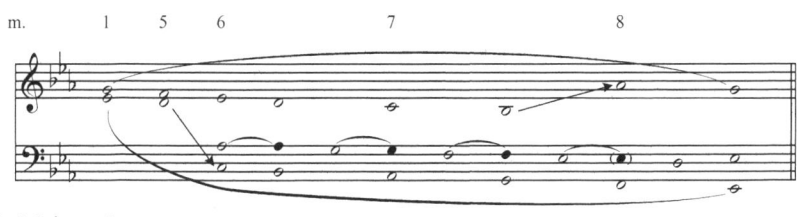

E♭ Major: I ————————————————————————————

initiating E♭>D bass motion coordinates not with upper-voice G ascending to A♭, as before, but instead with it descending to F. These thirds ($^G_{E♭}$ stated at the outset in the lower register and firmly entrenched in the upper register by measure 4; ^F_D stated first in the upper register – at 5$_3$ – and transferred to the lower register by the measure's end) expand into tenths and eventually seventeenths during the remainder of the linear progression [**2.9**].[15] (Though the texture thickens at 6$_1$, that moment is internal to the broader tonic-prolonging trajectory displayed in **2.9**. It is not the onset of a new thematic initiative.[16]) Through these strategies the tonic's $^G_{E♭}$ third is prolonged for over seven measures. The unfolded F>D third that concludes measure 8 is its successor.

Regarding **2.1d** (transposed in **2.10**):

|46| In the expositions that we have explored to this point, P projects the tonic through a stepwise progression downwards from 3̂. The tonic pitch in the soprano at the PAC (which occurs in all except

Example 2.10 Analysis of Haydn: (a) Piano Sonata in A♭ Major (H. XVI: 46), mvmt. 1, mm. 1–8; (b) Piano Sonata in E♭ Major (H. XVI: 49), mvmt. 1, mm. 2–14.

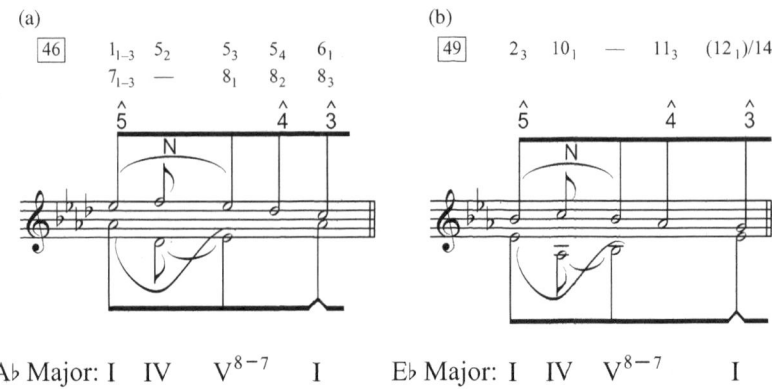

for [52)] does not serve as a background $\hat{1}$, however. Instead $\hat{3}$ is prolonged through this descending third-progression. The $\hat{2}$ that emerges in the following TR and S regions is its successor. When instead $\hat{3}$ sounds at the end of P, the possibility of a descent from $\hat{5}$ emerges. Since $\hat{2}$ still follows, a line from $\hat{5}$ through $\hat{4}$ to $\hat{3}$ within P will be the definitive statement of that trajectory within the exposition, and thus it may form part of the movement's background structure. The two-pronged connection of the tonic bass note's stem below $\hat{3}$ in **2.1d** (and **2.10**) conveys that this pitch is both the endpoint of one I–V–I bass arpeggiation (supporting the $\hat{5}$–$\hat{4}$–$\hat{3}$ span within P) and the point of origin for another (supporting the descent through $\hat{2}$ as the exposition continues and eventually to $\hat{1}$ during the recapitulation).[17]

In [46] E♭ (*Kopfton* $\hat{5}$, first stated at 1_3 against one of the tonic's embellishing chords) serves as the point of origin for a series of tonic-prolonging motions: the stepwise descent E♭>D♭>C (with continuation to A♭) in measures 1 through 3; the prolonged E♭ extending via arpeggiation upwards through A♭ to C during 4_1; and an interior E♭ (measure 3) extending through F and G to A♭ in measures 4 and 5, followed by C during 5_2 (thereby reprising the contour of the earlier arpeggiation).[18] That lower E♭ then connects with neighboring note F during 5_2, followed by E♭, D♭, and C to form an IAC at 6_{1-2}, completing the structure displayed in **2.10**.[19] Whereas the model shows only an 8–7 motion emanating from V, in this instance a $\genfrac{}{}{0pt}{}{6-5}{(4-3)}$ embellishment is employed as well.

Often an IAC will be replaced by a PAC during a partial or full repetition of a phrase. (See the P of 45.) Yet here $\hat{3}$ remains the terminus (at 8_{3-4}) during the reiteration. This $\hat{3}$ will be hoisted two octaves higher for the onset of TR (at 9_1). During the repetition Haydn sacrifices the IV chord to permit a soaring connection between the upper and lower E♭s (at 7_3 through 8_1).[20] In retrospect the E♭<A♭<C arpeggiations of the first phrase may be understood as incomplete traversals of a full-octave E♭<A♭<C<E♭ connection, attained only in the second phrase.[21]

49 Haydn establishes $\hat{5}$ as the *Kopfton* through an ascending arpeggiation to B♭ in the opening two measures of 49. A middleground B♭>A♭>G descent coordinates with a local harmonic progression (I IV V^7 I) that extends I-space into measure 8. B♭ is then reinvigorated through a brief yet impressive flourish to a high B♭ and back, at which point B♮ intervenes to direct the line to B♭'s upper neighbor, C (coordinating with IV$^{5-6}$). The return of *Kopfton* B♭ is omitted when V arrives at 11_3. The dominant's seventh, A♭, sounds in its place. This dissonant seventh of course should resolve to G (as displayed in **2.10**). Haydn omits that resolution at the cadence (12_1). He makes amends during TR (measures 14 and 16), twice presenting the A♭>G that one expected at the close of P.

Regarding **2.1e** (transposed in **2.11**):

28 The introduction of the *Kopfton* has been a prominent – and seemingly essential – feature in all of the P sections we have explored thus far. In most cases $\hat{3}$ has served as the *Kopfton*, though in 46 and 49 $\hat{5}$ fulfills that role. In 28 a different structure emerges during P: the principal melodic line descends from the fifth to the first scale degree. Since a background $\hat{3}>\hat{2}$ trajectory transpires during the remainder of the exposition, I propose that in this situation the *Kopfton*'s arrival occurs not during P, but instead during the tonic's 6 phase at the outset of TR. The B♭ that serves as the point of origin for the descending fifth-progression during P may be regarded as interior to a gradually emerging background structure that culminates in the G (*Kopfton* $\hat{3}$) at 17_1. (Though B♭ moves up an octave from its starting point during P, the cadence at measure 16 is in the lower register. The B♭ of 1_1 and the G of 17_{1-2} form an ascending sixth.)

Example 2.11 Analysis of Haydn: Piano Sonata in E♭ Major (H. XVI: 28), mvmt. 1, mm. 1–16.

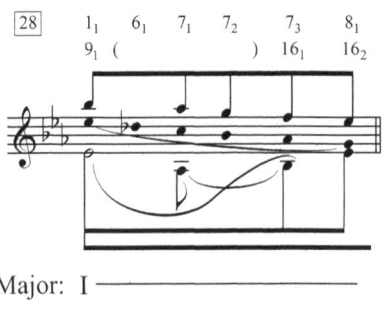

E♭ Major: I ─────────────────

(= $I^{8-7\flat}$ IV^{10-9}_{8-7} V^7 I)

Two similar phrases, both ending in PACs, shape P during this exposition. The first begins with a local B♭>E♭ fifth, traversed twice. Then E♭ leaps over the B♭ register (during 4_1), followed by B♭ leaping over this E♭ register (during 6_1). As this two-phase upward register transfer is accomplished, a descending interior line from E♭ through D to D♭ imbues the tonic chord that re-emerges in measure 6 with a dominant-emulating character. (See **2.11**.) With this momentum, the descent to the PAC occurs without a hitch in measures 7 and 8. (The F>E♭ second that concludes the descending fifth undergoes a routine expansion, as F>D<E♭, echoing the end of measure 1 into measure 2.)

During the phrase repetition that follows, Haydn's modifications are extensive and may seem disconcerting. At first all goes well: the descending fifth from B♭ that opened the first phrase is repeated in measures 9 and 10 (now traversed only once), and the upward transfer of B♭ is efficiently accomplished by 12_1. Complementing the B♭<E♭<B♭ ascending contour of measures 3 through 6, descending B♭>E♭>B♭ occurs during measures 12 and 13. Yet the harmonic foundation seems to have run amuck. In the first phrase the B♭ transfer transpires during a $I^{8-7\flat}$ expansion. One would think that the chord of measure 13 should, like that of measure 5, lead to $I^{7\flat}$. No such tonic restoration occurs. Instead Haydn pursues an alternative path to the dominant, displayed in **2.12**. This seems a better explanation for the succession from measure 13 to measure 14 than that the model of the earlier phrase is repeated with a gaping hole at the place where the chord of measure 6 should recur.[22]

Example 2.12 Analysis of Haydn: Piano Sonata in E♭ Major (H. XVI: 28), mvmt. 1, mm. 9–16.

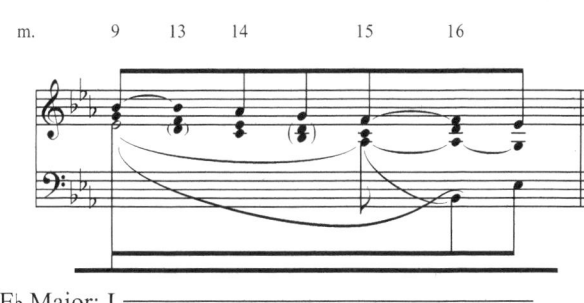

Some general observations about Haydn's P sections can be culled from this data, as follows:

(1) The opening tonic harmony may flourish in as simple a presentation as mere arpeggiation, with some modest passing or neighboring embellishment; or it may be prolonged by means of a local harmonic progression that supports a linear connection between chord members (most often a descending third-progression from $\hat{3}$) or neighboring motion. Though the *Kopfton* often is present at or near the outset of P, it also may serve as the goal of a linear motion ascending from $\hat{1}$ or, when $\hat{3}$ serves as the *Kopfton*, descending from $\hat{5}$. When P incorporates a second phrase that opens like the first, one should expect alterations within its initial tonic presentation, perhaps incorporating insertions of new content that increase the number of measures engaged.

(2) Within the phrase that establishes the tonic, the succession from I to IV or to II in first inversion is accomplished without fuss. Since those chords employ the fourth scale degree as bass, one modest gesture that promotes their attainment is to present the tonic chord in its first inversion. Modifications of greater potency include raising the tonic chord's fifth by a half step (thereby targeting the IV chord's third, as in G<G♯<A in C Major) or incorporating a minor seventh (targeting IV's third from above).

(3) When IV comes between I and V, it may be extended via its 6 phase. In the sonatas under consideration this is done without chromatic modification: that is, F-A-C in C Major may proceed to F-A-D (perhaps unfurled to D-F-A) but will not evolve further into D-F♯-A or F♯-A-C-E♭. (It seems that Haydn is reserving F♯ for the II♯ harmony within TR.)

(4) The V chord often is of brief duration. Especially when the $\hat{2}$ of a middleground third-progression is present in the melody during the preceding II or IV^6, it may be omitted at the top of the texture during V.

(5) The concluding I will not be prolonged within the phrase. If the tonic is to be extended, Haydn will embark upon a phrase repetition or codetta.

The transition (TR)

The sonatas under consideration were selected because their transitions all follow the same basic tonal trajectory: from the tonic's 5 phase through its 6 phase to a major chord on the supertonic. The exposition's energy abates temporarily on II♯, in a significant event called the medial caesura (MC), which may or may not incorporate a moment of total silence. The energy reignites with the onset of the secondary-theme zone (S) in the dominant key. (From a broad tonal perspective the harmonic progression is represented as I$^{5-6}$ II♯ V. In that the goal V is invariably tonicized, the preceding II♯ often is interpreted as V in the key of the dominant, as is the Hepokoski/Darcy notation "V:HC MC" – a medial caesura at a half cadence in the dominant key.) These signature events appear in their most normative formulation in **2.13**. Haydn's realizations of TR range from simple and brief to complex and extended. The five TR prototypes presented in **2.14** reveal the range of his practice within the twelve expositions we are considering.

Regarding **2.14a** (transposed in **2.15**):

|30| The first half of the exposition's two-part structure in |30| is ternary: a₁ b a₂. Though a₂, which corresponds to TR, begins like a₁ (at 16₂),

Example 2.13 Model for the structure of an exposition.

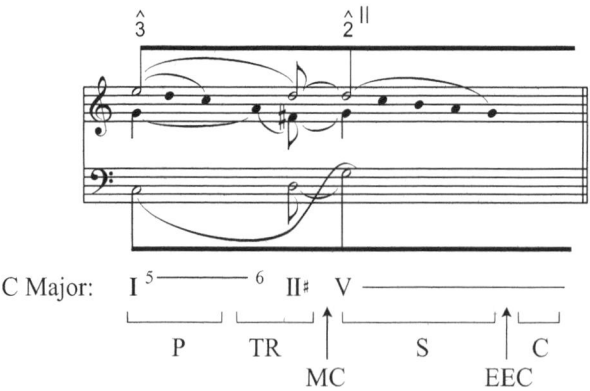

Example 2.14 Five models for the transition (TR) within Haydn's expositions.

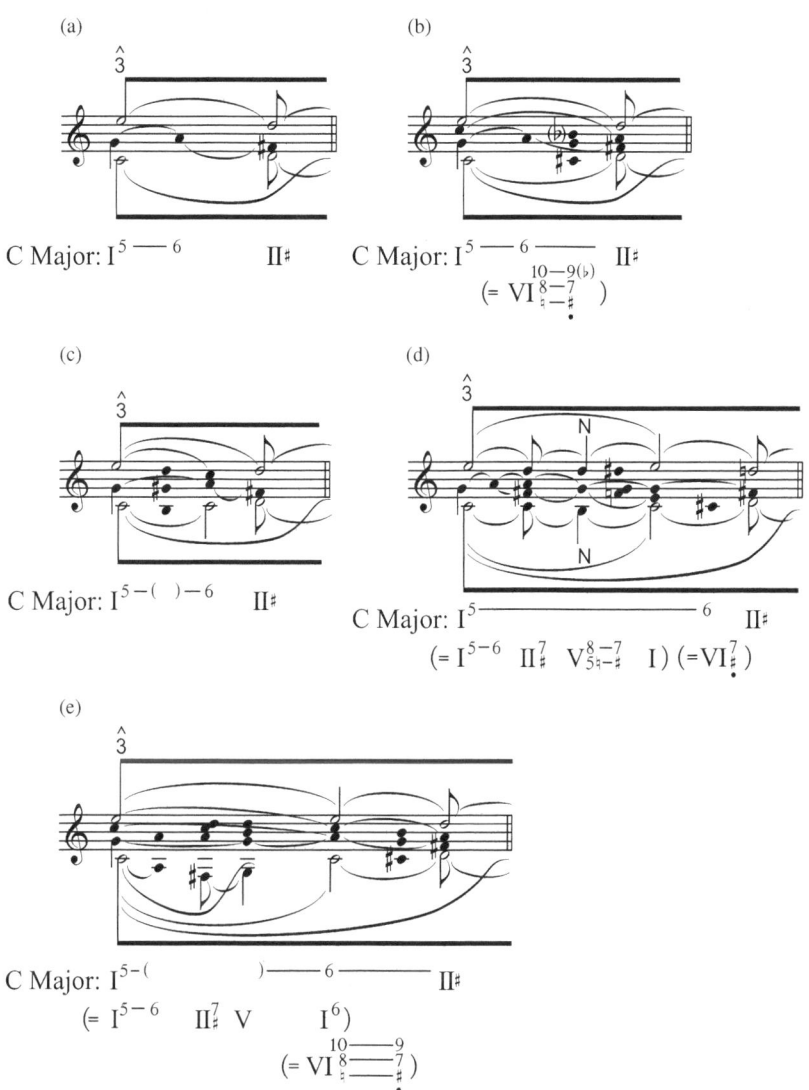

the harmonic progression soon takes a new course: an upward register transfer is pursued, leading to the emergence of the tonic's 6-phase chord and then II♯. (At some point during TR – perhaps sooner for some auditors than for others, or sooner on the second hearing than on the first – the broad I$^{5-6}$ II♯ progression may begin to resonate as IV$^{5-6}$ V in the tonicized dominant key.) Here, as is often the case (and a contributing factor in the energy loss at the MC), $\hat{2}$ does not sound at the top of the texture during II♯. Though C♯ (= *Kopfton* $\hat{3}$) is

Example 2.15 Analysis of Haydn: (a) Piano Sonata in A Major (H. XVI: 30), mvmt. 1 (a) mm. 17–21; (b) Piano Sonata in E♭ Major (H. XVI: 25), mvmt. 1, P through m. 14; (c) Piano Sonata in E Major (H. XVI: 30), mvmt. 1, P through m. 11.

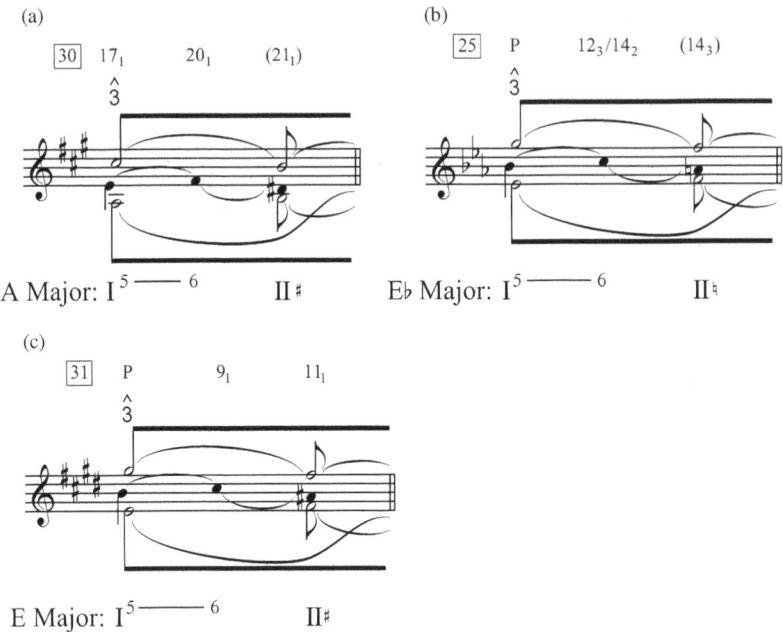

understood to have descended to B at 21_1, that pitch is absent from the upper register until 33_1, well into S. Despite that quirk, this TR gets the job done with minimal fuss, deploying the chords essential to the transition's task and little else.

25   The TR in 25 differs in two principal respects from that in 30. First, the tonic does not extend even minimally into TR: material reminiscent of the opening of P inaugurates TR on the 6-phase C minor chord, rather than the E♭ tonic itself.[23] (Consequently the grid of measure numbers above the graph in **2.15** displays "P" as the initiating tonic's location.) Second, the 6-phase chord is extended via a B♮-D-G embellishing chord that supports the filling-in of the C triad's upper third (G>F>E♭). High G (= 3̂, first sounded in this register during 5_4) emerges only at the end of this 6-phase extension (at 14_2), and, like the situation in 30, its successor (F) is absent during the major supertonic and will not establish itself in the upper register until well into S (at $18_{1–2}$). In this instance the MC that separates TR from S is made more emphatic through a rest in all parts at the end of measure 14.

Example 2.16 Analysis of Haydn: Piano Sonata in E♭ Major (H. XVI: 49), mvmt. 1, mm. 13–21; Piano Sonata in E♭ Major (H. XVI: 52), mvmt. 1, mm. 9–14.

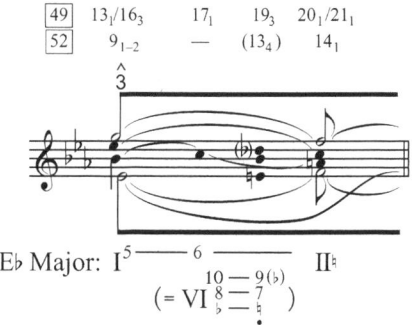

| 31 | Haydn extends the 6-phase chord more vigorously in 31 than in 25. Measures 9 and 10 present a full-fledged tonicization of C♯ Minor, supporting a G♯>F♯>E>D♯>C♯ melodic descent. (Observe how the concluding D♯>C♯ is embellished by unfolded upper thirds, as D♯<F♯ to E>C♯, echoing the cadence in E Major during measure 8.) The II♯ goal harmony is extended as well. Whereas in 30 and 25 only a $_{4-3\sharp}^{6-5}$ embellishment extends the major supertonic, in 31 a more expansive structure supports the melody's foreground F♯>E>D♯>C♯ fourth, as follows: |

m. 11_1 11_2 11_3 12_3

8 — 7 — 6 — 5

3♯ ——— 4 — 3♯

root: F♯ ————

The $^6_4$ chord is unfurled, first into $^5_3$ position and then into $^6_3$ position. What may seem to be a B major arrival at 11_{3-4} is not the equivalent of the genuine B major chord that inaugurates S at 13_1, following the MC. The B at 11_{3-4} (and continuing in the upper registers in measure 12) is a neighbor to the F♯ chord's third (A♯), to which it returns during 12_3. It is not asserted as a root.

Regarding **2.14b** (transposed in **2.16**):

| 49 | In 49 TR must accomplish a special task before proceeding to its transitional duties: namely, to make amends for the aberrant cadence that concludes P. The A♭>D dissonance of 11_3 is only half resolved by E♭ at 12_1. By rights, A♭ should descend to G, and in fact Haydn |

belatedly fulfills that obligation, in two registers, during measures 14 and 16. Once that is accomplished, the tonic's 6-phase chord emerges. In 31 we observed how Haydn extends $\hat{3}$ during the tonic's 6 phase via a downward fifth that touches upon all three of its members (G♯, E, and C♯). In 49 he inverts the direction of that initiative, ascending from G through C (at 17_1) to E♭ (at 19_1). The major supertonic supports G's successor, F (at measures 21 and 22), after a gradual descent from the upper register.

One crucial event, not yet mentioned, inspired me to create a separate template for this TR [**2.14b**, **2.16**]. Namely, the 6-phase chord *evolves* during 19_3: from diatonic C-E♭-G into chromatic and dissonant E♮-(G)-B♭-D. Variants of this surge are deployed as embellishing chords during an expansion of II♮: G-B♭-C-E♮ in measures 20 through 22, G-B♭-D♭-E♮ in measures 22 and 23, and G♭-B♭-(D♭)-E♮ in measure 23. That expansion confirms soprano F (= $\hat{2}$), after which minor seventh E♭ emerges (held by a fermata), guiding the progression towards the imminent tonicized B♭ Major.[24]

52 Recall that in 30 the a_2 of the exposition's ternary first part veers off in the direction of II♯, performing the duties of TR. Likewise in 52 the a_2 of a binary (a_1 a_2) first part corresponds to TR. Much of the content of measures 9 through 13, with variants, omissions, and rearrangements, corresponds to content from the opening eight measures, until the tonic's evolved 6-phase chord E♮-(G)-B♭-D♭ emerges at 13_4, in place of the 5-phase chord of 8_2. (The diatonic 6-phase chord is elided, represented in **2.16** by the dash in place of a measure number above that segment of the template.)

The prolongation of the major supertonic from 14_1 through 16_1 is similar to that which occurs in 31, 11_1 through 12_3, though here it is stated twice. Note that Haydn adds a dollop of modal mixture: whereas the descending fourth in 31 proceeds as F♯>E>D♯>C♯, that in 52 proceeds as F>E♭>D♭>C (in the tenor register), making S's arrival in tonicized B♭ Major at measure 17 all the more radiant. The passing $^6_4$ chord here absorbs additional content: G♭ and E♮ (connected by passing note F, echoing bass pitches from measure 13) sound with F, B♭, and D♭ for a potent dissonant effect.[25] During these repetitions the soprano twice resolves as E♮ to F. The third time (at 16_{3-4}) E♮ instead descends to E♭. This reprises Haydn's strategy during the supertonic prolongation in 49, where twice E♮ proceeds

Example 2.17 Analysis of Haydn: Piano Sonata in D Major (H. XVI: 51), mvmt. 1, mm. 20–25.

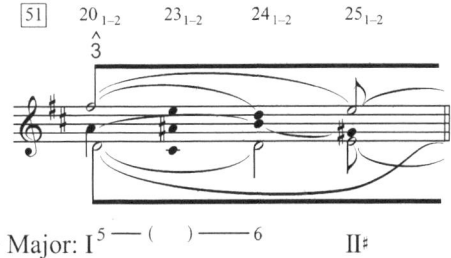

to F and then, as TR concludes, the F is elided and seventh E♭ emerges.

Regarding **2.14c** (transposed in **2.17**):

|51| A strategy deployed in |49| – namely, upward arpeggiation from $\hat{3}$ for a melodic unfolding of the 6-phase chord – is called into service in |51| as well: F♯<B<D extends from 22_2 through 24_2. Every phrase-opening traversal of D<F♯ (1_1 through 2_1, 5_1 through 6_1, 11_1 through 13_1, 15_1 through 17_1, and now 20_{1-2}) is followed by an upward thrust. Here that motion results in a register transfer in the midst of the middleground F♯>E>D third displayed in **2.17**. Though II♯'s E (= $\hat{2}$) does sound among the melody's eighth notes in measure 25, it is more dramatically stated at 28_2 (within S), the goal both of a broad stepwise ascent from A and of a local stepwise descending flourish from C♯.

The embellishing chord of measure 23, which connects the tonic's 5- and 6-phase chords, has no precedent in the TRs we have explored thus far, and thus a new template is warranted [**2.14c**, **2.17**]. Whereas a similar chord followed the 6-phase chord in |31| (at 9_2) as a means of extension, now it heralds its arrival.

Regarding **2.14d** (transposed in **2.18**):

|29| The six remaining TR sections are more complex than those we have examined thus far, and they present a serious analytical challenge. Comparing the first three prototypes of **2.14** and the fourth, note that only the latter contains two II♯ chords, both preceded by the tonic's 6-phase chord. Which II♯ corresponds to that of the first three prototypes? My analysis in **2.14d** proposes that it is the second.[26]

Example 2.18 Analysis of Haydn: Piano Sonata in F Major (H. XVI: 29), mvmt. 1, mm. 6–14.

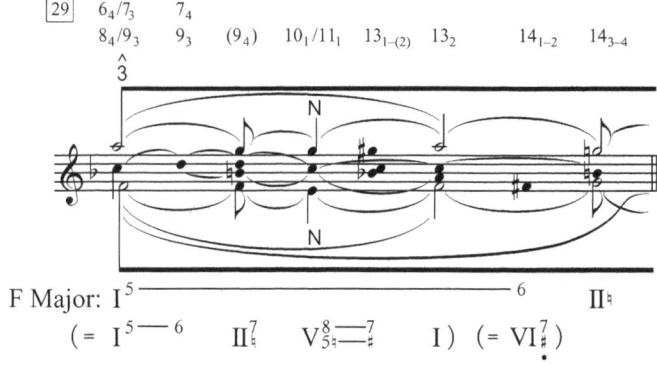

The first II♯ falls within a prolongation of the initial tonic; that prolongation's internal dominant is *not* the onset of the background dominant that will extend through S; the II♯ that concludes TR *precedes* the arrival of the background dominant. The content of 10_1 through 13_1 in 29 so dynamically tonicizes C Major that one may well suspect that "the" dominant has arrived, followed by a I→ IV$^{5-6}$ V progression in C Major during the remainder of TR [**2.18**]. Yet the role of TR is to come *between* the tonic and dominant regions. The dominant ought not to arrive before its herald.[27]

The initiating I$^{5-6}$ motion within the local tonic prolongation that opens TR in 29 is stated twice. (Consequently there are two rows of measure numbers in **2.18**.) Whereas the 6 phase is extended the first time, its second presentation is brief (at 9_3), followed by a swift onward push through II♮ to V. Though soprano G does not sound during this II♮, it eventually shines forth during V. The restored A (= $\hat{3}$) at 13_3 is transferred an octave lower during the tonic's evolved 6 phase (at 14_2), and its successor, G, humorously appears two additional octaves lower (at 14_4).

Regarding **2.14e** (transposed in **2.19**):

23   Whereas I-space extends through a restored tonic in **2.14d**, the tonic's 6-phase chord comes immediately after the local dominant in our final prototype, **2.14e**. Again there is a danger of interpreting that dominant (during measure 18 in 23) as the arrival of background V. I propose instead that the $_F^A$ outer-voice structure at 13_1 connects

Example 2.19 Analysis of Haydn: (a) Piano Sonata in F Major (H. XVI: 23), mvmt. 1, mm. 13-20; (b) Piano Sonata in E♭ Major (H. XVI: 28), mvmt. 1, P through m. 24; Piano Sonata in E♭ Major (H. XVI: 45), mvmt. 1, mm. 12-18; (c) Piano Sonata in C Major (H. XVI: 35), mvmt. 1, mm. 16-35; (d) Piano Sonata in A♭ Major (H. XVI: 46), mvmt. 1, mm. 9-17.

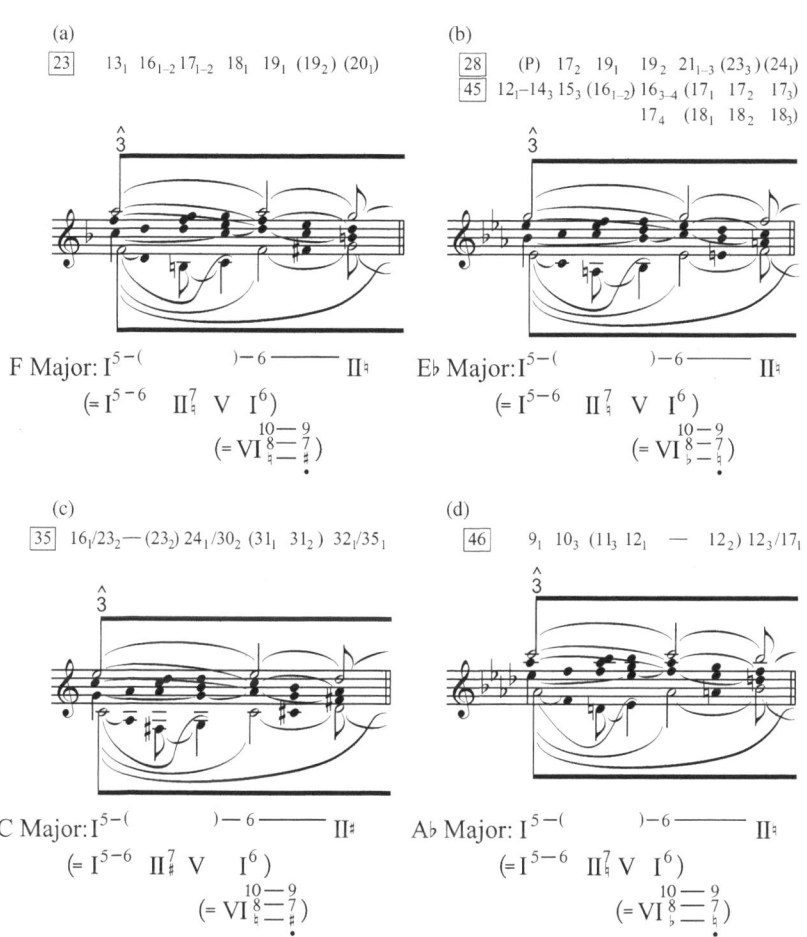

with that at 19_1, where the F-A-C chord absorbs sixth D. As often happens, *Kopfton* A's successor, G, is absent from the top of the texture during measure 20. It is restored quickly, as the melody's first pitch at the outset of S in measure 21.

|28| Despite shifts in the durations of the various events, the structure of TR in |28| is closely allied to that in |23|. For example, the one-beat B♮-D-G chord at 17_1 in |28| corresponds to the more potent A-C♯-E-G chord that is prolonged for two measures (14 and 15) in |23|. (This

embellishing chord functions at the structure's surface and consequently is not displayed in the prototype graph.) Though soprano G sounds in measures 21 through 23 (embellished by upper third B♭), its successor, F, is absent during the major supertonic (measure 24). As in $\boxed{23}$, we do not need to wait long for its reinstatement, at the outset of S (25_1).

$\boxed{45}$ Varying the temporal weighting of structural components during TR, noted above, persists in $\boxed{45}$, where I-space luxuriantly fills three measures, while the remaining chords leading to the major supertonic take up only three measures. (The latter part of the progression is then repeated, starting at 17_4.) TR opens with an extension of P's initiating G<B♭<E♭ sixth, now spanning a thirteenth between 11_3 and 12_1. Whereas during P that sixth collapsed downwards into an E♭<G third, during measures 13 and 14 Haydn attains the G *above* the register of the sixth/thirteenth. For a while the upper and lower Gs compete for supremacy. Only when the upper one gains ascendency (during 14_3) does TR continue with the tonic's 6-phase chord. *Kopfton* G sounds three times in the upper register during the opening tonic expanse and again during the tonic's 6 phase (at 15_3). The F during 16_4 is the last we hear from this upper strand: though F is a passing note to E♭, no E♭ sounds in the upper register during 17_1, nor does the *Kopfton* G return above it. (Compare with the prominent sounding of equivalent F and A during measure 19 of $\boxed{23}$, or E♭ and G during measure 21 of $\boxed{28}$.) The approach to the MC is reduced to a bare minimum: $\substack{B♭ \\ E♮}$ to $\substack{A \\ F}$. Fortunately the texture is refortified at the onset of S: *Kopfton* G's successor, F, sounds during 19_2.

$\boxed{35}$ Two events in measure 23 of $\boxed{35}$ warrant comment: first, the local 6-phase chord that has occurred at this point in the other TR regions corresponding to prototype **2.14d** or **2.14e** is absent; second, the melody does not descend to D, but instead begins an ascending trajectory that eventually reaches D an octave higher (repeated numerous times between 26_2 and 30_2). As was also the case in $\boxed{45}$, the C that is passing note D's goal is absent (at 31_1). Again the structure's upper strands disappear, though in this case their restoration falls within TR rather than S: E's successor D *does* sound prominently during the major supertonic chord, in several registers, and A sounds as well. Despite the duration of its prolongation, the dominant harmony of measures 24 through 30 is internal to a tonic-extending 5–6 shift, as displayed in the model of **2.19**.[28] In this case the 6-phase chord evolves not into C♯-E-G-B, as presented in the model, but instead into the less complex form C♯-E-G-A.

| 46 | The structure of TR in | 46 | relates to that in | 52 | and | 29 | in that no diatonic 6-phase chord sounds between I-space and the major supertonic. Much happens during the span from 11_3 through 12_3: the unfolding of two strands ($^{A♭>G}_{D♮<E♭}$) transpires in the bass against its complement ($^{D♮<E♭}_{A♭>G}$) in the soprano, at the end of which the local dominant is embellished by a double suspension ($^{A♭>G}_{F> \ E♭}$) whose resolution occurs after root E♭ gives way to the evolved 6-phase's A♮. (The diatonic 6-phase chord would be A♭-C-F. Its evolved state is here A♮-(C)-E♭-G.) Though the upper-strand C (= $\hat{3}$) is absent during this chord, its successor B♭ arrives at the end of TR (at 17_1). The major supertonic is prolonged for several measures, pursuing repetitions of a progression similar to one that Haydn deploys in | 31 | and | 52 | as well:

m.   (12_3) 13_1 13_2 13_3
m.   (13_3) 14_1 14_2 14_3
m.   (14_3) 15_3 15_4 16_2
m.   (16_2) 16_3 16_4 17_1
          8 – 7 – 6 – 5
          5————————— 4 – 3♮
root: B♭ ————————

In my reading of 12_{1-2}, a B♭>A♭>G line fills in the $^{B♭}_{G}$ third within the **2.19** model's fourth chord. There is no A♭>G>F line, corresponding to the second-highest strand in the model's fifth through seventh chords. (The fifth chord has been elided.) As if to compensate, Haydn presents A♭>G>F four times during an extension of II♮. The first two, in measures 13 and 14, are easy to spot. But note also those that occur from 15_3 through 16_2 and from 16_3 through 17_1.

The secondary-theme zone (S)

In the expositions under consideration, TR prepares for the arrival of the dominant, which will be tonicized during the secondary-theme zone (S). In each case $\hat{2}$ serves as the structural soprano during S. (See **2.13**.) Just as a middleground third-progression often emanates from $\hat{3}$ within P (E>D>C in C Major, as shown in **2.1**), the $\hat{2}$ within S will serve as the starting point for a fifth-progression (D>C>B>A>G) whose close is the exposition's most crucial cadential point, the essential expositional closure (EEC).[29] (When reiterations extend S, the last of multiple cadences is designated as the EEC.) A brief closing zone (C) will follow.

The bass support for a D-to-G fifth-progression may take one of two forms: it may transpire as a single arpeggiation (I–V–I in the tonicized dominant key) or as a double arpeggiation (I–V–I–V–I). With either harmonization the structure may be extended by means of an interruption:

$$\hat{2}$$
$$D > C > B > A \parallel (D > C > B > A) > G$$

The basic structures that Haydn employs for S in the sonata expositions under consideration are displayed in **2.20**. In the transpositions of these models that follow, the arrays of measure numbers reveal that repetition is a more prominent feature of S than of P and that such repetitions often focus on segments of the fifth-progression, D>C>B and B>A>G being the most common reiterations. Because multiple PACs often occur, the point of division between S and C may be difficult to determine. Rather than seeking exact melodic parallels in the repetitions, it is more productive to consider the agenda of S – that is, the traversal of the descending fifth-progression. If that span holds sway over the structure of a passage, then that passage likely resides within S. In these sonatas the agenda of C will be modest and generally distinct from that of S.

Regarding **2.20a** (reproduced in **2.21**):

|35| Soprano D at 33_1 (within TR) anticipates the arrival of $\hat{2}$ at 41_1 (within S), while the interior A>F♯ unfolding of 31_1 through 32_1 is complemented by G<B in 37_1 through 40_1. The stepwise connection of G and D (measures 37 through 41) will recur, either ascending or descending, several times (measures 45–48, 50–56, and 57–58), a key factor in determining that what begins during 45_2 should be regarded as an extension of S, rather than as the onset of C.[30] A simple form of dominant emulation emerges at the end of measure 41: the local tonic's fifth is raised a half step, helping direct the progression to IV (D<D♯<E). (Note how Haydn picks up the chromatic D♯<E as a motivic device starting in measure 45 and continuing through most of the remainder of S.) Soprano E at 42_1 is a neighbor to D, extraneous to the broader descending-fifth trajectory. The *fortissimo* C on

Example 2.20 Eight models for the secondary-theme zone (S) within Haydn's expositions.

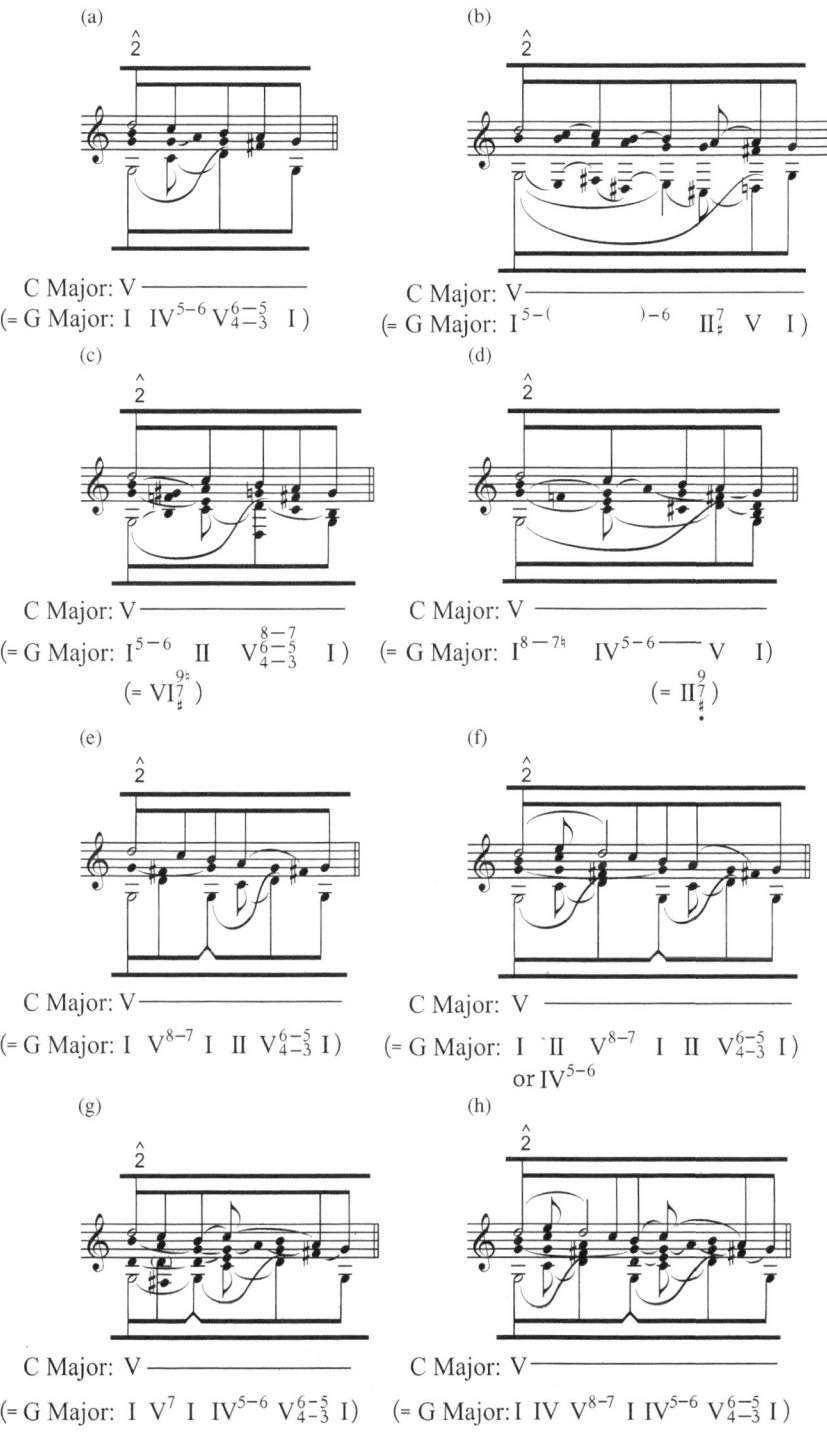

Example 2.21 Analysis of Haydn: Piano Sonata in C Major (H. XVI: 35), mvmt. 1, mm. 36–62.

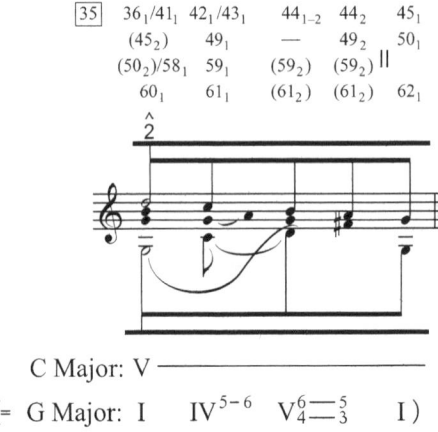

the following downbeat directs the line on its downward course. (By this point the IV chord has shifted to its 6 phase.[31]) Though B "belongs" in the soprano at 44_1, it is withheld until the grace note embellishing the following beat. A PAC is achieved at 45_1.

The extensions of S that follow this cadence employ a different means of extending I-space (a parallel progression of $^6_3$ chords, similar to that which connects I and II in **2.12**), though the melodic fifth between D and G is traversed in all cases. The D of the preceding measures extends conceptually (though not in sound) into 45_2: D♯ is a chromatic passing note from that retained D, leading to neighbor E before the line proceeds downwards to G. (This D is explicitly stated once again during 58_1.) Each of the three cadential attempts after that of 45_1 is in some way defective. (The measure numbers in **2.21** indicate their locations.) In measure 49 Haydn jumps from C to A in the melodic descent, with no connective B.[32] In measure 59 the C>B>A portion of the descent occurs in the tenor register, and the cadence is withheld. On yet another try, again with a diversion into the tenor register, the EEC is achieved (at 62_1).

Regarding **2.20b** and **2.20c** (transposed in **2.22**):

25   It is characteristic for Haydn to repeat – often several times – various segments of the foundational descending-fifth line during S. One version of this phenomenon is so pervasive in tonal music – and so

Anatomy of the I–II♯–V two-part exposition 71

powerful a tool in shaping a binary division – that it has earned a special name: *interruption*. After the line traverses the path from the fifth to the second scale degree (perhaps with internal repetitions), it begins again on the fifth scale degree, this time reaching the first scale degree. Though the repetitions that Haydn pursues during S generally reiterate not only segments of the structural melodic descent but also the corresponding harmonic support (so that multiple sets of measure numbers may be placed above the various model transpositions, such as **2.21**), the two downward trajectories during S in $\boxed{25}$ are supported in contrasting ways. These alternatives are displayed in **2.20b** and **2.20c**: one that in $\boxed{25}$ continues only so far as the dominant (HC); and another that ends in a PAC. Despite the contrasting support, an interruption-induced binary construction results nevertheless. Though the initial I^{5-6} leads to the supertonic in both, in the first phrase that supertonic arrives at a later point during the structural melodic descent than it does during the second. (See **2.22**.) The strategies of the two phrases are diametrically opposed: whereas the first is luxuriant and slow-paced, the second rushes towards the cadence only to be thwarted in achieving resolution, requiring backtracking before the V^7 ultimately leads to I.[33] Observe how much time is devoted to the opening tonic expansion in the first phrase: each tonic-triad pitch in turn is the goal of a descending fourth during the melody of measures 15 through 18: E♭>D>C>B♭, G>F>E♭>D, B♭>A♭>G>F. Those maneuvers fill less than two measures during the second phrase (22_1 through 23_3).

The voice leading that restores tonic B♭ during 18_{1-2} is developed sequentially along a descending path to the tonic's 6-phase chord at 19_2. The bass E♮<F from 19_3 to 21_1 continues this pattern, though the considerable emphasis placed upon the E♮ warrants the chord's interpretation as an evolved supertonic, rather than as a voice-leading chord within a more extended sequential descent.[34] Sounding along with the structural F>E♭>D>C melodic descent is the inner strand D>C>B♭>A♮, which Haydn transfers to the top of the texture during measures 18 through 21.

The abrupt diminished seventh chord at 23_4 thwarts any hope that the consequent phrase might employ the same harmonic trajectory as the antecedent. This evolved tonic 6-phase chord pushes towards II before the structural melody has left the starting gate, and thus the supertonic supports E♭ (at 24_{1-2}) rather than C (as in 19_3 through 20_4). Though the dominant at 24_{3-4} supports the continuing descending

Example 2.22 Analysis of Haydn: Piano Sonata in E♭ Major (H. XVI: 25), mvmt. 1, mm. 15–27.

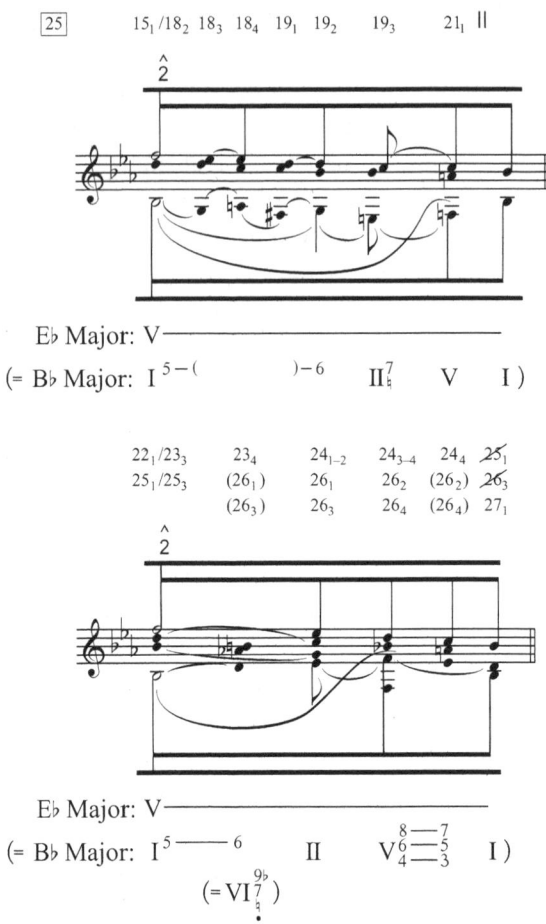

trajectory in an exemplary manner, the expected PAC does not materialize at 25_1. The measure numbers in **2.22** document how two further attempts are required before closure is achieved at 27_1. (The tonic's 6-phase chord reverts from its evolved state to diatonic G-B♭-(D). E♭-G during 26_1 and 26_3 stands for (C)-E♭-G.[35])

Regarding **2.20d** (transposed in **2.23**):

| 31 | An interruption establishes a binary division within S in 31. As was also the case in 25, the two downward trajectories are harmonized in contrasting ways, as **2.23** displays: in the antecedent phrase the middle pitch of the fifth-progression is supported by the supertonic,

Anatomy of the I–II♯–V two-part exposition 73

Example 2.23 Analysis of Haydn: Piano Sonata in E Major (H. XVI: 31), mvmt. 1, mm. 13–21.

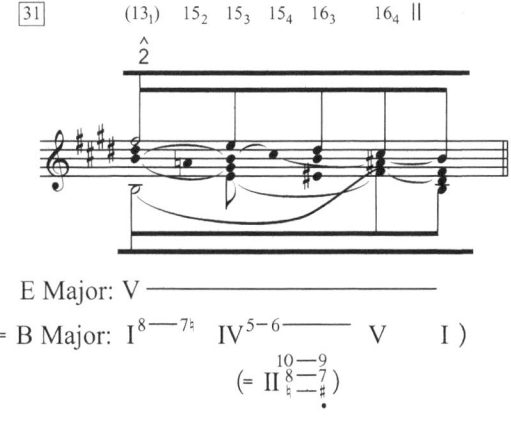

E Major: V ─────────────────────
(= B Major: $I^{8\text{—}7\natural}$ $IV^{5\text{–}6}$ ──── V   I)
$\quad\quad\quad\quad\quad\quad\quad (= II^{\begin{smallmatrix}10\text{—}9\\8\text{—}7\\\natural\text{—}\sharp\end{smallmatrix}})$

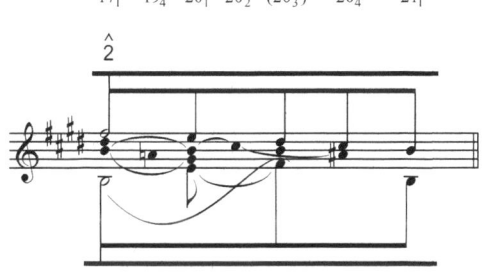

E Major: V ─────────────────────
(= B Major: $I^{8\text{—}7\natural}$ $IV^{5\text{–}6}$ $V^{6\text{—}5}_{4\text{—}3}$ I)

the asserted and evolved 6-phase chord of IV (E-G♯-C♯, represented by E♯-(G♯)-B-D♯), whereas in the consequent a cadential $^6_4$ supports that pitch, in what appears in **2.23** as a **2.20a** prototype infused with elements from the **2.20d** prototype. (The $^6_4$ occurs at 20₃, where a downward dip in the melody allows us to imagine a D♯ to connect the preceding E and the trilled C♯ that follows.[36] Because the cadential $^6_4$ is unfurled into $^6_3$ position, D♯ occurs in the bass.) In both phrases the initial tonic eventually takes on a minor seventh, surging towards the subdominant. Because an upper-register F♯ is not stated during the establishment of B Major in measures 13 through 15, a prolongation of F♯ from TR (at 11₁) into S will hook up with the E>D♯>C♯ of

Example 2.24 Analysis of Haydn: (a) Piano Sonata in E♭ Major (H. XVI: 28), mvmt. 1, mm. 25–51; (b) Piano Sonata in F Major (H. XVI: 29), mvmt. 1, mm. 15–30; (c) Piano Sonata in D Major (H. XVI: 51), mvmt. 1, mm. 26–39.

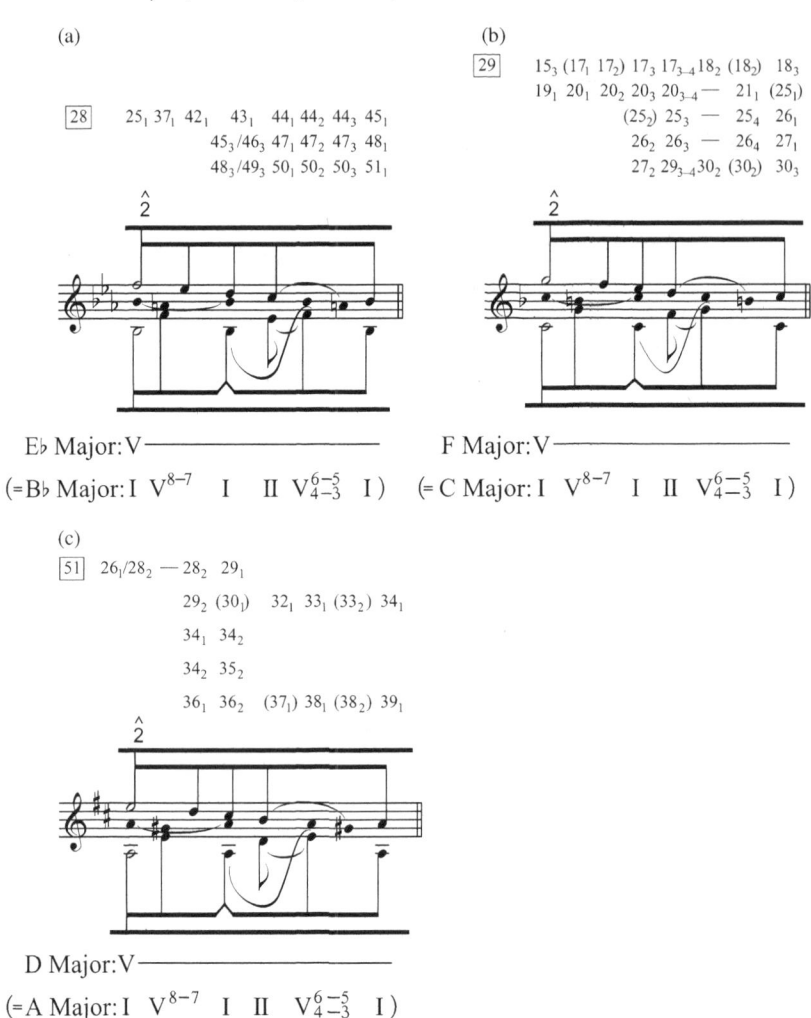

15_3 through 16_4. (F♯ is emphasized in the alto register at 14_1 and 15_1, but not in the register in which the line descends.)

Regarding **2.20e** (transposed in **2.24**):

[28] The structural model **2.20e** incorporates a double arpeggiation (I–V–I–V–I), sharing features with **2.20g** in the D>C>B segment of the fifth-progression and with **2.20f** in the B>A>G segment. In [28], S's

initial I-space alternates between tonicized B♭ Major's $\smash{\overset{F}{\underset{D}{}}}$ and $\smash{\overset{D}{\underset{B\flat}{}}}$ thirds, above root B♭. The latter third sounds at the top of the texture during 28_1, a register revisited during 34_{1-2}, at the end of a local I–II→V^{8-7}–I progression that transpires between measures 29 and 34. In this initial traversal that harmonization supports a melodic line with an ascending contour: F>E♮<F<G<A<B♭<D.[37] A repetition of the same harmonic progression then supports another F-to-D line, this time descending: F (measure 34), E♮ (measure 36), F (measure 37), E♭ (measure 42), D (measure 43).[38] The fifth-progression's lower third is traversed quickly, from measure 43 through measure 45. In compensation, Haydn repeats that segment two additional times during the remaining measures of S, as shown in **2.24**.

Measures 34 through 38 offer some especially intriguing writing. I propose that the progression $I^{5-(\ )-6}$ II→ V transpires. The initial tonic is extended through a descending fifth-progression: F>E♭>D>C>B♭. An elision occurs at the B♭: instead of the B♭ tonic root, the bass instead sounds a G (at 36_1), which joins with B♭ to form the tonic's 6-phase chord, directing the harmonic motion towards II→ and then V. Once V is achieved the forward momentum dissipates: Haydn indicates *Adagio* and allows the F to persist during a half-note chord with fermata. Will this progression be revived, or must we begin anew? It turns out that the dominant is not an endpoint. Little by little it is reenergized, ultimately attaining its minor seventh in the melody (at 42_1), after which the progression continues without a hitch.

| 29 | The S of 29 shares not only the deep structure of 28, as displayed in **2.20e** and **2.24**, but also various foreground features. For example, in 28 several projections above F (to B♭, then higher to D in measures 26, 28, and 34) precede the structural descent through E♭ to D. Likewise in 29, a C and then an E (in measures 15 and 16) soar above G before the descent through F to E. During II in 28, the structural melodic pitch C is embellished by upper-third E♭ (44_1) and later by a flourish from G through E♭ down to C (47_1). In 29, a similar flourish from A through F down to D occurs in 17_{3-4}. In 28, a hiatus induces concern regarding whether a structurally deep V harmony (measures 37 through 42) will succeed in resolving to I. In 29, an equally vital V harmony (measures 21 through 24) is similarly extended.

The structural descent transpires in its complete form during the first four measures of S, despite two mild aberrations: the dominant during 17_{1-2} is represented in the bass only by a belated leading tone (B♮); and the C of 18_{1-2}, which "should" descend to leading tone B♮ before the resolution to the tonic, is muted by the insurgence of E>D above that strand. Both issues are resolved in the restatement: the dominant's root G sounds during 20_1, and C descends to the leading tone at 21_1. The second tonic closure (at 25_1) is tentative. Several reiterations of the second half of the structure occur in the measures that follow, strengthening the cadential effect.[39]

$\boxed{51}$ The stepwise filling-in of the perfect fifth ^E_A establishes tonicized A Major during the opening measures of S in $\boxed{51}$. The ascending melodic line A<B<C♯<D<E is broken between D (at 27_2) and E (at 28_2), allowing the insertion of a subsidiary downward sixth from C♯. After the diminished fifth $^D_{G♯}$ during 28_2 we may expect a resolution to $^{C♯}_A$. At first Haydn is reticent to supply that resolution directly, though in repetitions it is freely stated (starting at 34_2). In **2.24** I propose that the structural fifth-progression has reached the halfway point as early as 29_1. The descent's remaining two pitches occur for the first time at 32_1 and 34_1, respectively. Most of this tonal terrain is then traversed again. As mentioned above, the D>C♯ segment of the descent is prominently presented during these repetitions. Yet now C♯'s successor, B, is absent (at 37_1). Though one may imagine it (regarding measure 37 as a variant of measure 32, where B fills the first beat), B does not sound until 38_2, just before the cadence.[40]

Regarding **2.20f** (transposed in **2.25**):

$\boxed{46}$ The structural model **2.20f** is only modestly different from that displayed in **2.20e**. It is distinctive in that a harmonically supported upper neighbor embellished its initiating melodic pitch before the descending fifth is traversed. Characteristically, Haydn incorporates considerable internal backtracking in his pursuit of this structure in $\boxed{46}$, as the abundance of measure numbers above the transposed model in **2.25** suggests. Note that there is a reluctance to proceed beyond the first dominant chord. The II and V^7 of measure 20 support a dramatic drop from the upper neighbor, C, to the dominant's leading tone, D♮. (No B♭ sounds in the upper register to resolve the neighboring C.) The milling about in measure 21 sounds like the chatter of spectators who have witnessed an amazing feat. Then, after an energetic reinstatement of the upper-register C in measure

Example 2.25 Analysis of Haydn: (a) Piano Sonata in A♭ Major (H. XVI: 46), mvmt. 1, mm. 18–37; (b) Piano Sonata in A Major (H. XVI: 30), mvmt. 1, mm. 22–55.

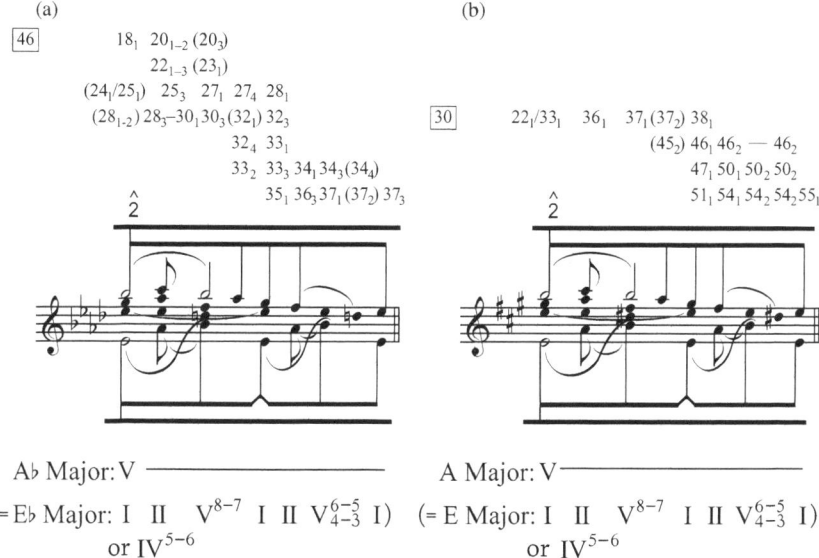

22, that feat is repeated. This time the progression comes to a standstill, with fermatas extending the dominant harmony's whole notes in measure 23.[41]

Haydn compensates for the aberrant behavior of neighbor C by twice reinstating it with a normative continuation. Observe how C descends by step to the dominant's B♭ at 27_1 and at 30_3. The B♭ proceeds through the dominant's seventh A♭ to G (at 28_1 and 32_3), supported by the tonic's root E♭ in the bass. Because neighbor C is now presented in the context of IV^{5-6}, the preceding tonic may be dominant emulating (I→IV). Note that Haydn has planted a high E♭ as early as measure 18. Now E♭ (two octaves lower) serves as the starting point for an approach to neighbor C from above.[42] This is most clearly stated in measure 28, where E♭>D♭>C occurs instead of B♭<C. I regard the earlier statement in measures 24 and 25 as a variant upon that normative voice leading: the essence, E♭>D♭>C, is embellished by an incomplete neighbor attained via chromatic filling-in, E♭<E♮<F>D♭>C, in which the initiating E♭ is elided.[43] After reiterations of the A♭>G resolution in measures 32 and 33, the line proceeds to F, the penultimate pitch of the structural descent, in measure 34, supported by a II–V progression. Though poised for resolution, this segment likewise undergoes repetition, delaying the EEC until 37_3.

[30] The I-space that opens S in [30] is extensive, its melody only gradually attaining structural B in the upper register at 33_1, the goal point of a local I^{5-6} II^7 V I harmonic progression beginning in measure 22. (The tonic's 5- and 6-phase chords sound in alternation for several measures before the 6-phase chord's tendency to lead to II is activated at 30_2.) Supported by IV^{5-6}, the structural B's upper neighbor C♯ occurs in the middle register during measure 36.[44] The return of B is supported by a cadential $^6_4$ embellishment, here unfurled into $^6_3$ position (at 37_1). The A that would connect this B and the G♯ at 38_1 is absent (above B and D♯). During a reiteration, that A (in the upper register during 45_2) does sound prominently. Then, after a brief supertonic, the dominant harmony during 46_2 is the first of three approaches (in two registers) to the PAC, which, secured at 55_1, serves as the EEC.

Haydn's humor was in rare form during measures 26 through 28. Chords containing a "wrong" note occur during all three of these measures! F♯ is a stable member of a local dominant harmony in measures 24 and 25. G♯ reaches over this F♯ in measure 26. Listeners will expect the F♯ to resolve to E, as a 9–8 suspension. Neither as ninth against E nor as fourth against C♯ does the F♯ budge. The resolution is postponed until measure 29. Though a similar second occupies the same chordal position in measure 31, that context is not the same. The F♯ in measure 26 is an *incidental* dissonance: it may (and usually will) resolve within the chord. The E in measure 31 is an *essential* dissonance: it is a member of the II^7 harmony and will resolve only with the shift to V.[45]

Regarding **2.20g** (transposed in **2.26**):

[45] In **2.20f** the fifth scale degree is embellished by an upper neighbor; in **2.20g** the third scale degree is. A quick B♭<D<F arpeggiation establishes the tonicized key of B♭ Major during measures 18|19 of [45]. That ascending perfect fifth is matched by a descending E♭>C>A♮ diminished fifth as measure 19 continues. The second half of measure 20 supplies its resolution: D>B♭. Though S extends for a total of 24 measures, the first half of its structural soprano (F>E♭>D) and the first bass arpeggiation (I–V–I) have transpired already during its first two measures. A modified reiteration of this segment (through 24_1) imbues that content with greater weight. For example, soprano F is embellished by neighbor G during measure 21, while an evolved

Anatomy of the I–II♯–V two-part exposition 79

Example 2.26 Analysis of Haydn: (a) Piano Sonata in E♭ Major (H. XVI: 45), mvmt. 1, mm. 19–42; Piano Sonata in E♭ Major (H. XVI: 49), mvmt. 1, mm. 25–60; (b) Piano Sonata in F Major (H. XVI: 23), mvmt. 1, mm. 21–44.

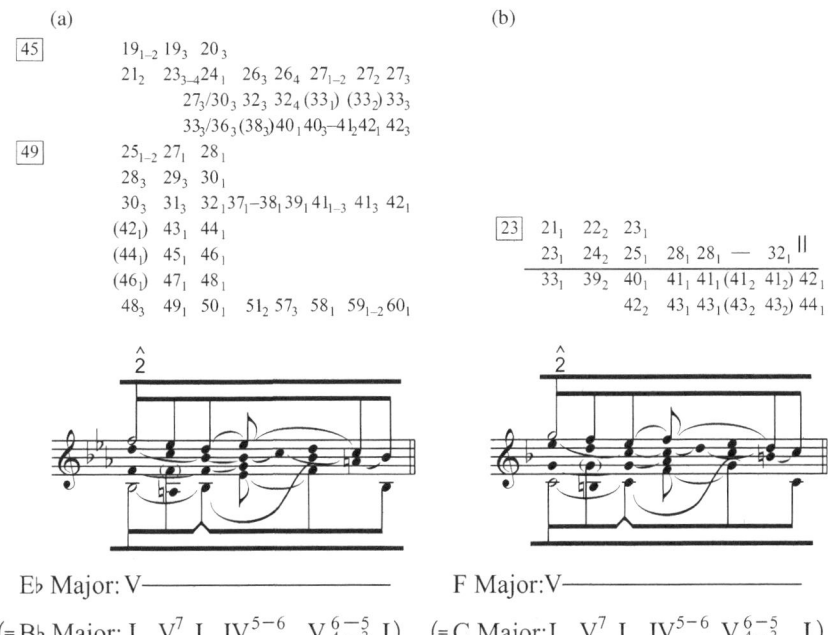

II→ harmony (E♮-G-B♭-D♭) comes between I and V in measures 22 and 23. Measures 24 through 26 offer $\genfrac{}{}{0pt}{}{D<E♭>D}{B♭>A<B♭}$ undulations. Then two significant shifts occur: first, the $\genfrac{}{}{0pt}{}{D}{B♭}$ third that is unfolded during 24_1 and 25_1 is inverted into a $\genfrac{}{}{0pt}{}{B♭}{D}$ sixth during 26_1; and, second, the diminished fifth $\genfrac{}{}{0pt}{}{A♭}{D}$ sounds within I→, resulting in a G>E♭ unfolding within IV as resolution. Of those two pitches, it is E♭ that again displaces D, this time as an *incomplete* neighbor, since the line now passes through D (supported by an unfurled cadential $^6_4$ at 27_{1-2}) to C and finally B♭ for a PAC.[46]

What occurs next may seem to be new material (and thus potentially the onset of C); yet, once I-space has been extended during measures 27 through 30, the same sort of undulation that we encountered in measures 24 through 26 returns, followed by a reprise of the D<B♭ sixth and arrival of incomplete neighbor E♭ (at 32_4). The approach to the cadence in measure 33 matches that of measure 27 in the bass, though the soprano omits several of the structural notes that were vital to the earlier cadence. In the enhanced repetition that follows, the stepwise descent to B♭ is restored in the melody,[47] this

time with the support of a conventional cadential $^6_4$ (bass F – not D – at 40_3!).

The interactions between the pitches E♭ and D form a vibrant component of Haydn's tonal strategy within S. The first E♭ (in two registers during measures 19 and 20) forms a dissonant diminished fifth with A♮, motivating the resolution during the second half of measure 20. A D<E♭>D neighboring motion occurs in the figuration of measures 21 and 22, followed by another diminished fifth at the end of measure 23. Though by this point it is clear that the structural line has descended from F through E♭ to D, Haydn invokes E♭>D motions for several additional measures, propelled by $^{A♮}_{E♭}$ augmented fourths and $^{E♭}_{A♮}$ diminished fifths in alternation. The first challenge to D's hegemony in the melody occurs during measure 26, where a diminished fifth $^{A♭}_{D}$ motivates the move from the tonic to the subdominant (as I→ IV). The resolution pitch E♭ occurs not only in the bass at 26_3, but also among the melody's sixteenth notes during 26_4. The latter functions as an incomplete neighbor: that is, the D that follows in measure 27 is not a restoration of the earlier tonic third, but instead serves as a passing note connecting E♭ and C.

Our contentment in the PAC at 27_3 is brief, since D is reinstated even during the same beat. Two more traversals of the D-through-B♭ span will occur. First, however, D is prolonged via a magnificent descending-octave line, supported by an elaboration of the basic B♭>F<G>D<E♭>B♭ sequential pattern in the bass. D migrates downwards during 27_4, followed by C and then B♭, which migrates upwards during 28_2, followed by A♮. Interlocking descending fourths (D>A♮, B♭>F, G>D) extend I-space within tonicized B♭ Major between 27_3 and 30_3, at which point the $^{E♭}_{A♮}$ diminished fifth returns, prolonging the tonic for two additional measures. Despite its extended prolongation, D eventually gives way (again motivated by a $^{A♭}_{D}$ diminished fifth) to E♭ during the second half of measure 32. The cadence that follows is negligent in its presentation of the structural descent, thereby motivating yet another – and a significantly more elaborate – cadential approach at the end of S. Could Haydn's two-beat trill on C during measure 42 be compensation for that pitch's absence during the cadence of measure 33?

49　The S theme in 49 bears a strong resemblance to the P theme – a common event in Haydn's expositions. At the medial caesura that concludes TR (at 24_1), the II♮ chord's minor seventh E♭ sounds in the

Example 2.27 Analysis of Haydn: Piano Sonata in E♭ Major (H. XVI: 49), mvmt. 1, mm. 32–60.

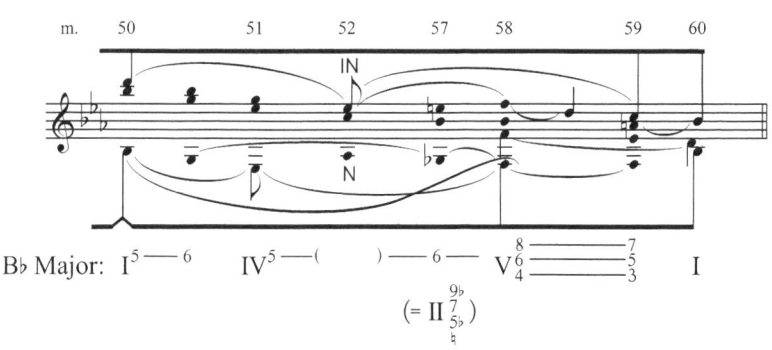

soprano. The structural F (= $\hat{2}$) is restored above E♭'s resolution pitch D at the outset of S. Several traversals of the F>E♭>D third occur during measures 25 through 32, as is noted in **2.26**. The succession from I to IV that follows utilizes a descending fifth in the bass (B♭>E♭), which Haydn divides into two thirds (B♭>G>E♭). (A local harmonic progression transpires during measures 32 through 36: I^{5-6} II V^7 I^6, connecting the B♭ and G. The 6-phase chord internal to that progression appears as dominant-emulating G-B♮-D-F in measure 34.) The IV harmony that arrives at 37_1 behaves conventionally, proceeding from its 5 to its 6 phase. (A graph of this passage is presented in **2.27**.) The structural melody's incomplete neighbor, E♭, is prolonged through 40_3, after which passing note D (whose arrival in the upper register is delayed until 41_3) directs the line to C for the cadential dominant, followed by B♭ at the PAC in measure 42.

The entire structure is traversed a second time with interesting modifications. Though the left-hand part in measures 42 through 48 restores the texture of measures 28ff., and though some of the right-hand material resembles what occurred earlier (for example,

C>A♮>F>E♭>D in measures 43 and 44 is a simplification of the line in measures 27 and 28), the omission of a high F might arouse concern. Haydn belatedly supplies that F at 48_3. The three chords of measure 50 and the second chord of measure 51 correspond to chords from the earlier traversal of the structure: 32_1, 36_{1-2}, 36_3, and 37_1. In the earlier traversal the IV chord undergoes a 5–6 shift, which potently directs the progression towards V. An ever-present danger with a major IV chord is that it instead will take on dominant-emulating tendencies and descend by perfect fifth: E♭ to A♭![48] That is what appears to happen in measure 52. A stark A♭-C-E♭ chord persists for over five measures, with no melodic embellishment whatsoever. Haydn seems to be stalling to ponder the predicament he has gotten himself into. Fortunately a highly evolved variant of IV's 6-phase chord, which arrives at 57_3, saves the day. (C-E♭-G is transformed into E♮-G♭-B♭-D♭, leading to F as II⇒ V.) In retrospect one may come to understand that the E♭ chord has not resolved to an A♭ chord after all, but instead that an embellishing chord (a subdominant version of **1.2**, Model 2 or 4) connects the E♭ chord and its evolved 6 phase. (This passage and the simpler structure of the first traversal are juxtaposed in **2.27**.[49]) Thus the IV^{5-6} V succession of measures 37 through 41 does occur in this restatement, though in a highly altered form.

The F>E♭>D third is traversed numerous times, even during the connection between TR and S. Closely observe how this line is embedded within the figuration. The flowing sixteenth notes during 25_{2-3} do not project a descending sixth (G>B♭), but instead an appoggiatura embellishes F, followed by a descending fifth ($\underline{F}$>B♭). The F is the point of origin for the broader F>E♭>D line that extends through 28_1. Likewise the eight sixteenth notes during 28_{2-3} do not constitute an octave, but instead a fifth (B♭<$\underline{F}$), followed by an upper-fourth extension that places inner-voice B♭ temporarily in the upper position. (Inner-strand B♭>A<B♭ from 25_3–26_1–28_2 sounds above the principal F>E♭>D strand at 28_3–29_2–30_3.) Whereas the sixteenth notes during measure 30 function in the same way, the context of measure 32 is different. Since the line continues upwards in measure 33, I suggest that structural F is not reinstated at 32_3. Instead the D of 32_1 is transferred up an octave, arriving at the end of 33_3. (The C during 33_{1-2} is a bold accented passing note connecting B♭ and D.) This D is the last in a succession of Ds, after which the structural descent concludes, as shown in

2.26.[50] Due to the upward transfer, the incomplete neighbor E♭ that follows D in that broader progression is attained through the traversal of a descending seventh, segmented into thirds: D (at 33_3), B♭ (at 36_3), G (at 37_1), E♭ (at 38_1). This E♭ is prolonged through 40_3, followed by the descent to B♭ for the cadence, as shown in **2.27**.

|23| An interruption creates a binary division within the S of |23|. The long horizontal line among the measure numbers above the model in **2.26** shows how the fifth-progression is segmented into two regions: from 21_1 through 32_1 (HC), and from 33_1 through 44_1 (PAC).

In this case the first of the two regions is more elaborately realized than the second. Looking first at the second region, we observe how G is reinforced repeatedly in two registers by upper neighbor A (measures 33 through 38), followed by the traversal of the descending fifth's upper half, G>F>E.[51] Given that IV$^{5-6}$ follows the internal I (supporting E), the line ascends to incomplete neighbor F (a thirty-second note) during 41_1. That strand's continuation occurs in the tenor register (F>E>D) before the PAC at 42_1. (Compare with the normative and modified cadences in measures 43–45 and 61–62 of |35|.) Part of this span is then repeated, placing the EEC at 44_1.

The first half of S exhibits several extraordinary passages, above and beyond the foundational structure documented in **2.26**. Note first that the E of 25_1 (midway through the descending fifth-progression from G) is extended by means of a full-octave stepwise descent. (Because an ascending register transfer occurs, the descent concludes during 27_2 exactly where it began.) E>D>C in measure 25 engages in a voice exchange with the bass; B follows, resolving to A during 26_1; A, G, and F all receive their own internal octave flourishes before the descent concludes on E during 27_2. A wondrous cadential passage follows. Though initially one might interpret measure 28 as a conventional cadential approach, the phrase unexpectedly extends through 32. Consequently a reassessment of the cadential initiative is in order. (See **2.28**.) IV's diatonic 6-phase chord, F-A-D, evolves into F♯-A-C-E♭ in measure 31. The potential dominant of 28_2 serves as a linear chord within the prolongation of IV^6 that precedes the asserted V. Such an interpretation comes about only by considering the broad context, assessing the relative merits of bass G's potential as asserted dominant root in measures 28 and 32. Though the conventional cadential formula is overridden during measures 28 and 29, it is used to good effect in measures 43 and 44.

Example 2.28 Analysis of Haydn: Piano Sonata in F Major (H. XVI: 23), mvmt. 1, mm. 25–32.

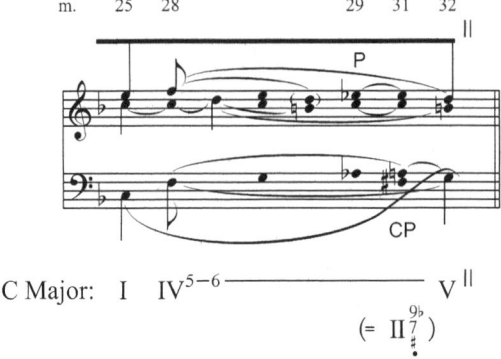

Example 2.29 Analysis of Haydn: Piano Sonata in E♭ Major (H. XVI: 52), mvmt. 1, mm. 17–40.

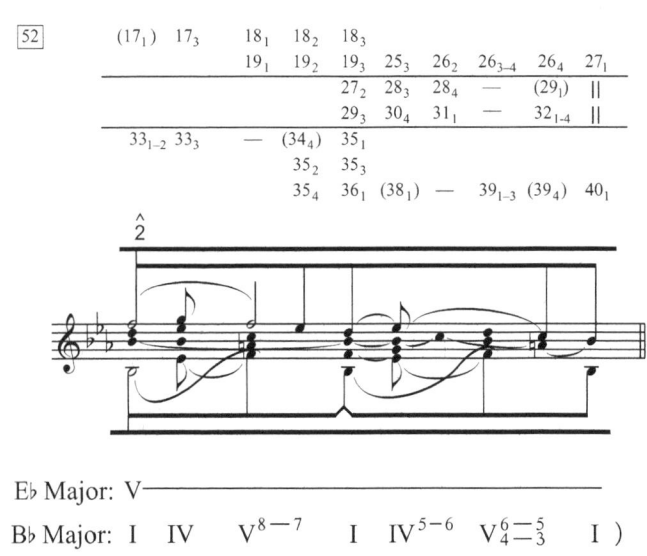

Regarding **2.20h** (transposed in **2.29**):

52 The prototypes displayed in **2.20f** and **2.20g** contain one neighboring note – embellishing either the fifth or the third scale degree. The **2.20h** prototype incorporates both. The S of 52 is the most complex among the twelve such regions we are examining. Haydn has organized it as a ternary form, as indicated by the horizontal lines among the measure numbers in **2.29**. The middle section is

distinguished from the outer sections by its application of interruption – melodic descent only as far as the second scale degree (HCs in measures 29 and 32) – and by the distinctive character of its contents: first an exploitation of the keyboard's upper register, reminiscent of a musical clock, and then a *furioso* passage in the parallel minor key. Were it not for the return of material from the opening of S in measures 33ff., it would be appropriate to regard measure 27 as the onset of C. I propose instead that S extends to 40_1.

In this exposition Haydn carefully integrates TR and the opening of S. Observe how C, the sixth scale degree in E♭ Major, is inserted within the second statement of the P theme (now functioning within TR) at 9_4. When this theme is called back into service for S, G (the sixth scale degree in tonicized B♭ Major) likewise occurs during 17_4. This G has been prepared by the emphasis on the modally modified G♭ during measures 14 and 15. In fact, the G♭>F>E♮<F motive introduced and repeated during TR recurs as G>F>E♮<F during S (measures 20 through 22).[52] An F>E♮>E♭>D line straddles TR and S. (Haydn does not reinstate F during the opening measures of S, though he does so when a variant of the theme begins in measure 33.) The F>D third is answered by an E♭<G third in measure 17, as displayed in **2.30**. Observe how the tonic harmony assumes a dominant-emulating character: minor seventh A♭ arrives along with the tonic's D at 17_2. That dissonance helps push D up to E♭ (outward resolution of the augmented fourth), which in turn guides F up to G (as shown in **2.30**).

The motivic G>F>E♮<F embellishment enhances the potency of F's arrival at 22_3. In this instance the F resides within a D<A♭ unfolding (measures 18–25) that resolves into a G>E♭ unfolding in measures 25 and 26. (Note the unfolding symbols in **2.30**.) The phrase concludes in a conventional manner, with a PAC at 27_1. (As we have seen in other expositions, the 6 in the cadential $^6_4$ arrives late.)

The ternary form's middle section engages two phrases of contrasting texture and rhythm that nevertheless both proceed from the B♭ tonic to the F dominant. What comes between those perimeter points is more fully developed in the first phrase: the tonic takes on dominant-emulating tendencies during 28_2, proceeding to IV in 28_3. The 6-phase C that extends IV arrives at 28_4, after which dominant-emulating tendencies emerge, dynamically pushing towards V.[53] The second phrase, distinctively transformed into the parallel minor key, reaches D♭'s upper neighbor E♭ through the motion of a descending

Example 2.30 Analysis of Haydn: Piano Sonata in E♭ Major (H. XVI: 52), mvmt. 1, mm. 14–27.

E♭ Major: $II^{8\,\,-\,\,7}_{\natural}$ V———
(= B♭ Major: $I^{8\,-\,7♭}$ IV $V^{8\,-\,7}$ I^{8}————————$^{7♭}$ IV^{5}———6
(= I IV^{5}—( )—6 V I)
(= $II^{7}_{\natural}$)

TR S $V^{8}_{4}\!\genfrac{}{}{0pt}{}{6}{}\!\genfrac{}{}{0pt}{}{-\,7}{-\,5}\!\genfrac{}{}{0pt}{}{}{-\,3}$ I) seventh during the second half of measure 30. As was also the case in the preceding phrase, this E♭ is supported by the subdominant. Its 6 phase emerges on the following downbeat. The dominant's A♮ and F gradually fall into place in the bass, against a $\genfrac{}{}{0pt}{}{E\flat}{C}$ third that is shared by both harmonies.

A full traversal of the F>B♭ fifth shapes the ternary form's final section. Haydn alters the musical surface while maintaining the essence of the structure from the ternary form's opening statement. Whereas an F>D unfolding transpired during the passage from TR into S, D<F is unfolded at 33_{1-2}. F's neighbor, G, is delayed by a flamboyant leap up to B♭. Distinct yet related melodies from the opening statement are integrated in these measures:

G♭	F	E♮	E♭	D	(15_3 through 17_2)
G	F		E♭	D	(17_{3-4} through 18_3)
G	F	E♮	F		(20_1 through 22_3)
G	F	E♮	E♭	D	(33_{3-4} through 35_1)

As was the case in measures 20 through 22, IV^{5-6} transpires in such a way that the 6-phase chord takes on dominant-emulating tendencies at 34_3. The dominant harmony at the end of measure 34 is not fully fleshed out. Haydn adds detail in two reiterations of the $V^7 \rightarrow I$ progression in the following measure. That tonic ($\genfrac{}{}{0pt}{}{D}{B\flat}$) is extended via a voice exchange (to $\genfrac{}{}{0pt}{}{B\flat}{D}$) between 36_1 and 37_2, after which a doubled G represents the IV^{5-6} harmony of 25_3 through 26_2. Though the V^7 chord of 39_4 lacks the soprano C that occurred during the first statement (at the end of measure 26), the following C section offers several C>B♭ resolutions during measures 41 and 42. Even with C "missing," the PAC at 40_1 serves as the EEC, concluding S.

The closing zone (C)

It is characteristic for multiple cadences to reside within S in Haydn's sonata expositions, as the measure numbers affixed to the transposed models above affirm. The last of these cadences, the essential expositional closure (EEC), is followed by a brief closing zone (C) that offers further confirmation of the tonicized dominant key, often in a way that contrasts the cadential formula of the preceding S.

After the sustained and vigorous descending motion of S, Haydn may elect to provide a contrast via ascending motion. In the C of 45 (from the middle of measure 42 to the double bar), a I–IV–V^7–I progression supports the stepwise ascending path from $\hat{5}$ to $\hat{8}$ in tonicized B♭ Major. The same notion, more daringly realized, prevails in 46 (starting in the middle of measure 37), where $\hat{6}$ to $\hat{7}$ is presented as a descending seventh rather than as an ascending second. (The C>D♮ seventh reiterates material from S: see measures 20 and 22–23, where the seventh is filled in by step.) A permutation of the $\hat{5}<\hat{8}$ connection ($\hat{6}>\hat{5}$ $\hat{7}<\hat{8}$) offers a double return of the tonic in 23 (measures 44–46).

In other cases the content of C will more closely mimic the close of S. As mentioned above, the cadential $\hat{2}$ within S in 25 is omitted (measure 26). Reiterations of $\hat{3}>\hat{2}>\hat{1}$ during C (measure 27) repay that debt.[54] In 28 (measures 51–58), Haydn luxuriantly achieves a high $\hat{3}$ and then pursues a $\hat{3}<$IN$>\hat{2}>\hat{1}$ descent. During the extended span up to $\hat{3}$, this closing zone offers neighboring embellishment (E♭>D and G>F) and both ascending and descending traversals of the span between $\hat{5}$ and $\hat{8}$. (The ascending version continues upwards to $\hat{3}$.) $\hat{3}>\hat{2}>\hat{1}$ is the basis for C in 29 (starting in the middle of measure 30), where both the $\hat{3}$ and the $\hat{2}$ are preceded by their upper thirds. C in 30 (measures 55–60) traverses the path between $\hat{3}$ and $\hat{1}$ in both directions, while also recalling the middle section of P (measures 11|12 through 16). $\hat{3}$–$\hat{1}$ likewise is the focus of C in 35 (measures 62–67), where B is presented not only as an ascending third from tonic G, but also (in the final measure) as a descending sixth, reached via arpeggiation. Arpeggiation of the tonic triad's pitches is the sole melodic content of C in 51 (measures 39–42).

The C in 31 (measures 21–24) offers a more substantial structure, twice traversing the same fifth-progression that formed the basis of S. Likewise in 49, F (during 60$_1$) leads through E♭ (61$_3$) to D (covered by F in 62$_1$). C follows (63$_1$), leading to a cadence on B♭ (64$_1$). A similar line is embedded within the C of 52 (measures 40–43).

In all cases C is characterized by brevity and simplicity. Though the agenda of C is not prescribed in the way that those of P, TR, and S are, clearly Haydn does not regard it as an appropriate venue for launching complex or innovative content. His C sections offer a respite from challenging material, an opportunity to catch one's breath before returning to the start of the exposition or forging ahead to the new challenges of the development.

3 | Composition in a minor key: six arias in G Minor from operas by Mozart

Our comparison of twelve similarly constructed sonata expositions by Haydn in chapter 2 was facilitated by transpositions into C Major. For our introduction to composition in a minor key, Mozart kindly has supplied six superb soprano arias all in the same key: G Minor.[1] Their formal constructions are varied: some of these arias, which span his career as an opera composer, are in binary form, while others are instead ternary. Though the tonic and dominant regions occur in predictable places within these structures, a range of tonal paths connect those pillars. We will take special note of how and when Mozart deploys the mediant, which is encountered frequently in minor keys, and also keep a close watch on the supertonic, which, due to the diminished quality of its diatonic form, often will mutate: A-C-E♭ may be replaced by A-C-E♮, A-C♯-E♮, or A♭-C-E♭, as well as more evolved states such as C♯-E♭-G-B♭ or C♯-E♮-G-B♭.

In that our focus is on works in G Minor, we will not assemble data that would allow us to compare how composing in one minor key might differ from composing in another. Yet the similarity of the predicaments in which these female protagonists find themselves (in each case she confronts an impediment to living happily ever after with the man she loves) offers a clear indication of the intensity of feeling that Mozart associated with G Minor.[2] Consider how the pitches of G Minor sit within the soprano vocal range: when either B♭ ($\hat{3}$) or D ($\hat{5}$) serves as the *Kopfton*, there is abundant room *above* the fundamental structure for melodic development. In all six of the arias, a high G plays a prominent role within the opening melody, hovering above descending linear progressions that emanate from the *Kopfton*.

"Nel sen mi palpita dolente il core" from *Mitridate, re di Ponto* (K. 87/74a)

Though betrothed to Mitridate, the king of Pontus, Aspasia's affections migrate to his son Sifare after she hears rumors of Mitridate's death in battle. Those rumors turn out to be false, and consequently Aspasia faces a wrenching dilemma. The text of her aria, "Nel sen mi palpita dolente il core," conveys two notions, arranged within a ternary form:

A_1: a description of her lamentable state, presented squarely in the tonic key, G Minor;
B: altruistic concerns regarding Sifare's peril, in a progression that extends from the mediant (B♭) to the dominant (D Minor), which is tonicized;
A_2: a reprise of the opening text and musical content, with variants and extensions, in G Minor.

The three lines of text that Mozart sets during A_1 are presented within a local $a_1 - b - a_2$ ternary form, as follows:

m.	3	11	13	19	23	28	29
						33	34

$\hat{3}$ ——————————————————————————————

	(=	3		IN	2 ‖	(3	2)	1)
		I————		IV	V♯,	I	V♯	I
		A_1						
	(=	a_1	b		a_2			)
Text lines:		1	2		3			
Example:		3.1a—						
		3.1b ———————					
					3.1c———————————————			

The first line establishes $\hat{3}$ as the *Kopfton*, incorporating a I–IV–V♯–I progression at two structural levels and ending in an IAC [**3.1a**]. The vocal melody's numerous upward leaps evoke Aspasia's distraught state. For the second line the progression proceeds through IV to V♯ (HC), coordinating with a middleground interruption on $\hat{2}$ [**3.1b**]. The third line, with more repetition of both words and harmonic activity than the preceding lines, completes the structure begun during the first two lines with a middleground descent to $\hat{1}$, coordinating with a PAC [**3.1c**]. Here the upward melodic trajectory peaks on a high B♭ in the first violin line. Mozart highlights the a_1 and a_2 initiation points by employing local dominants preceding the initial tonics. (Compare measures 1–2 and their more elaborate realization in measures 19–22.) *Kopfton* B♭ is emphasized through the resolution of the dominant's dissonant seventh.

IV is the principal intermediary between the tonic and the dominant within each phrase. At first Mozart proceeds from I to IV directly, without dominant emulation (measures 3 and 4). Thereafter I→IV prevails, with either G-B♮-D-F

Example 3.1 Analysis of Mozart: "Nel sen mi palpita dolente il core" from *Mitridate, re di Ponto* (K. 87/74a), (a) mm. 1–10; (b) mm. 3–19; (c) mm. 19–34.

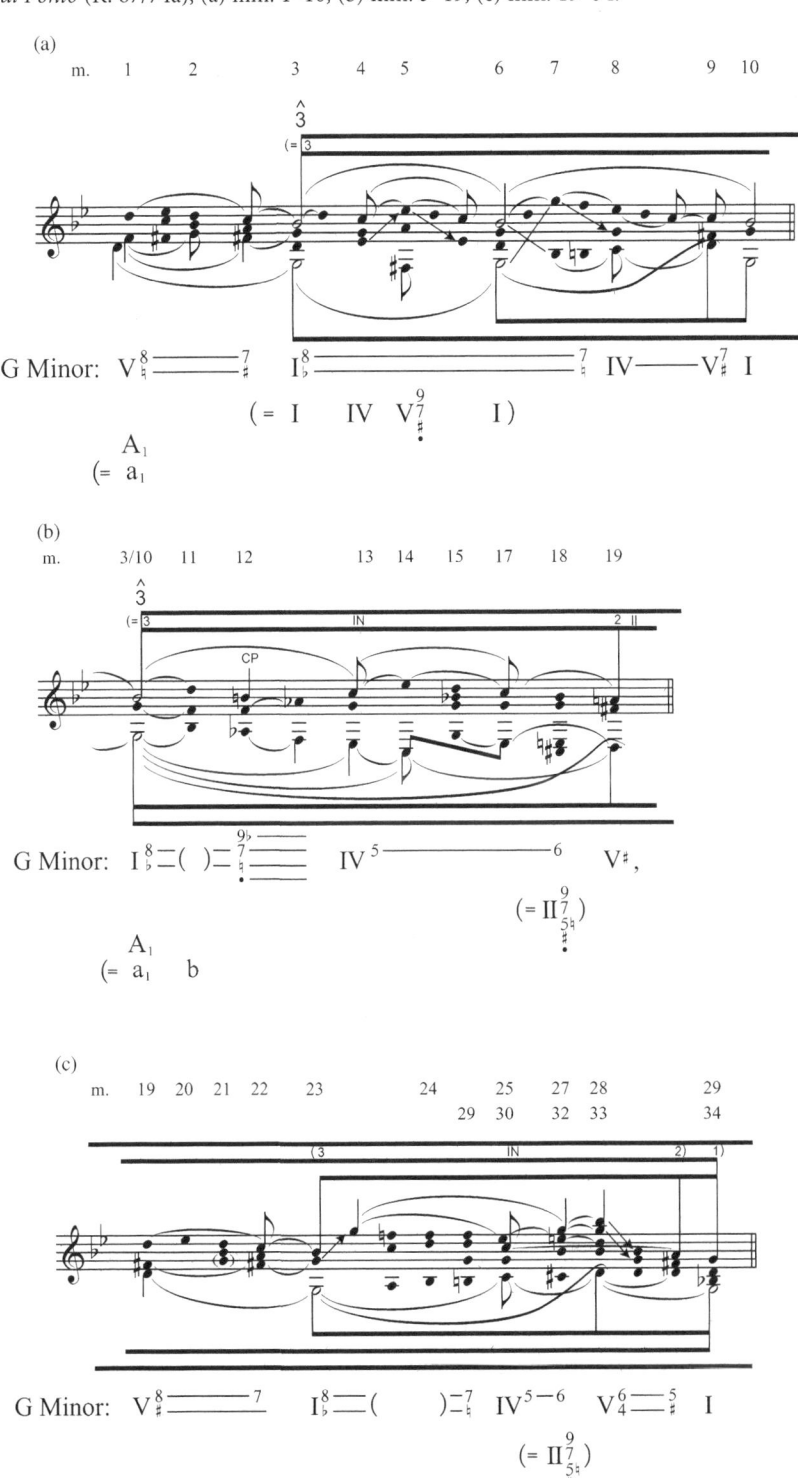

(measures 7, 24, and 29) or B♮-D-F-A♭ (measure 12) creating a surge on the path to IV. In measures 11 and 24 the tonic's upper-third chord (B♭-D-F) comes between the diatonic tonic chord and its dominant-emulating extension, allowing G's minor seventh (F) to be introduced in a consonant context before its downward tendency is activated once B♮ arrives ($^{B♮}_{F}$ resolving outwards in measures 12–13, $^{F}_{B♮}$ resolving inwards in measures 24–25).

The turbulent vocal melody often extends upward from the pitches that my graphs display as components of the foundational melodic line. For example, the B♭ in measure 3 is followed by upper-third D before C, B♭'s upper neighbor, arrives. (Note that the first violin proceeds directly from B♭ to C.) That C is embellished by an upper-third excursion to E♭ at 5_1. This tendency is heightened in measures 6 and 7, where a high G extends a sixth above *Kopfton* B♭ in the context of a voice exchange. The melody's resultant craggy shape underscores the text's vivid and painful emotional content while concurrently often covering the foundational structural melody. The high G is prolonged via descending G>F>E♭ when it returns in measure 23 and leads onward to B♭ in measure 28, as graphed in **3.1c**.[3] Observe how the quick vocal E♭>D>C third that opens measure 14 is extended as E♭>D>C♯>C in the following three measures, thereby prolonging the subdominant. Whereas the subdominant proceeds directly to the dominant in measures 4–5 and 8–9, IV extends through its 6 phase (in the evolved state C♯-E♮-G-B♭) during measures 18, 27, and 32. Mozart audaciously invigorates the IV$^{5-6}$ motion by deploying an embellishing chord like that introduced in **1.7b** during the second half of measures 26 and 31. Though C-E♭-F♯-A normally would return to C-E♭-G *before* the shift to the 6 phase, here the return of the 5-phase chord is elided. Since the 6-phase chord is highly evolved, two diminished seventh sonorities are juxtaposed.

The tonal world that I propose for Mozart's (and Haydn's) music is characterized by a range of hierarchical relationships among pitches. No markings in the score confirm definitively that what I propose actually exists. Only through analyzing music – lots of music – can one become convinced that such relationships do abound. Consider, for example, Aspasia's melody in measures 3 through 6. I suggest that the essence of the line is B♭<C>B♭ and that each of these pitches is embellished by an upper third. (The final third extends into a sixth – B♭<D<G during measures 6 and 7 – further separating B♭ from its neighbor C at 8_2.) Though B♭'s upper third D is itself embellished by an upper third during measure 11, the essence of the chromatic line extending into measure 13 – B♭<B♮<C – shines through. The integrity of the E♭>D>C third (heard in measures 5, 8, and 14) helps one to make sense of measure 16, where the chromatic passing note C♯ occurs

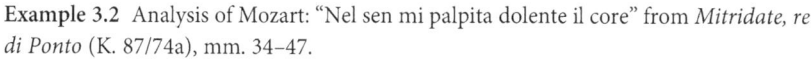

Example 3.2 Analysis of Mozart: "Nel sen mi palpita dolente il core" from *Mitridate, re di Ponto* (K. 87/74a), mm. 34–47.

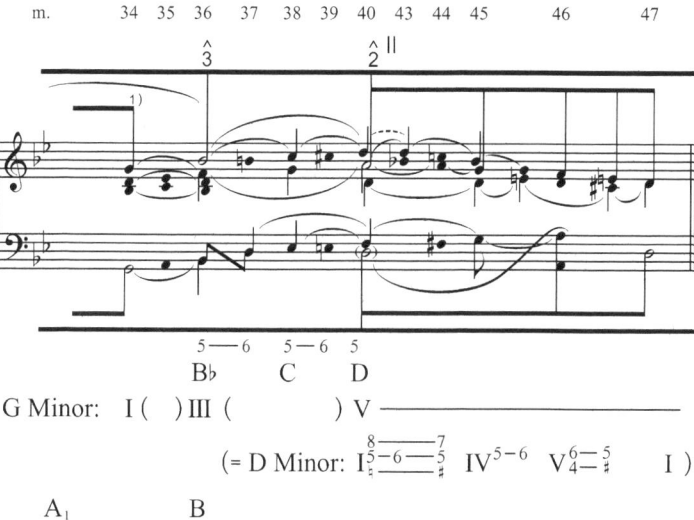

within yet another traversal of that third. The E♮-G-C♯ chord in that measure does not assert itself as a harmony: it is just passing through. Such hierarchical relationships may be established in any line. For example, in the bass of measures 10 through 13 the foundational G>F>E♭ descent (emphasized by the stemmed noteheads in **3.1b**) is expanded into G<A<B♭ A♭>G>F E♭.

Though a B♭-D-F chord occurs twice during the A_1 section, it there performs a foreground role within I-space. One might expect that during the B section a more assertive mediant will occur, providing some relief from the long-persisting minor. In fact Aspasia enters with the support of a B♭ major chord in measure 36 [**3.2**]. However, since the four lines of text that she sings during the B section offer no respite from the prevailing troubled mood, Mozart does not allow this chord to develop into a tonicized key (as he does in the other arias addressed in this chapter) but instead immediately continues in the trajectory to the minor dominant, which arrives four measures later as the culmination of a sequential ascent (an ascending 5–6 sequence with dominant-emulating 6-phase chords: B♭ G→ C A→ D). This V supports the aria's background $\hat{2}$.[4] Though the D chord is presented in its first inversion in measure 40, its tonicization during the ensuing measures leads to the root D at 47_1, in coordination with a fifth-progression that prolongs $\hat{2}$ by descending from A to D in the vocal melody. (As was also the case during the A_1 section, part of this line sounds below pitches that extend a fourth or a third higher, as noted in **3.2**.)

The tonicized D Minor's initial I-space is displayed in **3.2** as extending from measure 40 through measure 44. A local I–IV–V$^7_{\sharp}$–I^6 progression (not graphed) supports an ascending vocal connection between A and D before the tonic evolves into I→, igniting the progression to the PAC in measure 47. Then Mozart offers a varied repetition. The content of measures 47 through 52_1 integrates elements from two earlier passages, as follows:

	Melody	Chords	
mm. 36–40:	B♭<B♮<C<C♯<D	B♭ G→ C	A→ D
mm. 40–43:	A<B♭< C♯<D	D G	A→ D⁶
mm. 47–52_1:	A<B♭<B♮<C<C♯<D	D G→ C	A→ D

Then a replication of measures 45 through 47 is attempted in measures 52_3 through 54. The lack of closure at 54_1 leads to another attempt at the PAC, which duly occurs at 56_1. During that second approach Aspasia's melody charts an upward – rather than downward – course to the concluding D (reminiscent of the woodwind approach to the tonic G in measures 1 through 3), while the first oboe's line preserves the conventional stepwise descent. The open fifth (^A_D) at the cadence is filled by an F♯ (56_2), thus aligning the close of the B section with the chordal evolution of measures 1 and 2. Just as the pitches G, B♭, and D constitute the arrival of the G Minor tonic in measure 3 – *not* measure 2 – so also the tonic that initiates the A_2 section arrives in measure 59 – *not* measure 57. The vocal A<C♯<D close in D (measures 55 and 56) is transposed and enhanced to become D̲<E♭<E♮<F<F♯<G in the oboe line, resulting eventually in the restoration of tonic G Minor.

In analyzing the B section I at first resisted establishing D Minor at measure 40, wanting instead to prolong tonic G through measure 45. Only by listening to the progression many times and drawing graphs representing the alternative hypotheses I had about its structure did I eventually feel confident in the interpretation I have presented above.[5] Several significant features of measure 40 heighten its structural importance: (1) the melody's chromatic ascent ends there; (2) the bassoons are relieved by the oboes there; and (3) a middleground stepwise descent from A to D begins there. (The vocal A of measure 40, reiterated in measure 44, descends to G in measure 45, followed by F, E♮, and D in the following two measures. The relationship between the descent's A>G initiation and an upper D>C>B♭ strand in measures 40 through 45 is clarified in **3.2**.)

The A_2 section follows the general arrangement of A_1, with occasional novelties. Perhaps the most interesting variant occurs during measures 63 through 65, where diatonic $^5_3$ and dominant-emulating $^{4♮}_2$ statements of the G tonic are connected via linear filling-in: G<A♭<A<B♭<B♮, B♭<C<D, and D̲<E♭<F<G̲. Though the internal chordal simultaneities are poignant (especially A♭-C-E♭ against bass G), none of them are asserted harmonies. The

passage instead extends the I$^{8-7}_{b-\natural}$ first heard in measure 7. Whereas that event now fills additional measures, other passages from A$_1$ are omitted: for example, measure 65 corresponds to measure 7, measure 66 to the first half of measure 13, and measure 67 to measure 15. The PAC corresponding to that of measure 29 occurs in measure 81, with recurrences in measures 86 and (after two failed attempts) 95. Whereas the B♭>A>G structural descent during A$_1$ was interpreted as a middleground prolongation of $\hat{3}$ (as displayed in the graphs of **3.1**), its recurrence during A$_2$, after the background $\hat{2}$ of the B section and occurring near the end of the aria, no longer prolongs the *Kopfton*. G – rather than B♭ – now plays a role within the background structure, concluding the aria's $\hat{3}>\hat{2}>\hat{1}$ fundamental line. A brief orchestral coda offers a confirming PAC.

"Vorrei punirti indegno" from *La finta giardiniera* (K. 196)

Arminda is furious at Count Belfiore. Intent upon marrying him, she discovers that his earlier relationship with the Marchesa Violante Onesti (who is residing at the same palace, disguised as a gardener) has not subsided. The text of her aria, "Vorrei punirti indegno," expresses two contrasting notions: her anger at and love for Belfiore. Mozart juxtaposes these sentiments in the keys of G Minor and B♭ Major, respectively, within the aria's A$_1$ section. The B section continues the upward bass trajectory to the major dominant, D Major, as Arminda laments the state of her personal affairs. The concluding A$_2$ section reprises the text of the A$_1$ section, now in the key of G Minor throughout, thereby achieving tonal closure and also hinting that Arminda won't get her man. The overall shape of the movement may be represented as follows:

m.	1	21	41	42	71	92–93	94	102	103	124	125
	$\hat{5}$		$\hat{4}$	$\hat{3}$		$\hat{2}$ ‖	($\hat{5}$	$\hat{4}$	$\hat{3}$	$\hat{2}$)	$\hat{1}$
G Minor:	I	III			( )	V♯	I―――――――――――――				
							(= I	V♯ I	V♯	I)	
	A$_1$				B		A$_2$				
Text lines:	1–2	1–5			6–9		1–2		1–5		
Example:	3.3–										
	3.4 ―――――――――										
				3.5 ―――――――――							
				3.6 ――――							

A ten-measure orchestral prelude introduces the music that will support Arminda's expression of fury in the coming measures. The two presentations are differentiated by their orchestration and their cadences. The complete

Example 3.3 Analysis of Mozart: "Vorrei punirti indegno" from *La finta giardiniera* (K. 196), mm. 1–20.

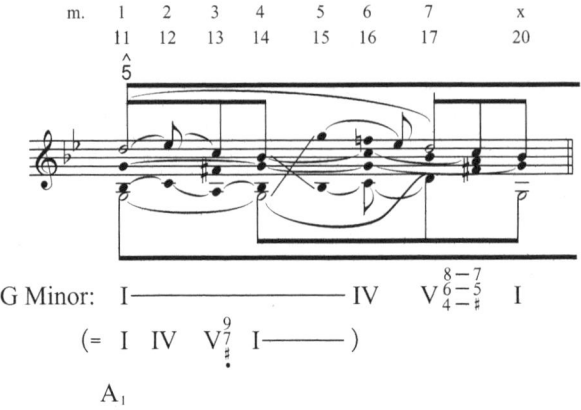

version of the structure, which accompanies Arminda's opening tirade, is displayed in **3.3**. The D>B♭ and C>A unfoldings of measure 17 (repeated two measures later, thereby extending the phrase to ten measures) are answered by a G<B♭ unfolding in the upper strings during measure 20, resulting in an IAC. (The broad D>C>B♭ third displayed in **3.3** occurs in place of the prelude's D>C>B♭>A fourth, where B♭ is transferred up an octave during measure 9, while A is an interior pitch within the closing V♯ harmony in measure 10, as is B♭ within the I of measure 20.) How Mozart establishes tonic G Minor here is very similar to his strategy in "Nel sen mi palpita dolente il core" [**3.1a**, measures 3 through 10]. The harmonic progressions are virtually identical, and the melodies differ only in their respective focus on $\hat{3}$ versus $\hat{5}$ as *Kopfton*. (D is especially suitable as the *Kopfton* when the mediant key, B♭ Major, is to be tonicized, since the $\frac{D}{B\flat}$ third is available for traversal when the bass ascends from G to B♭.)

The B♭ Major region within the A_1 section – extending from measure 21 through measure 70 – dwarfs the preceding G Minor phrase in length, though the essence of both its textual content and its musical structure is complete by measure 42, where the first root-position B♭ major chord sounds. The shift to B♭ Major is achieved without a transition. Again there are structural similarities with "Nel sen mi palpita dolente il core": compare **3.1b** (in G Minor) and **3.4**, measures 21 through 29 (in B♭ Major).[6] In the latter, the progression continues beyond the dominant, reinstating the B♭ tonic in a dominant-emulating form at measure 36, from which a IV–V–I progression, supporting the background structural descent from $\hat{5}$

Example 3.4 Analysis of Mozart: "Vorrei punirti indegno" from *La finta giardiniera* (K. 196), mm. 1–42.

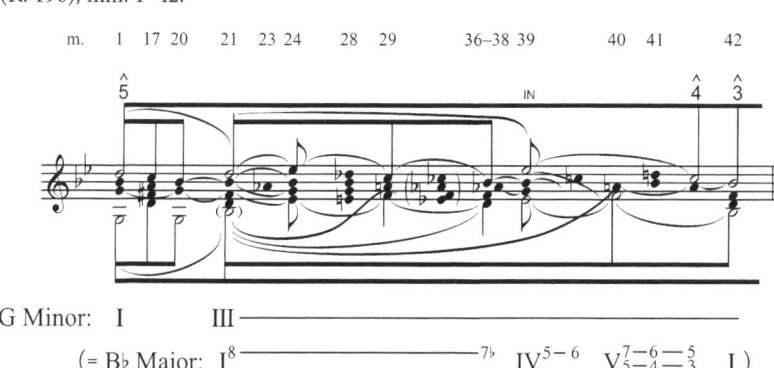

through $\hat{4}$ to $\hat{3}$, transpires. (Though the D>C>B♭ third is traversed repeatedly in both the G Minor and B♭ Major regions [**3.3** and **3.4**], that which reaches B♭ in measure 42 is more definitive than those that precede it.) The D-F-B♭ chord at 41_1 serves not as an asserted tonic, but instead as an unfurled passing/neighboring $^6_4$ chord. (Compare with the unfurled cadential $^6_4$ at 51_1.) In the numerous cadential reiterations after measure 42, the $\hat{5}>\hat{4}>\hat{3}$ descent to B♭ often is absent from the vocal line, which more freely approaches B♭ while one of the instrumental lines supplies the more conventional descent. (See, for example, the violin line from 51_3 through 52_1 and during measures 62 and 69–70, and the oboe line during measures 64 and 65.)

Imagine how Arminda must feel as she confronts this situation. She loves Belfiore, but at the same time she finds his conduct to be unacceptable. The responses of anger (*ira*) and pity (*pietà*) both seek the upper hand. Though at first she may think she has settled on how to proceed, misgivings and second thoughts emerge, and so she remains indecisive. This seems to be what Mozart wants to convey during the aria's B section. For a while (measures 71 through 78) he pursues a straightforward and goal-directed course. An ascending 5–6 sequence meant to connect III and V♯ leads up to, but does not quite achieve, the dominant goal [**3.5**, measures 71 through 78]. (Compare with the similar sequential connection between III and V in "Nel sen mi palpita dolente il core" [**3.2**, measures 36 through 40].) Some moments of silence along the way allow Arminda time for reflection. She

Example 3.5 Analysis of Mozart: "Vorrei punirti indegno" from *La finta giardiniera* (K. 196), mm. 42–93.

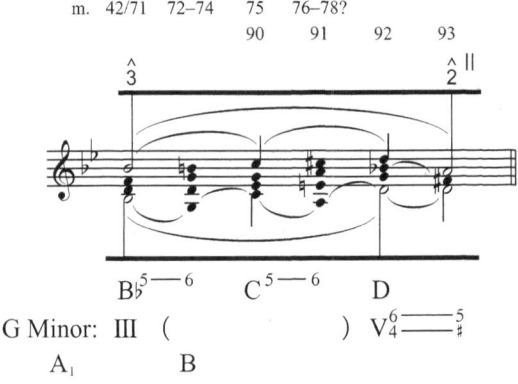

Example 3.6 Analysis of Mozart: "Vorrei punirti indegno" from *La finta giardiniera* (K. 196), mm. 75–90.

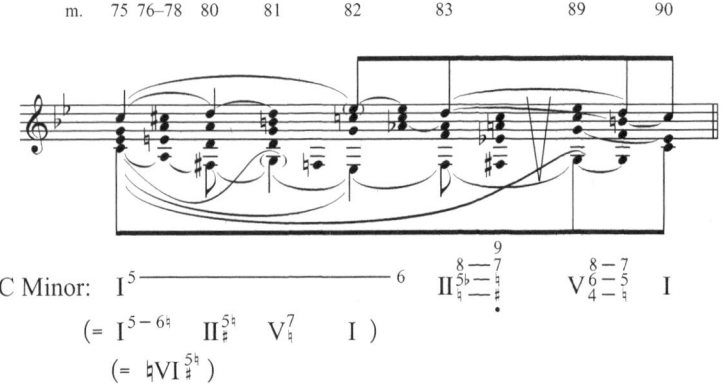

hopes that Belfiore will respond to her plea and that they will be reconciled. That hope is dashed, and consequently she abandons the dominant goal, backtracking to the C^5 chord that was stated in measure 75. The A major chord of measures 76 through 78 leads not to D major as dominant within the broad G Minor tonality but instead to D major as II→ within a conventional progression in tonicized C Minor.[7] (See **3.6**.) What *is* unconventional is Mozart's glide into the II→ harmony from above (measures 79 and 80). Yet upper-third extensions have been prominent throughout the B section: B♭<D in measure 71, B♮<D in measures 72 through 74, C<E♭ in measure 75,

and C♯<E♮ in measures 76 through 78. The melody's F>D in measures 79 and 80 reverses the direction of the unfolding, while the D chord's inverted state distinguishes this moment from the intended D-F♯-A arrival proposed in **3.5**. The measure numbers that annotate that model reveal that after the tonicization of C Minor runs its course the sequence picks up where it left off and the D-F♯-A dominant is attained after all. Yet note that it does so without Arminda's participation. She remains indecisive: three attempts are required to attain a PAC for the C Minor tonicization (measures 84, 87, and 90), after which she bows out, allowing the orchestra to complete the B section's tonal trajectory without her.

Though the G performed by the oboes and lower horns at 94_1, within the restored tonic that initiates the A_2 section, provides a modest voice-leading successor for the background $\hat{2}$ of the B section, Arminda concurrently reinstates $\hat{5}$ (D). Consequently a full descent from $\hat{5}$ to $\hat{1}$ will transpire during the A_2 section, as is conventional in the context of an interruption. The structure of the A_1 section, graphed in **3.4**, easily accommodates this new trajectory. Since there was no transition between the G Minor and B♭ Major regions, the latter can be transposed down a third and converted into minor without fuss during A_2. The D>C>B♭ from the initial G Minor region and the newly transposed B♭>A>G from the former B♭ Major region together span the D>G fifth. B♮ in measure 104 connects the B♭ of measure 103 (= $\hat{3}$) and incomplete neighbor C in measure 105 (corresponding to the E♭ in measure 24, graphed in **3.4**). Closure on $\hat{1}$ is achieved first in measure 125 and is then repeated numerous times during the remainder of the aria, including the lively orchestral postlude.

"Tiger! wetze nur die Klauen" from *Zaide* (K. 344/336b)

In *Zaide*, Mozart's first harem opera, Zaide and her beloved Gomatz are thwarted in their attempt to escape the clutches of Sultan Soliman. Consequently a most unpleasant fate awaits them. Zaide likens Soliman's anger to that of a tiger during the A_1 and A_2 sections of her aria "Tiger! wetze nur die Klauen." The contrasting B section shifts the attention from Soliman to Gomatz. Though death awaits them, at least their torment will be quelled.

In compositions in a minor key, the mediant often is an important point along the path between the tonic and the dominant, as is the case (with sharply contrasting levels of emphasis) in "Nel sen mi palpita dolente il core" [**3.2**] and "Vorrei punirti indegno" [**3.4** and **3.5**]. Given the text

Mozart sets in "Tiger! wetze nur die Klauen," that course would place references to Soliman and Gomatz, who of course represent opposite poles within Zaide's emotional world, within the same trajectory. Whereas Mozart proceeds conventionally from G Minor to B♭ Major during the A_1 section to set text concerning Soliman's feigned affection, he takes the unusual step of returning to G before proceeding a third in the *opposite* direction – to E♭ – at the outset of the B section, starting in measure 63.[8] This latter route, supporting text that focuses on the love that she and Gomatz share, is Zaide's preferred means of meeting her fate. Mozart proceeds eventually to a PAC resolution in G Minor (at 93_1). Yet this closure represents no more than Zaide's imaginings, not the reality of her situation. The dominant that would have been a more conventional goal of the B section holds sway briefly thereafter (measures 94 through 97), though more in the character of a transition or interlude than as a structural goal. (Compare with measures 1–3 and 56–59 of "Nel sen mi palpita dolente il core," noting especially the upward melodic line D<E♭<F♯<G.) With a crescendo and the addition of the dominant's dissonant minor seventh, Soliman's wrath comes to the fore again at the outset of the A_2 section. (Though the complete libretto for this unfinished work is missing, the literary source for the plot suggests that Soliman eventually will release Zaide and Gomatz, matching the kindness of Pasha Selim in *Die Entführung aus dem Serail*.)

Zaide's D>G fifth in measure 3 establishes the contour and boundaries of the structural melodic line that will transpire during the opening presentation of tonic G Minor, through 15_1, during which the text's first two lines are set. In that Zaide anticipates torture and death, it is not surprising that her vocal line often departs from the staid path of the linear descent as displayed in **3.7a**. D<G in measure 7 opens the upper register, a feature shared with the other arias we have explored [**3.1a**, measure 7; **3.3**, measure 5]. The cadential $_4^6$ chord of measure 9 is unfurled into $_3^6$ position. Note the relationship between unfoldings: C<D<E♭ (fully stated only in the first violin line in measure 8) proceeds to an upper-third pitch, while D>C>B♭ (at 9_{1-3}) proceeds from an upper-third pitch while engaged in a voice exchange with the bass. The F♯-A-C-E♭ chord at the end of measure 8 does not assert itself as a harmony. Instead, F♯ is a neighbor between the G of II^7 (stated in the upper register) and the G of the cadential $_4^6$. Nevertheless, the $\genfrac{}{}{0pt}{}{F\sharp}{C}$ augmented fourth propels the bass downwards to B♭ rather than directly upwards to the dominant root, D.[9]

We have seen how Mozart employs an ascending 5–6 sequence to connect III and V(♯) [**3.2** and **3.5**]. In "Tiger! wetze nur die Klauen" that device

Example 3.7 Analysis of Mozart: "Tiger! wetze nur die Klauen" from *Zaide* (K. 344/336b), (a) mm. 3–15; (b) mm. 3–17; (c) mm. 17–46; (d) mm. 17–62.

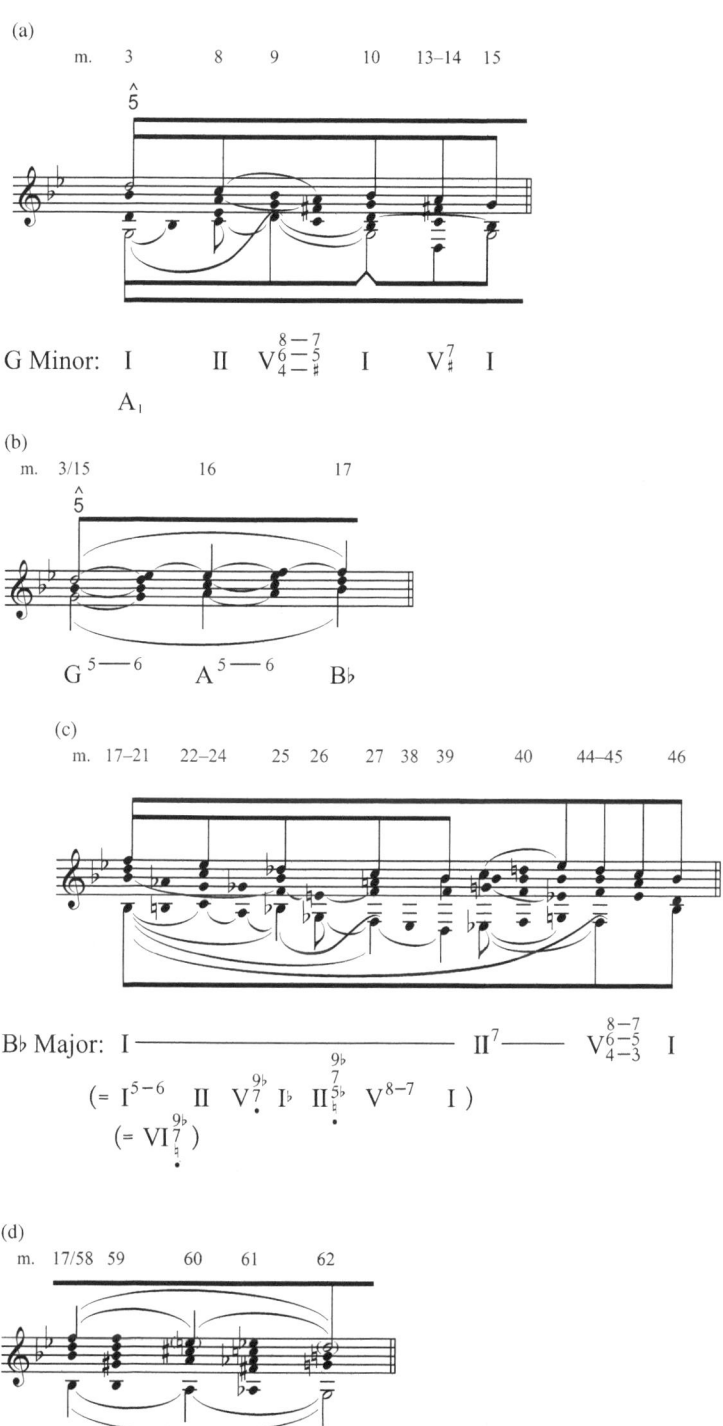

connects I and III [**3.7b**]. Observe that the entire structure is hoisted upwards two scale degrees: the fifth-relationship between the soprano and the root is maintained, so that during the B♭ Major region, where Mozart delivers the third through eighth lines of the text, a linear progression descends from F to B♭. D's role as the aria's *Kopfton* is submerged within that fifth, which transpires during measure 17 through 46 (to be explored below). Consequently the B♭ region is less integrally connected to the foundational structure than is the case in the structures displayed in **3.2** and **3.4**. In this instance what goes up comes back down: the G root and D *Kopfton* are restored in measure 62 (the latter implied as E♭'s successor, though not actually sounding), before Mozart proceeds to the aria's B section.

The structure of the B♭ Major region, displayed in **3.7c**, has much in common with the B♭ Major region in "Vorrei punirti indegno," displayed in **3.4**. Starting respectively on F or D, the broad soprano line proceeds with E♭>D>C>B♭, supported by bass (B♭)<D<E♭<F>B♭. (Bass E♭ in one case is the root of IV, in the other case the third of II.) Also shared is the halt on V within the initial tonic prolongation (measure 29 of **3.4**, measure 27 of **3.7c**). The rendition in the "Tiger!" aria has a more foreboding quality, with an infusion of elements from B♭ Minor, starting with the G♭ in measures 18 and 20 and including a minor tonic in measure 25 and a II⇒V succession in measures 26 and 27 (repeated in measures 34 and 35). Only with the G♮ in measure 36 (at the word "Herz" – heart) is that spell broken, leading to a return of the B♭ Major tonic at 39_1.[10]

A varied repetition of the passage leading up to the PAC extends the B♭ Major region through measure 58. The measures that follow, displayed in **3.7d**, represent a negation of the tonal progress towards the dominant that the extended B♭ Major region seemed to have accomplished. A chunk of the descending circle of fifths leads back to G. The circle replicates that B♭ chord's quality in the succeeding A and G chords. The G tonic's minor third B♭ is not restored until the arrival of its 6-phase E♭ in measure 63. Despite its major quality and its arrival via an augmented-sixth resolution (D⇒G) the G chord does not assert a dominant-emulating tendency towards C, though that might be a reasonable supposition during the fermata of measure 62.[11]

The E♭ Major region that initiates the B section may seem a curious successor of the G major chord of measure 62. Yet, as mentioned above, G major may be interpreted as a displacement of G minor. G minor's diatonic 6-phase chord is, of course, G-B♭-E♭. The B♮ of measure 62 functions as a wobble, as shown in **3.8**. Though B♮ has the potential to ascend to C, it does not do so. A tonicization of E♭ is established through a stepwise descent

Composition in a minor key 103

Example 3.8 Analysis of Mozart: "Tiger! wetze nur die Klauen" from *Zaide* (K. 344/336b), mm. 3–93.

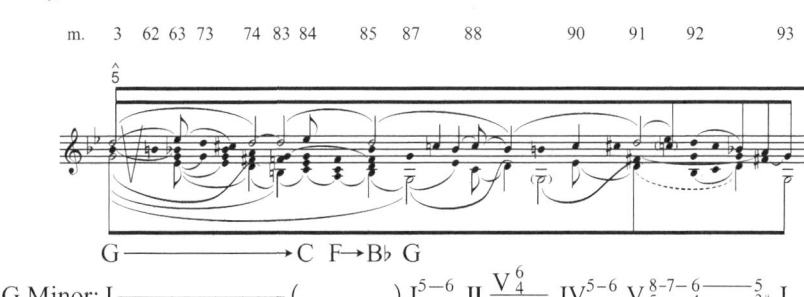

connecting E♭ and G in the vocal melody of measures 63 through 68, where the first two of the three lines of the aria's text set during the B section (lines nine and ten) are first presented. The E♭ chord retains its role as the G Minor tonic's 6 phase. Consequently a likely successor would be the supertonic. In the minor mode, that supertonic often will be a chord containing an augmented sixth, such as the chord at the end of measure 73. C♯-E♭-G-B♭ is a highly evolved supertonic chord (absent root = A), here functioning in its conventional role. This passage supports the final line of the text. During the broad E♭>D>C♯ melodic line in measures 63 through 73, E♭'s upper-third chord, G-B♭-D (attained via an ascending 5–6 sequence in measures 69 through 73), supports the interior pitch D.

Even in the small sampling of scores by Mozart that we have examined thus far, one is struck by a tendency for prolongation via the bass motion from 8 (or 1) through 5 to 3 [**1.5b**, measures 1 through 8; **3.4**, measures 21 through 38; **3.6**, measures 75 through 82; **3.7c**, measures 17 through 39]. That trajectory is pursued during measures 3/62 through 83 of the "Tiger!" aria as well [**3.8**]. Though the dominant harmony of measure 74 is prolonged through measure 80 (extended to 82) via a descending fourth-progression (D>C>B♭>A, with upper neighbor E♭ and chromatic C♯, thus incorporating elements of measures 63 through 73), the tonic is restored soon thereafter. Consequently the I chord of measure 83 is not a mere local event, but instead the culmination of an extended prolongation, at which point a surge initiates a descending circle of fifths leading to the tonic's upper-third chord (G→C-F→B♭). The tonic is reinstated soon thereafter. The progression of measures 87 and 88 seems to be heading towards a PAC. Yet something unusual happens at 88_3, delaying the cadence until 93_1: the

Example 3.9 Analysis of Mozart: "Tiger! wetze nur die Klauen" from *Zaide* (K. 344/336b), mm. 98–136.

$$
\begin{array}{l}
\text{m.} \quad 98\ 104\ 106\ 107\ 109\ 115\ \ 116\ \ 117\ 128\ 129 \qquad 130 \qquad 135 \quad 136 \\
\hat{5} \qquad\qquad\qquad\qquad\qquad\qquad\qquad\qquad\qquad\qquad\qquad \hat{4}\ \ \hat{3}\ \ \hat{2}\ \ \hat{1}
\end{array}
$$

G Minor: I ————————————————————— II^7 ——— V$^{8-7}_{4-\natural}{}^{6-5}_{}$ I

(= I (   ) IV$^{5-(\ )-6}$ V$^{8-7}_{\sharp}$ I)

(= II$^{9}_{5\natural}{}^{7}_{\sharp}$)

A$_2$

cadential $^6_4$ at 88$_2$ does not resolve to the dominant $^5_{3\sharp}$, as expected, but instead proceeds directly to an evolved tonic, B♮-D-F-A♭. (This could be interpreted either as an elision of the dominant $^5_{3\sharp}$ or as an assertion of the $^6_4$'s G as a root.) As **3.8** shows, this evolved tonic initiates a conventional progression that supports the reattainment of *Kopfton* D at 91$_1$, from which a middleground descent to G transpires during the following two measures. Its melodic course and the unfurling of the cadential $^6_4$ in these latter measures resemble the structure in measures 8 and 9. Here the close on G allows for an interpretation of C>B♭>A as a middleground $\hat{4}>\hat{3}>\hat{2}$, rather than as motion to an inner voice, prolonging $\hat{4}$, as in **3.7a**.[12] Mozart correlates Zaide's imagining of death with the most decisive cadence available. The quick progression from that PAC to the dominant of measures 94 through 97 represents a rejection of this poignant Zaide/Gomatz love-death and a return to the turbulent rage of Soliman, the focus of A$_2$.

Whereas the A$_1$ section juxtaposes two keys, G Minor and B♭ Major, a unified presentation of the G Minor tonic transpires during the A$_2$ section, which reprises the first eight lines of the text. Mozart melds together two descending-fifth structures: the D>G fifth displayed in **3.7a** and a lower-third transposition of the F>B♭ fifth displayed in **3.7c**. The result is displayed in **3.9**.[13] Though its internal harmonic progression is distinctive, the G>D>B♭ arpeggiation in the bass matches that of the **3.7c** model, from which the same II–V–I continuation leads to the definitive structural close (PAC) at 136$_1$. Attempts at cadential confirmation are deflected at measures 144 and 147 before a second PAC at 151$_1$ succeeds in quelling the harmonic activity.

Composition in a minor key   105

"Padre, germani, addio!" from *Idomeneo* (K. 366)

Not only has the Trojan princess Ilia lost her father and brothers in the recent struggle; she now is being held captive on Crete, which is ruled by her father's enemy, Idomeneo. To make matters worse, she has fallen in love with Idomeneo's son, Idamante. In the aria "Padre, germani, addio!" she laments her unfortunate state, unable to stifle her benevolent feelings for someone she ought to hold in contempt.

Unlike the three arias explored above, which are set in a ternary form ($A_1 - B - A_2$), "Padre, germani, addio!" is a binary structure ($A_1 - A_2$). The aria's full text is presented in both parts. Regions within A_1 that I label as a_1 and b_1 below are in the related keys of G Minor and B♭ Major, respectively. Yet the A_1 section proceeds beyond the tonicized III to attain V♯.[14] (This passage, measures 56 through 58, concludes the A_1 section structurally while prematurely initiating the textual presentation of the A_2 section.) In the A_2 section the progression to V♯ occurs earlier, within the transition. The b_2 region is presented in G Minor rather than in B♭ Major.

The aria's overall structure is laid out as follows:

m.	5	13	32	56	58	59	66	72	73	83	92/115
G Minor:	I	( )	III	( )	V♯, I		( )	III	V♯	I———	
	A_1					A_2					
(=	a_1	transition	b_1	leads to HC,	a_2		transition		b_2	PAC)	
Text lines:	1–2	3–4	5–8	1	2		3–4		5–8		
Example:	3.10a———										
	3.10b———————————										
			3.10c———								
				3.10d———							
	3.11————————————————————————————————										
										3.12———	

Ilia's melody during a_1 (measures 5 through 13) is characterized by an open fifth (G<D) followed by the stepwise descent of a third (D>C>B♭, stated twice).[15] (In **3.10a**, parentheses mark these fifths and square brackets mark these thirds.) These features are repeated on B♭ and on C during the opening phase of the transition. The contrasting elements of the text ("Padre …"; "Grecia …") set by similar musical structures results in a poignant juxtaposition of Ilia's allegiance to her family and her current domination by the Greek enemy. As was the case in **3.7b** as well, the sequential motion leads the melodic line upwards from the *Kopfton*, D. In

"Padre, germani, addio!" the $\hat{5}>\hat{4}>\hat{3}$ segment of the fundamental descent occurs below a highly developed voice-leading structure in this upper register, a situation that is not put aright until the end of the b_1 region's descending fifth-progression (F>B♭) in measure 41 (and again in measure 56). Consequently the foundational structure for A_1 displayed in **3.10b** starkly contrasts the surface of the composition, wherein the innards of the graph reside above the open noteheads. The tonic (a_1) and mediant (b_1) regions are connected via a descending circle of fifths whose chords all evolve, either as → or as ⇒. Whereas G leads to C via an ascending 5–6 sequence [**3.10a**],[16] C first extends to its upper-third chord via its own internal descending circle of fifths (C→F–B♭→E♭ in measures 23 through 27) before the C chord is restored in a highly evolved state, as G♭-B♭-D♭-E♮. A medial caesura occurs in measure 30, in anticipation of b_1's arrival.

Ilia's romantic attachment to Idamante justifies the tonicization of a major key during the b_1 region [**3.10c**]. A broad F>B♭ fifth-progression is stated three times (as indicated by the measure numbers above the graph), with some variants. Note especially that I IV in measure 38 becomes I→ IV in measure 49. I interpret the chord at 40_1, 51_1, and 55_1, as an unfurled cadential $^6_4$, rather than as a first-inversion tonic. In the first two instances a local F-A-C-E♭ chord paves the way for its arrival. Though this may seem to be a V^7–I continuation from the preceding IV^{5-6}, it is instead a voice-leading strengthening of the unfurled cadential $^6_4$'s arrival.[17] The fact that Mozart finds it dispensable in measure 54 supports this interpretation. The PAC at 56_1 concludes the B♭ tonicization.

That repose lasts for only half a beat. A *sforzando* chord (bass A♭) disrupts the cadential moment, initiating the A_1 section's final initiative, the connection between III and V♯. Three models for this passage are displayed in **3.10d**. Again melodic activity transpires above the analytical open noteheads. In Model 1 the background structure is presented without embellishment. Model 2 shows three lines moving upwards in a parallel $^6_3$ formation. The structural A ($\hat{2}$) is not connected to B♭ ($\hat{3}$) via direct voice leading, but instead emerges from the interior. Model 3 incorporates Mozart's sequential connection.[18] Though the chords at 57_1 and 58_1 are presented in $^6_3$ position, they correspond to 5-phase chords within the sequential pattern. The 6-phase chords are highly evolved: for example, instead of diatonic B♭-D-G, Mozart deploys dominant-emulating B♮-D-F-A♭. He heightens the emotional impact by overlapping the attainment of the A_1 section's structural goal and the opening textual content of A_2. His intent likely was to intensify the clash between Ilia's familial duty to be repelled by

Composition in a minor key   107

Example 3.10 Analysis of Mozart: "Padre, germani, addio!" from *Idomeneo* (K. 366), (a) mm. 5–19; (b) mm. 5–58; (c) mm. 32–56; (d) mm. 56–58.

(a)
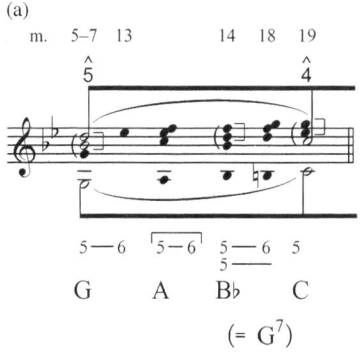

(b)
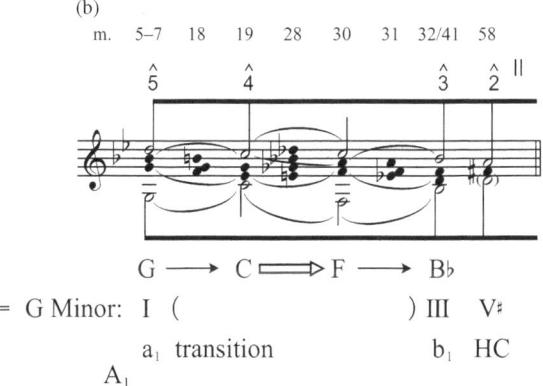

(c)
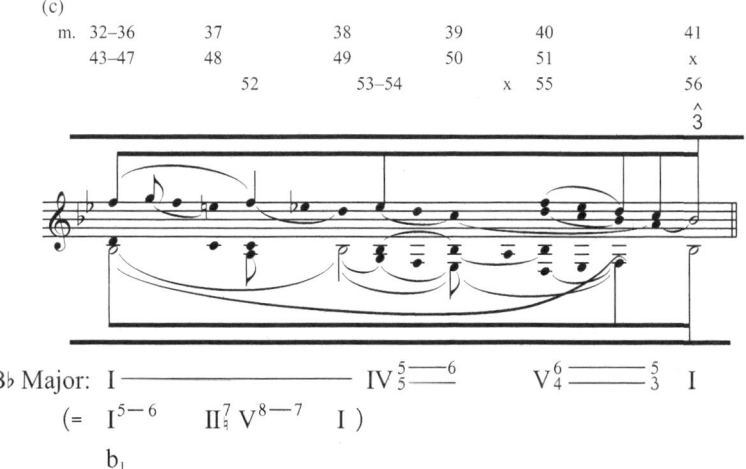

Example 3.10 (cont.)

(d)

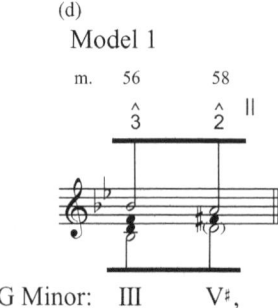

Model 1

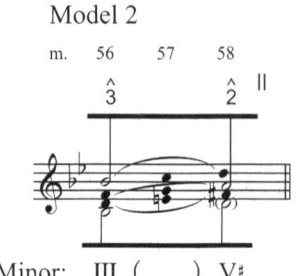

Model 2

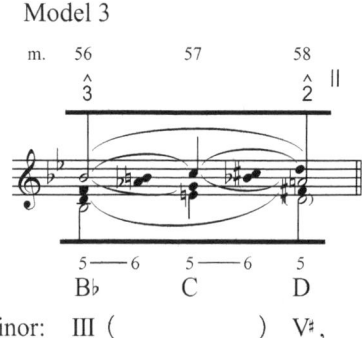

Model 3

her captor and the tender feelings that the B♭ Major region has just conveyed.

A central premise of a binary construction is that the incomplete structure of the A_1 section will be brought to a suitable close during the A_2 section, where the various elements reprised from A_1 will undergo alterations to make room for the final tonic. As mentioned above, in "Padre, germani, addio!" the b_2 region is presented in the tonic key. Consequently elements of the structure displayed in **3.10b** shift: whereas the transition in A_1 prepares for the mediant, that in A_2 proceeds through the mediant to the dominant, so that the tonic arrival coincides with the onset of b_2. Melodically, the fundamental descent from $\hat{5}$ is interrupted at $\hat{2}$ during A_1. That span is traversed again during A_2, this time achieving $\hat{1}$ [**3.11**].

It is heartening to see how Mozart can, when it is called for, boil his structural ideas down to their essence. My analysis of measures 13 through 32 is based upon the premise that a segment of the descending circle of fifths guides the progression from the tonic to the mediant, even if numerous

Example 3.11 Analysis of Mozart: "Padre, germani, addio!" from *Idomeneo* (K. 366), mm. 5–115.

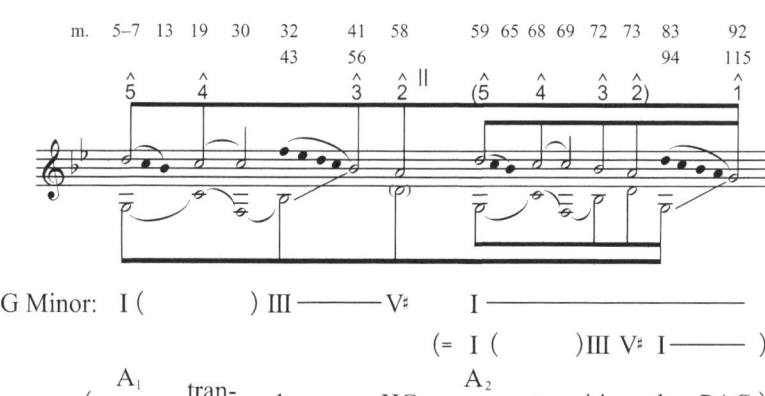

additional chords sound during this passage. The transition during A_2 speeds that process along, so that the major dominant that follows can be suitably prolonged. Consequently Mozart's progression (measures 65 through 72) dispenses with the additional chords of A_1 and comes to resemble the foundational structure presented in **3.10b**.

Sometimes Mozart will insert a specific chordal relationship at a key structural moment even when the context has changed. For example, during the initial circle of fifths, C⇒ F paves the way for the arrival of the mediant key, B♭ Major, for b_1. The progression to the dominant of measure 73, which paves the way for the arrival of the tonic key, G Minor, for b_2, is *not* circular, and thus dominant D lacks a → preparation. Yet Mozart inserts an A⇒D succession – functioning as an embellishment of the dominant – twice during an extension of this D chord (measures 77–81). On other occasions we may observe Mozart tending to specific pitch relations that transcend the transposition of the moment. For example, even though $\hat{5}$ serves as the *Kopfton*, the tonic G's upper octave plays an important role during the a_1 and a_2 thematic statements (measures 7, 10, 11, etc.). During b_1, in the tonicized key of B♭ Major, this G serves as an upper neighbor to the B♭ triad's fifth (measures 32, 34, 36, etc.). When that theme recurs in the key of G Minor during b_2, Mozart finds a suitable means to retain the high G (measures 83, 85, 87, etc.). This theme, whose presentation during b_1 is graphed in **3.10c**, is stated four times during the b_2 section, with PACs at 92_1 and 115_1. Two separate graphs account for its varied statements [**3.12a** and **3.12b**]. Observe that a neighboring note – F♯ in measures 90 and 101 (the equivalent of A in measures 39 and 50) – is absent from the final statements. To heighten the impact of the final statement, Mozart resorts to a wobble

Example 3.12 Analysis of Mozart: "Padre, germani, addio!" from *Idomeneo* (K. 366), (a) mm. 83–102; (b) mm. 83–115.

during the 6 phase of IV: A♭ displaces A♮ at 108_1. Diatonic A is restored in measure 112, at the end of an extended, partially chromaticized glide of $^6_3$ chords (not shown in the graph). The approach to the final PAC proceeds in a conventional fashion: the stepwise descent to $\hat{1}$ is traversed in the vocal line; the cadential $^6_4$ is no longer unfurled.

"Traurigkeit ward mir zum Lose" from *Die Entführung aus dem Serail* (K. 384)

Abducted by pirates, the noble Constanze finds herself in the seraglio of Pasha Selim, whose sexual restraint is on the verge of wavering. She is as yet unaware that, having been informed of her fate, her fiancé Belmonte is within the compound planning her escape. In "Traurigkeit ward mir zum Lose" she laments her sorrowful state: without Belmonte her life will wither away. As was also the case in "Padre, germani, addio!," the aria is in binary form ($A_1 - A_2$), both parts of which present the full text. The broad harmonic progression I III V♯, I V♯ I prevails.

The a_1 region within A_1 conveys Constanze's sadness in a progression whose middleground structure is highly developed yet conventional [**3.13a**]. The initial I-space, through measure 8, is prolonged via a local descending fifth-progression notable for the temporary positioning of inner-voice G at the top of the texture during 3_2 (an event that occurs in all the arias we have examined) and by the temporary wobble of A to A♭ during the supertonic harmony at 7_1. (A♮ is restored in the second violin line later in the measure.) The mediant that follows is attained via a circular progression (G–C–F→B♭ in measures 8 through 10). The first attempt at cadential closure fails. (The dominant of measure 12 leads not to a tonic close, but to the tonic's 6-phase chord, unfurled as E♭-G-B♭, at 13_1.) Only in the second attempt is a PAC attained. The B♭ and A of the melodic descent from *Kopfton* $\hat{5}$ are stated only in the viola line (measure 18), as the vocal line pursues a more dramatic course, from the cover tone D to inner-voice F♯.[19]

The b_1 section, which tonicizes the mediant key, begins in measure 33. The transition between a_1 and b_1 reprises some content from the a_1 region, where the root progression G–B♭–C in measures 3 through 16 extends the tonic (I) via its upper third (III) before proceeding to IV.[20] A local circular progression (G–C–F–B♭) connects the tonic and the mediant in both measures 8 through 10 (within a_1) and measures 20 through 22 (during the transition). The latter progression is internal to a broader circular trajectory extending from measure 19 through measure 33 [**3.13b**]. The C chord of measure 28 leads to F, not to D, as did that in measures 16 and 17. The medial caesura in measure 32 prepares for b_1's arrival in the tonicized mediant key, while the melody in measures 29 through 32 leads upwards above the fundamental line to a high F, making an F>B♭ fifth available for traversal during the b_1 region. (Compare with the similar situation during the transition and b_1 region in "Padre, germani, addio!")

Two complete traversals of the F>B♭ fifth occur during b_1 [**3.13c**]. Although Constanze's lament continues, her mention of the breeze ("Luft") at the outset of the second stanza is sufficient grounds to justify Mozart's setting of the passage in B♭ Major – an expected event in a G Minor aria of this period – and to convey the wafting of the breeze through a suggestive melodic gesture stated four times during measures 33 through 40. The negation of the breeze's positive potential is powerfully conveyed

Example 3.13 Analysis of Mozart: "Traurigkeit ward mir zum Lose" from *Die Entführung aus dem Serail* (K. 384), (a) mm. 3–19; (b) mm. 3–62; (c) mm. 33–62.

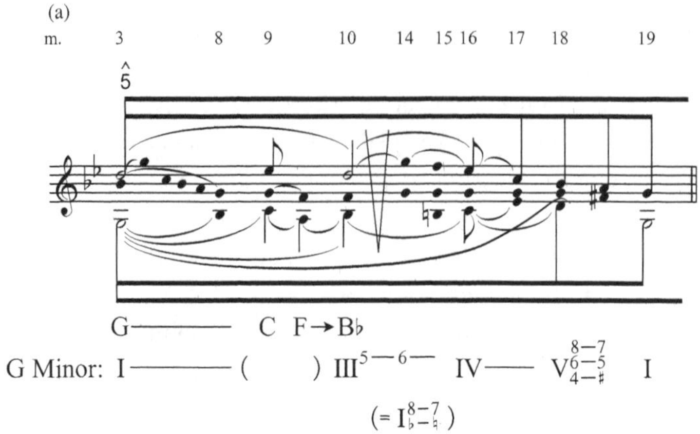

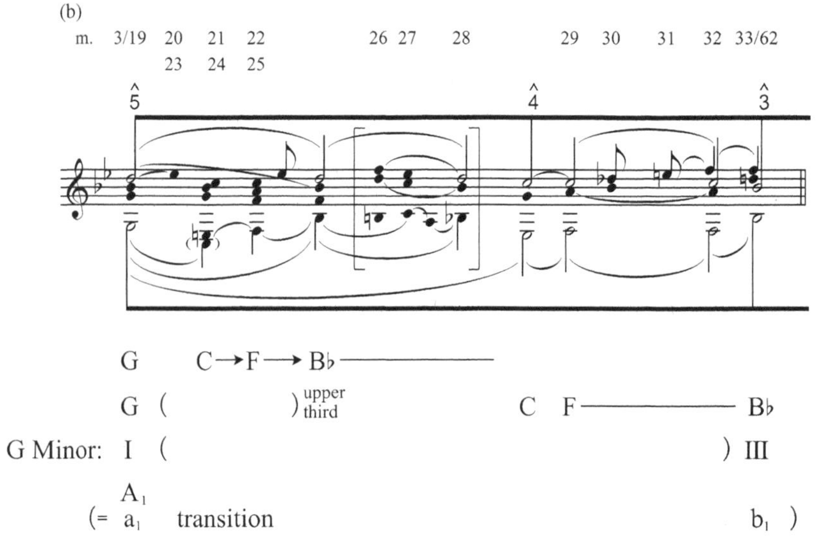

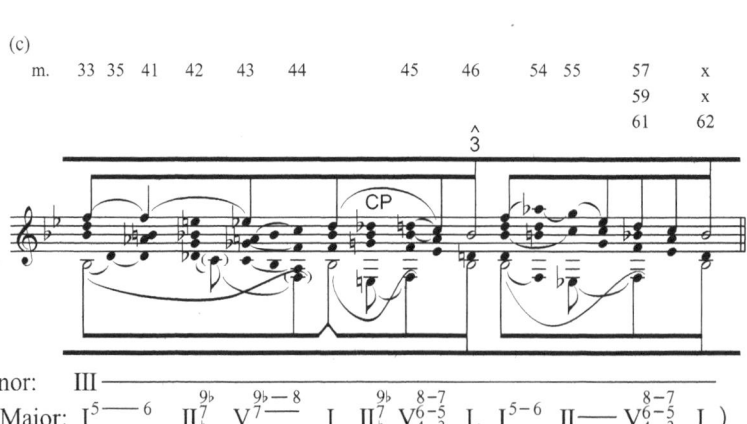

through a descending progression of diminished seventh chords in measures 41 through 43. In their context these chords represent a conventional progression expressed in an unconventional manner: from the B♭ tonic's 6-phase extension through the supertonic to the dominant, all highly evolved [**3.13c**]. After the resolution of the dominant to the tonic at 44_2, the structural line's chromatic descent continues with D♭, here stated only by the second basset horn. (The substitution pitch G occurs in the vocal and upper woodwind parts.) The following C is embellished by upper neighbor D♮. Goal B♭ arrives in conjunction with the PAC at 46_1. F is restored immediately, and consequently a second fifth-progression to B♭, this time with simpler harmonic support, occurs. (Note especially the predominance of diatonic chords and the single, as opposed to double, B♭–F–B♭ arpeggiation in the bass.) This descent is distinguished by its hesitancy to close. Neither at 58_1 nor at 60_1 does the expected root-position B♭ tonic chord occur. Mozart twice backtracks in the progression: whereas measure 54 contains an evolved tonic 6-phase chord and measures 55 and 56 present a diatonic supertonic chord, the diatonic tonic 6-phase chords (substituting for the PAC resolution chord) at 58_1 and 60_1 are followed by evolved supertonic chords. In each case a dominant $^{6-5}_{4-3}$ comes next, yet the B♭-D-F tonic harmony emerges only on the third try, at 62_1.

The final event in A_1 is the completion of the bass ascent to the dominant, D major. We can dispense with an elaborate discussion and even a new graph, since Mozart's strategy here (measures 62 through 66) is virtually identical to the structure in the corresponding spot in "Padre, germani, addio!" (measures 56 through 58). Model 3 of **3.10d** displays that structure, which Mozart now presents in a more solid form, with bass B♭<G>C<A>D. The dominant arrival is displayed within its broader context in **3.14**.

A comparison of **3.11** and **3.14** reveals a close relationship between the basic structures of "Padre, germani, addio!" and "Traurigkeit ward mir zum Lose." The chief difference occurs during the transition between a_2 and b_2: in one case, $\hat{3}$ is supported by the mediant; in the other, it transpires during a prolongation of the dominant. Closer to the musical surface, we note further differences in construction between the A_1 and A_2 transitions in "Traurigkeit ward mir zum Lose." Note especially the incorporation of the D<G>F♯ motive that opens a_1 and a_2 within the latter. That motive continues to evolve within b_2: D>G>F♯ in the oboe line of measures 96 and 97 becomes the D<G>F♯ motto in the vocal line of measures 98 and 99, while a more extended D<G>G>F♯ occurs during measures 113 through 117 and

Example 3.14 Analysis of Mozart: "Traurigkeit ward mir zum Lose" from *Die Entführung aus dem Serail* (K. 384), mm. 3–133.

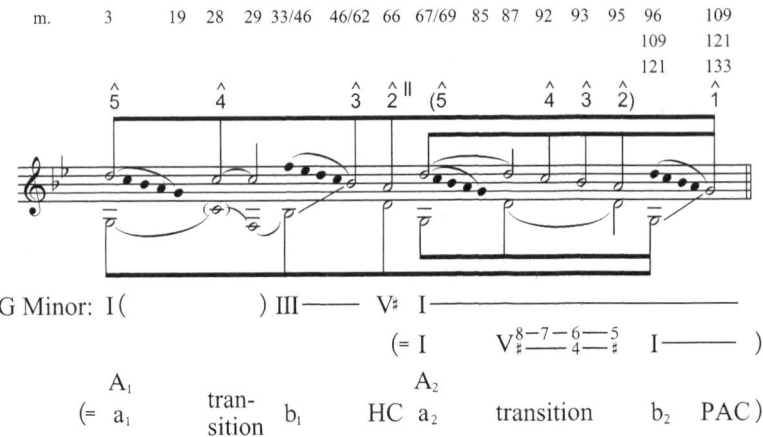

125 through 129. In addition, the C<D♭<E♮<F line from the first transition (measures 29 through 32) is transposed down a third and filled in to become A<B♭<B♮<C<C♯<D during the second (measures 92 through 95).

Whereas the a_1 and a_2 regions are the same, b_2 is not a routine transformation of b_1 from B♭ Major to G Minor. Mozart manages to preserve some absolute pitch relationships despite the lowering of the tonal center by a third. For example, compare measures 41 through 44 and measures 104 through 107. Because a diminished seventh chord contains nothing but minor thirds (or their enharmonic equivalent, the augmented second), *the same* progression of diminished seventh chords supporting *the same* melodic line is used in both cases, representing the harmonic progression I⁶ II V (leading to I) in B♭ Major and then in G Minor! Also compare the vocal line of measures 55 and 56 with that of measures 118 and 119. In the context of B♭ Major, a II chord is employed throughout, whereas in the context of G Minor a I–IV$^{5-6}$ approach to the dominant is employed instead. In addition to the shared melody, a C-E♭-G chord plays a prominent role in both cases.

Once the definitive closure is secured at 133_1, further enhancements of the cadential progression ensue for an additional fourteen measures. Whereas bass D at 135_1 supports a cadential $^6_4$ (the successor of the preceding II→), the D$^6_4$ during 137_2 functions as a passing chord within a II→⇒ transformation. When the cadential $^6_4$ does arrive at 139_1, it is prolonged as support for over three measures of mostly descending passagework that suggests Constanze's assumption of an impending demise. The vocal close at 143_1 is echoed by two orchestral descents in succession to conclude the aria.

"Ach ich fühl's, es ist verschwunden!" from *Die Zauberflöte* (K. 620)

Though Tamino and Pamina have by now fallen in love, a ritual in which Tamino is engaged does not allow him to speak. Pamina misinterprets this as a repudiation of their love. Without Tamino her life will not be worth living, and so she contemplates plunging a dagger into her heart. In "Ach ich fühl's, es ist verschwunden!" we encounter her lamenting her situation.

The A_1 section of the aria's binary form displays a normative tonal construction for a work set in a minor key: it proceeds from the tonic through the mediant to the dominant. This dominant, unlike that in the other binary-form arias we have explored, is extended for several measures. In fact, two of the text's eight lines (the sixth and seventh) are presented during this V-space. The A_2 section does not restate the opening material: neither the musical nor the textual content reprises that which opened the A_1 section. Yet A_2 does resolve the tonal tension caused by the interruption at the close of A_1 by concluding with a PAC in the tonic key, which is achieved only during a second attempt (measure 36, not measure 27). The structure is laid out as follows:

```
m.        1    7      8  13  16   17      20       24   26   26   ||
                                                   30   32   32   36-38

          5̂            4̂   3̂            2̂ ||     (5̂   4̂   3̂   2̂) 1̂
G Minor:  I   (    )  III    (    )      V♯       I ─────────────────
                                                (=  I   II   V♯   I   )

          A₁                                       A₂
Text lines: 1-2         3-4       5     6-7        8 ───────────────
Example:  3.15a─
          3.15b ─────
          3.15c ──────────────            3.16a ──────────
                                          3.16b ───────────────
```

The first two lines of the text, which bewail the lost love, are set within a conventional local harmonic context: from I through IV to V♯ [**3.15a**]. The sense of sorrow is conveyed by the staid string accompaniment, by the numerous descending seconds in the vocal line, and by several melodic diminished fifths (C>F♯ in measures 3 and 4, G>C♯ in measures 5 and 6). Some potent chords are employed: the diminished seventh in measure 2 (representing V➔)[21] and the augmented sixth in measures 5 and 6 (serving as an embellishing chord). The aria contains several extraordinary passages of lingering on the dominant. To resolve is to confirm that Pamina's situation is hopeless – a signal for her to kill herself. To hold off is to await the longed-for reconciliation. The embellishing-chord expansion of V-space (E♭, G, C♯, also B♭ the second time) will be restated in a variety of forms as the aria proceeds.

The transition between the tonic and mediant regions begins as a varied reiteration of this local dominant embellishment, in which the inward motions of measures 5 and 6 are transformed into outward motions in measure 7: bass D>C♯ and first violin D<E♮. Mozart negotiates the ascending third between tonic G and mediant B♭ by transforming G's local dominant into B♭'s local dominant [**3.15b**]. Instead of reverting to the D dominant, its A-C♯-E♮ embellishing chord morphs into F-A-C♮-E♭, the dominant in B♭ Major.[22] Consequently E♮, which initially seemed to function as a neighbor to D, ultimately functions as a wobble, temporarily displacing the F dominant's seventh, E♭. Likewise bass C♯ at first may seem to function as a neighbor but ultimately behaves as a chromatic passing note.

The third and fourth lines of the text hark back to the time when Pamina had no doubts about Tamino's commitment. Though she acknowledges that it has ended (or so it appears to her), this contrasting notion justifies Mozart's setting of these lines in the tonicized key of B♭ Major [**3.15c**]. From a broad perspective, the $\hat{3}>\hat{2}>\hat{1}$ structural descent (in B♭ Major) during this region serves as the $\hat{5}>\hat{4}>\hat{3}$ segment of the fundamental line. The principal difference in the local harmonic progressions of the G Minor and B♭ Major regions is the greater incidence of 6-phase chords in the latter. For example, the initiating succession in measures 8 through 11 is I$^{5-6}$ II rather than the I$^{8-7}_{♭-♮}$ IV of measures 1 and 2.[23] Mozart continues the extraordinary treatment of dominant harmonies during measures 14 and 15, where the word heart ("Herzen") induces a wondrous extension of a modest B♭<D unfolding (followed by a straightforward C>A unfolding during the second half of measure 15).

The transition from the mediant to the dominant (measures 16 through 20) engages a segment of the ascending 5–6 sequence, as often has been the case in the arias we have explored. Graphs from several other arias may be compared with this passage: **3.2**, measures 36 through 40; **3.5**; and **3.10d**, Model 3. In each case the structural line descends to $\hat{2}$, covered by D.[24] Pamina presents the fifth of the text's eight lines, in which she implores Tamino to take notice of her deplorable state, during this transition. The dominant prolongation that follows continues that thought with the next

Composition in a minor key   117

Example 3.15 Analysis of Mozart: "Ach ich fühl's, es ist verschwunden!" from *Die Zauberflöte* (K. 620), (a) mm. 1–7; (b) mm. 1–8; (c) mm. 1–16.

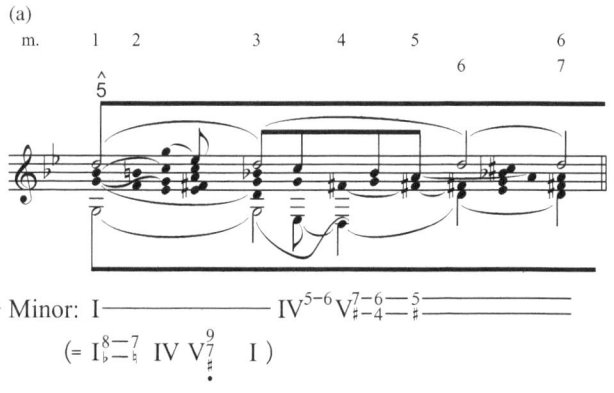

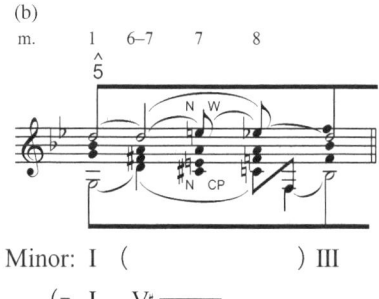

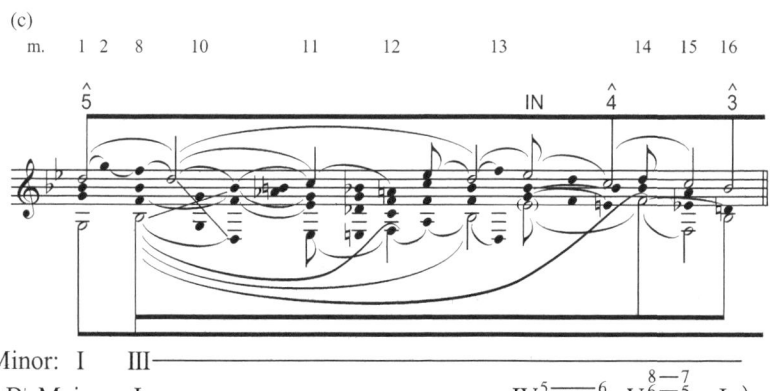

Example 3.16 Analysis of Mozart: "Ach ich fühl's, es ist verschwunden!" from *Die Zauberflöte* (K. 620), (a) mm. 20–30; (b) mm. 20–38.

two lines of the text. During measures 20 and 21 embellishing chords extend the dominant, in coordination with the filling-in of the dominant's upper fourth (D>C>B♭>A), reminiscent of the fourth-progression in measures 3 through 5 [**3.16a**]. Then a new variety of embellishing chord is employed. Whereas measures 5 and 6 incorporate the dominant root D's neighbors E♭ and C♯, and measure 7 incorporates its neighbors C♯ and E♮, C and E♭ shape the neighboring motion in measures 22 through 24 (along with inner-voice G, neighbor to F♯).

The eighth (final) line of the text coordinates with the return of the tonic for the A_2 section. The progression of measures 24 through 26 gives the impression of pressing towards a PAC, which is averted at 27_1 [**3.16a**]. Yet another embellishing-chord prolongation emerges, with neighbors E♭ (extended by an E♮ wobble in measure 28) and C♯, thereby continuing Pamina's stall tactic. What we at first take to be the final cadential dominant turns out to extend the dominant of measures 20 through 24 [**3.16b**].[25] Even the text backtracks to line 7. The closing progression is restated (with a ♭$\hat{2}$ wobble in measure 32), and though its cadential dominant is again extended (measures 33 through 35), this time it succeeds in driving to the PAC. This long-awaited, long-dreaded tonic sounds on three consecutive downbeats (36_1 through 38_1). The $\genfrac{}{}{0pt}{}{A}{F\sharp}$ third among the G<B♭ A>F♯ G unfoldings of these measures expands first into a diminished triad (A<C>F♯) and ultimately into a diminished seventh chord (A<C<E♭>F♯) for Pamina's final utterance: "peace comes only in death."[26] The orchestral postlude presents an adaptation of the melody from 1_2 through 3_1 (focusing on its descending-second "sighs") followed by a cadence that borrows the ♭II–V♮ of measure 32, which now resolves directly to I.

4 | The happy ending: three sonata-rondos in D Major from piano concertos by Haydn and Mozart

When a rondeau or the more developed rondo takes on symmetrical characteristics (AB–AC–AB′–A, in which B is in a contrasting key and B′ is in the tonic key), it begins to align itself with the exposition–development–recapitulation–coda arrangement that characterizes the Type 3 sonata.[1] Both Haydn and Mozart further develop that tendency, writing movements that are sufficiently distinct from either a normative rondo or a normative Type 3 sonata that they warrant classification as what is now called a sonata-rondo or, in Hepokoski and Darcy's terminology, a Type 4 sonata. The abbreviated Type 1 sonata (exposition–recapitulation–coda) may also develop along these lines, creating a sonata-rondo category distinguished from the more common Type 4 via a superscript label: the Type 4^1 sonata. (The designation Type 4 otherwise represents Type 4^3.) Because the composer is negotiating a path between two more congealed formal strategies, one encounters a wide range of variants, especially in the later rotations. The most stable element is the expositional rotation, which in a major key generally will match the Type 3 (or Type 1) juxtaposition of the tonic and the dominant, with intervening transition. In fact, Hepokoski and Darcy abandon the rondo letter designations for the Type 4, instead employing the sonata designations P^{rf} TR ' S / C, in which superscript rf acknowledges the refrain function of the primary-theme zone. In contrast to a conventional exposition, the expositional rotation in a Type 4 sonata will not be repeated.

Hepokoski and Darcy offer numerous astute observations regarding the wondrous creativity of Haydn and Mozart within this arena. As a complement to their overview and with greater emphasis upon structure and harmony, I present close analyses of the closing movements from three piano concertos in the key of D Major: Haydn's H. XVIII: 11 of the early 1780s and Mozart's K. 451 of 1784 (both Type 4^3 movements), as well as Mozart's K. 537 of 1788 (a Type 4^1 movement with an internal expansion that Hepokoski and Darcy acknowledge in the label Type $4^{1\text{-exp}}$). Readers may elect either to study each movement in turn, as presented below, or instead to explore first the three expositional rotations, then the two

The happy ending 121

Example 4.1 Analysis of Haydn: Piano Concerto in D Major (H. XVIII: 11), mvmt. 3, mm. 1–60.

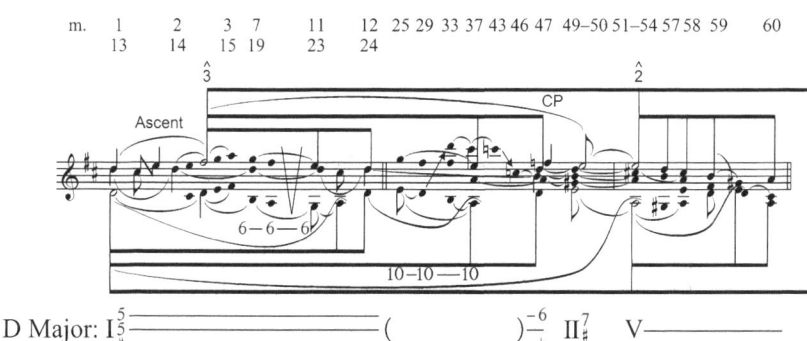

developmental rotations, and finally the three recapitulatory rotations and abbreviated coda rotations.

The expositional rotation in H. XVIII: 11 (measures 1–77)

The sprightly P^{rf} theme signals a movement full of good cheer. What might have been an eight-measure theme is expanded to twelve measures through internal repetitions (measures 5–6 and 9–10). Though all the pitches between $\hat{1}$ and $\hat{5}$ occur during the melody's opening tonic presentation, the broader context suggests the reading of an ascent to *Kopfton* $\hat{3}$, followed by an upper-third extension. (See **4.1**.) Note especially how F♯<G<A is complemented by G>F♯>E in measures 7 through 11, proceeding to D in measure 12. The chromatic F♮ in measure 47 leads the background line from long-extended F♯ towards E. Careful consideration of the *Kopfton* issue is especially important in this movement, since the same melody (with a revised continuation) will inaugurate S, in a context that gives priority instead to the fifth (E in the tonicized dominant key, measures 53 and 54).

The G>F♯>E third is subjected to severe interference. Because the content of measure 7 is repeated in measure 8 (with the outer voices exchanged), and because those two measures are then repeated, the listener may be tempted to regard F♯ and A as restorations of the tonic third and fifth. I propose in **4.1** that they instead function as passing notes within IV^{5-6}. (Compare with **1.1d**, 2_2 through 3_1.) The orchestra and piano appear to be of two minds on the matter: whereas the soloist proposes a tonic extension in measures 8 and 10 (echoing 3_2 through 4_1), the orchestral lines extend onward to complete the outer-voice thirds at 11_1, compelling the piano to comply. The IV harmony's 6-phase E extends through the V♯ that follows, leading to the PAC's tonic D. The orchestra then repeats the entire phrase.

Looking ahead, note that the medial caesura that concludes TR occurs on II♯ (Hepokoski and Darcy's V:HC MC) at 50_1. From the insight attained through our study of sonata expositions of this sort in chapter 2, we should expect II♯ to be preceded by the tonic's 6-phase chord. Indeed, that is exactly what Haydn offers during measures 47 and 48. (As mentioned above, the chord's third is lowered.) His method of connecting the tonic 5- and 6-phase chords is motivically related to events from the opening P^{rf} section. Recall that the initial F♯<G<A third was answered by G>F♯>E, supported below in parallel sixths (as displayed in **4.1**). The same G>F♯>E third returns in an expanded form to initiate TR (measures 25 through 37), this time supported by what begins as a lower line in parallel tenths, though midway through the progression its middle pitch, D, is transferred to the top of the texture, so that the third "tenth" – C♯ – sounds as a sixth. After chromatic inflection to C♮ it is transferred to the texture's interior. (See the arrows in **4.1**.) Whereas the G>F♯>E third within P^{rf} is supported by IV^{5-6}, the harmonic context II ( ) V prevails within TR. Though V's C♯ could resolve to D for a restoration of the tonic (as was the case in measures 11 and 12), or the A chord potentially could serve as the medial caesura (of the alternative I:HC MC type), here instead C♯ is lowered to C♮, a downward trend that continues with B at 47_1. This is exactly what is called for in this context: we *need* to attain I^6 as predecessor of II♯. Haydn here approaches the 6 (= B) from above. (Note in **4.1** the concurrent descending thirds that are traversed from the opening of the movement through measure 47: an outer-strand F♯>E>D displayed as upward-stemmed notes connected by a beam; and an inner-strand D>C♯(C♮)>B displayed as downward-stemmed notes connected by a slur.) Despite the logic that guides the underlying strategy here, one may admire Haydn's audacity in juxtaposing E minor and D major chords in measures 25 through 32. In fact, a "peculiar juxtaposition" of E minor to D major and B minor to A major occurs during measures 25 through 40.[2] Though one might temporarily question which of the two chords E or D – or B or A – is hierarchically deeper (a quandary similar to that which might arise in the context of measure 7 as well, as noted above), once the dominant prolongation begins at the endpoint of the motivic G>F♯>E third, one may succeed in perceiving that the perimeter chords rooted on E and A – II and V – guide the progression.[3]

The soprano E of measures 49 and 50 is a crucial element in the exposition's structure. Through its strength the thematic content during the S that follows may be understood as an ascending gesture to E (not to C♯, as was the case when this material occurred during P^{rf}). The soloist registrally broadens what would normally be a stepwise D>C♯>B continuation into a succession of filled-in ninths during measures 57 through 59. In **4.1** the normative register is used to display this non-normative means of descent, whose conclusion on A in measure 60 corresponds to the EEC.

As is typical, the structure of the closing zone (C) that follows contrasts that of S. Here Haydn focuses on melodic presentations of the tonicized A triad's lower third: numerous C♯>B>A̲ descents (some supported by I$^{5-6}$ II^7 V^7 I) confirm the EEC. In a departure from the rondo norm, a refrain in D Major does not follow at the outset of the developmental rotation. Consequently there is no retransition. At this juncture the movement resides closer to the "sonata" than to the "rondo" side of this hybrid form. From what has occurred thus far, the vivacious thematic content and the absence of a repeat sign after C are the chief indicators (besides Haydn's rondo label) that we are here dealing with a Type 4 rather than a Type 3 sonata movement.

The developmental rotation in H. XVIII: 11 (measures 78–253)

Inquiring minds benefit in many ways from undertaking analyses of musical scores. At a basic level, an analytical inquiry will help performers and listeners to take note of a movement's signature events, which might confirm assumptions about how the form proceeds or, when something unusual occurs, raise flags. During the developmental rotation in Haydn's rondo, the sudden shift from a D Minor episode to the return of the D Major P^{rf} theme at measure 201 may signal a potential – though odd – start of the recapitulatory rotation. Yet this P^{rf} theme does not behave as would one that opens such a rotation. Before its cadence, a new whirl of shifting chordal activity emerges. A more suitable location for the onset of the recapitulatory rotation is measure 254, where a well-behaved P^{rf} theme is stated in its entirety in D Major. (Another normative trait is that it is followed by a transition.) But, if that is so, then why is it preceded by an F♯ major chord? Clearly a deeper level of analysis is required, lest we conclude that Haydn was eccentric in his tonal and formal constructions.

Experienced analysts develop a sense of what to be on the lookout for. (For example, during TR in the expositional rotation one might well expect

Example 4.2 Analysis of Haydn: Piano Concerto in D Major (H. XVIII: 11), mvmt. 3, mm. 1–309.

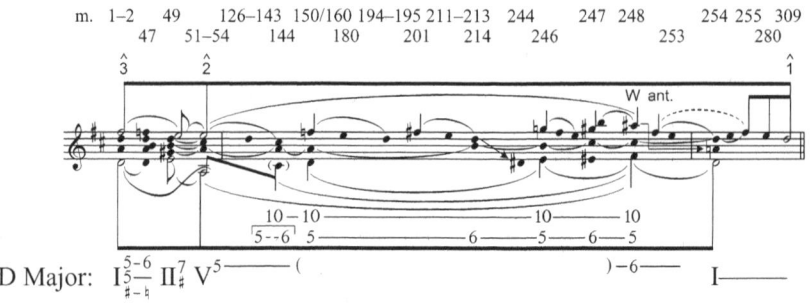

to find a progression that proceeds broadly as I^{5-6} II♯, as turned out to be the case in this movement.) Development sections tend to be havens for circular and sequential progressions, sometimes proceeding at a wondrously slow pace. Thinking broadly, one might discern that the A major dominant chord first introduced at measure 51 extends through measure 149. (Details will follow presently.) Its immediate successor is not a D Major tonic resolution, but instead a substantial episode in D Minor (measures 150 through 200). D Major follows (measure 201), though it soon shifts to its 6-phase B Minor (measure 214). This data suggests that the development is guided by an ascending 5–6 sequence, connecting the dominant's 5-phase A-C♯-E and chromaticized, unfurled 6-phase F♯-A♯-C♯ (measure 248), a construction that is displayed within its broader context in **4.2**. As is often the case with a 5–6, the sequential ascent is abbreviated, taking advantage of the convenient fact that its first and sixth chords share the same pitch content:

$$A^5 \quad (A\sharp^6 \quad B^5 \quad B\sharp^6 \quad C\sharp^5) \quad C\sharp^6 \quad D^5 \quad D\sharp^6 \quad E^5 \quad E\sharp^6 \quad F\sharp^5$$

A sonata-rondo integrates two distinct formal shapes, with a flexibility that allows the composer to emphasize one or the other when their normative formal parameters differ. In a rondo the tonic key and the refrain theme (P^{rf}) would be restored at measure 78. Haydn's maintenance of the dominant through measure 149 is indicative of a sonata-form emphasis during this region, though at least the motivic content stems from P^{rf}. Consequently from a rondo perspective there is a P deficit throughout the beginning stages of the developmental rotation. Aware of his debt, Haydn offers an abbreviated P^{rf} when the sequential ascent reaches D Major. (The

D Minor of measures 150 through 200 delays that arrival.) Despite this strong signal that the recapitulatory rotation is beginning, the broad sequential initiative continues, not even allowing the P^{rf} theme to cadence in D. Though the thematic deficit has been offset, Haydn obeys the sonata-form norm that a tonic restoration does not occur during the developmental rotation. The sequence allows for a presentation of the theme in a D Major context that functions not as the resolution of the dominant, but instead as a region that is being passed through during the connection of the dominant's 5- and 6-phase chords. Thus ingeniously both the sonata- and rondo-form norms are fulfilled.

Though the broad V^{5-6} of **4.2** might have proceeded upwards by step to a chord rooted on B, a possibility that here is strengthened through the presence of dominant-emulating A♯ and the emergence (at 253$_2$) of E, F♯'s minor seventh, Haydn instead treats the 6-phase F♯ as an anticipation of the D Major tonic's third. The A♯, indifferent to the diminished fifth that it forms with E, behaves as a wobble, returning to A♮ at the onset of the recapitulatory rotation. Because the 6-phase chord is unfurled, a broad connection between dominant root A and tonic root D, via two descending thirds, is achieved in the bass, as shown by the downward-stemmed A, F♯, and D in **4.2**.

This crucial F♯>D versus F♯→B choice of succession is in fact an issue that Haydn has planted within the developmental rotation early on. In a breathtaking correlation, the sequential ascent to dominant A's 6-phase chord occurs not only in the broad trajectory displayed in **4.2**, but also within the initial dominant prolongation, displayed in **4.3a** and **4.3b**. Note first that in this case the F♯ chord (measures 118 through 125), which begins diatonically but evolves to incorporate both major third A♯ and minor seventh E, *does* proceed to a B chord, labeled as II in the context of the A Major tonicization. Though the sequential progression of **4.3b** does not incorporate quite the same level of chromaticism as that which spans the entire developmental rotation, it instead accommodates modal mixture. The A chord is presented with a C♮ from measure 78 onwards, and its upper-third chord C♮-E-G♮ is prolonged beginning at measure 90. Consequently this version of the sequence (unlike the broader one, which commences with the tonic) proceeds obstinately in whole steps, from C♮^{5} to F♯^{5}. (By its endpoint, the modal mixture has dissipated, allowing the sequence to span an augmented fourth from wobbly C♮ to diatonic F♯.) Another uncommon traversal occurs during the prolongation of II that follows. Note in **4.3a** that II is extended by its upper-third chord (measure 140). Haydn's ingenious local connection of those chords involves an obstinate circular progression of two

Example 4.3 Analysis of Haydn: Piano Concerto in D Major (H. XVIII: 11), mvmt. 3
(a) mm. 51–144; (b) mm. 51–126.

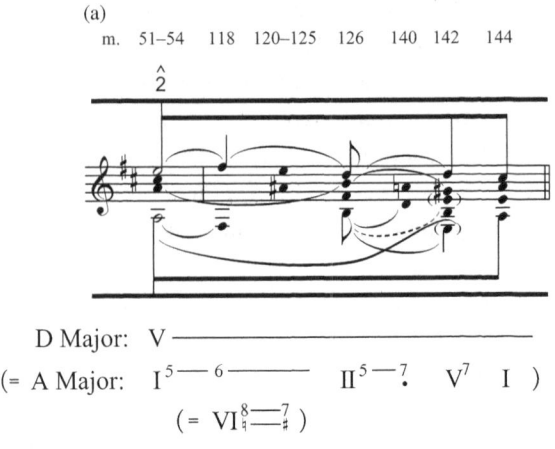

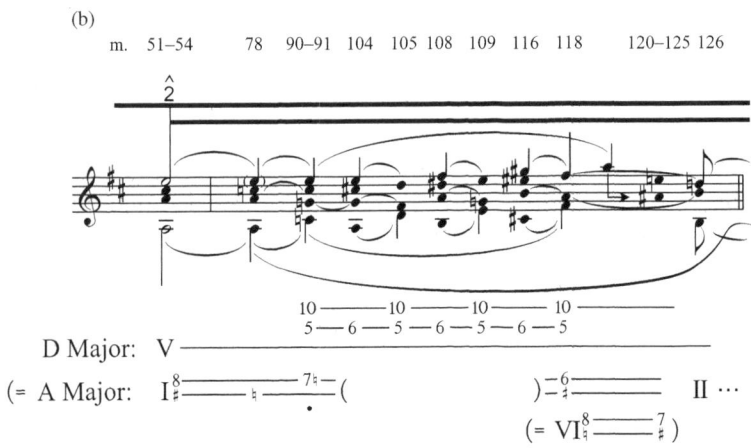

descending major thirds, with an internal modal shift: b–G–g–E♭. Clearly he has strayed quite far from the B minor chord. Yet E♭ is immediately incorporated within a brief tonicization of B's upper-third chord: ♭II V⁷ I in D Major in measures 134 through 140.

Several of the individual chords encountered during the broad sequential ascent of **4.2** are themselves tonicized. Haydn offers an extended episode in tonicized D Minor. (See **4.4**.) Since the mode is minor, it is not surprising that the mediant is emphasized during the traversal of the span from I to V♯. In this case the structural soprano pitch F♮ arrives at the outset of III. (The structure of the III prolongation has several features in common with the

Example 4.4 Analysis of Haydn: Piano Concerto in D Major (H. XVIII: 11), mvmt. 3, mm. 151–194.

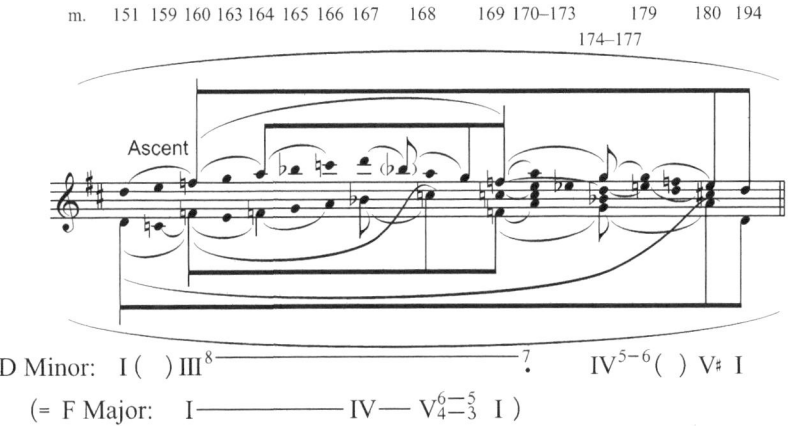

D Major P^{rf} theme, graphed in **4.1**.) The A minor chord prolonged during measures 170 through 173 is peculiar. (One wonders if the explicit Hungarian flavor of the rondo allowed Haydn some uncommon freedom in his chordal successions. Here A minor and G minor chords are juxtaposed, as were E minor and D major during TR.) Is this A minor the arrival of the dominant, with conversion to major quality in measure 180, after an embellishing chord on G? I resist that reading, instead interpreting the G chord (which is extended via a conventional 5–6 shift) as the link between the tonic-to-mediant D<F and the dominant A that follows, as shown in **4.4**. From this perspective the A chord of measures 170 through 173 serves as the mediant's upper-third chord, supporting passing note E.

A tonicization of D Major, starting in measure 201, barely gets off the ground before the swerve to D's 6-phase B Minor. (See **4.5**. Locate within **4.2**.) A descending circle of fifths from 211_1 through 213_1 simply moves the entire structure down a third, though soprano E is retained as the F♯ dominant's seventh. (The newly attained bass E consequently passes between the initial D, which retrospectively may be understood as the root of B Minor's III, and F♯ within an auxiliary progression – that is, one starting away from the tonic.) The tonicization of B Minor extends further, leading from I through II➔ to V in measures 214 through 232. Though at first it appears that Haydn is planning to restore the B tonic via two descending thirds (F♯>D>B), his progression exceeds that target, instead hitting B again in measure 244, where an evolved B chord surges towards

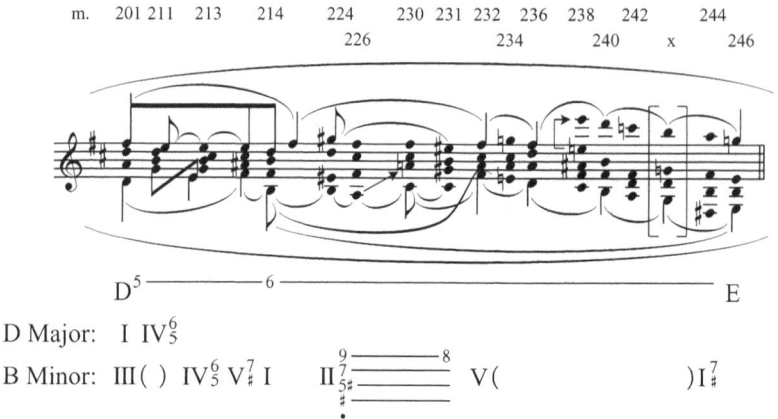

Example 4.5 Analysis of Haydn: Piano Concerto in D Major (H. XVIII: 11), mvmt. 3, mm. 201–246.

E, the next chord within the broad sequence. The remainder of the sequence transpires quickly, as shown in **4.2**. The F♯ goal is attained in measure 248.

The recapitulatory and coda half-rotations in H. XVIII: 11 (measures 254–321)

The PAC at 265_1 gives the statement of P^{rf} that begins in measure 254 a solidity that was lacking in that which occurred during the developmental rotation. The immediate onset of TR material confirms that the recapitulatory rotation is under way. (See **4.6**.) Typically the recapitulatory TR will be modified so as to prepare for the presentation of S in the tonic key. In this work Haydn achieves a medial caesura on D Major's dominant seventh chord at 295_1. The fermata on the dominant's ninth B at 297_1 invites a cadenza. Because the expositional rotation's P^{rf} and S are thematically identical at their outsets, Haydn has the option to truncate the structure at this point. The TR cadenza turns out to function as an RT (retransition) cadenza, proceeding not to S, but instead to the coda half-rotation's modified statement of P^{rf}. The fundamental structure concludes with the cadence – the ESC – at 309_1, which is followed by a brief coda.[4]

Recall from **4.1** that during the expositional rotation's TR a local V harmony (arriving at 37_1) comes between the tonic 5- and 6-phase chords. Attentive listeners may have considered the possibility of that TR's conclusion in a I:HC MC, a hypothesis that would need to be abandoned once

Example 4.6 Analysis of Haydn: Piano Concerto in D Major (H. XVIII: 11), mvmt. 3, mm. 254–309.

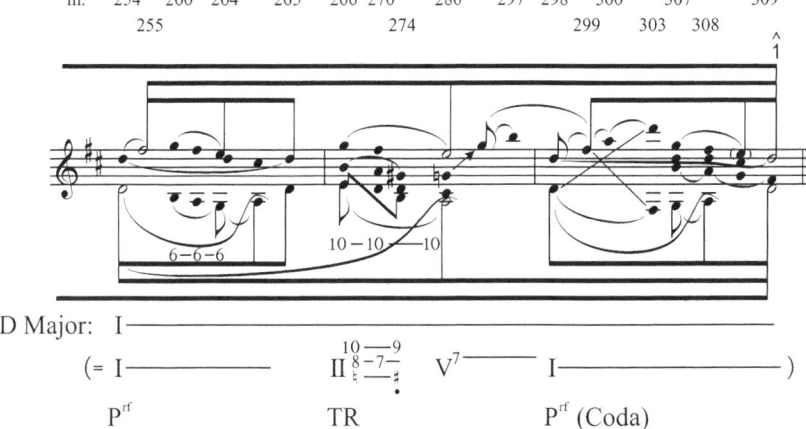

the V's C♯ proceeded through C♮ to the tonic 6-phase B (at 47₁). Haydn's reworking of TR for the recapitulatory rotation offers a second chance for that rejected potentiality, since the revised tonal course requires that S (or its substitute, the coda half-rotation's P^{rf}) be presented in the tonic key. The instigator of this V's migration to a deeper structural plane is the chord of measures 274 through 278. Whereas a modest B-D-F♯ occurs at that location during the expositional rotation (measures 33–36), here a surging B-D-G♯-(F♮) sounds instead. In a conventional analysis such a chord might be labeled dutifully – though myopically – as vii^{o7}/V. In **4.6** it is instead interpreted as an evolved state of the supertonic that inaugurates TR. This vitalization and the dramatic rests that Haydn inserts in measures 278 and 279 give the V^7 chord that emerges at 280₁ a structural weight that was missing during the expositional rotation. Indeed, this V^7 now confidently extends for nearly twenty measures of notated score, plus whatever addition the soloist might provide during the cadenza. Clearly the D-F♯-A chord that sounds at 289₁ is not a tonic resolution. It instead is part of the sequential sweep upwards to V^7's first inversion at 291₁, like the D Major region that occurs during the developmental rotation (measures 201ff.).

A further surprise awaits the listener during the coda statement of P^{rf}. Whereas the *Kopfton* F♯ has been embellished by upper-third A numerous times during the movement, here that ceiling is punctured: F♯<A<D transpires during measures 299 through 307 (with highpoint D thrice stated), in the context of a $_D^{F\sharp}X_{F\sharp}^D$ voice exchange in the outer voices.[5] (The definitive arrival of the upper D is at measure 303, anticipated by B's upper third, D, in

measure 300.) Though this extension leads to a somewhat blurred stepwise descent to the lower D for the PAC at 309_1, which serves as the ESC, the measures that remain within the coda make amends. (The structure has been tidied up through the removal of cover tones B and A and the addition of E within parentheses for presentation in **4.6**.)

The expositional rotation in K. 451 (measures 0|1–103)

Whereas sometimes (for example, in K. 537, which is next on our docket) Mozart will present several tonic-key themes in succession as a sonata-rondo's opening P^{rf}, in K. 451 a single sixteen-measure entity arranged as

|: a_1 :|: b a_2 :|
D Major: I————   II♯ V————   I————

serves to introduce the tonic key, D Major. (See **4.7**.) Though the *Kopfton* F♯ arrives on a weak beat, the relationship between the unfolded thirds D<F♯ and E>C♯ in the first four measures helps the listener to comprehend that the principal linear strand will emanate from F♯, not from the A that emerges above it at 2_1. (In the piano statement starting in measure 104, a new slur begins on the second downbeat, subtly supporting the interpretation D<F♯, A>F♯, rather than D<F♯<A>F♯.) The A will play many roles within the expositional rotation: it appears six times in **4.7** and will return in **4.8** through **4.10** and **4.12**. But it is not the *Kopfton*.

The a_1 section is constructed as two four-measure I-to-V motions, the latter more definitive than the first. Note how the E>C♯ third of measures 3 and 4 becomes E>D>C♯ in measures 7 and 8, where the D and C♯ are presented an octave lower by the second violins (covered by high A>G♯<A in the first violins) and where the E is supported by II♯ before the arrival of V. (The configuration of an A covering a structural E will recur at the outset of the S theme in measures 55 and 63, as displayed in **4.9**.)

The A>F♯ third (first heard in measure 2) is the guiding force during measures 9 through 11, where F♯ serves as the upper neighbor to $\hat{2}$ during an unfurled $^6_4$ embellishment of V, as shown in **4.7**. Mozart departs from the normative script during measures 12 and 13. After downbeat A, G, and F♯ in the preceding three measures, E "should" arrive at 12_1, as restoration of $\hat{2}$ after the $^6_4$ embellishment. Yet no E sounds in that register. (It is placed within parentheses in **4.7**.) Sometimes fastidiousness leads to dullness, and here Mozart apparently felt that neglecting the E, instead emphasizing

Example 4.7 Analysis of Mozart: Piano Concerto in D Major (K. 451), mvmt. 3, mm. 1–16.

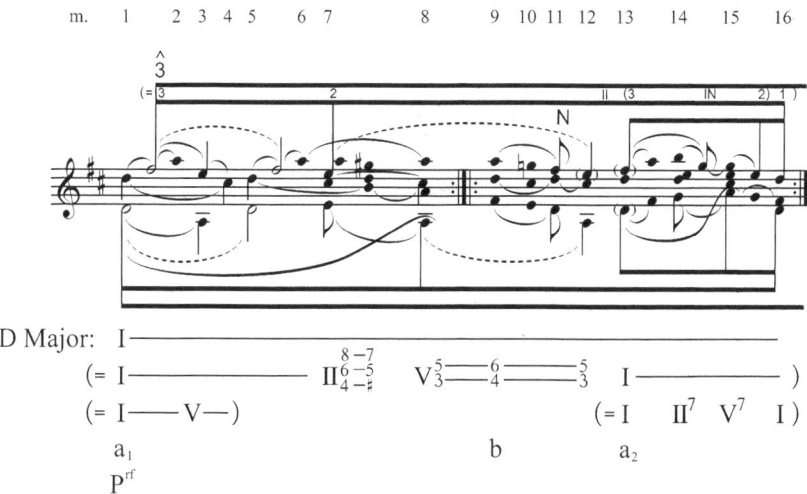

an $_A^{C\sharp} X_{C\sharp}^A$ voice exchange, would appeal more.[6] That neglect continues in the tonic restoration. Because leading tone C♯ is the prominent melodic pitch in measure 12, D rather than F♯ initiates the tonic presentation in measure 13. The analyst is here called upon to discern what melodic shape Mozart has deformed. Both as a compression of measures 1 and 2 and as antecedent to the B>G third of measure 14, I propose that F♯<A should be regarded as the normative melodic content for measure 13 and thus have placed an F♯ within parentheses at that spot in **4.7**. Though a literalist analyst may be concerned that so important a note as this F♯ is absent, an imaginative analyst will understand that there is not always a one-to-one correspondence between a work's guiding structure and that structure's surface realization.

The transition begins immediately after the PAC in measure 16b. A dependence upon the structure of measures 1 through 8 may be discerned. (See **4.8a**.) The filling-in of the initial A<D fourth relates both to the filled-in D>A fourth of measure 9 and to the dominant-key filling in of A>G♯>F♯>E that will transpire during S (measures 55 through 58). The high A is embellished by repeated upper neighbors in measures 21 through 24 (where the tonic's prolongation via $^6_4$ embellishment is reminiscent of the dominant's prolongation during the b section of P^{rf}). F♯ is restored during the second half of measure 24, just before the descent to E. Given the proportions of the movement thus far, we might surmise that the rests in all parts at 28_2 signal the transition's medial caesura. (An MC may occur either

Example 4.8 Analysis of Mozart: Piano Concerto in D Major (K. 451), mvmt. 3 (a) mm. 17–28; (b) mm. 29–55.

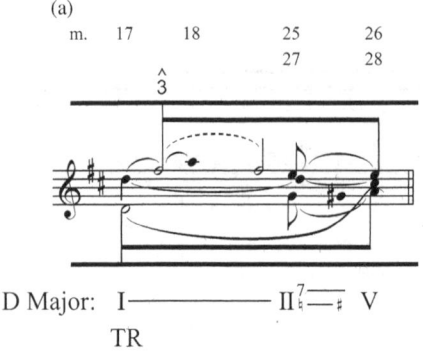

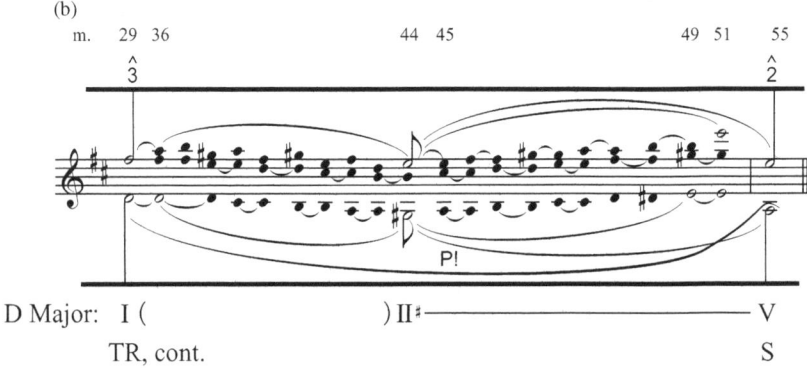

on II♯, as in the examples we explored in chapter 2 and the Haydn movement in this chapter, or on V.) That turns out to be a false assumption. (The MC is denied.) Mozart instead returns to the opening TR material. This time the F♯ is not restored in measure 36, as it was in measure 24. The more extended continuation that ensues (as graphed in **4.8b**) takes the high A as its melodic starting point, working its way downwards via a circular progression to an E corresponding to that of 25_2 (now without G♮ as diatonic predecessor of chromatic G♯ in the bass).[7] What Mozart does next is astonishing. In that P^{rf} was presented with repeats, he has set up his TR to incorporate repetition as well (so that 28|29ff. matches 16|17ff.). The circular progression in measures 36 through 44 consequently comes across as an *expansion* within a repetition of the basic structure, not jeopardizing the ultimate outcome. Listeners may still expect an A major chord at the medial caesura (what Hepokoski and Darcy refer to as a I:HC MC).[8] The chord at

The happy ending   133

45_1 projects that very outcome! (Compare **4.8a** and **4.8b** through 45_1.) Yet Mozart proceeds not *to* that chord, but instead *through* it.[9] With the patience to hear the progression to its end, we come to understand that the E major chord is extended from measure 44 through measure 54, via an ascending 5–6 sequence.[10] Despite setting the passage up as a varied repetition, Mozart nevertheless elects to alter the TR goal, so that a medial caesura on II♯ (Hepokoski and Darcy's V:HC MC) occurs at 53_1. Elaborately expanded, the tonal plan here corresponds to the TRs we explored in chapter 2. (Compare with **2.13**.)

We may expect that the S region that follows will be guided by a descending fifth-progression from E (= $\hat{2}$) to A. Given that repetition has been a factor both in P^{rf} and in TR, we may further expect repetition to occur here as well. The theme of measures 55 through 62, presented by the strings, offers a special challenge: it contains an example of a "peculiar juxtaposition" in which two modules at different pitch levels appear to be identical in structure, yet function differently in the broader context. The theme's first four measures project the root progression A B➔ E, while the next four project D E➔ A. Clearly A in the first half is hierarchically deeper than the B that follows it. Yet is D in the second half likewise deeper than the following E? As **4.9** reveals, I think not.[11] I read the first module as an extension of the opening tonic (in which an upward excursion in the melody – another instance of a high A in the limelight – leads back to E). The essential descent to A, supported by a conventional IV–V–I progression, is accomplished in the second half. The piano, with some support from the woodwinds, repeats the entire theme.

Though some analysts might regard the material that begins at 70_2 as a closing zone (C), I am struck by the similarity of its deeper structure to what has occurred thus far within S. In **4.9** note especially the upward leap after the initial E (to A in measure 55, to E in measure 78), the prolongation of the initial E (through measures 58 and 80), and the eventual presentation of the full fifth-progression. Consequently I propose that S continues to a definitive cadence – the EEC – at 88_1. The contrasting arpeggiations that begin in measure 88 constitute a brief C, which segues into the role of retransition with the arrival of G♮ at 93_2.

The second phase of S begins with the reestablishment of E (= $\hat{2}$) via an ascent incorporating reaching-over in measures 70 through 76. (An ascending-octave prolongation of C♯ transpires between 74_2 and 76_2 before the piano's E, the summit of the line, reaches over it. E then undergoes a similar prolongation.) The harmonic progression that follows supports lines emanating from E in two adjacent octaves, as shown in **4.9**. All through the

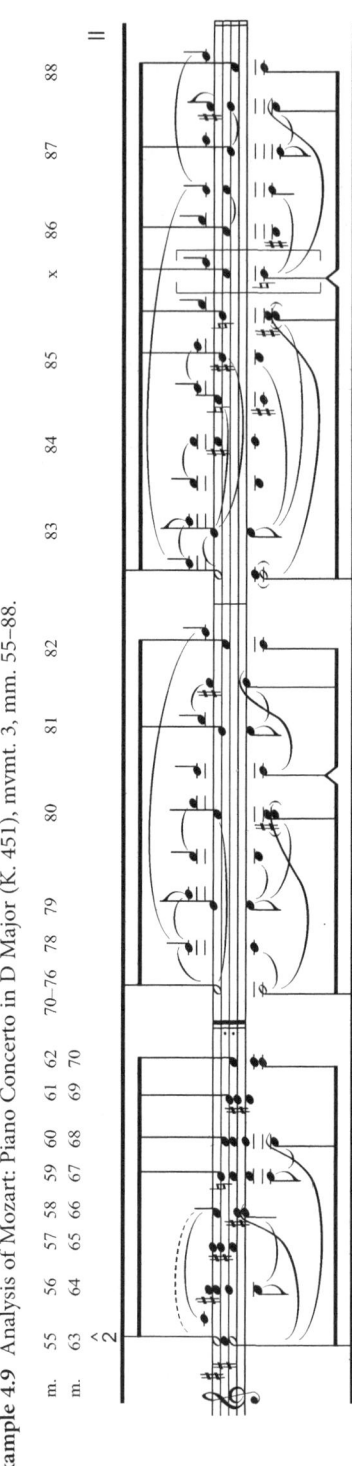

Example 4.9 Analysis of Mozart: Piano Concerto in D Major (K. 451), mvmt. 3, mm. 55–88.

The happy ending 135

expositional rotation we have encountered notes above the register of the fundamental line. Whereas fourth A arises above E in measure 55, octave E emerges in measure 78. In my reading the principal strand is the lower one, maintaining the register that was active during the first phase of S.[12] In this phrase it descends only so far as C♯ (IAC at 82_1). That imperfection is removed during an expanded repetition of the phrase, which achieves the desired PAC (= EEC) at 88_1. Note in **4.9** how the I chord that would support the melody's C♯ is elided during the repetition. Instead the preceding dominant, G♯-B-D at 85_2, leads to E♯-G♯-B-C♯, an embellishing chord of I^6.

For several measures after the EEC, a closing zone (C) offers resolutions of dissonant $\smash{\genfrac{}{}{0pt}{}{D}{G\sharp}}$, extending the tonicization of A Major. The G♮ at 93_1 annuls that tonicization, initiating a retransition during which A's broader role as dominant is asserted.[13] Tonic D Major returns at the onset of the developmental rotation in measure 104.

The developmental rotation in K. 451 (measures 104–213)

In contrast to H. XVIII: 11, in which the developmental rotation begins with an extended dominant more characteristic of a Type 3 sonata, in K. 451 Mozart offers the rondo form's normative tonic-key restatement of P^{rf} at that juncture. Despite the contrasting internal paths of their progressions, both the expositional and developmental rotations proceed broadly from I to V. Now III (measure 200) – rather than the expositional rotation's II♮ – serves as connector. Note in **4.10** how the motivically significant F♯<A third is chromatically filled in during the I–III traversal. The chordal support for that span is an extraordinary realization of a segment of the descending circle of fifths.[14] Whereas in a minor key the tonic-to-mediant connection proceeds without a hitch (e.g., D–G–C–F), the major key's diminished triad on $\hat{7}$ is a significant obstacle, especially when dominant emulation is employed. Though the obstinate variant D→G→C♮→F♮ is feasible, in that scenario the major key's *lowered* mediant must be accommodated within the broader progression. Mozart's alternative is breathtaking. Each build-up of the dominant-emulating surge is gradual. During the D prolongation (displayed within the first "measure" of **4.10**), a drawn-out 5–6–7♮ connection pauses on the 6 (unfurled) for an extended new theme, to be explored below. Yet eventually D's minor seventh, C♮, emerges, guiding the broad trajectory from D to G. The G expansion is identical, though now

Example 4.10 Analysis of Mozart: Piano Concerto in D Major (K. 451), mvmt. 3, mm. 104–214.

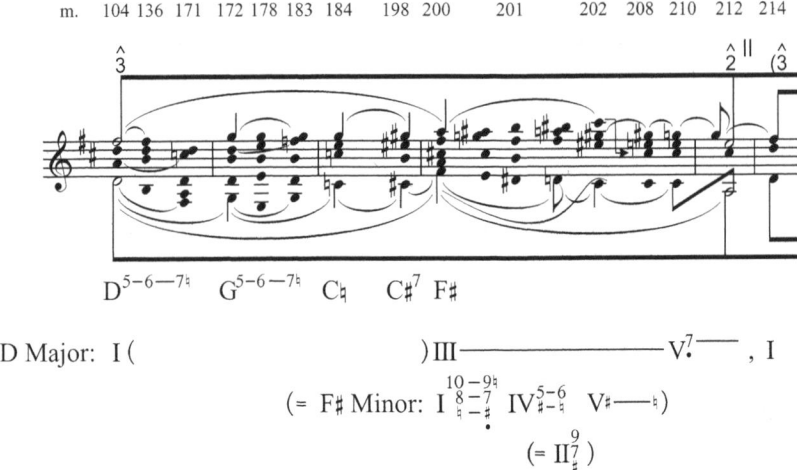

without a new theme emerging during the 6 phase. Because G also takes on dominant-emulating characteristics, the next chord must be rooted on C♮, from which Mozart had the choice of letting the circle continue obstinately further out of D Major (C♮→F♮), or intervening. He chose to intervene, proceeding in his broad trajectory from C♮ (measure 184) to F♯ (measure 200), achieving the diatonic III. Because dominant emulation is not possible in that context, his strategy of connection shifts to an ideal means of traversing an augmented fourth, namely a segment of the chromaticized ascending 5-6 sequence, pursued obstinately:

C♮⁵ C♯⁶ D⁵ D♯⁶ E⁵ E♯⁶ F♯⁵
         (= C♯→)

Whereas in a diatonic sequence the sixth chord (E⁶) would restore the pitch content of the first chord, here the root has shifted from C♮ to C♯, facilitating a surge heralding the F♯ mediant arrival at measure 200.

The succession from III to V results from the transformation of a chord that is related both to III and to V. The major dominant in tonicized F♯ Minor (III) is quickly attained: C♯-E♯-G♯ in measure 202. In the following measures this chord is transformed into V's diatonic upper-third chord: from C♯-E♯-G♯ first to C♯-E♮-G♯ and then to C♯-E♮-G♮. Root A's arrival at 212₁ concludes the development's tonal agenda.

The recapitulatory rotation will have a double resolutional duty, since both of the preceding rotations proceed from $\hat{3}$ to $\hat{2}$. The dissonant G above $\hat{2}$ in measures 212 and 213 sets up a third P^rf presentation of $\hat{3}$. The long-

The happy ending 137

Example 4.11 Analysis of Mozart: Piano Concerto in D Major (K. 451), mvmt. 3, mm. 136–157.

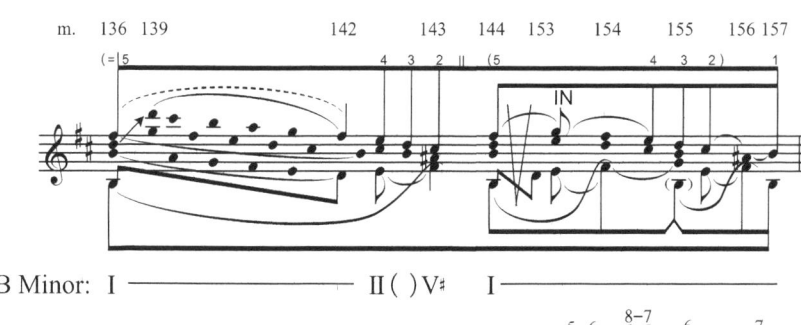

awaited resolution on background 1̂ will occur with great force (at the end of a cadenza) later in that rotation.

Returning now to the theme in B Minor (measures 136 through 157), note that Mozart employs a conventional antecedent-consequent binary structure, with an expanded consequent. (See **4.11**.) Whereas the S theme, also guided by a fifth-progression, emphasizes the upper octave at the outset (A above E in measure 55, as shown in **4.9**), B Minor's fifth F♯ is covered by an even higher pitch: tenth D in measure 139. Just as S's E is restored before the deeper progression begins its move to the dominant, so also in this B Minor theme F♯ is restored in measure 142 before II and then V emerge to complete the phrase.[15] (Mozart explicitly invites listeners to compare the structures of these two themes: beginning in measures 157, just after the B Minor theme concludes, he presents the S theme in B Minor.) During the consequent phrase the line from F♯ proceeds upwards to neighbor G (at 153$_2$), lengthening the route to the cadence. An elision occurs at 155$_1$: instead of a tonic resolution of the preceding dominant seventh as the midpoint of this double-arpeggiation support for the descending fifth-progression, *followed by* its 6-phase chord as segue to the upcoming supertonic, the tonic 5-phase chord is elided.[16] Thus bass F♯–B–G becomes F♯–G. My parenthetical B in **4.11** offers a reminder that the G–B–D chord ultimately derives from root B.

One of the unsettling aspects of analysis is that there often is no direct correlation between an event's duration and its structural importance. For example, the B Minor region that arises in measure 136 and does not slip away until measure 171 is displayed in **4.10** as the prolongation of a mere passing note (B between A and C♮). On the other hand, the F♯ minor mediant harmony that I interpret as the principal interior moment between the tonic and dominant perimeter points in this 110-measure developmental rotation lasts a mere measure (200), half of which is surging towards its local successor (F♯ Minor: I→ IV). The situation here is especially challenging because the F♯ chord is surrounded by C♯ chords (measures 198–199 and 202ff.). In other contexts one might interpret the F♯ chord as an unfurled $^6_4$ embellishment of the C♯ chord. Yet here it serves as support for the broad melodic F♯<A third's endpoint, from which a descending A>G♯>G♮ chromatic line emanates. (See **4.10**.) The F♯ chord is the successor of the preceding C♯→, rather than its embellishment.

The recapitulatory and coda rotations in K. 451 (measures 213|214–394)

In accordance with the norms of both the sonata and rondo forms, both P^{rf} and S are presented in the tonic key during the recapitulatory rotation. One small detail within P^{rf} warrants special mention. Whereas in all of its previous statements the theme's opening eight measures have emphasized the A above *Kopfton* F♯, during measure 219 that trajectory proceeds further upwards, to D. That incidentally is the same expansion that Haydn pursued during the coda half-rotation of H. XVIII: 11 (measures 303 through 307). Within K. 451 Mozart employs this D to establish an unanticipated parallelism between the P^{rf} and S themes: not only are they now both presented in D Major; they also both exhibit a prominent D>C♯>B>A line supported by the progression I II♯ V. (Compare measures 219–221 and 271–274.)

The transition must be reconstructed to prepare the tonic-key statement of S that will follow. Whereas in the expositional rotation the two common choices of TR trajectory were I V and I II♯ (recall that Mozart presented the I V possibility before proceeding definitively to the I II♯ alternative), during the recapitulatory rotation I V will be used because it provides the tonic-pointing tonal focus equivalent to the earlier dominant-pointing I II♯.[17] Consequently there can be no ploy of dangling an eventually rejected dominant medial caesura candidate before the listener during the early stages of TR. Mozart instead begins with material corresponding to the second phase in the expositional TR. (That is, 246_1 corresponds to 29_1, not 17_1.) The circular progression that in the earlier instance proceeded to II♯ is here revised so as to extend to the tonic, as follows:

measures 36ff.:	D	b	E	A	D	g♯°	c♯	f♯	b	E
measures 253ff.:	D	b	E	a	D	G	C♯	f♯	B	e	A	D

Example 4.12 Analysis of Mozart: Piano Concerto in D Major (K. 451), mvmt. 3, mm. 298–315.

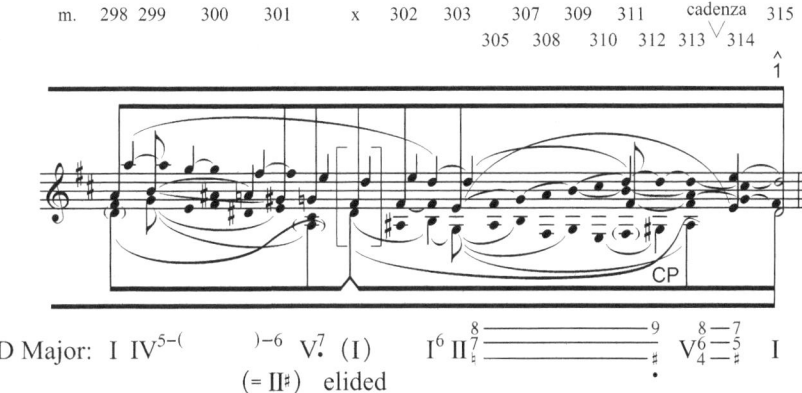

That tonic prolongation (concluding at measure 263) is followed by material like the expositional rotation's rejected motion to V: bass G<G♯<A in measures 264 and 265 corresponds to that of measures 25 and 26.[18] The medial caesura occurs at 269_1, followed by the onset of the tonic-key S two measures later.

At first the presentation of S in D Major proceeds without incident. Only in the approach to the final cadence – the ESC – does Mozart begin to broaden, in preparation for a cadenza. The content of measures 82 through 88 in **4.9** corresponds to measures 298 through 315 in **4.12**. Due to the inserted cadenza – Mozart supplied one that extends for forty-seven measures – the projection of this phrase in the latter context is highly charged. Two initiatives are of special interest during this broadening. First, the two melodic lines (emanating from the pitch A in adjacent octaves) are here connected via a stepwise-ascending seventh that transpires between measures 303 and 311. (By the time the upper-register's D is reached, the lower-register's E has been displaced by its upper neighbor, F♯.) Second, the supertonic chord eventually develops strong dominant-emulating tendencies, surging towards V. (Diatonic E-G-B-D evolves into chromatic G♯-B-D-F♯.) Of special note in my analysis is the rejection of the literalist reading of the chord at 311_1 as I. Though not sounding until beat 2, the pitch B is a chord member, and bass D substitutes for a passing F♯ connecting the E of 310_2 and the G♯ of 312_2.

The structural close (ESC) occurs at 315_1. The coda rotation that follows has a distinctly lighter feel, caused in part by the shift to $\frac{3}{8}$ meter. Note that the excursion to high D, introduced in measure 219, is retained during P^{rf}.

Measures 347 through 361 offer a theme that incorporates features of both P^{rf} and S. Tonic-key statements of the first part of S (first by the orchestra, then by the pianist) follow on its heels. Residual I–IV$^{5-6}$–V–I progressions contract first into I V I and then into repetitions of I as the movement comes to a close.

The expositional rotation in K. 537 (measures 0|1–151)

Whereas most rondos commence with a tonic-key refrain followed by a contrasting-key episode, in a sonata-rondo these elements are invariably connected by a transition. The resulting P^{rf} TR' S / C formal unit – the expositional rotation – is understood to be the start of a sonata-rondo (a Type 4 – rather than Type 3 – sonata) more by the character of its themes than by any distinctions within its formal design. One might even imagine the fermata rest during 151_1 in K. 537 followed by a repeat sign, with all that has preceded it constituting the exposition of a Type 3 sonata movement. Since the P^{rf} theme (like that which would sound during an exposition repeat) follows directly after the rest, it is some time before listeners can be absolutely certain that this movement is *not* shaped as a Type 3 sonata. Because S is in the dominant key, Mozart not surprisingly uses I II♯' V as the tonal plan (familiar to readers from our exploration of sonata expositions of this type in chapter 2). TR (which accommodates a sizeable I-space extension) begins at 48_1, S at 74_1, and C at 136_1.

P^{rf} offers a vivid display of Mozart's ability to create seemingly new content through the reshaping of existing material. The essence of his tonic prolongation is the traversal of an F♯>E>D third, from *Kopfton* $\hat{3}$ to the tonic root. Observe in **4.13** that three distinct harmonizations of that third occur within P^{rf}. Each is repeated with altered keyboard participation, revised orchestration, and increased bravura display, and the harmonizations become gradually more elaborate. Melodic upper thirds (A after or before F♯, G before E, and F♯ above D) play a vital role in shaping this thematic content.

The piano initiates the movement without orchestral support. During the opening two measures the melody emphasizes in turn the F♯ *Kopfton* and inner-strand D. (See **4.13**.) Each is followed by its upper third. D's neighbor E and F♯'s neighbor G embellish reiterations of these two pitches before the descent to $\genfrac{}{}{0pt}{}{E}{C\sharp}$ for the half cadence at 4_1. The consequent phrase is modified so as to end on the tonic (PAC), completing the F♯>E>D third-progression that was interrupted in measure 4. At 7_2 the melody's G, which at 3_2 served as a neighbor to F♯ within the initial tonic prolongation, finds itself in a new context: an asserted V^7. This G now serves as upper-third to E (rather than neighbor to F♯), within a motivically significant pairing of unfolded chordal thirds: F♯<A followed by G>E. The piano's clear D at 8_1 confirms for the listener that the principal melodic strand spans F♯ to D, *not* A to F♯. The orchestra undertakes a second statement of the theme, with modest variation.

The second segment of P^{rf} dispenses with the local interruption, instead offering more developed harmonic support for the F♯>E>D descent. Though numerous pitches jutting above the principal line conceal the exact path of the descent, I propose the course displayed in **4.13**, measures 16 through 22. (Note again the repetition of the entire structure.) Here the first segment's unfolded F♯<A and G>E thirds take on a deeper role within the structure: the direction shifts in the first third (A>F♯), both are filled in by step, and G is supported by IV. The tonic's 6-phase B, whose arrival coincides with the restoration of *Kopfton* $\hat{3}$, here serves as a divider within the bass descending fifth connecting the roots of I and IV. This IV is followed by its upper-fifth chord (which should not be interpreted as a restoration of the tonic) as support for passing note F♯. Mozart makes an issue of closure. F♯ covers D at the cadence in measure 22. (Thus an IAC results.) A PAC occurs only during the repetition. Note the extraordinary manner in which Mozart connects the initial D and A chords (measures 16–19): a parallel progression (chordal glide) of $^6_3$ chords with suspensions whose span exceeds an octave. Once the PAC is achieved at 28_1, a two-measure synopsis of this phase is presented (that is, a quickie I IV V I that emphasizes the melody's B of 20_1 and F♯ of 22_1). The IAC close at 30_1 motivates a repetition. Still no PAC at 32_1, so another repetition ensues. Mozart abandons his aberrant synopses when this third try refuses to come to rest in a PAC. The matter will be set aright in measure 46.

The A hovering above the F♯ synopsis goal is picked up as the starting point for another A>G>F♯ third during the third segment of P^{rf}. (See **4.13**.) The passing G migrates to the bass, resulting in a first-inversion tonic chord at 37_1. As in the second segment of P^{rf}, the attainment of a PAC occurs only during the repetition, which also offers a more prominent presentation of the answering G>F♯>E third. (In the initial statement G and F♯ sound in the second violin an octave lower.) Though the revised synopsis that follows ends in an IAC at 44_1, a PAC is achieved during a second try, at 46_1. The multiple Ds in measure 47 signal the end of P^{rf}.

Contrasting the sonata expositions we explored in chapter 2, the expansiveness of this movement's opening justifies an extension of I-space well

Example 4.13 Analysis of Mozart: Piano Concerto in D Major (K. 537), mvmt. 3, mm. 1–42.

D Major: I ——————————————————, I^5———^{6} IV( )V^7 I , I ——— IV V ——— I)

(= I ——— V^8———^{7} I) (= I V^7 I) (= $I^{8-7\natural}$ IV V^7 I)

P^{rf}

Example 4.14 Analysis of Mozart: Piano Concerto in D Major (K. 537), mvmt. 3, mm. 48–77.

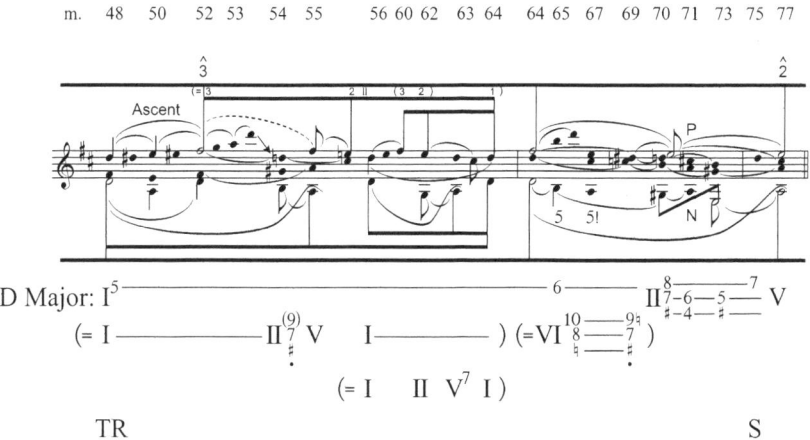

beyond the P–TR divide at measures 47–48.[19] In fact, measures 48 through 64 offer a fully developed thematic statement that is closer in basic structure to measures 1 through 8 than were the later segments of P^{rf}. (See **4.14**.) Note especially how the motivic F♯<G<A third in measures 52 and 53 now extends onward to D. (The distinctive ascent to D will be reiterated in a new harmonic context during measures 64 and 65, helping to confirm that this tonic expansion belongs within TR rather than P^{rf}.) This D is transferred an octave downwards (with stepwise filling-in) before the F♯ is reinstated as a suspension at 55_1.[20] Note also that eventually the ascent to the *Kopfton* is matched by a descending third from E to C♯ (measures 62 and 63).

Perhaps even more pertinent to the transitional process is the conversion from the employment of IV as intermediary between I and V, which was characteristic of P^{rf}, to the employment of II♯ in measure 54. The I–II♯–V progression of TR's opening phrase is a local manifestation of the broader I^{5-} ^{6}–II♯–V progression that transpires during the course of the entire expositional rotation.[21] (Compare the utilization of the subdominant in **4.13** and the supertonic in **4.14**, both at multiple levels.) Though the models of **2.14** correspond to various traversals of TR by Haydn, indeed Mozart here is pursuing exactly the same course. Though I display the upward arpeggiation to D in measure 65 (to correlate with that of measure 53), for the remainder of TR the graph focuses upon the voice leading that accomplishes first the transformation of the tonic 6-phase chord into a surging VI➔ and then the expansion of II♯. Mozart's deployment of what seems to congeal as an A major chord in measures 67 and 68 is an astonishing construction. What is A major doing directly after the B minor 6-phase arrival? I propose that the harmonic trajectory involves chordal evolution from B-D-F♯ to D♯-F♯-A-C♮. Thus the A-C♯-E chord's bass A is a chord member (the submediant's dissonant seventh, which I show resolving to the supertonic's third, G♯, though note in the score, measure 69, that an F♯ intervenes in the cello and bass line), whereas the C♯ and E are *passing notes* within D>C♯ (tenth to lowered ninth) and F♯>D♯ (fifth to third) spans that serve to extend VI♯. Note also the elision at measure 70: D♯ does not resolve to II's root (E), but instead descends by half step to its seventh (D♮). Thus Mozart has truncated the conventional prolongational device that in full would transpire as

```
8   7♮   6    5
♯ ─────  4    ♯
```

by beginning after its normative consonant initiation point. My placement of abbreviations N and P in the graph is intended to help prevent the interpretation of the A-C♯-E chord of measures 71 and 72 as II♯'s resolution, which comes later. In fact, Mozart extends this II♯ for several measures into the domain of S. As **4.14** displays, the resolution to A-C♯-E occurs in measure 77. The silence in all parts during 73_2 may be interpreted as a conventional medial caesura, even if A-C♯-E does not follow directly thereafter.

The three distinct F♯>E>D descents within P^{rf}, as displayed in the three "measures" of **4.13**, are complemented by three distinct E>D>C♯>B>A descents within S, as displayed in the second through fourth "measures" of **4.15**. If S is to balance the earlier P^{rf}, then we should regard 136_1, *not* 89_1, as the location of the EEC.

As mentioned above, the II♯ chord that concludes TR extends for several measures into S. The dissonant seventh D sounds during measures 75 and 76 before the resolution to A major in measure 77. This portion of S will not be repeated as a whole. Instead, the opening E➔A harmonic succession is repeated in measures 79 through 81. Thinking now in terms of the A Major tonicization, the progression then continues in measures 83 and 84 with the subdominant, D major, which serves as the platform for an upper-third excursion (bass D<E<F♯ in measures 83 through 87) before IV's 6-phase chord leads onward to V and I, supporting a fifth-progression descending from E, as shown in **4.15**.

The second segment of S is distinctive in two ways. First, the theme's two presentations are differentiated by modal mixture, with the first statement (measures 89 through 97) taking on a minor-key hue. (Note that this is the movement's third theme shaped by an interruption.) Second, until near the end the melody emphasizes only the pitches of the E>A fifth's lower third.[22]

(See **4.15**.) Once E is reinstated during 104_1, the descent to A is quick and conventional.

The third segment of S contains the expositional rotation's only interruption of a fifth-progression. The initiating E is fleetingly presented during 107_1, attained via an ascent that incorporates reaching-over: A descends to G♯, B reaches over G♯, B descends to A, C♯ reaches over, and so on. As in the first segment of S, compensation for the non-repetition of this segment is provided by some internal repetition, here of the *Kopfton* attainment, in measures 107 through 109, where the high E's arrival is tardy, above bass G♯. The A tonic is extended by means of the descending sequential progression of 109_1 through 112_1.[23] The interrupted descent occurs in measures 113 and 114. The continuation does not reiterate the *Kopfton*-attainment ascent, but instead picks up with the descending sequence. The harmonic progression supporting the descent to A is much expanded from its antecedent formulation. (See **4.15**.) This is the only instance within the expositional rotation of Mozart supporting a descending fifth-progression using a double bass arpeggiation (A–E–A–E–A). The progression is teeming with vitality. Note especially how the initial tonic surges during measure 119 (thus I➔ IV), how Mozart spends several measures pondering a circular continuation (perhaps A➔D➔ will lead to G♮) before instead leading from IV to V via IV's 6-phase chord, how that 6-phase chord surges and thereby puts into question what we had assumed was a secure D♮ in the melodic descent, how the surge's D♯ falters in attaining E so that instead D♮ is restored, how a minor hue emerges during the prolongation of the internal tonic, and how that infiltration of minor lingers into the supertonic realm, where B♭ and F♮ temporarily darken the mood before II➔ dynamically steers the progression to its V^7–I close.[24] As mentioned above, that close may be interpreted as the EEC.

The closing zone (C) that follows is distinctive in its lack of directed linear progressions. Though the fifth E>A and its filled-in E<A inversion are stated several times, the character of this passage – in particular its lack of propulsive harmonic activity – is that of a temporary lull. Yet the emergence of A's minor seventh (which negates the A Major tonicization) in measures 148 and 149 signals that something is brewing. But what?

The recapitulatory rotation and coda half-rotation in K. 537 (measures 151|152–374)

The fermatas in measure 151, which invite a cadenza, mark the dividing line between the movement's expositional and recapitulatory rotations. As in a

Example 4.15 Analysis of Mozart: Piano Concerto in D Major (K. 537), mvmt. 3, mm. 1–136.

D Major: I II$\frac{8-7}{\sharp}$ — V
(= A Major: I IV$^{5-6}_{}\frac{8-7}{}$ V$^{6-5}_{4-3}$ I) (= I♮ II$^{9\sharp}_{5\sharp}$ V♯ I♮ — ♯ II V I II V   I)(= I II V — I
S   (= I$^{8-9\flat}_{8-7\natural}$ IV$^{7}_{5-6}$ V$^{9\natural}_{7}$ I♯–♮ II$^{5\natural}_{3\natural}\frac{9\sharp}{7}$ V♯ I)
                                                                                                                                                                                         (= II$^{7}_{\sharp}$)

Type 1 sonata, the most obvious difference between these two rotations in a Type $4^{1\text{-exp}}$ sonata is the placement of S, which here begins in measure 225, squarely within the tonic – rather than the dominant – key. Consequently Mozart's chief creative project during the recapitulatory rotation was to reconfigure TR to achieve a medial caesura on V, rather than on II♯. To be more explicit: whereas I^{5-6} II♯ precedes the expositional rotation's tonicization of the dominant, the opening tonic of this recapitulatory rotation will first lead *down a fifth* to the subdominant, so that IV^{5-6} V may transpire during the latter part of the transition. Fortunately the succession from I to IV is one of tonal music's most natural paths. Yet the very ease of its attainment makes IV – especially when its quality is major – a somewhat treacherous location within tonal space, because we ask that it *not* follow its natural tendency to perpetuate the descending-fifth motion by which it was attained (thereby creating an obstinate circle of fifths: D→G→C♮→...), but instead to allow a 5–6 shift to redirect the tonal trajectory towards the stepwise-related V.

Given that this movement lacks a developmental rotation, it is not surprising that the transition region within the recapitulatory rotation takes on developmental characteristics, triggered by issues relating to the IV–V succession. (These characteristics are what justify the "exp[anded]" designation within the Hepokoski and Darcy formal label: the Type $4^{1\text{-exp}}$ sonata.) Mozart commandeers the IV that occurs in measure 177, during what initially seems to be the second segment of P^{rf}, to enter into transitional space. Yet this IV refuses to facilitate the broader tonal agenda. As will be explained below, IV instead takes on dominant-emulating characteristics that Mozart deals with in a surprising way. Eventually the D tonic is restored (measures 202 and 203). Now with dominant-emulating minor seventh C♮, it surges towards another IV – one that *will* be harnessed and expanded via a chromaticized 5–6 shift to attain the TR's dominant goal. That dominant (measure 224) is displayed in **4.16**, along with other essential elements of the expositional and recapitulatory rotations.

During the recapitulatory P^{rf} Mozart proceeds along the path of the expositional rotation far enough to restate the normative course from IV to V and I (measure 171 through 173: compare with measures 20 through 22 in **4.13**). Yet during that theme's second statement – after the IV at 177_1 – Mozart hurls the listener unexpectedly into a whirl of extraordinary tonal activity. Compare the chords of 177_1 and 179_2. If E♯ is interpreted as F♮ (Mozart's reason for using the enharmonic spelling will be explained in a moment), then one may interpret this passage as the emergence of the G chord's dominant-emulating tendency towards C♮, an option that was

Example 4.16 Analysis of Mozart: Piano Concerto in D Major (K. 537), mvmt. 3, mm. 1–228.

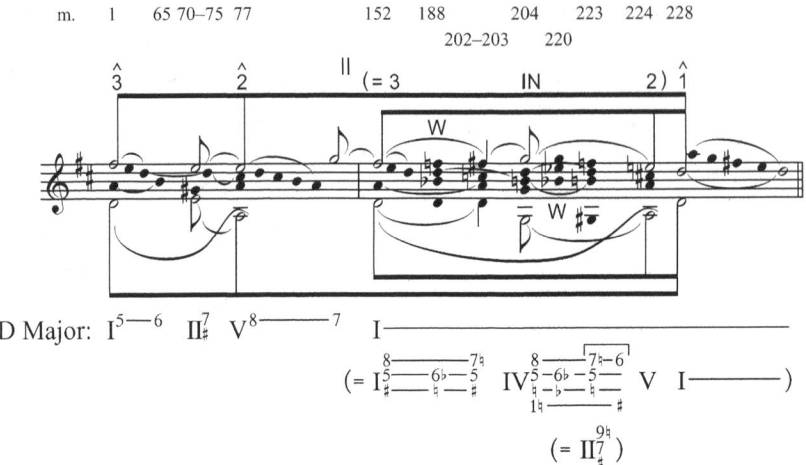

mentioned above. $G^{8-7\sharp-7\natural}$ is traversed over these three measures, with the internal $7\sharp$ supported by G's upper-third chord, B-D-F$\sharp$. Having brewed up this potent G→ force, Mozart astonishingly foregoes resolving it. He instead shoves it downwards: first to F$\sharp$→, then to F$\natural$→. The mechanism that he employs explains the enharmonic spellings. If G-B-D-F$\natural$ is interpreted as G-B-D-E$\sharp$, then its root shifts from G to (absent) C$\sharp$. In this manner an obstinate, chromatic circle of fifths transpires between measures 177 and 188, as follows:

m.   177   179———   180   186———   187   188

    G^8 ——— $^{|7\natural}$ $C\sharp\Rightarrow$ $F\sharp^8$ ——— $^{|7\natural}$ $C\natural\Rightarrow$ $F\natural^8$ — $^{7\flat}$ $B\flat$

Whereas the proposed resolution to C$\natural$ would have put a considerable strain on the D Major tonality, the substitute B$\flat$ goal is easily accommodated, since it is the second chromatic variant of the D Major tonic's 6-phase (lower-third) chord.[25] The diatonic 6-phase chord of measure 65 is transformed into its surging first chromatic variant (B-D$\sharp$-F$\sharp$, which sounds in the further evolved state, D$\sharp$-F$\sharp$-A-C$\natural$) in measure 69 to serve as the connector between I and II$\sharp$ (as shown in **4.14**). Here B$\flat$-D-F$\natural$ instead serves to prolong the D tonic: its B$\flat$ is a neighboring note, while its F$\natural$ is a wobble. Mozart reinforces the transitional nature of this region by using the B$\flat$ oasis to present the theme that opened TR during the expositional rotation (as displayed in the first half of **4.14**). Yet during its consequent phrase the 5-phase D tonic is restored (as shown in **4.16**), now with added minor seventh C♮ (measures 202 and 203).²⁶ We are finally ready to proceed to the structurally deep IV that will carry the transition onward to the dominant.

Note how Mozart averts the danger of a second mishap in the continuation from IV in **4.16**. Whereas the resolution of the wobble F♮ and chromatic neighbor B♭ of measure 188 is accompanied by the addition of D's dominant-emulating minor seventh in measures 202 and 203, facilitating the I➔IV harmonic succession, it is exactly that scenario that must be *prevented* during the prolongation of IV if V is to be achieved. The context requires IV$^{5-6}$ (with dominant emulation applied to the 6-phase chord), not IV$^{8-7♮}$. Yet note that wobble B♭ and chromatic neighbor E♭ in measure 220 resolve exactly as did their predecessors, and that at the same time G's minor seventh F♮ emerges (measure 223). This time, however, one additional shift occurs: bass G ascends to G♯. I propose that here Mozart achieves IV$^{5-6}$ via the route IV$^{8-7♮-6}$, and that instead of presenting each of these components successively, in an orderly fashion, he rambunctiously merges the second and third components, which might have appeared as G-B-D-F♮ followed by G♯-B-D-E, into a single entity: G♯-B-D-F♮, wherein ninth F♮ substitutes for root E.

The local connection between tonicized G's diatonic 5- and chromatic 6-phase chords during measures 204 through 220 engages a chord progression similar to that employed by Haydn in H. XVIII: 11, displayed in **4.1** (measures 24 through 49). Note in that example how the tonic chord in D Major inaugurates a progression that proceeds through a minor supertonic to a dominant that shifts from major to minor quality before the restored tonic returns in a 6-phase variant. In K. 537, I in tonicized G Major (measure 212) leads through a dominant-emulating II (measure 218) to a dominant that likewise shifts from major to minor (measure 219) before the restored tonic returns in a chromatic 6-phase variant (measures 220 through 222). In this version the connection of I and II➔ is expanded into I$^{5-6}$ II➔, following the model of measures 64 through 70. (Compare with **4.14**.²⁷)

The recapitulatory rotation continues with an S and C that, except for their presentation in D Major, follow their expositional precedents closely. The retransition that follows in measures 295 through 302 traverses the path from I to V⁷ to set up the tonic arrival of the coda half-rotation. Another cadenza opportunity emerges at the fermata in measure 302.

None of the three rotations presents all the themes that Mozart has created for this movement in the tonic key of D Major. During the expositional rotation, the S themes are presented in the dominant key. During the recapitulatory rotation, in which the S themes are presented in the tonic key, P^{rf} is abbreviated: TR emerges with the second of the three tonic-key themes, and the third is not heard at all. Also, the theme that opened TR in the tonic key during the expositional rotation is stated instead in the tonicized submediant (measures 188ff.) and subdominant (measures 204ff.) keys. During the coda half-rotation, which begins at the upbeat to measure 303, only the themes from P^{rf} are utilized. (Mozart makes a point of presenting all three of them this time, as well as the synopsis statements, in compensation for his early initiation of TR during the recapitulatory rotation.) Measure 344, where the last of the P^{rf} themes cadences, competes with measure 287, where the last of the recapitulatory rotation's S themes cadences, as the site of the ESC. The merger of sonata and rondo principles within the sonata-rondo form leaves some flexibility regarding the relative strength of those two principal cadential moments. Either way, Mozart continues after measure 344 with coda material that emphasizes dominant-seventh resolutions, incorporating the opening of the first P^{rf} theme into the mix.

PART TWO

Masterpieces

5 | Haydn: Symphony No. 45 in F♯ Minor ("Farewell"), movement 2

in response to James Webster

Not only has Haydn's "Farewell" Symphony attained a popularity exceeding that of most of his other works; it also has received intense analytical scrutiny from one of the leading Haydn scholars of our time, James Webster.[1] A thorough assessment of Webster's analytical writings on Haydn might warrant a hefty monograph. They are thought-provoking and extend well beyond the themes of my study. I here limit myself to assessing his treatment of one relatively uncomplicated movement (the slow movement from the "Farewell"), focusing especially on his harmonic perspective.

The exposition's primary-theme zone (P, measures 1–16)

Haydn extends I-space through the first six measures of P by means of a local I–IV$^{5-6}$–V^7–I progression that closely resembles measures 1 through 4 of his String Quartet in D Minor (op. 42), movement 3. (Compare **1.2c** and **5.1**.) In both contexts the *Kopfton* $\hat{3}$ is extended via its upper third, followed by $\hat{3}$'s upper neighbor preceded by that neighbor's upper third. A passing chord containing the pitches (but not asserting the function) of the tonic comes between IV's 5- and 6-phase chords. The symphony's progression continues with II and V during the antecedent phrase, extending to I in the consequent phrase. Observe how three of the four principal melodic notes are allied motivically through stepwise descents from their upper thirds: E>D>C♯, F♯>E>D, and (more quickly and only in the antecedent phrase) D>C♯>B.

> Webster proposes that there are cadences in measures 4 and 6 (p. 60). I reserve the notion of cadence for phrase-ending events. In this case the phrases are eight measures in length. I propose that there are shallower and deeper levels of harmonic motion at play here, indicated by the multiple hierarchical levels in **5.1**. The chords at 1_3 and at 6_3 are the same. At the phrase level what occurs between them amounts to a

Example 5.1 Analysis of Haydn: Symphony No. 45 in F♯ Minor ("Farewell"), mvmt. 2, mm. 1–16.

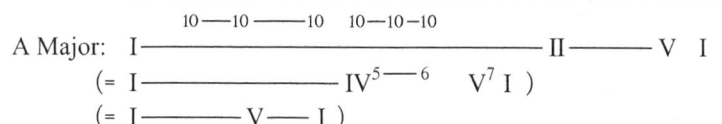

prolongation of I-space. The *first* deep structural motion away from the prolonged tonic is the II of measure 7, which leads to the *first* cadence of the movement – a half cadence – in measure 8. (In that **5.1** displays the structural entity that serves as foundation for both the antecedent and consequent phrases, the traditional interruption symbol appears in the grid of measure numbers above the staff.)

The highly developed motivic analysis presented in Webster's example 2.11 seems to me to overemphasize the composition's foreground relationships. Non-adjacent pitches (such as the descending thirds mentioned above) relate in meaningful ways that are not acknowledged in his presentation. Also consider the cello and bass contour C♯<D>C♯ over the first three measures. In my view it prefigures the E<F♯>E neighboring motion in the violin line of measure 3, and yet neither of these relationships is labeled as a motive. (At a deeper level, C♯<D>C♯ guides the melody of 4_3 through 6_3, as shown in **5.1**.) Webster instead displays that F♯ as the starting point for motive *e2*, contradicting the measure's harmonic foundation, emphasized through the filling-in of the E>C♯ third (which he labels parenthetically as *a5*). Whereas I process the passage as an embellishment of E followed by a structural third, Webster focuses on a fourth.

Haydn: Symphony No. 45 in F♯ Minor ("Farewell"), movement 2

Example 5.2 Analysis of Haydn: Symphony No. 45 in F♯ Minor ("Farewell"), mvmt. 2, mm. 1–28.

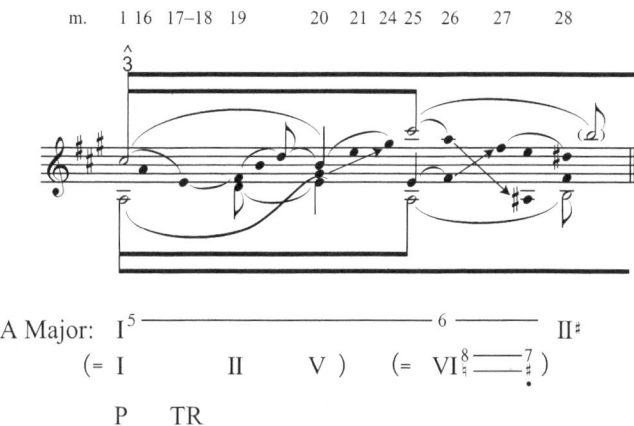

The exposition's transition (TR, measures 17–28)

From our study of keyboard sonata expositions by Haydn in chapter 2, we know that I^{5-6} II♯ is a common tonal trajectory during TR. Does it occur here? Indeed so, as **5.2** reveals. In this instance the tonic extends well into the domain of TR. The violin E of measures 17 and 18 continues the downward trajectory of P's filled-in C♯>A third. This descending sixth is followed by a reciprocal (and swift) ascending F♯<B<D, outlining II within a local I–II–V progression. An upward register shift transpires during the V that follows (measures 21 through 24, where the B>G♯>E dominant arpeggiation that would complement the preceding tonic and supertonic arpeggiations is replaced by B<E<G♯), after which the *Kopfton* C♯, supported by the tonic, is reinstated in the upper register (at 25_1). The tonic's 6-phase chord arrives in measure 26 and surges at the end of measure 27. As was also the case in some of the piano sonata expositions, C♯'s successor, B, does not sound at the top of the texture during the II♯ chord. (It appears within parentheses in **5.2**.) It is presented in the following measure, as the $\hat{2}$ from which a descending fifth-progression will emanate during S. Though not emphasized by silence in all parts, a medial caesura occurs upon the arrival of the major supertonic in measure 28.

Webster's and my readings of the transition do not concur. He places measures 17 through 20 within P (his **1Gr** [first group]: see his Example 2.10, p. 57), whose dominant endpoint continues into measure 21 to inaugurate TR (his **Tr**).[2] His somewhat sketchy harmonic analysis reads as follows (p. 57):

m.	1	17	[20]	21		[28]	29
	[P			TR			S]
	I		(V)	——————————	V/V	V

I offer the following alternative:

m.	1	17	19	20		25	26	28	29
		P	TR						S
		I^5	———————————————	—6		II♯	V
		(= I		II	V ——————)

In my reading the A major chord in measure 25, with radiant *Kopfton* C♯ at its peak, represents the final sounding of the initiating tonic. (As often happens, TR begins with an extension of the tonic from P.) Webster offers no interpretation of this A chord. Might the root progression E–A–B–E in measures 20 through 29 correspond to I IV V I in tonicized E Major? If so, why did he resist displaying the progression in that manner? I think such resistance was wise, because the A chord of measure 25 resides deeper within the structure than does the preceding E chord, which he analyzes as (V). If he disagrees, then readers would have benefited from seeing his reading of how the A chord functions within his proposed (V) to V/V context. On a more basic level, it seems to me inherently illogical that a TR whose purpose is to *come between* the I of P and the V of S should begin with that V chord. His placing of parentheses around the V numeral hints that he himself found this an awkward reading. My I^{5-6}–II♯ alternative sidesteps that dilemma and resonates with Haydn's TR trajectory in all the works explored in chapter 2.

The exposition's secondary-theme zone (S, measures 29–71)

When listening to a movement in sonata form one may engage in a dialogue between the expectations that the form induces and their unique realization

Haydn: Symphony No. 45 in F♯ Minor ("Farewell"), movement 2

Example 5.3 Analysis of Haydn: Symphony No. 45 in F♯ Minor ("Farewell"), mvmt. 2, mm. 29–71.

$$
\begin{array}{l}
\text{A Major: V} \longrightarrow \text{IV } V_{4-3}^{6-5} \text{ I)} \\
(= \text{E Major: I} \longrightarrow \\
\quad (= \text{I}^{5\sharp} \longrightarrow {}^{\sharp}\text{IV}^{5-6} \; V_{4-3}^{8-7} \text{ I)} \\
\quad (= \text{I}_{\sharp}^{5-6\sharp} \; \text{II}_{5\sharp}^{9\sharp} \; V^{8-7-} \text{ I)} \quad\quad (= \text{I}^{5-(\;)-6} \longrightarrow \text{II}_{\sharp}^{9\sharp} \; V^{8-7} \text{ I)} \\
\quad\quad\quad\quad\quad\quad\quad\quad\quad\quad\quad\quad\quad\quad (= \text{VI}_{\sharp}^{9\sharp})
\end{array}
$$

(or suppression) in the movement at hand. From our study of keyboard expositions by Haydn in chapter 2, we may expect that the S region in this symphony movement will reside squarely within the dominant key, E Major, and that it will be shaped by a fifth-progression descending from B (= $\hat{2}$ within the broad A Major tonality) to E. Because the *Kopfton* C♯ (= $\hat{3}$) was introduced in the middle register during P but then was transferred to the upper register during TR, we should be especially curious regarding which register Haydn will choose for the fifth-progression.

Haydn makes register a central concern during the opening measures of S. Though we may appreciate that B in the upper register during measures 29 and 31 fulfills the expectation established by the high positioning of *Kopfton* C♯ in measure 25, that height is forfeited soon thereafter: B in the middle register prevails during measures 36 through 38. Yet the high B sounds again during measure 40. Despite this vacillation, it is the lower register that prevails in the approach to the PAC of measure 46. Though 5.3 contains additional information that will be addressed gradually as we proceed, at this point take note of the wavering of B between two registers and the fifth-progression to the E of measure 46. That fifth-progression, divided between the first and second violins, is to some extent concealed by pitches a third higher. Before we proceed to a closer examination of the harmonic progression, observe also that the upper register eventually will prevail. Two stepwise traversals of the B>E fifth transpire during S: once in the middle register, the other – which I display as more definitive – in the upper register.[3]

The downward-stemmed notes in the bass of **5.3**, measures 29 through 46, tell a familiar story: the tonic sounds first in its root position (bass E) but then is destabilized through inversion. Bass G♯ is a half step away from A, the next point on the path towards the dominant. B and E quickly and conventionally conclude the progression. The tonic surges with the B♯ at 41_3, and IV undergoes its familiar 5–6 shift. The initial tonic and its first inversion are the endpoints of a local progression that engages pitches from the parallel minor key. Thus the tonic 6-phase chord at 34_3 is spelled as E-G♮-C♮, and the supertonic that follows is a potent II⇒ (an uncommon inversion of the chord often nicknamed the "German" augmented sixth).[4] The dominant eventually moves into its $^4_2$ position, poised for resolution to the inverted tonic of measure 40.

In measures 60 through 71 Haydn reprises the structure of measures 35 through 46, with modest adjustments. (See **5.3**.) Though the parallel-minor hue recurs in measures 48 through 52, the supertonic chord of measure 60 is built with C♯ instead of C♮. The upward registral shift that transpires later in the phrase results in a bolder statement of the stepwise structural descent to E for the EEC at 71_1.

The two versions of the initial local succession I^{5-6} II (measures 29 through 35 and 46 through 60) are presented in contrasting manners. The E tonic is extended during measures 29 through 33 using two back-to-back doses of neighboring-chord embellishment, in the midst of which the temporary shift to the parallel minor occurs. The tonic's 6-phase chord (E-G♮-C♮) and the evolved supertonic chord (E-G♮-A♯-C♮) both retain elements from the parallel minor. In measures 46 through 55 the embellishments of the tonic are more elaborately worked out and extended. (Note that the chord at 55_3, which concludes the extension, is a close approximation of what transpires during measure 32.) In measure 56 Haydn elides the tonic 5-phase restoration, substituting the tonic 6-phase chord, now highly evolved: dominant-emulating E♯-G♯-B-D♮. As is its tendency, this chord leads to the supertonic, also highly evolved: instead of diatonic F♯-A-C♯ or the minor-hued E-G♮-A♯-C♮ of measure 35, Haydn employs dominant-emulating E-G♮-A♯-C♯ in measure 60. Due to these chordal evolutions, two diminished-seventh chords (corresponding to C♯→F♯→) occur in succession.

One aspect of my harmonic perspective that remains imprecisely codified is the notion of harmonic assertion. Just when does a combination of pitches warrant a harmonic label? Three passages within S offer special insight into this issue. The first is measures 29 through 33, which are derived from measures 3 and 4. There is a melodic tension in bass D♯, as connector

Haydn: Symphony No. 45 in F♯ Minor ("Farewell"), movement 2

between two Es and as diminished fifth against the recently sounded soprano A, which functions as a passing note: at first thwarted in its quest to fill in the B>G♯ third, but then successful on a second try (where G♯ is displaced by G♮). I regard this passage as just barely within the realm of the harmonic. Consider next 46_3 through 52_2, whose melody uses the same pitch classes as in measures 29 through 32. Modal mixture recurs as well. Yet in this case the harmonic dimension is more pronounced, given the motion from tonic root E to dominant root B and the intervening conventional A<A♯ approach to B.[5] Finally, consider 62_2 through 69_1. I propose in **5.3** that the dominant is prolonged from $^6_3$ position in measure 62 through $^4_2$ position in measure 68, resolving to a first-inversion tonic chord in measure 69. But what is one to make of the G♯-B-E chord in measure 66? Is it, too, a tonic resolution, even though E never yields to leading tone D♯ in measure 65? Perhaps. Yet consider an intriguing alternative: that the $^6_3$ chord of measure 66 is an unfurling of the $^6_4$ in measure 65, prolonging the wait before the dominant is fully restored at 68_{2-3}. I retain some wiggle room within my notion of assertion because there are cases – such as this one – in which alternative views might be equally viable.

Webster and I agree that S is segmented into two parts (which he calls "paragraphs"), with the juncture occurring between 46_2 and 46_3, as shown in his example 2.11 (pp. 58–59).[6] Though I am mildly concerned about the lack of bass B within the first paragraph in his summary representation of the movement in example 2.10 (p. 57), since that phrase is as vibrant and structurally sophisticated as the one that follows, my more serious reservations concern the bass pitch B that he places in measure 50 of that example, since it appears that he intends for this B to extend until the cadence of measure 71.[7] I suggest that instead B (represented by bass D♯ in **5.3**) serves as an interior space between the tonic's 5 and 6 phases and that it by no means extends either to the local dominant of measures 62 through 68 or to the deeper dominant of measure 70. As in our interpretations of TR, Webster and I are at loggerheads regarding the hierarchical relationships among chords.

Nor do we always agree regarding local pitch hierarchies. Consider our contrasting interpretations of measure 35. Whereas Webster hears the first violin's C♮ resolving as a suspension to the immediately following B as part of an *e4* motive (see his example 2.11 and p. 60), I instead interpret that B as passing between chord members C♮ and A♯ of II⇒, as displayed in **5.3**. C♮'s resolution pitch is instead the B at 36_3. Observe that, from the outset of S, the first and third eighth notes of each measure are emphasized in the violin melody, at first through a quarter-plus-eighth rhythm, then through a subsidiary pitch being placed on the second beat: lower neighbor D♯ in measure 33, passing note D♮ in measure 34, *passing note B* in measure 35, and neighboring note C♯ in measure 36. (This relationship persists even when a tie connects the third beat of one measure and the first beat of the next.) That consistent pattern is broken by the temporary cessation of activity during measure 37, after which a contrasting eighth-plus-quarter rhythm emerges. Fortunately this phrase's twin follows, giving more data to help confirm one reading over the other. I contend that the progression from the tonic 6-phase through II⇒ to V during measures 34 through 36 (this the more somber, minor-hued twin) is complemented by the same progression (in a perkier, major-hued manifestation) during measures 56 through 62, as shown in **5.3**.

Webster and I agree that Haydn resorts to some extraordinary dissonance resolutions during S. The cello and bass D♯ in measures 36 and 37 is transferred to the first violin, where it resolves at 41_2. Indeed, one may sense that something has been "left hanging" in the original register (p. 62). Likewise the A of 45_2 is transferred before resolution (now down an octave from first to second violin). This time Haydn does provide a confirming in-register resolution: the second-violin G♯ at 46_3. Webster instead assigns that role to the first-violin G♯ in measure 47 (p. 62). To my ears, the dissonant context of that moment (and G♯'s role as a local passing note between A and F♯^{8}) prevents it from serving as a resolution. Perhaps in compensation for the unusual resolution in measures 45 and 46, Haydn will emphasize the A>G♯ resolution during the C section that follows immediately after S.

The exposition's closing zone (C, measures 71–76)

Reviving a rhythmic idea from TR, the exposition's brief C region emphasizes C♯>B (from 72_1 to 73_3) and A>G♯ descending seconds. As noted above, the latter may compensate for the abrupt transfer of the first violin's A at 45_2 to the inner register. Yet more potent associations emerge when C recurs in the tonic key at the end of the recapitulation. There the descending seconds are F♯>E and D>C♯, recalling melodic content from P, with the concluding C♯ serving as a lingering echo of the *Kopfton*.

Haydn: Symphony No. 45 in F♯ Minor ("Farewell"), movement 2   161

Example 5.4 Analysis of Haydn: Symphony No. 45 in F♯ Minor ("Farewell"), mvmt. 2, mm. 1–126.

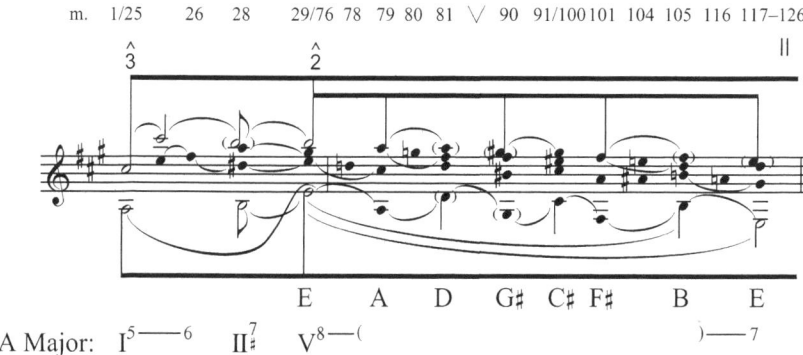

The development (measures 77–126)

I display the exposition's foundational harmonic progression as

A Major: I   II$^7_♯$ V   rather than as   A Major: I
                                                 E Major: IV   V^7 I

because, from a broad perspective, the E chord retains its tendency to resolve to tonic A throughout, even if it is tonicized during the exposition's S and C regions. The principal structural event of the development is the destabilization of that E chord, heralding the return of tonic A for the recapitulation. Though it contains some potentially diverting local chordal successions (to be explored below), the broad trajectory of the development corresponds to one of the most basic of all mechanisms for chordal progression: the descending circle of fifths. This circle connects the stable (through tonicization) E-G♯-B dominant of the exposition and the unstable E-G♯-B-D dominant seventh that ends the development, forming a broad V$^{8-7}$. The circle traverses chords rooted on each of the diatonic pitch classes of A Major (*not* E Major!): E–A–D–G♯–C♯–F♯–B–E. (See **5.4**.) Two of A Major's three minor triads (those on C♯ and F♯) and its diminished triad (that on G♯) either from the outset have evolved or eventually do evolve into major triads. Only the B triad (whose third, D, will become the minor seventh of the following restored E dominant) does not so evolve. In

Haydn's realization some of the chords sound only in an inversion, and in some cases a chordal ninth sounds in place of an octave doubling of the root. The model presented in **5.4** displays the foundational progression in its most normative formulation, omitting these surface variants. Pitches that are not literally present in the score appear within parentheses.

Haydn offers a wide range of treatments for the various points along the circle and their connection. During two-measure prolongations utilizing motivic content from the exposition's TR, the E and A triads, both major in their diatonic states, become dominant-emulating through the addition of their minor sevenths. In contrast, the D chord that follows (at 81_1) sounds for but one beat and only in first inversion. The D–G♯ link is the diatonic circle's one imperfect fifth, and here Haydn conceals that liability by dividing the fifth into two thirds (thus D̲–B–G♯). Though the B chord is hierarchically dependent upon the chords that it links, its presentation – from 81_2 through 89_3 – is much more extended than that of either the D or G♯ chord. The circle's G♯ chord is, like the D chord, both brief and presented in an inversion: diatonic G♯-B-D is represented by highly evolved B♯-D♯-F♯-A in measure 90.[9] The C♯ chord that follows is dominant-emulating not only in that its minor third is converted to major (C♯-E♯-G♯) but also by being presented using material derived from the prolongation of the dominant-functioning B major chord in measures 62 through 68. The C♯ chord extends through to the arrival of the circle's next member, F♯, at 101_1. It, too, eventually takes on dominant-emulating characteristics before resolving to B at 105_1. Haydn reveals further resourcefulness by the manner in which he projects the B chord through measure 116: against a descending first violin line he pursues a segment of an ascending 5–6 sequence, which possesses the special characteristic of restoring the pitch content of the first chord at its sixth chord. That is, B-D-F♯ occurs at both of the points marked by an asterisk below:

m.   105   107   110/114   115   –   116
      B⁵———6   C♯⁵———6   ⌈D⁵———6⌉
      *   *

B's 6-phase chord is transformed from diatonic B-D-G♯ into dominant-emulating G♯-B♯-D♯; C♯'s 5-phase chord serves as the venue for a reminiscence of S's opening theme; and D's 5- and 6-phase chords collide (B-D-F♯-A in measure 116, instead of D-F♯-A followed by D-F♯-B). The circle's concluding E chord, functioning as V^7 in the tonic key of A Major, retains F♯, prominently stated in measures 120 and 125, as chordal ninth.

Of the seven chordal roots that serve as the foundation for the development's structure in my perspective (as displayed in the second "measure" of **5.4**), Webster acknowledges only two: F♯ and E, which appear in his example 2.10 (p. 57). He shows a B notehead as well, but not until measure 116 – eleven measures too late, in my view. His example 2.12d (p. 61) suggests that he regards this B to be hierarchically inferior to the preceding C♯, apparently as no more than the E dominant's chordal fifth. (Likely he would have deployed the Roman numeral ii^7 had he interpreted this B otherwise.) In my discussion above I offer alternative interpretations of the three additional pitches that he displays (B in measure 81, G♯ in measure 107, and C♯ in measure 110). In my view they reside closer to the musical surface than do the seven foundational roots.

Clearly Webster and I have arrived at an impasse. There is no common ground between our views, except that the development concludes with a dominant chord. I shall let the matter rest here, allowing readers to ponder the relative merits of my circle-of-fifths reading and voice leading graph versus Webster's "V (ii) vi V/iii iii=I^6 V" reading and bass-line graph (Example 2.10, p. 57).

The recapitulation (measures 127–190)

If Haydn had constructed the recapitulation using a conventional format, he would have traversed both the C♯>B>A third of P and the E>D>C♯>B>A fifth of S (now in A Major), with an intervening TR region ending on a dominant MC to herald the reemergence of the tonic A for S. He has elected not to pursue this model in full. Instead he leads directly from the HC ending the antecedent phrase of P (which, like the potential MC moment, is a dominant chord) to the onset of S, thereby trimming the recapitulation by twenty measures. (The exposition's measures 8 and 29 – the latter transposed – become the recapitulation's adjacent measures 134 and 135.) The redundancy of separate P and S descents to A (background $\hat{1}$) is thereby averted. The $\hat{2}$ dangling at the end of the development (as shown in **5.4**) is resolved by inner-strand A at measure 127, but its melodic confirmation is delayed until measure 152 and reconfirmed during the second segment of S, with the arrival of the ESC in measure 185.

In partial compensation for this reduction in content Haydn extends the II→ chord of measure 166 (compare with that of measures 60 and 61), in two stages: first a filled-in voice exchange ($^{F\sharp}_{A}X^{A}_{F\sharp}$) occurs in the lower strings between measures 166 and 172; and then a further evolution of the chord is accomplished through the lowering of bass F♯ to F♮, resulting in II⇒.[10] Since the upward registral shift of the *Kopfton* occurred during the exposition's TR, the omission of TR during the recapitulation results in the retention of the lower register. In that S undergoes a downward transposition of a fifth, the recapitulation's goal A is in the register of the initial presentation of the *Kopfton* C♯ in measure 1.

> Webster does not address the recapitulation in detail. He does, however, provide reductive graphs – his Examples 2.12b and 2.12c (p. 61) – that offer a harmonic analysis of measures 158 through 177. By starting at measure 158, rather than the phrase-initiating tonic of 152₃, he gives the impression that the dominant is being extended throughout the passage.[11] As was also the case regarding the exposition's measures 56 through 59 (in the tonicized dominant key), discussed above, I instead regard the A♯-C♯-E-G♮ chord of measures 162 through 165 as an evolved tonic 6-phase chord within a broad I^{5-6}–II♯–V–I progression whose V (in measures 176 through 182) is unrelated to the E-G♯-B(-D) chord in measures 154 and 156–161.
>
> The label V°/V/V, which Webster employs in his examples, is unnecessarily complicated. Webster and I agree that the A♯-C♯-E-G♮ chord's root is F♯, three fifths away from tonic A. In the context of A Major, a chord rooted on F♯ (here an asserted 6 phase of I) warrants the label VI. The fact that this VI is dominant-emulating does not invalidate the scale-step label VI. I offer the symbols VI→ II→⇒ V as a more informative and less cumbersome alternative for the progression of measures 162 through 176. It is possible to acknowledge a chord's resolutional tendencies without resorting to multiple doses of applied-dominant notation.
>
> What occurs during measures 166 through 175, which Webster calls a "purple patch" (p. 61), is straightforward: an evolved supertonic chord is extended via a filled-in voice exchange, followed by further evolution, from II→ to II⇒. What might have occurred along the way is another story. The various internal chords within the voice exchange are constructions that, in other contexts, one would expect to behave in ways that contrast their linear roles here. Listeners should be alert to the possibility that one of those alternative tendencies might be asserted.

Haydn: Symphony No. 45 in F♯ Minor ("Farewell"), movement 2

Consider the following alternative continuations to become better attuned to exactly what is at stake along the path of this delectable progression.

- After measure 169, proceed to C♯ minor.
- After measure 171, proceed to a G major $^5_3$ chord and then to C minor.
- After measure 173, proceed to G major.
- After measure 175, proceed to B♭ major.

The arrival of root E at measure 176 is more gratifying because so many alternatives have been resisted.

6 | Haydn: String Quartet in G Minor (op. 20, no. 3), movement 3

in response to Robert O. Gjerdingen

Robert O. Gjerdingen charts a provocative new course for the analysis of eighteenth-century music in his *Music in the Galant Style*.[1] Having immersed himself in a vast array of mostly Italian *partimenti* (instructional basses) and *solfeggi* (vocal lines paired with *partimento* basses), he explores a range of schemata that he suggests served as the foundation for galant composition, in a mix-and-match process. Some of these schemata were recognized and named by eighteenth-century musicians, while others have come to the fore through modern analytical investigation and synthesis. Thus, though the conception dates from the eighteenth century, Gjerdingen works within a framework that is in part his own construction.

Given that I pursued a similar agenda for somewhat later music in *Thinking About Harmony*, I am of course favorably disposed towards Gjerdingen's initiative. That said, I must admit that I found his book frustrating to read. My concerns fall within three broad categories, as follows:

(1) Musical progressions of only superficial similarity are lumped together within a single schematic category. For example, consider the bass C>G<A>E in C Major. When the chord on E asserts itself as a first-inversion tonic, I would interpret the progression as an expansion of I^{5-6-5}. Yet the same notes may occur in a contrasting context, proceeding as C>G<A>E<F>C, a broader tonic expansion with no internal tonic assertion. (The E chord may in fact be realized as E-G-B.) Though their agendas are contrasting, each is labeled as a Romanesca in Gjerdingen's system.[2] Consider also his Prinner, which is characterized by a bass such as F>E>D>C in C Major. (Often a G will sound between the D and the C.) In some cases the E performs a passing role between F and D, in a context corresponding to what I would label as IV^{5-6} (with the 6-phase chord unfurled), followed by V and I. In other cases the F leads directly to E (supporting I in first inversion), followed by an E>D>C expansion of I-space.[3] Again, these seem to me to be highly contrasting roles for the same set of bass pitches.

Gjerdingen might have refined his labeling system (Prinner 1, Prinner 2, etc.) or coined more terms. (He invents names for a number of other schemata.)

(2) There are numerous instances in which Gjerdingen's application of scale degree numbers seems to me to be faulty.[4]

(3) Though Gjerdingen acknowledges that his perspective addresses only part of what constitutes galant music (p. 219), his 500-page tome does not offer samples of how a synthesis with other analytical methodologies might be achieved. When multiple perspectives offer complementary insights, this is not a problem. However, I often found that my perceptions did not sit comfortably alongside Gjerdingen's. Since he denigrates the conventional practice of harmonic analysis and the Schenkerian perspective (pp. 34, 59, 140, 370, 424–426, and 435), one might expect that readers accustomed to applying those tools will confront some wrenching challenges when entering into Gjerdingenian territory. Instead of critically assessing those other practices, exploring various points of contention, he simply asserts that traditional notions of harmony, form, and tonality are ill suited to this music and should be abandoned. (Readers are left with the sense that sometime around January 1, 1801, a radical shift in how music was conceived occurred.) Fortunately the format of *Harmony in Haydn and Mozart* fosters the very sort of comparative assessment that I think is needed. We shall proceed to that endeavor presently.

The exposition's primary-theme zone (P, measures 1–8)

Gjerdingen's analysis of the *Poco Adagio* from Haydn's String Quartet in G Minor opens with a quotation from Leopold Mozart.[5] I shall do likewise: "when your [Wolfgang's] music is performed by a mediocre orchestra, it will always come off poorly [*verlieren*], because it is composed sensibly for all the instruments and is not insipid [*platt*] as Italian music generally is."[6] Whereas Gjerdingen both resolutely rejects the "insipid" characterization of Italian music and seeks to place Haydn and Mozart within the mainstream of Italianate practice, we should keep in mind that one of their most alert and qualified contemporaries – Leopold – thought otherwise. Contrary to Gjerdingen's assertion (p. 21), various sorts of rudimentary harmonic analysis were practiced during the eighteenth century. Yet its principal practitioners (Lampe, Trydell, Daube, Holden, Vogler, and Portmann) wrote in English or German, not Italian.[7] Were northern and southern

Example 6.1 Analysis of Haydn: String Quartet in G Minor (op. 20, no. 3), mvmt. 3, mm. 1–8.

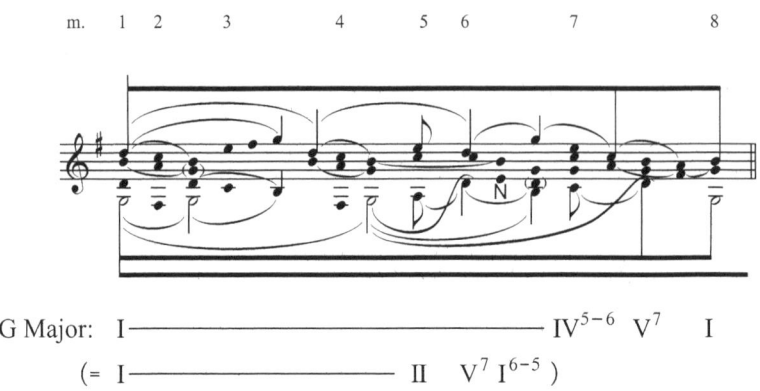

authors immersed in contrasting repertoires? Or did they possess contrasting manners of listening to and making sense of music? Or were northerners simply more industrious in writing down and circulating their perceptions through books? Whereas Gjerdingen emphasizes the southern aspects of Haydn's and Mozart's styles, I would argue that the qualities that Leopold Mozart appreciated resulted from the integration of southern and northern tendencies, thereby validating the utilization of northern analytical techniques, from which the perspective that I espouse has evolved.

I propose that Haydn's *Poco Adagio* conforms to the version of sonata form that Hepokoski and Darcy refer to as Type 2, which contrasts the more familiar Type 3 in its second rotation (what follows the exposition).[8] The G Major key is conveyed at the outset of the first rotation through the melodic filling-in of intervals from its tonic chord. D>C>B is prominently stated at multiple levels. Note especially the appealing interplay of thirds: D>B is unfolded repeatedly during measures 1 through 6, followed by C>A in measure 7 before the concluding $\frac{B}{G}$ at the cadence in measure 8. (See **6.1**.) The upper pitches of these local thirds span a broad D>C>B third, supported by P's foundational I–IV$^{5-6}$–V^7–I harmonic progression. Despite the prominence of the D-to-B third, another tonic-chord interval claims some attention as well: D<E<F♯<G, which is traversed over the course of the first three measures and hinted at again by the leap up to G during 6$_3$. The first four measures come across as a competition between these two alternative trajectories: the $\frac{C}{F\sharp}$ dissonance of measure 2, which leads the melody downwards, is inverted to $\frac{F\sharp}{C}$ in measure 3, propelling the melody upwards. Which route shall we take? Measure 4 confirms that, at least during P, the descending route will be featured. Yet later, during TR,

Example 6.2 Analysis of Haydn: String Quartet in G Minor (op. 20, no. 3), mvmt. 3, mm. 1–18.

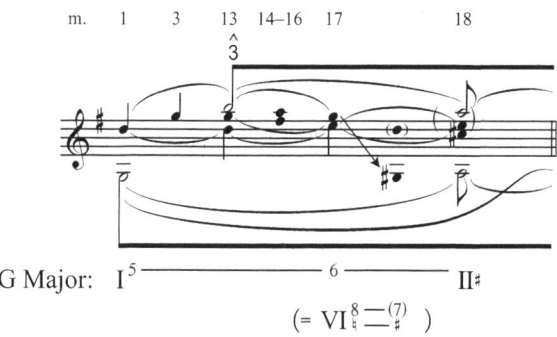

the ascending trajectory is revived and extended: a filled-in D<G<B arpeggiation is traversed during measures 9 through 11, and a high B (which serves as the movement's *Kopfton*) is attained in measure 13, just before the extended tonic gives way to the harmonic trajectory leading to the TR's goal II♯ in measure 18 (to be explored below). Though the D<G fourths are displayed in **6.1** as local events, retrospectively they supersede the beamed D>C>B third in structural importance. A broad D<G<B arpeggiation extending over the movement's first thirteen measures (as shown in **6.2**) is the path to the *Kopfton*, even if during P the D<G segment seems to lead nowhere.

> My comments on Gjerdingen's analysis of the *Poco Adagio* will focus on aspects of our readings that are irreconcilable. Yet some of my concerns stem from what seem to me to be an inconsistent or incorrect application by Gjerdingen of his own system. For example, in his annotation of the triad in measure 1, all three pitches are labeled, whereas in measure 5 only the top pitch is.[9] I cannot discern the logic behind Gjerdingen's determination of when to label and when not to label a pitch. In my perception, the B<D third of measure 1 is matched by the C>A third in measure 2. It makes no sense to me that B is labeled but A is not. Sometimes foreground pitches (e.g., B in measure 7) are labeled while pitches that reside deeper within the structure are not. In such decisions, I doubt that Gjerdingen is following explicit eighteenth-century precedents. He instead is relying on his innate musicality. It is the clash between his and my musical sensibilities, rather than his apparatus, that is at the heart of my discomfort.[10] Though I would find using his tools limiting – there are things I would want to convey that they could

not comfortably accommodate – my Gjerdingenian analyses would look much different from Gjerdingen's own.

In measure 3 Gjerdingen attempts to display a hierarchy among pitches: ❻ appears within a larger circle than ❼ or ❶. (In presentations of the theme later in the movement, Gjerdingen labels only the ❻.) In my view the goal ❶ (the endpoint of a slur in **6.1**) is structurally deeper than either the ❻ or the ❼. Gjerdingen was attentive to the E because, in his view, it initiates a Prinner. Yet he does not show a descent from ❻ to ❺ within measure 3. It appears, instead, that ❻ is retained against the cello's B. (Observe in **6.1** that with my more sophisticated analytical tools I was able to move the D that Gjerdingen labels as ❺ into measure 3, where it "belongs": it is performed there by the viola.)

The term Passo Indietro means "a step to the rear" (p. 167). This is a misleading description of what occurs in measure 3. From the tonic root G, the ascent to B in the bass often is the initial phase of a motion that eventually extends through C to dominant D (as occurs from 6_3 through 7_3). In my view the "step to the rear" is not the B of measure 3, but instead the restoration of G in measure 4. The ascent to G in the first violin at 3_3 likewise is a move forward on the path to the eventual attainment of a high B. It appears that Gjerdingen regards bass C at 3_1 as a note that ought to ascend to D. I instead regard it as a cello replication of the violin C from measure 2. In this interpretation the first violin's E is a local passing note to the F♯ that will form an augmented fourth against that C (an inversion of the diminished fifth from measure 2). Measure 3 extends measure 2 via a $^B_G X ^G_B$ voice exchange with registral shift. Both outer-voice lines have begun upward journeys, rescinded through the $^G_B X ^B_G$ voice exchange between 3_3 and 4_2. The role of the cello C in measure 3 is not the same as that in measure 7. If the latter had not proceeded to D, I would agree with Gjerdingen that a Passo Indietro had occurred.

Though the cello E at 6_3 might not be the pitch one expects to hear, I think the term Deceptive Cadence distorts the situation. After all, the E delays the full sounding of the tonic harmony by only half a beat. We expect to hear – and do hear – a cadence in measure 8, not measure 6. I propose a radically different Gjerdingenian interpretation: that the cello D<E>B of measure 6 represents the second through fourth pitches of a tonic-extending Romanesca whose initiating G>D is here expanded through the insertion of the supertonic in measure 5. My ear connects the cello G of measure 4 and B of measure 6, whereas for Gjerdingen there seems to be a chasm between E and B.

Gjerdingen's analysis of measure 7 focuses our attention on B, the *only* first violin pitch given a scale-degree label. Let's turn for a moment to species counterpoint. Above cantus firmus whole note C, two half notes C and B may occur, followed by a downbeat $_D^A$. Though B forms a dissonant seventh with C, it is permitted in this context because it connects two consonant pitches. In free composition that unaccented passing note may be shifted to an accented position, so that the B internal to the C>A third falls against the arrival of D below. Yet even here B remains hierarchically dependent upon C and A. (Haydn's harmonic succession is from IV^{5-6} to V^7, none of which claims B as a chord member.) Consequently I find Gjerdingen's omission of labels for C and A in measure 7 to be misguided. Though the sixteenth-note A is followed by a quarter-note A in measure 8 that Gjerdingen does label, the latter occurs in conjunction with the cello's G and thus functions as a suspension. A's structural moment has already concluded by that point.

By proposing a Cudworth for the cadential gesture, Gjerdingen asserts that an octave connection (not completed) is the fundamental melodic event of the passage. That notion is defensible. My alternative reading for measure 7 depends upon the ear's responsiveness to the repeated unfolding of the D>B third in the preceding measures. Coming after D>B and resolving into $_G^B$ at 8_1, C>A emerges as the essence of measure 7's melody. Clearly Gjerdingen finds delight in the B at the cadence (marked by an exclamation point), which in his interpretation is a departure from expectation. I instead regard B as the inevitable goal of the phrase, both as the resolution of the preceding dominant's seventh[11] and as the endpoint of a motivically significant D>C>B third. From my perspective, this B is not an unexpected swerve that spoils an intended PAC. Instead it adumbrates, in the context of an IAC, the arrival of *Kopfton* B an octave higher during TR: D>C>B̄ and D<G<B̄ are complementary paths to $\hat{3}$.

The exposition's transition (TR, measures 9–18)

The first violin B at the cadence in measure 8 is the melodic goal of a downward stepwise progression from the D at 1_3. A similar progression in the ascending direction achieves B in two registers: during 11_3 and at 13_1.

Example 6.3 Analysis of Haydn: String Quartet in G Minor (op. 20, no. 3), mvmt. 3, mm. 19–43.

G Major: V————————————————————————————————————
(= D Major: I ———————— IV V^8——————— 7 —— I ———— IV— V^7 I
                  (= A Major: I   II V^7 I)

Though the phrase that begins in measure 9 eventually veers away from the tonic, leading to a medial caesura on II♯ during measure 18 (thereby confirming its role as the exposition's TR), its initial measures complete the tonic expansion that was initiated during P. As mentioned above, the G of 3_3 (and 6_3) is a stepping-stone to the high B of 13_1, as shown in **6.2**.

From our study of major-key sonata expositions in chapter 2, we know that I$^{5-6}$ II♯ is a very common harmonic trajectory during TR. The model displayed in **2.14e** (omitting its second and third chords) closely resembles Haydn's procedure here. Whereas P contains descending stepwise trajectories of three thirds from ^D_B (in measures 1–2, 3–4, and 1–8) and from ^C_A (in measure 7), a similar progression starting on ^B_G (measures 13–17, as shown in **6.2**) is traversed during TR. The trajectories within P prolong a single harmony (I or V^7); that in TR connects the tonic's 5- and 6-phase chords.[12] Just before the arrival of II♯, the unfurled 6-phase chord evolves into dominant-emulating E-G♯-B. Because the first violin's D at 18_1 belongs with these pitches (though it arrives later), I place it within parentheses above G♯ in **6.2**.[13] Like the MC in several of the expositions we explored in chapter 2, the structural soprano (A) is absent at the MC. Here both A and E are supplied within parentheses in **6.2** to fully represent the structure that Haydn has incompletely presented. Perhaps in reference to the fact that *Kopfton* B initially was stated in the lower octave (at 8_2 and during 11_3), the belated arrival of A (= $\hat{2}$) during S is likewise in that lower register (at 19_1), preceding its upper-octave presentation during 24_1 (as shown in **6.3**).

The gap between Gjerdingen's and my perspectives is clearly in evidence in our contrasting interpretations of measure 13. For me, this moment is the culmination of a broad projection of the tonic harmony. The first violin's high B shines as a beacon, heightening the impact of the lower Bs of measures 2, 4, 8, 10, 11, and 12. This tonic B (the *Kopfton*) will find its successor in the dominant A of measure 24. (All measure numbers in this discussion correspond to Haydn's published score.[14]) For Gjerdingen this moment instead falls within the realm of the dominant tonicization. One should not underestimate the difficulty in deciding what hierarchical relationships are at play within a composition. Here Gjerdingen and I have made contrasting determinations: whereas he correlates the D chords of measures 14 and 19, I correlate the G chords of measures 1 through 13 (5-phase) and 17 (6-phase), which Haydn links via an even-paced descent of B>A>G>F♯>E in the first violin line.[15] Gjerdingen is responsive to the Prinner schema, which concludes at measure 16; I am responsive to the I^{5-6}–II♯ foundational progression (noted repeatedly during our study of Haydn transitions in chapter 2[16]), which places measure 16 within the connection of G-B-D and G-B-E. Readers should be cognizant of the fact that developing facility in analysis is not simply a process of accumulation, of absorbing the content of numerous books. In some cases one must make a choice. In this instance merging Gjerdingen's and my perspectives would lead to chaos.

The exposition's secondary-theme zone (S, measures 19–43)

Whereas the expansion of the opening G Major tonic during P and TR supports the traversal of an ascending melodic trajectory to *Kopfton* B (D<G<B), during S the tonicization of the dominant key, D Major, is the venue for a reciprocal downward trajectory (A>F♯>D). Though that fifth, filled in as A>G>F♯>E>D, may be harmonized in a variety of ways, Haydn here pursues a double arpeggiation in the bass (D–A–D–A–D), thereby emphasizing soprano F♯ as an internal nodal point. (See **6.3**, noting especially the double prong attached to bass D's stem at measure 30, indicating its role as endpoint of the first D–A–D arpeggiation and initiation point of the second.) Just as the upper-register *Kopfton* B arrives at the end of the initial tonic expanse (measure 13), so also its successor A arrives just before the harmonic progression within tonicized D Major begins its journey away from the tonic chord (measure 24). Another important similarity binds these two initiating regions: whereas the $\genfrac{}{}{0pt}{}{C}{F\sharp}$ and $\genfrac{}{}{0pt}{}{F\sharp}{C}$ dissonances and their resolutions are emphasized during measures 1 through 4, their D Major equivalents, $\genfrac{}{}{0pt}{}{G}{C\sharp}$ and $\genfrac{}{}{0pt}{}{C\sharp}{G}$, are juxtaposed in measures 19 through 22.

Given the relatively short durations of P (eight measures) and TR (ten measures), eight measures would be a viable duration for S. After the six-measure prolongation of I (in tonicized D Major) that opens S, measure 25 seems to be pursuing that goal. (An omission occurs at beat 2, where F♯, shown within parentheses in **6.3**, may be understood as an unstated connector between G and E.[17] The trill belatedly sounds that F♯.) The progression's continuation in measure 26 is a surprise. The A chord does not resolve, but instead is extended by means of a tonicizing I–II–V^7–I progression.[18] As is typical of any tonicizing progression, one of the intervals of its tonic chord is traversed: here E>D>C♯, during which a register transfer occurs (thus E>D<D>C♯). The full resolution of the descending unfolding of $\genfrac{}{}{0pt}{}{D}{G\sharp}$ in the first violin line of measure 26 extends through two measures: inner-strand A arrives on the second beat of measure 27, while outer-strand C♯ is delayed until the third beat of measure 28. Because of the register transfer, the restoration of E at the end of measure 28 occurs in the upper octave.

Whereas initially we might have interpreted the stepwise descent to E (slurred in **6.3**) as the deepest level of linear progression that will occur within S, the non-resolution of the dominant induces a reassessment. Haydn revives this dominant by adding a fresh seventh during measure 29 (where, in addition, a filled-in G>G octave restores the normative register). *That* G serves as the second note within S's deepest descending linear progression, resolving to F♯ in measure 30. (In **6.3** a beam joins the pitches of this line.)

A descending linear progression characteristically proceeds from a structurally deeper outer-strand pitch (here A = $\hat{2}$) to interior pitches. Thus it is not surprising that even after the midpoint of the descent (F♯ in measure 30), the initiating A sounds prominently during the prolongational play. Yet note how often the G>F♯ second is reiterated in the second violin and viola lines.[19] Then in measures 38 through 40_1 G sounds in all four instruments (covered by a B in the first violin). Whereas G ascends to A in the bass (leading from IV to V^7) and is retained as V's seventh in the viola, E sounds in both violin lines during 40_3. (Consequently the G of measure 38 serves as an *incomplete* neighbor to the preceding F♯, followed by the downward continuation to E.) Though E is covered by G in the first violin line during measures 40 through 42, the final cadence confirms that the second violin's E>D is the principal melodic line and that the viola – not the first violin – is responsible for the inner-voice G>F♯ resolution. This cadence serves as the EEC. Reiterations of the cadence here substitute for a separate C region.

Though he ended up not using it, the Monte Principale that Haydn sketched to open S (labeled as measures 19 through 22 in Gjerdingen's ex. 27.7) introduces the tonicized dominant key, D Major, through the traversal of the harmonic progression I$^{8-7♮}$ IV$^{5-6}$ V, in which IV's 6-phase chord evolves into a dominant-emulating II$^7_{♯}$.[20] I appreciate that, in his sketch, Haydn presents the D tonic chord in root position before proceeding to its rendering in second inversion ($^6_4$). Some of the $^6_4$ effect persists in the final version (measures 19 through 22), though mitigated by the viola line (not shown in Gjerdingen's reduction). In my view the broader tonal trajectory requires that the filled-in D>A>F♯>D arpeggiation in the Monte Principale's first measure be interpreted as I in tonicized D Major. The C♮ that emerges at the end of the measure induces a surge towards IV, one of the principal means of moving away from a major-key tonic. The difference between my I$^{8-7♮}$ IV and the familiar alternative analysis I V^7/IV IV is minute compared to Gjerdingen's refusal (1) to acknowledge the arrival of D Major as the local tonic during the Monte Principale's first measure (he instead labels the D as ⑤ in the key of D Major's IV, explicitly placing the onset of IV's domain at the beginning of the measure through a bracket placed above the score), and (2) to acknowledge that an important formal unit (S, following the medial caesura that concludes TR in measure 18) begins here as well. Gjerdingen is at loggerheads not only with me, but also with Hepokoski and Darcy.

Occasionally in the early days of harmonic analysis, authors would jump back and forth quickly among keys without informing their readers what they were doing, and consequently eccentric and hard-to-decipher rows of analytical symbols would appear in their analyses. (See *TAH*, **6.15a** and **7.11**.) For the most part, authors nowadays are careful to indicate the tonal context in which their numerical harmonic and scale-degree labels are to be interpreted. Gjerdingen's practice, as exemplified in measures 26 through 28, seems to me a step backwards. In measure 26, D is ❶; in measure 27, A is ❶; in measure 28, A is ❺. The lack of an apparatus to specify the key in which each number is to be interpreted during these quick shifts is problematic, especially in that Gjerdingen intends that his book will be accessible to non-specialists. Yet his methodology reveals a more basic problem: the need to choose just one number for a pitch. Compare Gjerdingen's perspective with my **6.3**. During a tonicization a pitch that serves as the root of V in its broader context (D Major) may concurrently function as the root of I in its local context (A Major).²¹ Though rarely invoked, I welcome Gjerdingen's "= ⑤" notation at the downbeat of measure 29.²²

Often two lines work concurrently in traversing intervals from a prolonged harmony. Whereas I propose that the cadence is achieved through the descent from F♯ through E to D in measures 30 through 43, another interval of the D Major tonic chord is traversed as well: A<D (an ascent that undergoes two descending register transfers, as shown via a dotted slur and an arrow in **6.3**). Gjerdingen does a good job of showing the latter ascent. Yet his ❷ at the downbeat of measure 43 seems disconnected from its context. Just as I proposed above that G Major's ❷ occurs during measure 7 (suspended into measure 8), so also I propose that D Major's ❷ occurs during measures 40 through 42 (suspended into measure 43 upon its third and final resolution). Though certainly Gjerdingen and I might disagree regarding whether ❷>❶ or ❼<❽ is the principal cadential gesture here, the lack of emphasis on ❷ above the dominant root A, a result of his selective omission of the second violin line as he transformed Haydn's quartet score into a keyboard reduction, leaves an important part of the story untold.²³

The development (measures 44–88)

At its most fundamental level, this development goes nowhere tonally: the same D Major that was tonicized during the exposition's S region persists through measure 88, just before the tonic return. (See **6.4a**.) As is characteristic of a Type 2 sonata, the development's thematic emphasis is upon material from P (measures 44–47, 51–54, etc.) and TR (48–50, 55–65, etc.). The restoration of root D at measure 84 leads to a medial caesura, heralding the return of the G Major tonic in measure 89. (Since the interface between thematic and tonal parameters in a Type 2 sonata contrasts that in the more familiar Type 3 sonata, Hepokoski and Darcy refer to the tonic return not as a recapitulation, but instead as a tonal resolution. Note that S – not P – is presented in conjunction with the tonic return. The development plus the tonal resolution together present the second complete rotation of the thematic content: P TR ' S.)

The first layer of Haydn's tonal expansion within the region labeled "b" in **6.4a** is displayed in **6.4b**. Not surprisingly, an interval from the D triad

Example 6.4 Analysis of Haydn: String Quartet in G Minor (op. 20, no. 3), mvmt. 3
(a) mm. 1–113; (b) mm. 24–84; (c) mm. 24–82; (d) mm. 51–81.

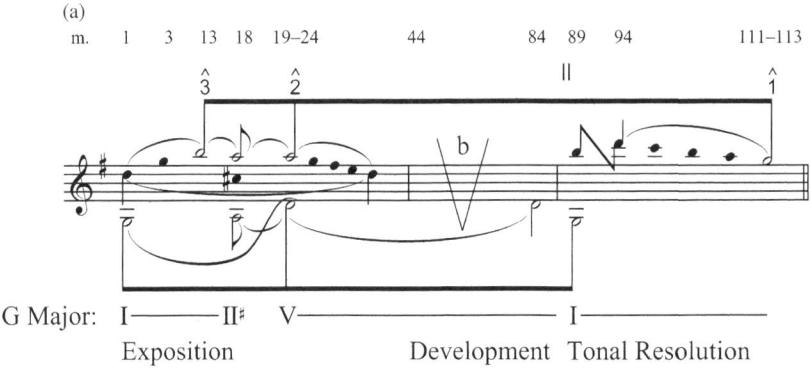

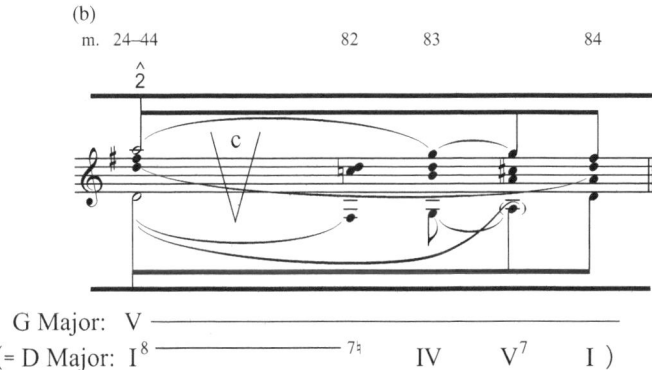

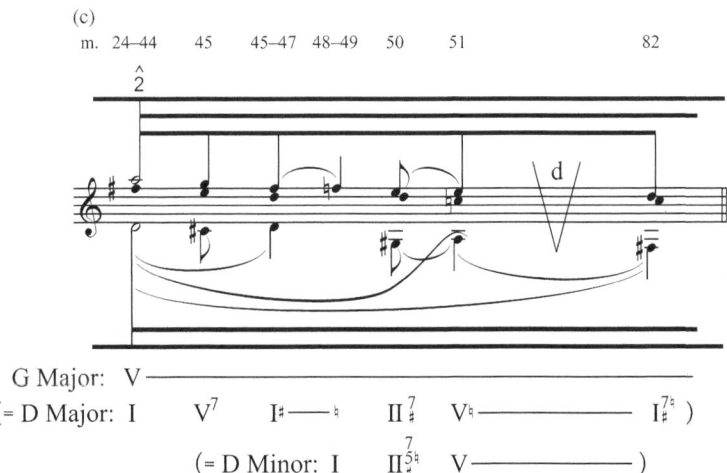

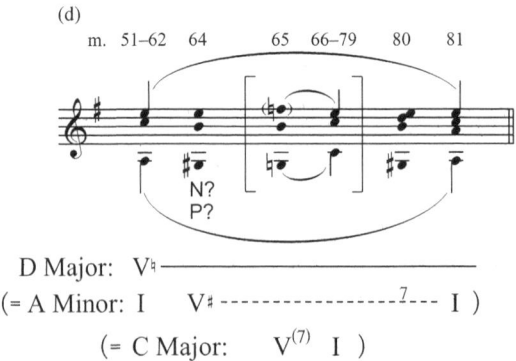

D Major: V♮ ─────────────────────────
(= A Minor: I   V♯ ----------------7---- I)
           (= C Major: V⁽⁷⁾ I)

(A>F♯) is traversed via stepwise descent in the melody, supported by a conventional harmonic progression in the tonicized dominant key. (In my graphs of the development, I have made a few adjustments in register and inversion to enhance clarity.) The G chord of measure 83 serves as IV within tonicized D Major, rather than as the return of the background G Major tonic. The preceding D⁷♮ chord functions locally as a surging tonic.

Observe in **6.4b** that the conventional traversal of the span between the tonic root and third in the bass is projected as a descending sixth, rather than as an ascending third. How Haydn fills in that space, which is labeled "c" in the graph, is displayed in **6.4c**. Again an interval from the D triad is traversed in the melody: this time A>D. The D tonic harmony supports the A, F♯, and D. A potent bout of modal mixture induces a temporary shift to D Minor, beginning in measure 48. Consequently the dominant of measure 51 contains a C♮, rather than a C♯. That C♮ will be retained as the minor seventh when D Major's dominant-emulating tonic arrives in measure 82.

It would be useful at this point for readers to reconstruct the structure of the movement as presented in **6.4a–c**. Listen to the merged content of these three graphs, noting especially that Haydn reinforces the D chord of measure 44 and the A chord of measure 51 through partial presentations of the P theme. The most pressing issue remaining regarding the development's harmonic plan is to make sense of the presentation of that theme in the key of C Major beginning in measure 66.

Though A Minor (tonicized beginning in measure 51) would have been regarded as a key closely related to tonic G Major by eighteenth-century musicians, I suggest here a more hierarchically sophisticated derivation: as diatonic dominant of the parallel minor of G Major's dominant key, D Major. The content of **6.4d** occurs where the label "d" appears in **6.4c**. At the outset the traversal of a broad I–II⇨V progression during measures 51 through 64 serves as a conventional expansion of tonicized A Minor.[24] A's leading tone G♯ may be expected to fulfill its upward tendency, restoring the A tonic. Yet in a minor context one very common way to launch a surge towards the mediant key (C Major) is to allow the G♯ instead to serve as a passing note leading to G♮, as **6.4d** displays.[25] Though Haydn assigns a prominent role to C Major (as noted, it supports a partial statement of the P theme), ultimately it is an upper-third extension of A Minor. I go so far as to place it within brackets in the example. A second chance at resolving A Minor's dominant chord (now with minor seventh) is offered in measure 80. This time it behaves conventionally, leading directly to the tonic. There is a danger that listeners will have lost the thread of the more basic progression shown in **6.4c** during this broad expansion of A Minor. Such an exaggerated discrepancy between duration and structural importance indeed can be troubling. Yet it seems that Haydn and other composers do occasionally go off on such tangents, as if a fermata were placed above the A minor chord in **6.4c**, inviting elaboration. After all, this dominant chord supporting 2̂ in D Major occurs within an even broader expansion of a dominant chord supporting 2̂, namely G Major's dominant, which holds sway over the entire development section (as shown in **6.4a**) before the tonic returns in measure 89.

> Since many of the schemata from the exposition recur during the development, Gjerdingen recycles his analysis of earlier measures. I am intrigued by his labeling of the B near the end of measure 49 as ❷ (in A Minor), an acknowledgment of its role within the proposed Indugio. Though I would instead retain D Minor here, accepting a chordal role for the labeled B would result in a move from the tonic's 5 phase to its unfurled 6 phase, proceeding normatively to a dominant-emulating supertonic. My ear, guided by Haydn's single slur joining the four notes of that beat, processes the passage as a D>A fourth filled in by passing notes. In Gjerdingen's A Minor perspective the motion might be interpreted either as ❹ ❷ ❼ (with ❶ serving as a B chord's seventh) or as a filling-in of the subdominant fourth (❹ ❶) followed by ❼. Perhaps the question mark that Gjerdingen places after the word Indugio in the example reflects his uncertainty on this point. My sparser presentation in **6.4c** would have included a superscript "5–6" to the right of the Roman numeral I if I had regarded the B as anything more than a local passing note.
>   Speaking of passing notes, the D at beat 3 of measure 53 performs that role within an E>C>A arpeggiation of the A minor chord.[26]

Consequently Gjerdingen's ❹ is misplaced, in my view. It belongs above the thirty-second note D in the following measure.

The passage from measure 55 through measure 65 proceeds from an A Minor tonic to its major dominant, via II⇒ in measure 63. Haydn employs abundant chromaticism, which Gjerdingen interprets as indicative of numerous key shifts: from A Minor to B Minor to E Minor back to A Minor. It was not a universal practice in eighteenth-century analytical thought to so freely shift among keys, especially when, as here, those potential tonics are not extended. Kirnberger, writing in 1771, presents an example (*TAH*, **6.10**) containing abundant chromaticism (including a passage that ascends to $\hat{2}$ via its leading tone, akin to measures 57 and 58 of Haydn's quartet). He states flatly: "If one abandons [the announced key] immediately, no modulation has occurred."[27] A conventional harmonic progression may be discerned if one retains the key of A Minor throughout this passage:

m.	55	57	58	59	60	61	62
A Minor:	I^5———^{6}		II♮——♯		V♮——♯		I
	(= VI→)						

Gjerdingen and I have similar views regarding how what I call the development concludes: we both employ a I or ① label for the C of measure 79, the A of measure 81, and the D of measure 84. (Our perspectives are reversed in measures 82–83, where Gjerdingen interprets G as ① and I interpret D as I→.) The chief difference between our purviews is that for me the various tonicizations are guided by a broader tonal outlook (C as upper third of A; A as fifth of D; etc.), whereas for him there appears to be no overarching tonal plan beyond the context of an individual schema.

Measures 78 through 84 offer an array of chords that would be interpreted in starkly contrasting manners by different analysts. Those who, like Gjerdingen, conceive of harmony within a single dimension might be struck by the close juxtaposition of four V^7→I successions:

G→ C   E→ a   D→ G   A→ D

They might note with satisfaction that C Major, A Minor, G Major, and D Major are four of the six diatonic regions within the tonal realm of G Major. (The other two, B Minor and E Minor, occur in measures 58 and 77, respectively.[28]) I instead espouse a broader, more hierarchical view. Based on the analytical graphs presented above, the first four chords in the series would all fall within the domain of A Minor. Juxtapositions of a minor tonic and its upper third are pervasive in music. Here C Major relates not to the movement's tonic, G Major, but instead to A Minor. That A is itself internal to a broad D–A–D arpeggiation (spanning **6.4c**). Thus the fifth chord in this series, though dissonant, is a reinstatement of the D Major chord that began the development and consequently is hierarchically deep. That D–A–D arpeggiation is embedded within a broader one (corresponding to **6.4b**), which reaches fruition in measure 84.

The tonal resolution (measures 89–113)

The exposition's S begins (in measure 19) with the four pitch classes of tonicized D Major's dominant seventh chord (A-C♯-E-G), thereby bringing the II♯ (A-C♯-E) of the medial caesura into the tonal context that will prevail for the remainder of the exposition. Likewise, when that theme is transposed to tonic G Major for the tonal resolution, the initiating dominant seventh chord D-F♯-A-C intensifies the D-F♯-A of the preceding medial caesura (measure 88). The traversal of S closely follows the exposition model, resolving in measures 111 through 113. (See **6.4a**.) Though the pitch B serves as the movement's *Kopfton*, S offers a descent instead from D to G. At this point in the movement, that traversal's endpoint pitch G completes the broad $\hat{3}>\hat{2}>\hat{1}$ fundamental line that extends through all the regions of the movement (as shown in **6.4a**).

In that Gjerdingen opposes imposing the notion of sonata form (let alone the Hepokoski and Darcy notion of the Type 2 sonata) upon music of the eighteenth century,[29] the medial caesura on D in measure 88 and the subsequent restoration of G Major in measure 89 are for him no more than successive components within the long string of events that shapes the movement.[30] I hold the opposite view, proposing that whereas some events are variable from work to work, others recur in the same position over a range of movements written by various composers and thus serve as form-defining characteristics. Hepokoski and Darcy have established the Type 2 category as a handy name for a specific set of characteristics. That is essentially the same sort of analytical enterprise as Gjerdingen labeling a set of more local events as the Meyer schema. No one in the eighteenth century would have understood what was meant by a Type 2 sonata – or a Meyer (named after Gjerdingen's mentor, Leonard B. Meyer). Yet we employ both notions fruitfully in an effort to make sense of this wondrous music. Carl Dahlhaus (no stranger to Gjerdingen) proposes: "how musical works are interpreted analytically … is a process that never achieves closure, in that the current state of composition inspires the detection of technical facts that do not cease to be facts even if none of the composer's contemporaries noticed them."[31]

7 | Mozart: String Quintet in C Major (K. 515), movement 1

in response to V. Kofi Agawu and Michael Spitzer

The insights attained through our study of twelve keyboard expositions by Haydn in chapter 2 serve as the foundation for this chapter's focus on the first movement from Mozart's String Quintet in C Major (K. 515). My study complements and assesses perspectives published by V. Kofi Agawu and Michael Spitzer, who address harmonic and structural issues in depth (though Spitzer's account extends only through the exposition).[1] Their agendas are broader than mine: Agawu considers musical topics such as fanfare, bourrée, and pastoral; whereas Spitzer focuses especially on his notions of thematic and cadential liquidation. Though I find these agendas interesting and encourage readers to pursue them, my commentary will focus on how the perspectives of Agawu and Spitzer intersect with my harmonic initiative.

The exposition's primary-theme zone (P, measures 1–57)

From its initiating tonic arpeggiation through its closing PAC at 57_1, Mozart projects the hegemony of tonic C throughout P. The foundational structure is defined by a stepwise ascent to *Kopfton* E (attained during 14_4), followed by a stepwise descent to the tonic pitch. Because that descending third is interrupted at $\hat{2}$, P is binary (a_1 a_2), as displayed by the positioning of the measure numbers in **7.1a**. The antecedent phrase projects I-space in the manner displayed in **7.1b**. Two principal initiatives fill out that skeletal shape: the *Kopfton* is attained by means of a stepwise ascending motion characterized by reaching-over (C descends to B, and D reaches over it; D descends to C, and *Kopfton* E reaches over it); and a descending stepwise octave, reinforcing the *Kopfton*, is traversed. (These details appear in **7.1c**.) Note especially how Mozart shifts to the tonic's 6-phase chord to support the conclusion of the octave descent (at 17_4), thereby initiating the tonic-expanding progression $I^{5\ 6}$ II V I, which fleshes out the bald I V I displayed within parentheses in **7.1b**. A more local – and more daring – realization of that progression occurs during the opening 16 measures, where the tonic's

Example 7.1 Analysis of Mozart: String Quintet in C Major (K. 515), mvmt. 1 (a) mm. 1–57; (b) mm. 14–19; (c) mm. 1–19; (d) mm. 21–57.

C Major: I   V   I

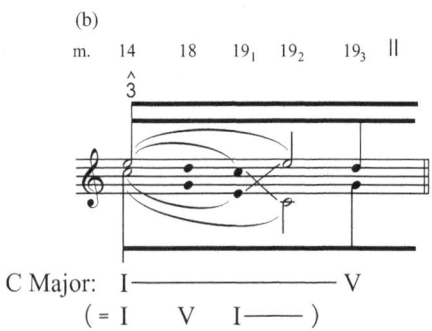

C Major: I ——————————— V
  (= I   V   I ——)

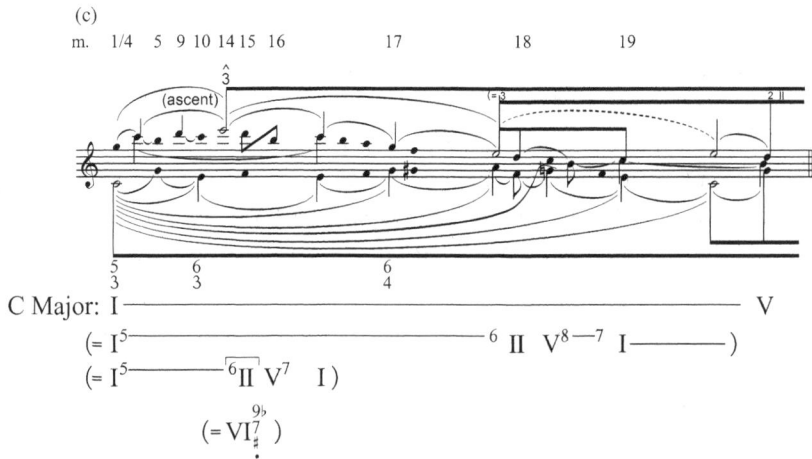

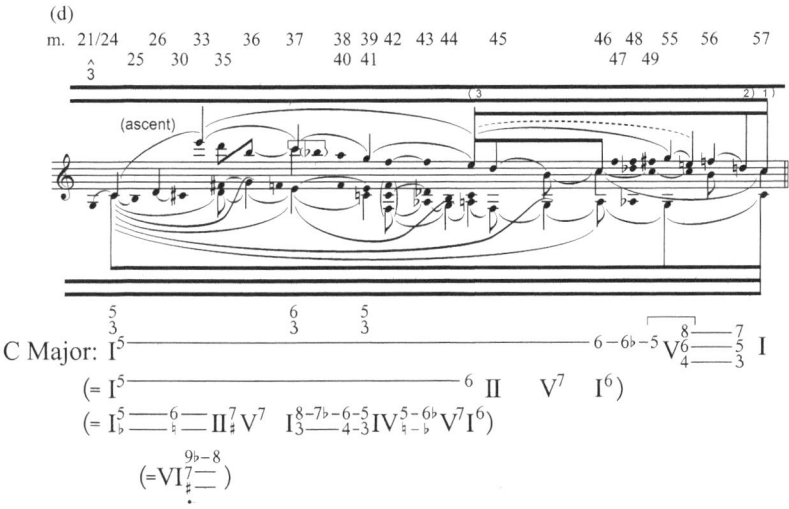

evolved 6-phase chord (C♯-E-G-B♭) and the supertonic's third (F) collide at 15_{1-2}.[2]

Though the consequent phrase closely follows the antecedent model until measure 46 (compare **7.1c** and **7.1d**), Mozart incorporates several creative variants and extensions: a glimmer of C Minor initiates the phrase (measures 21 through 24); the tonic's 6-phase chord arrives in measure 30 – well before II – instead of colliding with it; that II takes on dominant-emulating characteristics (measure 35); and a more developed harmonic progression supports the G>E span within the octave descent (measures 41 through 44). Equally consequential is the substitution of the tonic's 6-phase for its 5-phase chord at 46_1. (Compare with measure 19.) I interpret this passage as a near equivalent of a passage from Haydn's Quartet in A Major (op. 55, no. 1) that we explored in chapter 1. (It was written around a year after Mozart's quintet.) Compare the contexts of F♯-A-B-D♯ in **1.4d**, measure 158, and A♭-C-E♭-F♯ in **7.1d**, measure 49. In both cases an outward expansion prolongs the tonic.[3] Whereas in the quartet the progression continues with a second-inversion tonic chord (measure 159), in the quintet the arrival of the second-inversion tonic (which closely resembles that of 17_1) coincides with the assertion of G as the dominant's root (measure 55). Soprano F in measures 42 and 43 fills in a G>E third, while the F of measures 47 and 48 resides within a broader E<G third, an unfolding that is matched by F>D during the cadential dominant, preceding the PAC on C (as shown in **7.1d**). This region holds a special fascination because various potentialities for alternative harmonic trajectories are hinted at, though ultimately not realized. Potential tonicizations of D♭ Major and B♭ Minor yield to an affirmation of C Major. Because Mozart explores yet another harmonic potentiality later, a fuller exploration of this passage will be postponed until our discussion of its presentation during the recapitulation. (Readers may wish to take a preliminary look at **7.6a** at this point.)

> Though Agawu and I share the same broad conception of measures 1 through 57 as a period divided by an interruption, our readings of the internal content are vastly different, as are our conceptions of what a harmonic analysis ought to entail: whereas my 7.1c and 7.1d offer twenty-two Roman numerals, his example 4.2 displays only five. (He describes this section of his chapter as "focusing ... on harmony" (p. 91) and his presentation as a "close analysis" (p. 93). Two additional numerals are employed in his textual commentary.) The central tenet of my conception – that despite various modifications the two phrases convey nearly equivalent structures until their closing cadences – is irreconcilable with his reading. Agawu's example 4.2 (p. 93) instead juxtaposes a D>D registral shift in the melody (though measure numbers are in short supply, I think he is referring to 15_3 through 18_1) during the first phrase and a local D>C descent (35_4 through 37_4, after which the beam above is transformed into a dotted beam) during the second phrase. In the former I instead connect E>E within an expansion of I-space. The lower E is not displayed in Agawu's graph: it falls within his D>D span.[4] In the latter phrase my ear is guided by a recollection of the E>E connection of the antecedent phrase. Consequently I place more weight on the E arrival at 44_3 than does Agawu, who instead proposes a local $\hat{5}$-to-$\hat{1}$ descent within the broader $\hat{3}$-to-$\hat{1}$ descent. He even expresses concern that there is a "conflict of head tones [*Kopftons*]" (p. 92).
>
> Just how different are measures 21 through 30 from 1 through 10? Mozart appears to be presenting a study in contrasts: the mode switches from major to minor for the new phrase's first four measures (eventually wobbly note E♭ reverts to E); the first violin and cello trade melodic lines; and the tonic's evolved 6-phase chord (C♯-E-G-B♭), which arrived breathtakingly *late* during the first phrase (measure 15, colliding with the onset of II), now arrives so *early* that the 5-phase tonic expected as the culminating moment within the phrase's initiating I-space is elided (measure 30). Despite these deviations I accept these measures as the opening of a consequent phrase forming the second "half" of P. For me (and for Agawu) the PAC at 57_1 concludes a melodic initiative that was launched during measure 14. Not so for Spitzer. Swayed by the

discontinuities that emerge, he places the onset of TR at measure 21. (Just how untenable that perspective is will become apparent when we reach the condensed restatement of P during the recapitulation: if TR begins where Spitzer says it does, then I would think he would have to argue that there is no P during the recapitulation.) Furthermore he perceives measures 21 through 57 as a succession of two phrases (with a juncture at the end of measure 37, which in my view resides within the traversal of the E>E octave) rather than as a single extended phrase. His provocative commentary gives short shrift to harmony. Though he acknowledges the "extreme chromaticism" in measure 15, he offers no guidance regarding what harmonic trajectory Mozart is pursuing (p. 202); and the extraordinary passage beginning in measure 48 is perfunctorily described as "an exquisite Neapolitan 'purple patch'," with no assessment of its inner workings (p. 204). He also asserts that tonal ambiguity prevails during measures 37 through 54, to the extent that a "swing to B♭ major" is in the works (though averted), that there is a "cadence on F," and that the succession of measures 38 and 39 might be interpreted as I–V in F Major (pp. 203–204). In my view the C-E-G chords in measures 39 and 41 definitively assert the C Major tonic. They are *more* stable than their $^6_4$ equivalent at 17_1. (Both spots correspond to soprano G within the E>E octave descent.) Spitzer's Mozart is far less orderly than mine. Whereas he would have him perpetrating severe disjunctions within the second phrase, I envision him as calculating just how innovative he may dare to be in *varying* the structure of the first phrase for presentation during the more elaborate second phrase.

What constitutes a musical line? The lines that shape my analysis differ considerably from those in Agawu's. I propose in **7.1c** and **7.1d** that prominent E>E octaves, filled in by step, shape I-space (closing on the tonic's 6-phase chord). That line transpires within three measures during the antecedent phrase. The continuity within the E>E octave of the consequent phrase is more of a challenge to perceive because the descent's pace is much slower, filling just under eleven measures.

What constitutes a tonicization? Several chords within P are candidates for interpretation as a local tonic: D minor (15_3), A minor (17_4), D major (35_3), G major (36_3), F major (38_1), and D♭ major (48_1). My analysis refrains from imposing any of these key shifts. Spitzer is more swayed by the lure of tonicization, even to the extent of imagining that the F major chord of measure 38 might have fulfilled a dominant function within B♭ Major. I instead propose that the innate tendencies

> of various chords can be enhanced through added dissonance and chromatic shifts (shifts that are chromatic within C, rather than diatonic in a related key). My terms "dominant emulation" and "surge," as well as the symbol ➙, convey how the attributes that propel a V harmony may be transferred to other scale degrees whenever a descending-fifth root succession is at hand.

The exposition's transition (TR, measures 57–85)

A reward for our careful study of Haydn keyboard expositions is the clarity and speed with which comparable structures in other works may come into focus. The transition within the Quintet's first movement is structured in the manner of one of the templates we developed in chapter 2. (Compare **2.13/2.14b** and **7.2a**.) In this case I-space extends well into TR, while II♯ serves as host for a reprise of the sort of cello/violin dialogue that characterized the movement's opening measures. As if to signal that the latter portion of TR is not designed to sustain an extended thematic presentation, that dialogue breaks apart in measure 77.

The tonic region that opens TR integrates harmonic and circular progressions. From 57_3 through 60_2 Mozart traverses $I^{8-7\flat}$ IV^{5-6} V I [**7.2b**], wherein the opening I-space is expanded through a foreground I^{5-6}–II–V♭–$I^{7\flat}$ progression, coordinating with a chromatic ascent from C to *Kopfton* E.[5] (This structure is similar to, though more sophisticated than, that which opens P.) That foreground *harmonic* progression contains a segment that is barely distinguishable from a *circular* progression (A D G C F).[6] In the next phrase Mozart gives free rein to this latter construction: whereas C A D G C F from 60_3 through 62_1 replicates the equivalent passage from the preceding progression, broadly filling in the C➙F fifth, the continuation clearly follows a circular course: after the initiating C➙F it proceeds through B, E, A, D, G, C, F♯, and B to E. (Only the initiating C and concluding E chords are displayed in the model of **7.2c**.) This turn of events affects the broader harmonic course: unlike the dominant-emulating I targeting IV of the previous phrase, the E major chord prepares the tonic's 6-phase chord, which leads to II♯ (at 66_{1-2}) rather than to IV. Though the succeeding chordal roots continue the fifth-relationships (after E: A D G C), the downbeat of measure 65 corresponds to the apex of the phrase (the arrival of *Kopfton* E in the upper register), followed by a shift in the melodic direction and rhythm. These markers justify a shift from a circular to a

Example 7.2 Analysis of Mozart: String Quintet in C Major (K. 515), mvmt. 1 (a) mm. 14–101; (b) mm. 57–60; (c) mm. 60–67.

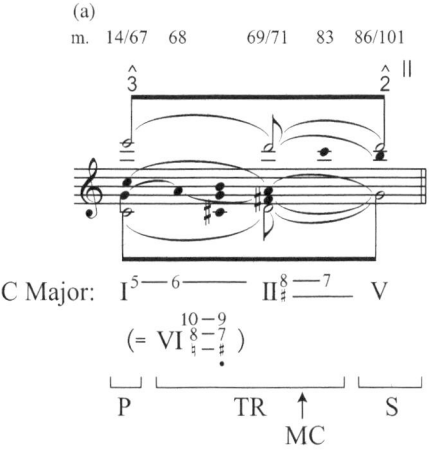
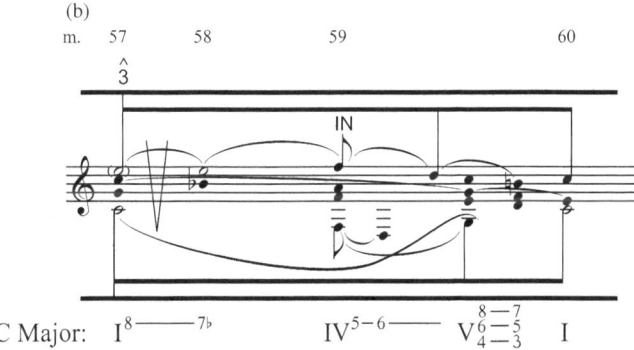
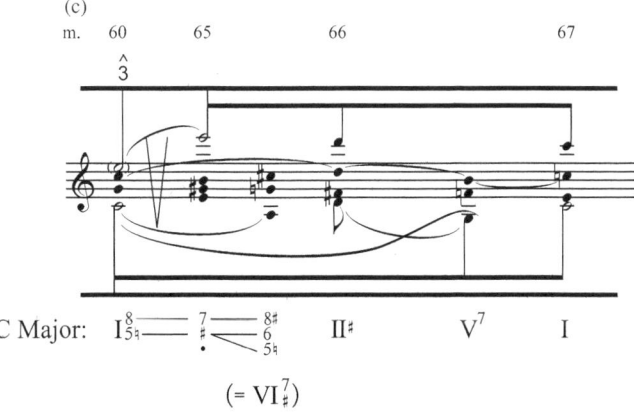

harmonic interpretation at that point, aligning the continuation with that of the preceding phrase. (Compare **7.2b** and **7.2c**.) This second phrase extends beyond the potential PAC moment (67_1) in order to carry out the essential duties of TR: the shift to the tonic's 6-phase chord and continuation to II♯ (as displayed in **7.2a**). The medial caesura occurs at 82_1, after which the first violin introduces the D chord's minor seventh and leads by step to the middle register.

That the two phrases graphed in **7.2b** and **7.2c** share significant content (in part content not graphed but denoted instead by hairpin symbols) is vital to the determination of where TR begins. That moment is 57_3, not 60_3. Though the first of the two phrases does not perform any of the tasks that distinguish TR from an extension of P, it introduces the structural framework that will do so during its varied and extended repetition.

My reading of P's melodic structure is dominated by two intervals: the ^E_C major third, traversed stepwise both ascending and descending; and the ^E_E octave, traversed stepwise descending. These intervals continue to play a vital role within TR's opening tonic region: ^E_C is traversed in both directions during the phrase of measures 57 through 60 (embellished by incomplete neighbor F at 59_1), while, in addition, an upward E<E extension occurs during the phrase that begins in measure 60. Take the time to map out the exact correlations between these events within P and TR: C<E from 4_4 through 14_4 is represented by the lines from 57_3 through 58_4 and from 60_3 through 61_4, whereas the E>E octaves from 14_4 through 17_4 and from 33_2 through 44_3 are complemented by the E<E line from 61_4 through 65_1; and so on. The first violin E at 58_4 is the endpoint of a tonic expansion, surging with dissonant $^E_{B\flat}$ leading into the ^F_A of IV (covered by A). Even with Mozart's legato slur (not to be confused with the structural slur employed in analysis) between 61_3 and 62_1, E is again the tonic's melodic anchor during TR's second phrase. The violin C at 64_1 is interior to the E<E octave traversal and consequently should not be given the weight of a goal, which falls instead on E at the following downbeat.[7] Whereas the descending E>E octaves during P coordinate with the succession from the tonic to its lower-third (6-phase) chord, A minor, the ascending E<E octave during TR coordinates with the succession from the tonic to its upper-third chord, E minor (at 65_{1-3}).

> Though he elects to analyze the transition in the context of the upcoming tonicized dominant key, G Major, rather than tonic C Major, Agawu's reading (within his example 4.1 on p. 92) matches the essence of my **7.2a**. My only urgent recommendation is that a D (which sounds in the first violin in measures 71 and 81–83) be placed at the top of his D major

chord. In his commentary Agawu proposes that the passage from 57_3 through 60_2 serves as "closing material" within P (pp. 81–82) and notes its similarity to the basic structure of the region that has preceded it. (Compare his examples 4.2 and 4.3.) As noted above, I coordinate the onset of TR with the initiation of the material that eventually will fulfill the vital role that TR plays within the exposition.

Agawu's treatment of the circle of fifths (see especially his example 4.4b on p. 96) seems to me insufficiently hierarchical (I suggest that I-space extends from 60_3 through 61_4, after which a circle of fifths transpires) and lacking in perspective regarding how this phrase expands upon the harmonically conceived preceding phrase. (That is, if the bass progression D G C in measures 59 and 60 is part of a harmonic progression, shouldn't D G C in measures 66 and 67 be also? Compare my **7.2b** and **7.2c**.)

Spitzer regards TR as extending from measure 21 through measure 85. The passage that is for me the focal point of TR – measures 67 through 69 – is minimally addressed in his commentary. A few words convey his interpretation: "the cadence at bars 59–60 expresses the confirmatory rhetoric of a codetta, a bluff which Mozart calls when the cadence is suddenly extended into a compressed harmonic sequence leading into the D major 'standing on the dominant'" (p. 204).[8] I suggest instead that the "harmonic sequence" has run its course before the tonic's reinstatement at 67_1, and that only after that point – during harmonic rather than sequential or circular activity – does the trajectory that leads into the D major supertonic transpire. For Spitzer the "most interesting point" is the dominant (my major supertonic) prolongation of measures 69 through 85, which he regards as the transition's "liquidation phrase" (p. 202), or even as "a 'meta-liquidation' of the opening sentence" (p. 204). Though he suitably correlates its $_{D>C\sharp}$ and $^{G>F\sharp}$ dyads with $_{C>B}$ and $^{F>E}$ in measures 4 through 19 and marvels at their stretto presentation beginning in measure 77, it is equally pertinent to note that the $^{G}_{C\sharp}$ diminished fifth has already played a prominent role within the movement: in measure 15, where it resolves directly to $^{F}_{D}$; and in measures 30 through 35, where the expected C♯<D resolution (against G>F♯) is elided, replaced by C♯>C♮.

The exposition's secondary-theme zone (S, measures 86–115)

Once the medial caesura concludes the vital business of TR, a four-measure extension (measures 82 through 85) both introduces the D chord's minor seventh C and features unfoldings of thirds that Mozart will develop further during S. Observe how a segment of the upper-strand descent, E>D>C>B from 85_2 through 86_1, recurs throughout the first phrase of S, now with E serving as a neighbor to D: from 87_2 through 88_1; from 89_2 through 90_1; from 91_1 through 92_1 (with upward register transfer and added chromaticism); and from 92_4 through 93_1 (with D suppressed and the B extending onwards to A).[9] (In **7.3a** some of the unfoldings are displayed as simultaneities.[10]) The inner-strand C>B>A>G is similarly deployed. Note that its concluding G does not occur in the first violin melody where expected (at 86_1), but instead is diverted to the upper register (during 86_3), foreshadowing the register transfer that will occur during measure 91. (An unfolding of B̲>G *does* occur in the upper register during 92_1.) These descending lines serve to prolong soprano D (= $\hat{2}$) via motion to the interior of the texture. A middleground harmonic progression (shown in **7.3a**) transpires during the latter part of the phrase in coordination with the stepwise descent from D, interrupted at A during this phrase.

At measure 94 the violin melody is transferred to the viola, against which Mozart juxtaposes a new melody in the violins. Whereas the antecedent phrase of S occupies a standard eight measures, the consequent is expanded to twenty-two. The region up to measure 101 corresponds more or less to that of the earlier phrase (as the measure numbers in **7.3a** indicate). Thereafter Mozart enlivens the progression using a marvelous descending-in-thirds strategy, summarized in **7.3b**. Though some might be tempted to interpret the passage from 101_1 through 106_3 as a free fall through tonal space, I discern sufficient markers (such as the reinforcement of some of the pitches in the upper register and the seams where the thirds transfer from the violins to the violas and from the violas to the second viola and cello) to warrant the perception of a straightforward harmonic progress, as **7.3b** displays. The dominant's trilled A signals the impending arrival of the PAC on G (corresponding to the EEC) at 115_1.

The major third $\genfrac{}{}{0pt}{}{B}{G}$ occurs in a wide range of contexts during measures 105 through 112, during which its pitches undergo a change of status from consonant to dissonant. At the outset $\genfrac{}{}{0pt}{}{B}{G}$ is a consonant component of the G Major tonic. Its stability is intact at 106_1, where E displaces the tonic's D during a descent in thirds to IV. The G and B do not budge even when C sounds in the bass. At this point B becomes a dissonant seventh. When C♯ sounds, the root transfers to A. Thus B becomes a dissonant ninth and G a dissonant seventh, both poised to resolve by descending step to the dominant's $\genfrac{}{}{0pt}{}{A}{F\sharp}$.[11] A cadential $^6_4$ intervenes, and then the pitches resolve one at a time: first B to A (at 113_1), and then G to F♯ (at 114_1).

Example 7.3 Analysis of Mozart: String Quintet in C Major (K. 515), mvmt. 1 (a) mm. 86–115; (b) mm. 101–115.

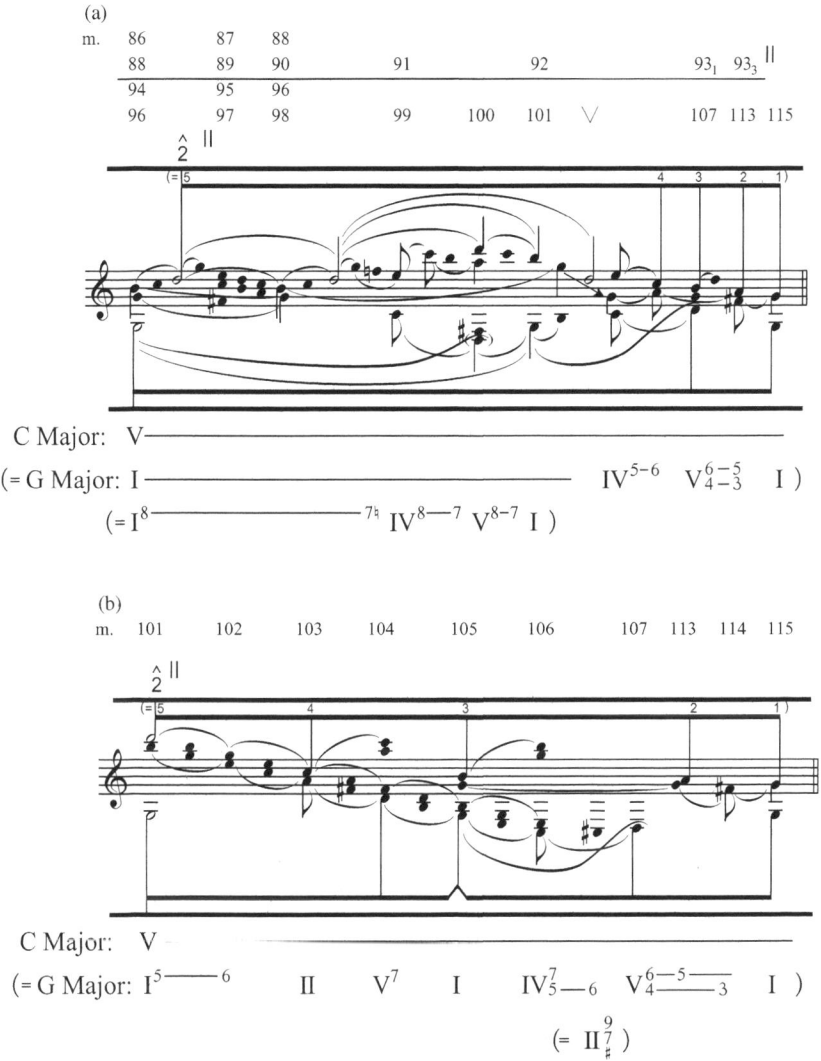

Agawu's example 4.1 offers a brief peek at his conception of the structure for S: B>A>G supported by I V I in the tonicized key of G Major. I instead subscribe to the notion that a pitch from the fundamental structure generally serves as the starting point for descending linear progressions during S. I suggest in **7.3a** and **7.3b** that D – not B – serves as the starting point for several descents. For example, within the first phrase a linear connection links D to the B of measures 88, 90, and 92, and through the B of measure 93 to A.

As does Agawu, Spitzer regards B as the starting point for a descent during S's antecedent phrase, though he and I agree that D performs that role in the consequent phrase. (Compare his examples 7.11a and 7.11b and my **7.3a**.) Whereas he shows a single C – labeled as a neighbor – in the treble clef during measure 91, I show two: the first a neighbor to B, the second a passing note from D. That passing role prevails again during 92_4, where the foundational descending line is interspersed with higher pitches: G>D̲ E>C̲ B<D̲ A. My perception of an essential similarity between the antecedent and consequent phrases until measure 101 allows me to use the same graph for measures $91-92_1$ and $99-101_1$. Spitzer does not concur: his graphs of those passages are strikingly different. On the other hand, our conceptions of measures 101 though 115 are similar. I suggest that his bass B>B connection of measures 105–106 should be replaced by B>C (here in accord with Mozart's legato slur).[12] From measure 101 to this point, the third and seventh eighth notes of each measure serve as lower neighbors. That precedent offers a strong incentive to interpret the B at 106_2 is a neighbor to the C that both precedes and follows it.[13] (Consult **7.3b** for my interpretation of the foundational structure.) I recommend also that soprano C in measures 108, 110, and 112 should be displayed as a passing note within the cadential $^6_4$'s (not I^6_4's!) ^D_B third – just as Mozart has slurred it – and not as a neighbor to B, as Spitzer proposes. This descending third is the retrograde of the ascending B̲<C<C♯<D third at 93_{1-2}, which also transpires during a cadential $^6_4$.

The exposition's closing zone (C, measures 115–151)

Listeners have encountered ascents to the third scale degree at several points during the exposition: C<D<E̲ heralds the *Kopfton*'s sounding at 14_4, at 33_2, at 58_4, and at 61_4. The closing zone's G<A<B̲ expanse from 115_4 through 118_1 will become C<D<E̲ during the recapitulation, where the content of C is presented transposed to the C Major tonic key. Consequently the arrival of B, the third scale degree in tonicized G Major, at 118_1 corresponds to some of the most significant arrival points within the exposition. (In this instance the ascent is covered by upper thirds B, C, and D, which double the bass ascent from the tonic's third to the dominant's root.) As **7.4** shows,

Mozart: String Quintet in C Major (K. 515), movement 1   195

Example 7.4 Analysis of Mozart: String Quintet in C Major (K. 515), mvmt. 1, mm. 115–143.

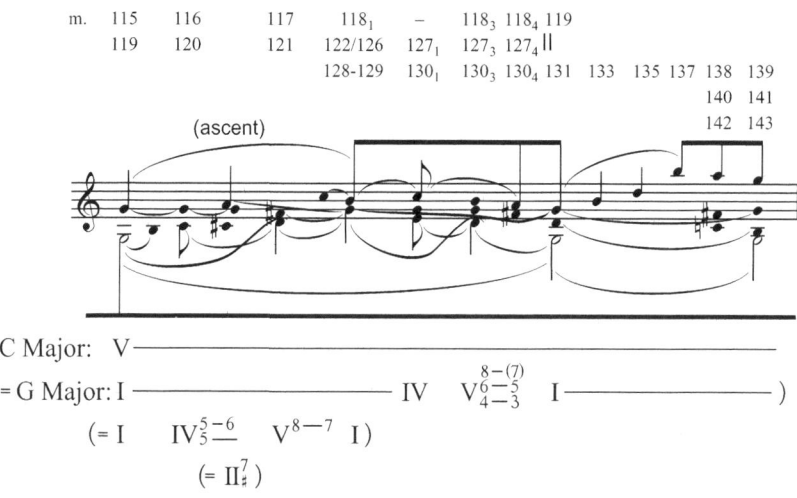

what goes up comes down: B is the starting point for the descending linear span B>A>G, thereby reinforcing the closure that was achieved during S. Though measure 131 could have served as the exposition's terminus, Mozart extends into the upper register: the high B>A>G third of measures 137 through 139 echoes that of the lower register. Repetitions of the A>G portion of that third keep the phrase alive for four additional measures.

The exposition concludes with retransitional material. Upward stepwise motion leads to G's minor seventh F♮, revoking the G Major tonicization and pointing towards the C tonic: C-E-G for the restatement of P or evolved 6-phase C♯-E-G-B♭ to set the development in motion.

> Agawu devotes a brief paragraph to C, commenting on its "surplus of closural signs" (p. 97). We agree that measure 131 is the principal moment of closure. His example 4.1 (p. 92) rewrites Mozart perhaps too freely: the G>F♮>E>D motion that he places just after the double bar actually belongs before it. Mozart's point is that this descent may continue another whole step to C, triggering the reiteration of the exposition, or instead a half step to C♯, inaugurating the development.
>
> Spitzer's example 7.11c contrasts my **7.4** by instead emphasizing a fifth-progression from D. My reading of the passage as ascending to and descending from B is based on the interplay with previous ascents to the third scale degree; the avoidance of parallel octaves with the bass; the unequivocal local B>A>G descent from 118_1 through 119_1; the upward

> transfer of B at 126₁; the maintenance of the upper-third notion with C<E (expanded into a tenth) during measure 127; and the echo B>A>G of measures 137 through 139. In our exploration of Haydn's sonata expositions in chapter 2, we encountered numerous cases in which the agenda of C contrasts that of S. The traversal of the $\frac{B}{G}$ third instead of the $\frac{D}{G}$ fifth helps to distinguish these two regions and prepares for the recapitulation's emphasis on $\frac{E}{C}$, the very interval that has been traversed by that point to shape the movement's fundamental line.

The development (measures 152–204)

Considered from a broad perspective the background $\hat{2}$ that arrives during the exposition's TR and the background V that arrives at the outset of S are prolonged through the end of the development. In the common dominant prolongation V $^{8-7-6-5}_{34-3}$ the $^6_4$ chord sometimes is unfurled into $^5_3$ position and may even assert itself as a tonic harmony. Yet given its context I resist regarding such a tonic as hierarchically deep – as, say, the equivalent of the tonic that will emerge at the onset of the recapitulation. The passage may instead serve as an internal *reiteration* of the path to the dominant. In this movement the principal roots from S through the end of the development are G (beginning at measure 86), C (elided at measure 152 and present during measures 182 through 184 and 191), D (192₄), and G (measures 193 through 204). Due to the D chord's quality and brevity I find the following analysis unconvincing:

```
m.              86         150      152     182      192         193
C Major:       V⁸₃———7———————6——    (                )  ⁻⁵₋₃
                                     4
(= G Major:    I⁸————————7♮         IV♮———♭     V⇨      I)
```

I instead endorse the following interpretation:

```
m.              86         150      152     182      192         193
C Major:       V⁸₃———7———————6——    (                )  ⁻⁵₋₃
                                     4
               (=                   I♮———♭     II⇨     V)
```

How Mozart launches the development is full of surprises. The arpeggiation in measures 152 through 155 is shaped as a modest reworking of the exposition's first four measures, which after all one has already heard as continuation after measure 151 (assuming that the performers follow Mozart's instruction to repeat the exposition). The disposition of C♯-E-G-B♭ within the score matches as closely as possible the original C-E-G-C, and one may attribute the added dissonance and chromaticism to Mozartean rambunctiousness: a passing over of the tonic 5-phase chord in favor of its more propulsive 6-phase, II-targeting extension (previously presented during measures 30 through 34, during the second phrase of the exposition's P). In measures 156 through 159 rambunctiousness gives way to deviousness. A magical property of the tonal system fosters some temporary ambiguity: this variant of the tonic's 6 phase (C♯-E-G-B♭, targeting II) is the enharmonic equivalent of one of its dominant-emulating extensions (E-G-B♭-D♭, targeting IV). Thus the unexpected F-B♭-D at measure 156, which one should assume will settle into F-A-C, compels a retroactive shift from one to the other interpretation of the preceding diminished seventh chord.[14] (Even during I→ IV, the diminished-seventh surge is often spelled as E-G-B♭-C♯ rather than E-G-B♭-D♭ when the D♭/C♯ is heading upwards to D, upper neighbor of the IV chord's fifth.) Further surprises are in store. The F-A-C resolution (measure 160) is elided: though A and C do fall into place as expected, that moment collides with the onset of F's evolved 6 phase: the bass ascends to F♯, while D sounds in the first violin line. It turns out that IV is not asserted as a harmony after all. As the passage continues it becomes apparent that a sequential progression – not a harmonic progression – is operative, with the C Major tonic's 6-phase A-C-E as its goal. A diatonic model and a chromaticized version corresponding to Mozart's score are juxtaposed in **7.5a**. Brackets denote the points where Mozart persists in his rambunctious upward striving, for example merging the stable F-A-C 5-phase moment with the propulsive F♯-A-C-D 6-phase surge. Though the initial soprano C is absent and though the chordal support contrasts that of measures 4 through 14, both the exposition and the development open with an ascent to E.

The arrival on A at 171_1 concludes the development's opening initiative, which Mozart marks by a switch from developing content from P to developing content from C. (Compare the cello line of measures 171 through 173 with the first violin line of measures 132 through 134.) Concurrently the tonal trajectory closely matches a region from S. The passage from 60_3 through 64_2 is organized as a tonic prolongation (underlined below) that leads seamlessly into a circular progression:[15]

<u>C   A   D   G   C</u>   F   B   E   A   D   G   C

Example 7.5 Analysis of Mozart: String Quintet in C Major (K. 515), mvmt. 1 (a) mm. 152–171; (b) mm. 152–193.

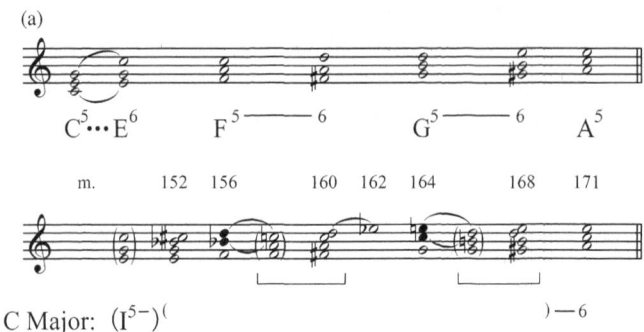

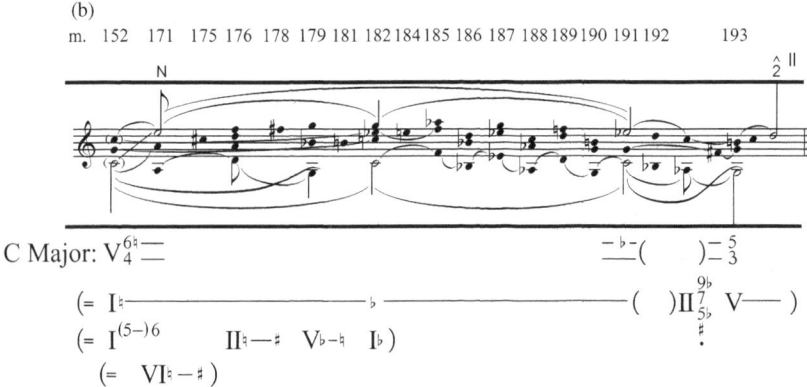

Though some of the chords contain chromatic elements, the progression of roots is limited to the diatonic pitches of C Major. Within the development Mozart follows a darker path. Not only do several of the chords waver between minor and dominant-emulating major quality, but the progression of roots also takes on a minor-mode character. As my analysis in **7.5b** reveals, Mozart now pursues the following trajectory:

C   A   D   G   C   F   B♭   E♭   A♭   D   G   C

This progression leads to a brief II⇛ at 192_4, announcing the V that is the goal of the development (restoring that of the exposition's S and C regions), as shown in **7.5b**.

The dominant's arrival coincides with yet another shift in the exposition content that is developed. Beginning in measure 193 the first violin presents material like that from the opening of S (measures 86ff.).[16] As in S, that content soon migrates to the violas, while the violins project (beginning at 197_4) the perky melody introduced at 94_4. A chordal progression like that of measures 90 through 92 (and 98 through 101) is traversed several times over a G pedal point, leading to the final borrowing from the exposition: the transitional stepwise ascent to F♮ that concludes C (measures 143 through 150). An astonishing stretto of three G<A<B<C<D<E<F♮ ascents occurs during measures 201 through 204: one in the cello, another in the second violin, and a third in the first viola (in part echoed by the second viola). The connection between measure 204 and measure 205 (the onset of the recapitulation) recalls that between measure 151 and measure 1 (the repeat of the exposition) and decisively corrects the aberrant connection between measure 151 and measure 152 (the onset of the development).

> Agawu and I are in agreement regarding the opening region of the development, through measure 171. His example 4.1 shows (at the right edge of its upper staff) a voice-leading model similar to that which I present in **7.5a**. We likewise both propose that the goal chord (A minor in measure 171) should proceed to a chord with root D. Yet at that point our perspectives begin to diverge: whereas the next chord in his reduction is the augmented sixth of 192_4 (whose root is D), I proceed instead from A (transformed into A➔ at measure 175) to the D chord of measure 176, as shown in **7.5b**.
>
> I am not sure how to integrate Agawu's example 4.4c (showing measures 184 through 190|191) into the space between the A minor and D⇛ chords displayed as adjacencies in his example 4.1. It appears that he is proposing an expansion of a C chord via a circular progression. My conception (**7.5b**) offers a suitable context for such an expansion. Since the progression works its way through all the roots within the diatonic C Minor circle, I am baffled by Agawu's commentary: "The circle of fifths also serves a prolongational purpose in the course of the development, where four contiguous fifths from B♭ to G (measures 184–90) lead to the retransition to the home key in measure 205" (p. 95). Why begin on B♭? Why end on G? Why is the model's concluding root C (measure 191) placed within parentheses?

The recapitulation (measures 205–368)

The exposition is built from two principal linear descents: P's E>D>C (in C Major) and S's D>C>B>A>G (in the tonicized dominant key, G Major). The stepwise relationship between *Kopfton* E ($\hat{3}$) and the dominant fifth D ($\hat{2}$) is the foundational melodic continuity within the exposition (as displayed in **7.2a**) and is replicated within the development (**7.5b**). The recapitulation also presents two linear descents, though their interrelationship contrasts that of the exposition. The prior establishment of $\hat{2}$ and the proximity to the movement's termination warrant the acceptance of $\hat{1}$, the endpoint of the recapitulation's linear descents, as a background event. The transposition of S from the tonicized dominant key to the tonic key prevents a recurrence of the previous E>D continuity while establishing a new continuity between the endpoints of the two linear descents: E>D>C (measures 217 through 242) and G>F>E>D>C (measures 273 through 305). This redundancy of closure on $\hat{1}$ makes amends for the prominent focus on the dominant in the latter parts of both the exposition and the development. Mozart underscores the tonic focus of the recapitulation through a considerable expansion of content within the C section, to be discussed below.

The recapitulation presentation of P (measures 205 through 242) is altered principally in that the binary (antecedent/consequent) construction of the exposition is abbreviated to a single phrase. Measures 205 through 213 reprise the exposition's opening nine measures, but measure 214 picks up the thread with content resembling measure 30, the tenth measure of P's *second* phrase. Consequently the exposition P's tinge of C Minor (measures 21 through 24) is bypassed. The phrase continues without incident until the passage dominated by the A♭-C-E♭-F♯ chord (compare measures 48ff. and 232ff.), which is more fully developed the second time around. Mozart explores various potential continuations from this chord. The three potentialities that are in play during the exposition (only one of which is fully realized) are presented in **7.6a**, along with a fourth possibility that Mozart introduces during the recapitulation. In addition to the familiar enharmonic shift from A♭-C-E♭-G♭ (which would resolve to D♭, as shown in Model 1) to A♭-C-E♭-F♯ (which would resolve to G, shown in Model 3), he demonstrates how A♭ may function as the upper minor third of root F (Model 2) and how G♯ may function as the upper major third of E (Model 4).[17] Despite those tantalizing alternatives, ultimately it is Model 3 (which is displayed in its broader context in **7.1d**) that moves the progression forward to the cadence.

Mozart: String Quintet in C Major (K. 515), movement 1

Example 7.6 Analysis of Mozart: String Quintet in C Major (K. 515), mvmt. 1 (a) mm. 49–236 (*passim*); (b) mm. 323–353; (c) mm. 308–353.

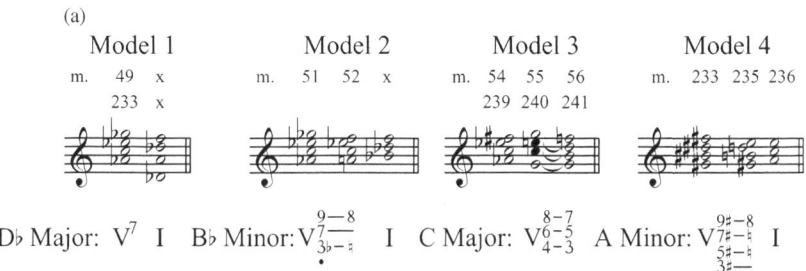

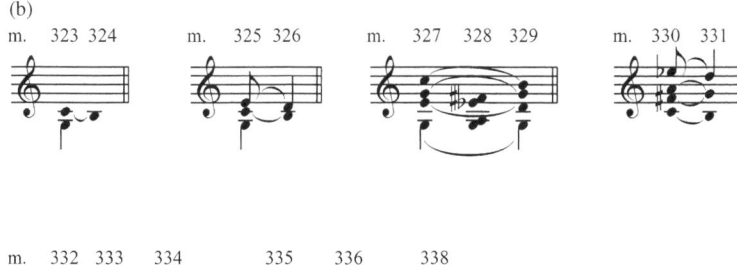

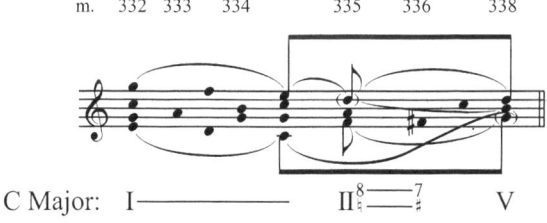

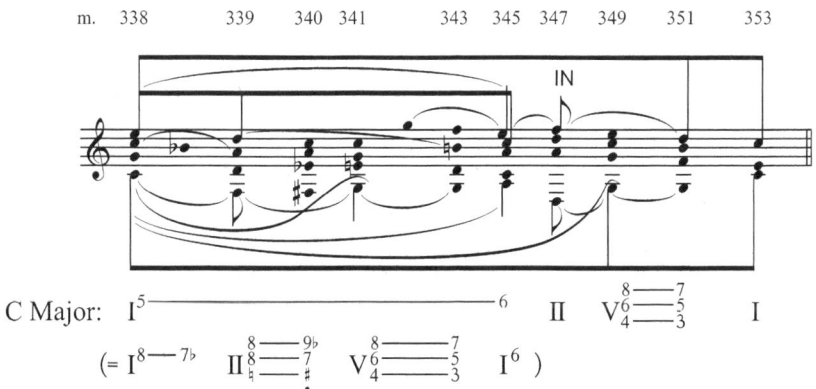

Example 7.6 (cont.)

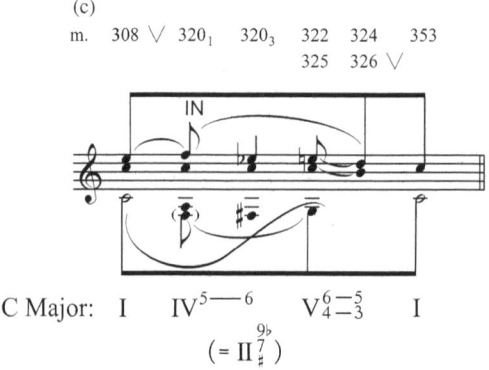

Because S will be presented in the tonic key, the recapitulation's TR requires an overhaul. The basic strategy remains the same: a phrase that resides within the realm of the tonic occurs first (242_3 through 245_2), followed by an expanded restatement that veers off in a new direction. In this case that expansion leads not to a return of C (as at 67_1), which inaugurated a I^{5-6}–II→ progression targeting the V of the exposition's S, but instead a fifth lower to F (at 253_1), which inaugurates a IV^{5-6}–V→ progression targeting the I of the recapitulation's S. Whereas the circular progression of 60_3 through 65_1 leads up a third from C to E followed by a descending third back to C, during the recapitulation an ascending 5–6 sequence (C→F D→G E→A), resembling that which opens the development (**7.5a**), leads downwards a third from C (at 245_3) to A (at 251_1), followed again by a descending third, now to F.[18]

The modifications within the recapitulation version of S are modest (besides the obligatory transposition) and for the most part are motivated by registral concerns. For example, the cello line of measures 92 and 93 spans an ascending fifth (G<D), whereas that of 279 and 280 instead descends a fourth (C>G). The ascent accommodates a stepwise filling-in in the bass (G<A<B<C<D), whereas the descent focuses on the essential notes of the I–IV$^{(5)-6}$–V progression (C>F<G). Mozart allows himself a freer treatment of the first violin melody against this bass, omitting the incomplete neighbor to E. (The essence of the melody in measures 92 and 93 is B>C>A; the equivalent in measures 279 and 280 would be E<F>D, though F sounds only in the bass.) An extension of the path to the cadence occurs near the end of S. Mozart resists the tendency of the cadential $^6_4$ to descend

Mozart: String Quintet in C Major (K. 515), movement 1

into the $\frac{5}{3}$. During the exposition version of S that resolution is achieved in measures 113 and 114 (the fifth arriving before the third), whereas during the recapitulation a flourish to the upper octave and back adds three measures to the musical fabric, with the $\frac{5}{3}$ falling into place during measures 303 and 304.

A more substantial extension occurs during C. The content of the exposition's measures 130 and 131 serves as the foundation for measures 320 through 353 during the recapitulation. Mozart employs a standard cadenza start with bass F♯ (a member of II→) at 320_3. A hush of primordial silence precedes the introduction of the germinal dominant root G. Over the next thirty measures Mozart expands gradually from the tiniest embryo[19] to a full-bodied progression, employing not only one of the closing motives from the exposition but also, beginning at 341_4, a motive from S. (The various stages are displayed in **7.6b**.) Though the broad context, shown in **7.6c**,[20] would lead listeners to interpret the G-C-(E) chord as an embellishment of the G-B-D dominant, eventually G-C-E is unfurled so that C resides in the bass, and in my view this C asserts itself as a root (as displayed in the fifth and sixth stages presented in **7.6b**). I interpret this as an internal reiteration similar to the one encountered during the development, as follows:

m.	305–308 V	320	322 V	332	—	335	—	338	
				338	345	347	349	351	353
C Major: I		IV$^{5-6}$	V$^{6-}_{4-}$	(				$^{-5}_{-3}$	I
			(=	I$^{5\text{———}6}$		II	V$^6_4$———$^{-5}_{-3}$)		
Example: 7.6c———————————————————————————————————									
				7.6b ———————					

Even those who reject this interpretation likely will agree that a PAC occurs at 353_1. The remainder of the movement follows the course of the exposition's close, minus the concluding transitional passage. The final utterances of the movement are projections of the tonic harmony, supporting an echo of the E>C third that was traversed over the course of the entire movement.

Agawu and I share similar conceptions of the recapitulation's P and TR. His notion that S pursues the descending third B>A>G during the exposition seemingly pays dividends during the recapitulation, where the transposition to C Major results in E>D>C, a local manifestation of the descent from the *Kopfton*. Even if my assertion that G – not E – is the principal soprano pitch during measure 273 is not accepted, I find the G>F>E>D>C descent of measures 288 through 305 to be unequivocal. I take that C (within S) as the ESC, not the C of measure 353 (within C), as Agawu proposes in his example 4.1.

8 | Mozart: *Don Giovanni* (K. 527), Act I, Scene 13: Donna Anna's recitative and aria

in response to Carl Schachter

Throughout the span of my development as an analyst these past forty years, Carl Schachter has stood as a superlative – perhaps *the* superlative – Schenkerian. I have gained much from his presentations, articles, and textbooks. Though publicly I have praised his work,[1] behind the scenes I have occasionally registered some complaints.[2] In this chapter, devoted to Donna Anna's recitative and aria from Act I of *Don Giovanni*,[3] I attempt to sort out my relationship with Schachter's perspective, as represented by his analysis of this scene. Somewhat to my surprise, my views have evolved in such a way that I find myself in disagreement with him on numerous points. Schachter's participation in a *Journal of Music Theory* analysis forum early in his career involved standing side by side with others who worked from starkly different premises.[4] The forum that I offer here involves standing side by side with someone who shares similar premises. Some of our disagreements stem from my extensions into post-Schenkerian domains, whereas others reflect my more orthodox application of Schenkerian principles.

Structural overview of the recitative (measures 1–70)

A modest two-measure transition leads from the B♭ Major of the preceding quartet and recitative to a new recitative in the closely related key of C Minor. Listeners may well expect that this recitative will proceed in its broad trajectory from tonic C to dominant G major, so that a cadence on C (perhaps shifting to C Major) may coincide with the onset of an aria. A possible realization of such a recitative structure appears as **8.1**. The measure numbers accompanying the graph assert that every chord used in forming this model appears within the score, though some (starting at measure 62) are hoisted up a step. This scene falls within a small class of compositions in which the tonal center shifts permanently during the interior of the movement.[5] As will be explained below, the A minor supertonic chord (measure 49) within C Minor's tonicized dominant

Example 8.1 Analysis of Mozart: *Don Giovanni* (K. 527), Act I, Scene 13, mm. 3–70.

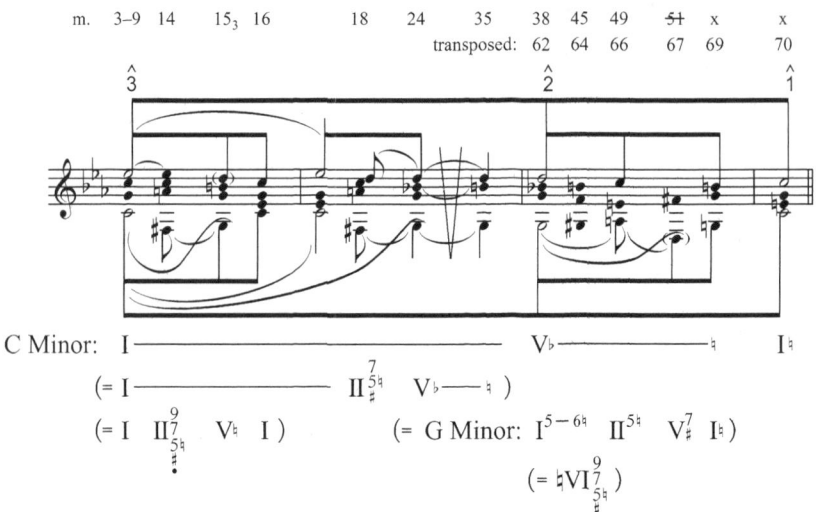

key, G Minor, ultimately overthrows G and takes over its role as dominant. Consequently the aria that is launched at measure 70 is not in C Major, as we might have predicted as early as measure 3, but instead in C's usurper, D Major.[6] This is not a conventional modulation from one key into another. Instead a seismic shift has occurred.[7] The spot on the graph labeled m. 62 lurches upwards a whole step and to the right to the position labeled m. 49. Imagine new open noteheads A♮ and E♮ displacing the filled-in noteheads at that spot. Root A is now charged with fulfilling the tonal duty that had been invested in G. Consequently the recitative will cadence in D Major.

The graph for the recitative is divided into four segments. Note that this structure bears a strong resemblance to a conventional sonata form: the first segment establishes the tonic key (as does any P section); the second segment leads to a medial caesura on the dominant (like a TR ending in a I:HC MC); the third segment tonicizes the dominant key, ending with a conversion from minor to major (features that in a minor-key sonata movement might be fulfilled by S followed by the development); and finally the fourth segment presents the tonic resolution (as occurs during a recapitulation). In this plan Donna Anna's aria would extend the resolution key, confirming tonal space already established during the recitative. As explained above, in Mozart's realization of this plan the normative C G→ C structure (the beamed open noteheads of the graph's bass) becomes C G→/A→ D.

In Schachter's perspective C Minor serves as a link connecting hierarchically deeper B♭ Major and D Major regions. He presents three graphs (examples 9.4a, 9.4b, and 9.5A) that propose a double utilization of "the 5–6–5 contrapuntal progression," first quickly from B♭ Major to C Minor, then slowly from C Minor to D Major. He notes with some concern that C Minor and D Major are not closely related (p. 222). My perspective is subtly different. I propose that Mozart projects the intent to juxtapose two closely related keys in successive scenes: B♭ Major and C Minor, reserving the right to execute the commonplace shift of mode from C Minor to C Major later. Consequently the process by which D Major instead emerges as the aria's tonal center seems to me highly idiosyncratic – a case of unexpectedly jumping off the scripted path in the middle of a progression, rather than a blithe sailing along to the intended goal via the reliable 5–6–5 device.

The recitative's opening C Minor tonic region (measures 3–16)

Dissonant $\genfrac{}{}{0pt}{}{F}{B\natural}$ during the two-measure transition into C Minor (measures 1 and 2) focuses the ear on the melodic resolution, *Kopfton* E♭, which is covered by the violin G (here given the potent dissonant embellishment of appoggiatura F♯) later in measure 3.[8] This E♭ and its tonic support are prolonged through measure 9. (See **8.1.**) Whereas E♭ extends into measure 15, its support shifts to the supertonic: at first F♯-A♭-C-E♭ (II⇒); then, after a passing chord in measures 12 and 13, F♯-A♮-C-E♭ (II→). In contrast to Mozart's practice later in the recitative, here I and II⇒ occur in direct succession, without an intervening tonic 6-phase chord. Yet the version of II⇒ that Mozart employs is a special case in this regard: the tonic's 6-phase C-E♭-A♭ is fully incorporated within the pitch content of II⇒, which consequently might be regarded as the merger (or "collision") of these roles. The V♮ of 15_{3-4} (with cadential $^6_4$ embellishment) leads to the tonic resolution at 16_1, completing the tonic-establishment phase of the recitative. This PAC marks the moment in the dialogue between Donna Anna and Don Ottavio in which her central point (and indeed a central point of the opera) has been uttered: the claim that it was Don Giovanni who attempted to rape her and who murdered her father.

The downbeat of measure 3 offers multiple E♭s to resolve the F of the preceding measure's diminished fifth, *before* F♯<G sounds in the first

violin. Either E♭ or G might be regarded as the more fundamental pitch. Indeed, for reasons that will be broached later the higher pitch is more fundamental in the context of the G Minor presentation of this content in measure 38. In its initial statement, however, E♭ emerges as the *Kopfton*, with G serving as its upper third.[9] Schachter instead regards the G both as the *Kopfton* and as the starting point for a fifth-progression descending to the tonic C of measure 16.[10] The choice of G results in both an awkward situation during the A Minor tonicization (note how background G apparently extends through the A Minor region in Schachter's example 9.4) and in a curious lack of deep structure during measures 16 through 24. A more orthodox view of the structure would be that the E♭ of the opening tonic region is reinvigorated by the E♭ at 16_3 (note my slur in **8.1**), proceeding to D over bass F♯ in measure 18. Any lingering doubts regarding whether E♭ or G serves as the *Kopfton* should be resolved by the reinstatement of E♭ *rather than* G during this TR-functioning passage. In choosing E♭ as the *Kopfton*, I propose that at the critical juncture of measure 70 the end of the recitative's broad descending third-progression to C (as graphed in **8.1**) would coincide with a reinstatement of the *Kopfton* for the aria. That initiative is modified in two ways: first, a conventional shift from C Minor to C Major would result in the transformation of the reinstated *Kopfton* into E♮; second, the extraordinary whole-step seismic shift during the latter portion of the recitative would result in the replacement of E♮ by F♯. The sum of these modifications is an augmented second, from E♭ to F♯. Whereas I propose that F♯ is *a highly modified reinstatement of* E♭, Schachter proposes that F♯ is *the voice-leading successor of* G. My E♭-to-F♯ transformation is adumbrated by the juxtaposition of E♭ and F♯ during measure 3. Whereas that F♯ dissonates against what we assume will be the governing tonic, ultimately it is the tonic that pulls itself upwards to accommodate the F♯.

In the opening chapter of *Schubert* I focused on the supertonic to conduct a much-needed overhaul of symbols for harmonic analysis. My point was that analysts impede comprehension by employing a wide range of incommensurable symbols and nicknames for chords that perform the same function. I proposed that a Roman numeral should reflect a harmonically asserted chord's root and that any modifications may be noted via Arabic numbers and accidentals placed beside the Roman numeral. During this recitative Mozart employs a wide range of supertonic chords. It is important to understand that they *all* perform the same function, and thus they all should be labeled as II. In my view, both F♯-A♭-C-E♭ and F♯-A♮-C-E♭ are built from root D. (This notion extends back to the eighteenth century, as documented in *TAH*.) I propose two alternative means of acknowledging such chordal evolutions: either by providing a complete listing of all modifications and additions beyond the diatonic triad (those for the versions of II that occur in measures 14, 18, and 49 are displayed in **8.1**), or by use of an arrow: → for a dominant-emulating chord, such as F♯-A♮-C-E♭; ⇒ for a chord containing an augmented sixth.[11] Schachter instead employs ♯IV for the chords of measures 10 through 15. Consequently his analysis does not reveal the continuity with the other supertonic chords within the recitative. (I will assess his non-II labels for the chords of measures 18 and 49 later.)

The recitative's transitional region (measures 16–37)

An important formal arrival point occurs at measure 38, where Mozart renews the content and tempo of the opening tonic region, transposed to the dominant key. This formal relationship resembles that which occurs in many sonata expositions. (Especially towards the end of the eighteenth century, P and S might present similar thematic content.) Preceding the onset of this "S" region, a transitional progression (I II♯ V) occurs, culminating in what Hepokoski and Darcy call a I:HC MC, a half cadence in the tonic key serving as a medial caesura. (See **8.1**.) Note that the recitative's deep structural $\hat{2}$ arrives *after* the transition, as is also the case in the context of a V:HC MC, explored in chapter 2.

This transition incorporates an extraordinary extension of the G dominant, dividing the octave into three equal segments. The chordal spellings for this conception include the awkward juxtaposition of E♭ and F♯:

m. 24   25   28   31   33   35
    G   B♭→ E♭   F♯→ B   D→   G

Mozart chooses E♭–F♯ as the place to "take the hit" (converting G♭ into its enharmonic equivalent, F♯) so as not to conclude on a chord notated as A♭♭-C♭-E♭♭ (rather than as G-B♮-D). Coincidentally the augmented second from E♭ to F♯ plays important roles elsewhere within this scene, as noted above. I propose that during an "obstinate" (as opposed to diatonic) circular progression the composer has exited the uneven terrain of modulo 7 diatonic tonality and entered a uniform modulo 12 realm. Because the notation that Mozart employs was designed to accommodate music that favors seven diatonic pitch classes, seemingly inexplicable enharmonic shifts are inevitable. If instead a music notation that makes no distinctions among the twelve pitch classes (for example, the numbers from 0 through 11) had been employed, this circular progression would transpire seamlessly:

$$7 \quad 10\rightarrow \quad 3 \quad 6\rightarrow \quad 11 \quad 2\rightarrow \quad 7$$

I suggest that the best way to make sense of such progressions is to shift conceptually from modulo 7 into modulo 12 tonal space and back. Fortunately here the modulo 12 passage begins and ends on the same chord (G, converted from minor to major quality).[12]

The two parts of this transitional region correspond to Donna Anna relating to Don Ottavio why she suspects Don Giovanni to be the perpetrator (supported by the I–II♯–V progression) followed by the first phase of her recounting what occurred in her bedroom (supported by the obstinate, dominant-prolonging circular progression, certainly a novel and potent mechanism for conveying in music the wrenching experience that she had endured). The medial caesura at 37_4 coincides with her recollecting that she shouted for help (which might also have induced a caesura in Don Giovanni's advances towards her). This is a fitting moment for the inauguration of a new formal section: without the call for help the crime, though serious, would have been limited to attempted rape. (Donna Anna ultimately succeeded in freeing herself on her own.) Her shouting triggers a new element – her father's arrival as she is chasing the fleeing Giovanni – that leads to the capital crime of murder. (The scuffle is depicted at the outset of the opera.)

> Whereas Schachter interprets earlier chords containing the pitch F♯ as ♯IV in the key of C Minor, the F♯ at 18_3 triggers a modulation to G Minor. I think it is important to retain an awareness of the broader context. Whereas in Schachter's analysis the G–B♭–D chords in both measure 24 and measure 38 are labeled only as I in G Minor, I regard them as statements of V in C Minor, at two distinct structural levels (as shown in **8.1**). Though the latter V is also interpretable as I in tonicized G Minor (as shown in the graph), its deeper structural role is that of V, which Schachter omits.[13]
>
> I agree with Schachter that the circular progression is "a remarkable portrayal of Anna's confusion and disorientation" (p. 226).
>
> A small error in Schachter's example 9.3 (namely, the measure number 38 should be placed above soprano C♯ at the beginning of the second

> system) affects the interpretation displayed in example 9.2, where it appears that the prolonged G chord shifts from minor to major and then *back to minor* quality before the new thematic initiative begins in measure 38. The attack on G-B♭-D at measure 38 attains greater potency because it cancels the shift to major (expressing that Donna Anna's hopeful call for help has not yet been answered).[14] The extraneous flat in Schachter's graph distorts the tonal relationship between the transition and the onset of the G Minor region.[15]

The recitative's G Minor region and tonal reorientation (measures 38–69)

Because the transitional region so strongly sets up the soprano pitch D, I accept the D of measure 38 as the successor of the *Kopfton* E♭ in the recitative's descending fundamental line. This analytical decision requires a contrasting interpretation of measures 3 (where the fifth G is the upper third of E♭) and 38 (where the fifth D is structurally deep).[16] The two contexts are, in fact, different. D is carefully prepared by what precedes it (note especially the first violin D during 37_2), and its usurper, E, is the starting point for an E>D>C♯ third in measures 62 through 69. (Keep in mind that **8.1** displays the structure as it would have transpired *without* the seismic shift described above. Beginning at measure 62, the score transposes this structure upwards by a whole step.)

Recall that a C Minor tonic chord is presented in both measures 3 and 9. Multiple neighboring notes (in the manner of but with greater dissonant intensity than the situation presented in **1.2b**, Model 1) come between these two statements of the tonic. The progression then proceeds directly to II⇒, without an intervening tonic 6-phase chord. Mozart modifies this plan during the G Minor tonicization, where the tonic chord of measure 38 is restored not in its original 5 phase, but instead as E♮-G-B♮, a chromatic variant of its 6 phase, in measure 44. The choice of E♮ (rather than diatonic E♭) relates not only to the upcoming supertonic A♮ (rather than "Neapolitan" A♭), but also to the means by which G's 5- and 6-phase chords are connected. The minor third between roots G and E♮ invites an enharmonic shift during the neighboring chord. Whereas F♯-A♮-C-E♭ would restore the G chord, its reinterpretation as D♯-F♯-A♮-C leads instead to the 6-phase E♮ chord. (Though Mozart employs the spelling D♯ from 40_1 onwards, initially D♯ will seem to function as E♭, like the A♭s in C Minor during measures 6 through 8. The emergence of root B♮ at 42_3 confirms the transformation of E♭ to D♯.) This 6-phase chord takes on a dominant-emulating character at 45_1, resolving to $II^{5♮}$ at 49_1. (The diatonic II in G Minor cannot be preceded by a dominant-emulating chord, because it is of diminished quality. The minor II borrowed from G Major is here employed as a substitute, a common occurrence in a minor key.) Despite the contrasting means of accomplishment, both the C Minor and the G Minor regions begin with the tonal trajectory from the tonic to the supertonic. We should expect that after $II^{5♮}$ at 49_1 a continuation to V♯ and I will transpire. Indeed, the downward motion in the lower strings during measures 49 and 50 seems to be heading to G Minor's dominant root, D.

The D♯ at 51_1 shatters the listener's expectations and induces a wondrous shift in the tonal trajectory, transforming the remainder of the scene. Whereas the expected A>D succession during measures 49 through 51 would have corresponded to $II^{5♮}$ V♯ in G Minor, the D♯ (as third of a B^9→ chord with absent root) that emerges instead helps shape a I–II→V♯–... progression in A Minor. Because the progression from the tonic through the supertonic to the dominant has been such an important key-defining feature within the recitative, A embarks upon the same prolongational rite that was in progress for G. This extraordinary shift in the tonal plan coincides with an extraordinary moment in the narrative: Donna Anna's success in escaping the hold of her oppressor. That uplifting outcome is conveyed via an upward whole-step jolt in the tonal plane: the broad tonal trajectory that we expected would lead from C Minor's dominant G back to tonic C for the aria proceeds instead from the elevated dominant A to tonic D.

Before that happens at measure 70, the A Minor tonicization continues. The I–II→V♯–... progression discussed above resolves to I^6 at 52_1. (The emergence of A Minor's diatonic 6-phase chord here is reminiscent of the arrival of G Minor's modified 6-phase chord at 44_1.) Whereas I^{5-6} often leads to II, here an alternative use of the 6-phase chord is called upon: I^{5-6-5}. A sequential ascent from 52_1 through 62_1 connects the 6-phase and restored 5-phase chords.[17] A Minor still awaits a harmonic confirmation, which is provided by the progression of measures 62 through 69. A's 5- and 6-phase chords (bass A at 62_1 and A♯ at 64_3) are connected by a local harmonic progression similar to the one connecting the same-functioning chords of 49_1 and 52_1. Yet note a significant alteration: whereas the 6-phase chord in measure 52 is rooted on diatonic F, that in measure 64 is rooted on F♯. The latter leads to $II^{5♮}$ at 66_3 and V♯ at 67_3. This tonicizing progression's close on A at 69_4 incorporates D Major's leading tone, C♯: as A's role as a local tonic ends, its broader role as dominant in the uplifted home key of D Major is made manifest. The cadential D of the recitative's fundamental line (at 70_1) interlocks with the arrival of the aria's *Kopfton* F♯ as the scene's next section begins.

In his example 9.3, Schachter clearly displays the connection between the G minor and E minor chords in measures 38 through 44, along with the intervening enharmonic shift. Yet he does not interpret the G>E<A motion through measure 49 as a segment of a conventional harmonic progression. The A minor chord is for him I in tonicized A Minor from the outset, whereas for me that chord at first registers as $II^{5♮}$ in tonicized G Minor (as shown in **8.1**).

Whereas Schachter and I agree that A Minor is prolonged from measure 49 through measure 62 (note the dotted slurs in his graph and the absence of internal content from those measures in his example 9.4b), we perceive contrasting internal organizations. For Schachter the dominant at 51_4 is the deepest event between the A tonics, whereas for me A Minor's 6-phase F-A-C chord at 52_1, which I regard as a substitute for the 5-phase A-C-E, is. Schachter's graph is not entirely convincing as a projection of the hierarchy he proposes. Whereas his long slur from root E to root A is consistent with the slur from V to I among his Roman numerals, the slur above the upper line's C>(B)>A third in measures 51 and 52 not only makes the "deep" dominant's fifth B (shown within parentheses) appear as a local passing note, but also outlines an $\genfrac{}{}{0pt}{}{C}{A}$ third that would seem to support my reading of I^6 (or (VI) in Schachter's notation) as hierarchically deeper than the V that precedes it.

Whereas Schachter proposes A<B>G♮<A as the foundation for the bass in measures 62 through 69 and begins analyzing in the key of D Major in measure 66, I regard the passage as the projection of a conventional harmonic progression in A Minor, as shown in **8.1** (transposed). Our principal disagreement centers on the role of bass G♮ in measure 68. Though I agree that this pitch functions as a lower neighbor (Schachter's "LN" notation), I regard it not as a whole-step neighbor to A, but instead as an F𝄪, leading tone G♯'s chromatic lower neighbor, in disguise. The V♯ in my local progression arrives near the end of measure 67. If G♯-B-E serves as the dominant, then F𝄪-A♯-C♯-E (Mozart not only spells F𝄪 as G♮, but also A♯ as B♭) is an embellishing chord that, using Schachter's terminology, might be called a "common-tone diminished seventh" chord.[18] Mozart further complicates matters in two ways: first, the embellishing chord does not arrive all at once, but in phases, with the

F𝄪 [G♮] first and the other pitches later; and second, the restored dominant has evolved, so that instead of hearing G♯-B-E at 69_1, we hear the more propulsive G♯-B-D-F♮. Consequently two diminished-seventh sonorities sound in succession. In my view the first one is an embellishment of the second one. Schachter instead interprets the leading tone G♯ as a passing note between the G♮ and A. (See the slur in his example 9.4b.)

The aria's A_1 section (measures 70–86)

Mozart deploys two stanzas of text in shaping the aria's ternary structure. The A_1 section presents the first stanza, in which Donna Anna calls for vengeance. In D Major throughout, the section ends in a PAC. The contrasting B section presents the second stanza, in which Donna Anna reminds Don Ottavio that it is her father's murder that makes vengeance mandatory. A shift to D Minor occurs early in this section, which closes in a half cadence. In the A_2 section both the D Major tonality and the first stanza of text are restored. (Some structural and textual complications within A_2 will be addressed below.) A coda, beginning in measure 125, follows A_2's PAC. The aria projects a complete and normative form, restoring order after the extraordinary recitative that has preceded it. Measure 70 is concurrently the endpoint of the recitative's seismic structure and the initiation point of the aria's orthodox structure.

Though these two structures are independent, they both begin by establishing $\hat{3}$ as the *Kopfton* on their respective opening downbeats (3_1 and 70_1). Whereas G promptly covers the recitative's E♭ (via E♭<F♯<G), the upper third is attained more gradually during the aria (as F♯<G<A during measures 70 through 75). A similar third, in the minor-key form F♮<G<A, will grace the aria's B section as well. (See **8.2**.)

The harmonic path from I to V within the A_1 section utilizes IV^{5-6} as connector, with IV's 6-phase chord taking on dominant-emulating (II→) characteristics. Because an upper third emanates from *Kopfton* F♯, the incomplete neighbor G that comes between the tonic's F♯ and the dominant's E has an upper-third association as well (the oboe B>A>G in measures 76 and 77). From G the line passes through F♯ to E for the section's internal half cadence.[19] The dominant – with minor seventh – is extended for four measures. Mozart repeatedly unfolds its dissonant $\frac{G}{C\sharp}$ diminished fifth, followed by the tonic restoration (emphasizing the resolution third, $\frac{F\sharp}{D}$)

Example 8.2 Analysis of Mozart: *Don Giovanni* (K. 527), Act I, Scene 13, mm. 70–125.

in measure 84.[20] The cadence comes at 86_1, at the close of a local I–II–V^7–I progression. Overall, measures 70 through 86 are conventionally shaped as an interruption structure, as shown in **8.2**.

> Schachter and I are to a large extent in agreement regarding the path from the tonic to the dominant in measures 70 through 79. (See his example 9.7.) I am especially pleased that he uses the IV$^{5-6}$ notation. My addition of the Roman numeral II within parentheses and Arabic numbers and accidentals to show how this II evolves is simply a more detailed analysis, not a contradiction of Schachter's reading. However, I am concerned about how Schachter and most other analysts use Arabic numbers. Note that at measure 75 a 6 appears below the graph's music notation. This 6 (like those at measures 84 and 85) indicates inversion. That of measure 77 does *not* indicate inversion, but instead charts a voice-leading process. I find it inherently confusing to use the same symbol in such contrasting ways, and thus make a clear distinction in my analyses between Arabic numbers that chart linear relationships (which appear in the same row as the Roman numerals) and those that indicate an inversion (which I seldom use, but when I do I place them in a separate row above that of the Roman numerals).
>
> Schachter and I do disagree on one point: the melodic path during the approach to the dominant. We both acknowledge a G>E third in measures 77 and 78. (He displays G>F♯>E melodically, whereas I display $\smash{\genfrac{}{}{0pt}{}{G}{E}}$ as a simultaneity.) He interprets that third as the first half of a descending diminished fifth formed with C♯ at 79_3; I instead regard it as the first of three unfolded thirds (the latter two being Donna Anna's F♯>D and E>C♯) whose upper strand (G>F♯>E) leads to $\hat{2}$ for an interruption at the half cadence.[21]
>
> Consistent with my reading of an interruption, one would expect that $\hat{4}$ (as neighbor to the restored $\hat{3}$ that will emerge in coordination with the return of the tonic) will participate in a dominant prolongation.[22] Peaking Donna Anna's melodic line and the bass melody in alternation during measures 80 through 83, dissonant G extends and intensifies the dominant's tension. Schachter instead reads the passage as a tonic expansion. The chief means of prolonging a harmony in music is to fill in its intervals. Two of V^7's intervals are so treated here: $\underline{E}$<F♯<G and E>D>C♯. Donna Anna's F♯ at 80_1 is a connector between her E of 79_2 and G of 80_2. Due to its metrical positioning, this F♯ functions as an *accented* passing note. Her D at 81_1 similarly connects the E of 80_4 and an imagined C♯ at 81_2. (The $\underline{E}$>D>C♯ third is stated without imaginative

filling-in by the violas, who are joined by the first violins in measure 83.) Her A (in the lower octave at 81_2 and upper octave starting at 83_1) represents a separate strand that equally supports the dominant and the tonic (as is apparent in its extension into measure 84). The lower strings form a canon with Donna Anna's line, so that ascending and descending passing notes (F♯ and D) meet on the downbeats of measures 81 through 83. Had Mozart intended a tonic restoration at this point, certainly he would not have slurred the strings' ascending sevenths (filled-in A<G) the way he did. Schachter's analytical F♯<G slurs, unflagged and flagged stems, and open and closed noteheads give a prominence to the F♯ that the score takes pains to prevent. I propose that the tonic resolution occurs instead in measure 84, where a $\smash{{}^{F\sharp}_{D}}X\smash{{}^{D}_{F\sharp}}$ voice exchange aptly resolves the $\smash{{}^{G}_{C\sharp}}$ diminished fifths that have pervaded both the upper and lower registers during the preceding dominant expansion.

The aria's B section (measures 86|87–100)

The shift to the minor mode and the text's new focus on the bloody murder give rise to the perception of a contrasting B section. Just as the half cadence (supporting middleground $\hat{2}$) within the A_1 section serves as a division point (interruption), resolving during the conclusion of the section, the half cadence that ends the B section (supporting background $\hat{2}$ in measures 98 and 100) creates a deep division point, at the level of the aria as a whole. An entire section (A_2) is required to resolve that interruption.

Mozart achieves a sense of continuity among contrasting passages through the means by which he shifts from D Major to D Minor. Recall that in the recitative the embellishing chord B♮-D-F-A♭ comes between two statements of the opening C Minor tonic. At the outset of the G Minor dominant region, the embellishing chord F♯-A-C-E♭ is reinterpreted as D♯-F♯-A-C, leading to a chromatic variant of G's 6-phase chord in measure 44. We encounter the same embellishing chord a third time and with a third outcome in measure 87 (now in the context of D Major). Preceded by D-F♯-A, C♯-E-G-B♭ here resolves to the minor-hued D-F♮-A.

In a minor key the tonic often is extended via its upper-third chord. Mozart employs a descending circle of fifths (D G C♮ F♮) in measures 90 through 95 to achieve this goal. Observe in **8.2** how that progression supports the upper-third extension from the minor-mutated *Kopfton*: F♮<G<A. (The voice-leading operation of reaching-over is employed twice, resulting in G above

E and A above F♮.) Though usually a composer will lead from the third scale degree in the bass upwards to the fourth and then fifth scale degrees, here Mozart instead leads downwards two thirds in quick succession to B♭ for D Minor's diatonic 6-phase chord, which here serves in its customary role as a link between I and II⇛.[23] As mentioned above, during the opening progression within the recitative Mozart proceeded from I to II⇛ without incorporating an intervening tonic 6-phase chord. Now, in the aria's B section, that more developed course is realized. Among the various instances of passing notes filling in chordal intervals during this scene, perhaps the most interesting is the chromatic F♮<F♯<G<G♯ that transpires in the viola line during measure 97, connecting the II⇛ chord's minor ninth, F♮, and raised third (tenth), G♯. Composers often are hesitant to write parallel fifths during the resolution of a II⇛ chord.[24] The F♮ in measure 97 resolves to E indirectly, via a pair of unfoldings: F>D in the vocal line answered by C♯<E in the first violin line. The vocal F♮ in measure 99 is similarly resolved, though an octave lower, in the viola line, with resolution in register delayed until 100_4 (oboe).

> Among the differences between Schachter's and my readings of the B section, our interpretations of soprano F♮ in measure 90 and bass B♭ in measure 97 are the most critical. Regarding the former, I correlate the deep structure of the B section with the *Kopfton* much earlier than Schachter does. The parallelism of the A_1 section's initiating F♯<G<A and the B section's F♮<G<A motives is strong evidence that the F♮ of measure 90 is more than an interior divider within an ascending fifth-arpeggiation.[25] Regarding the latter, I interpret what Schachter labels as ♯IV instead as II⇛. This leads me to expect I^{5-6} as its predecessor, with the tonic's 6-phase chord deployed in its normative role. (Mozart's writing in measures 116 through 118, to be discussed below, offers further confirmation of this reading.) That 6-phase chord is not acknowledged in Schachter's graph. Whereas his symbol ♯IV$^6_{(5)}$ is positioned below both bass B♭s, I display a shift from B♭-D-F♮ to B♭-D-F♮-G♯ (from I^6 to II⇛) below my bass B♭ (which corresponds to both measures 97 and 99: I see no reason to favor the latter, as Schachter does, since Donna Anna's F♮ is as vital a presence at 97_3 as it is at 99_2).

The aria's A_2 section and coda (measures 100|101–140)

In life, one often repeats oneself when one has something urgent to say. Under Mozart's guiding hand, Donna Anna jumps back to content from the

B section at the very moment we expect A$_2$'s PAC (at 116$_1$). Clearly she is intent on pressing her case to Don Ottavio. The intricate structural situation here is better described in words than represented in a graph. (Consequently **8.2** is much abbreviated in this region.)

Measure 115 corresponds to measure 85. We are on the verge of the PAC that would conclude the A$_2$ section and lead directly into the coda. Instead Mozart inaugurates a brief reminiscence of the B section, both in text and structural content. Through an elision (omitting both the cadential measure and the first ten measures of B), he jumps directly to the tonic's 6-phase chord in measure 116. Instead of measure 97's B♭-D-F♮ (diatonic in D *Minor*, the key of the B section), he employs D *Major*'s 6-phase chord B-D-F♯. Given that he has been in D Major throughout the A$_2$ section, this is a logical alteration. Whereas B♭-D-F♮ led to II⇒ and then V♯ in D Minor (as shown in **8.2**, measures 97 and 98), B-D-F♯ leads to II➔ and then V in D Major (measures 116 through 118). In both contexts the supertonic-to-dominant succession is repeated. (Because a different variant and inversion of the supertonic is employed – one that does not present the danger of parallel fifths – Mozart does not shy away from a direct F♮>E descent in the melodic line.) Mozart's abbreviation of the structure here supports my analytical decision during the earlier B section to regard I$^{5-6}$ II⇒ V♯ as the essence of the progression.

This abbreviated reminiscence of B is followed by an abbreviated restatement of A, in which the initial tonic-to-dominant progression is elided. The dominant that closes the B reminiscence assumes the role of the dominant at the A interruption (that is, measure 118 = measure 79 or 109). The remainder of A$_2$ follows the model of the final measures of A$_1$ (measures 79|80 through 86). The PAC occurs at 125$_1$, followed by a coda rich in local I$^{5-6}$–II–V^7–I progressions.

One final point: we noted how in the C Minor recitative B♮-D-F-A♭ serves both as an embellishing chord expanding the C-E♭-G tonic and as the venue for an enharmonic shift (to G♯-B♮-D-F) that resolves to a chromatic variant of the tonic 6-phase chord. In the D Major aria C♯-E-G-B♭ similarly functions as an embellishing chord expanding the D-F♯-A tonic and also during the conversion from D-F♯-A to D-F♮-A. Mozart adds one more context to this list in measures 116 and 117, where C♯-E-G-B♭ occurs in its enharmonic guise as A♯-C♯-E-G, embellishing the 6-phase B-D-F♯ chord.

> Because my notion of the supertonic is more inclusive than is Schachter's, I perceive similarities among progressions that do not register as such from his perspective. As noted above, I regard the B section's harmonic progression to consist of four segments: the tonic

(with shift from major to minor quality and an upper-third extension), the tonic's 6-phase chord, the supertonic, and the dominant. I distinguish between what occurs at the beginning of measure 97 (the tonic's 6-phase chord) and at its end (the evolved supertonic chord). Schachter's neglect of the former is problematic. In his analysis of the A_2 section (his example 9.7), the opposite omission prevails: the tonic's 6-phase chord is emphasized, but the supertonic chord that it prepares (where Schachter provides the outer-voice pitches G♯ and F♮ of 117_4) is left unanalyzed. Whereas the chord on A♯ is a local embellishment of B, that on G♯ plays an important role within the broader harmonic progression. In my view, the long line connecting Schachter's VI and V numerals should end a bit sooner, leaving room to acknowledge the II➔ that leads to V. The chord that Schachter labels as VI concludes a I^{5-6} expansion of I-space, whereas my II➔ is the intermediary between I-space and V-space.

9 | Mozart: Symphony No. 40 in G Minor (K. 550), movement 3, Trio

in response to Leonard B. Meyer

Seldom have so few notes generated so many words of commentary as in Leonard B. Meyer's sixty-seven-page analysis of the forty-two-measure Trio from Mozart's Symphony No. 40 in G Minor.[1] His article was published in the summer of 1976, a significant moment in my personal musical development: it was then that I transferred my principal focus from music performance to music theory.[2] For me Meyer's style of harmonic analysis exudes a nostalgic familiarity: it corresponds to the methodology of Walter Piston,[3] through which I first explored the topic during my undergraduate years. Back in 1976 I did not imagine that eventually I would be so critical of my elders, so intent upon exposing the faults of the literalist approach to harmonic analysis and upon developing an imaginative alternative.

The A_1 section's first phrase

I-space extends through much of the Trio's opening phrase: *Kopfton* $\hat{3}$, supported by the tonic root G, is stated at the first downbeat and extends through measure 4, at the end of which the tonic's 6-phase chord leads the way to a II^7–V–I cadence, supporting a middleground third-progression in the melody [**9.1**]. Mozart's deployment of upper-third extensions (D above B at 1_2, E above neighbor C at 3_2) should not be confused with the establishment of $\hat{5}$ as the *Kopfton*.[4] His reduction of the melody for performance by the first horn in measures 26|27 through 32 emphasizes the deeper structural notes. At that level another type of embellishment is clarified: incomplete upper neighbors conclude measures 1, 3, and 5 (and 27, 29, and 31). The $\genfrac{}{}{0pt}{}{C}{A}$ third at 1_3 plays a purely embellishing role, though (as we shall see below) in the context of measure 25 it will contribute to the assertion of II.

The first violin's A at 2_1 is a note that one would expect to lead downwards to G, within a traversal of the tonic's $\underline{B}$>G third. Because dissonant seventh C reaches over it at 3_1, the A's downward continuation is relegated

Example 9.1 Analysis of Mozart: Symphony in G Minor (K. 550), mvmt. 3, Trio, mm. 1–6.

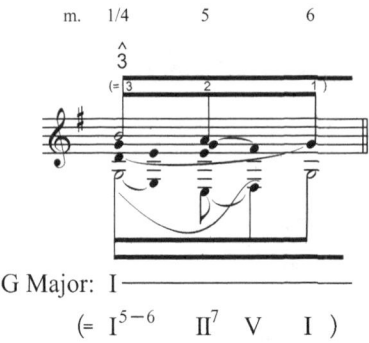

to the second violin line. Supported by root D, which is understood to prevail throughout measures 2 and 3, the pitches F♯, A, and C strive for a tonic restoration, within a projection of I-space that extends through the Trio's first four measures.

Assessing how larger intervals break up into smaller units is an important and not necessarily straightforward aspect of interpretation. Whereas the first violin melody's first three pitches may superficially represent the arpeggiation of the tonic triad, their context suggests that the performer should project the ascent of a third (to *Kopfton* B), followed by an upper-third extension.[5] (The horn line in measure 27, discussed above, reinforces this interpretation.) The B – not the D – should make the deepest impression upon the listener. Clearly performers do something beyond what the music notation explicitly indicates (all notes of equal duration, uniform dynamic level, and legato connection) in order to create this effect. Whereas one may effortlessly learn from the score where the downbeats fall and take that information into account when shaping the phrase, one must contemplate the music more carefully to know which pitches participate in the projection of the structural framework (for example, the pitches that are represented in **9.1**) and which others do not. Consequently pitches such as D at 1_2 and B during 5_3 should come across as embellishments. As another example, note that the downbeat first violin notes of measures 3 through 6 traverse the descending fourth from C to G. Through analysis one may come to understand that this fourth is not a meaningful interval. The C, as a dissonant upper neighbor, resolves to the restored *Kopfton* B, which is then extended via a third-progression.[6]

Not only do Meyer's Roman numerals (displayed in his example 1, pp. 696–697) cling closer to the musical surface than do mine (displayed in **9.1**); they also lack any sense of hierarchical differentiation. For me there is a considerable difference between how D-F♯-A(-C) functions in measures 2–3 and in measure 5, to the extent that I am reluctant even to use the V numeral in the former case.[7] My presentation of how harmony shapes this phrase is accomplished using four Roman numerals, whereas Meyer requires ten. This difference stems in part from the built-in redundancy of the system that he employs. When a harmonic function is projected by two consecutive chords in different inversions, an inevitable stutter occurs: for example, ii ii in measure 5, the first with and the second without an indication of chordal inversion.[8] In addition, from my perspective his I vi ii is a motion from I to II via the tonic's unfurled 6-phase chord. In this instance the pitch E does *not* assert itself as a root.

An important premise of a hierarchical analytical perspective is that through careful score study a performer may decide upon and project a specific set of relationships among pitches, thereby eliminating other potential sets of relationships. For example, I propose that in this phrase the restoration of the tonic harmony and *Kopfton* $\hat{3}$ at 4_{1-2} extends I-space into measure 4. If this is the case, then the internal $V^{(7)}$ of measures 2 and 3 cannot be extended through to the V of 5_3. Consequently I have difficulty coming to terms with the multiple perspectives that coexist within Meyer's example 5 and the related commentary on pages 702 through 704. I applaud the connection of B>A>G in his graph 4, which matches the perspective that I display in **9.1**. Yet I am bewildered by the concurrent presentation, in his graphs 1 and 2, of a connection between the A of measure 2 and the A of measure 5, which requires that the B of measure 4 be interpreted as a "fill" of the "gap" between C and A. In my view these perspectives, which Meyer regards as "complementary and converging," are mutually exclusive. If I in measure 4 resolves the V of measures 2 and 3, then the A *must* resolve to a member of the tonic chord. It is not available for prolongation into the next V.

The A_1 section's second phrase and extension

The dominants of measures 5 and 14 perform similar roles, though at different structural levels and employing contrasting projection by the

Example 9.2 Analysis of Mozart: Symphony in G Minor (K. 550), mvmt. 3, Trio, mm. 1–14.

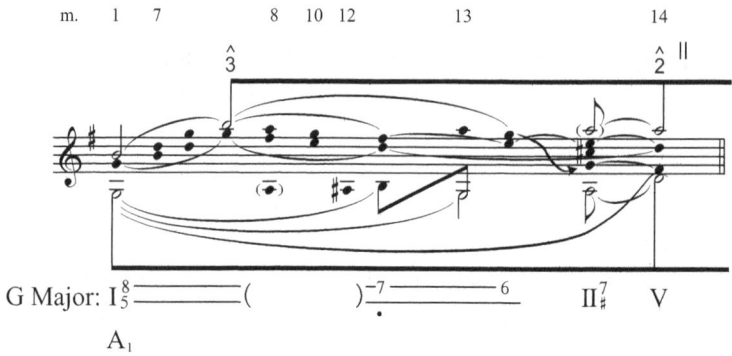

orchestra. That of measure 5 participates in a G–D–G sacred triangle (to borrow Schenker's term) within the G Major tonic prolongation of the opening phrase, while that of measure 14 plays the same role within the tonic prolongation of the entire Trio, utilizing the expanded range that emerges during the second phrase. Only the latter V is tonicized. (The cadential progression during the second phrase's extension in measures 14 through 18 is a somewhat simplified dominant-key equivalent of that presented in the tonic key during the first phrase.) Mozart attains the second dominant with greater vigor: whereas A-C-E-G suitably projects II^7 in measure 5, dominant-emulating A-C♯-E-G (II$^7_\sharp$) performs that role in measure 13. Compare these contexts in **9.1** and **9.2**, noting that both supertonic chords are preceded by the tonic's diatonic 6-phase chord.

The chief difference between these two contexts is the broader expansion of the tonic between its 5- and 6-phase chords in the latter. Though the A major chord that emerges in measures 8 through 11 could have served as the herald of the goal dominant, it instead resides within a linear connection (via contrary motion) between the tonic and its upper-third chord, which offers local consonant support for the passing note F♯. (Observe in **9.2** that the tonic's 6-phase E is attained via an 8–7–6 motion: G>F♯>E.) In both phrases a D (at 1_2 and at 10_1) emerges above the principal melodic strand. Another notable feature of this phrase is the temporary neglect of the upper register. The downward cascade during measures 13 and 14 is brought to order only through the reemergence of the strings, with the first violin's A (at 14^2) corresponding to background $\hat{2}$, the successor to *Kopfton* B. The expanded range (*Kopfton* B stated in the middle register during measures 1, 4, and 7 and in the upper register during measure 8) is acknowledged during the second phrase's extension, where

Example 9.3 Analysis of Mozart: Symphony in G Minor (K. 550), mvmt. 3, Trio, mm. 14–26.

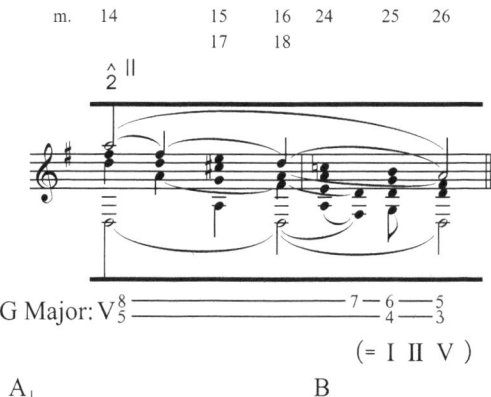

the first violins present A>F♯>E>D in both registers (measures 14 through 18).[9] The structure of this extension and its continuation within the Trio's B section are displayed in **9.3**.

> Meyer's harmonic analysis of the second phrase, presented in his example 1, is vastly different from mine [**9.2**]. In my view the dominant arrival (D major) occurs during measure 14, just before the onset of the extension. In Meyer's view the dominant arrives during measure 8, after which it is prolonged via an internal "deceptive cadence" (measure 12) preceding the "complete cadence" of measures 13 and 14. (See his commentary on p. 714.) Note, however, that A emerges as the bass – performed by the flute – at 8_3. (I place A within parentheses in **9.2** because I imagine its impact beginning two beats earlier, at 8_1.) I propose that in its context A-D-F♯-A does not assert itself as a D major dominant harmony (or as the tonic in tonicized D Major). It instead serves as a $^6_4$ embellishment of the A major chord that emerges in measure 10. Though this chord could have been asserted as "the" II♯ that leads to the phrase's goal dominant (or, from Meyer's perspective, V leading to I in tonicized D Major), the bass/root A here instead participates in a chromatic line that extends over six measures: G<A<A♯<B. (These pitch classes are sounded by various instruments and in various registers between 6_2 and 12_2.) Once goal B is attained, the line quickly reverts to its origin (B>A>G from 12_2 to 13_{1-2}), coinciding with the emergence of the tonic's 6-phase chord, from which a normative path to the dominant ensues. In my reading this phrase develops organically as an evolved repetition of the I^{5-6}–II^7–V progression of measures 1 through 5. In

Meyer's reading the phrase abruptly introduces the tonicized dominant, without even the herald of a dominant-emulating chord on A.

Both Meyer and I are cognizant of downward motions that pervade this phrase and continue during the remainder of the Trio. My perspective is more hierarchical than his: despite the woodwind arrival on D at 14_1, my ear is drawn to the A that emerges above it (when the first violin line resumes) as successor to *Kopfton* B. Viewing both **9.2** and **9.3**, observe how the upward B<B octave during the opening tonic prolongation is answered by a downward A>A octave that extends from 14_2 through 26_2 (to be discussed below). Meyer's most detailed analysis appears in his example 22, graphs 1a and 1c (pp. 726–727). Though almost all the pitches he displays in those graphs are accounted for also in my graphs (including **9.4** for the closing measures), his assemblage forms a more or less one-dimensional descending tenth, whereas I propose a conventional interruption structure – $\hat{3}$ $\hat{2}$ ‖ ($\hat{3}$ $\hat{2}$) $\hat{1}$ – that migrates between the middle and upper registers. From my perspective the least viable of Meyer's assertions is that the A of measure 26 extends through to the A of measure 41. I instead perceive the potent reemergence of the tonic harmony and *Kopfton* $\hat{3}$ beginning at 27_1.[10]

The B section

If one were to remove 18_3 through 26_2 from the Trio, a coherent *binary* structure would emerge, emanating from the foundational

$\hat{3}$ $\hat{2}$ ‖   ($\hat{3}$ $\hat{2}$) $\hat{1}$
I   V   I─────────────
                (= I   V   I)
A_1 A_2

interruption scheme. The inclusion of those measures transforms the Trio into a *ternary* form (what many analysts, including Meyer, instead call rounded binary), in which the B section extends the dominant that is established in the concluding measures of A_1. Two types of prolongation confirm the initial tonic during A_1: first, a melodic descent from $\hat{3}$ to the tonic root, as shown in **9.1**; and second, an ascending registral shift, as shown in **9.2**. The prolongation of the dominant during the latter portion of A_1 corresponds to the first of these strategies: a descent from $\hat{2}$ to the dominant root, as shown in **9.3**, measures 14 through 18. Only during the

B section is the second of the tonic's prolongational strategies replicated: the completion of an A>A registral shift spanning measures 14 through 26, complementing the ascending B<B span of the opening tonic prolongation. (Compare **9.2** and **9.3**.)

Given that the portion of the dominant prolongation that occurs during the latter part of A_1 supports the connection of $\underline{A}$>F♯>D, the B section may be devoted to the concluding fourth of that octave: D>$\underline{A}$. (In its realization this fourth is reinforced at the upper octave by the flute.) We have observed how Mozart filled in that fourth during a dominant prolongation in the parallel key of G Minor in "Tiger! wetze nur die Klauen" from *Zaide* [**3.8**, measures 91 and 92].[11] An important aspect of that prolongation is the support of $\hat{3}$ (B♭ or B♮) by means of a $^6_4$ chord that connects statements of the dominant without serving as the dominant's resolution. The principal analysis in **9.3** conforms to that notion. (The $^6_4$ is unfurled into $^5_3$ position.) However, I propose that at the foreground level the Trio's pitches G, B, and D do assert themselves as the tonic, in a subdued reminiscence of the Trio's opening. It is important that the dominant, prolonged since measure 14, not give way to the background tonic until the onset of A_2 at 26_3. Consequently I intend my example's parenthetical I II V in measures 25 and 26 (an expansion of measures 1 and 2) as a reiteration of the approach to the dominant, rather than as the dominant's resolution followed by the presentation of a "new" dominant.

Finally, keeping in mind that any harmony may be prolonged via motion to its upper-fifth chord and back, note that the connection of V^{8-7} in measures 18 through 24 incorporates an A minor chord at 24_{1-2}. In a common voice-leading strategy, the pitches A and E provide consonant support for the melody's C before it assumes its role as dissonant seventh upon the restoration of the dominant root, D. (I interpret the oboes' B and D at 24_3 as upper neighbors to chord members A and C. An $^C_{F♯}$ diminished fifth, though not literally sounded, is understood to prevail at 24_3.) Mozart connects the initial D dominant and its upper-fifth chord using a segment of the chromaticized ascending 5–6 sequence: $\overline{D^5/F♯^6}$ G^5 $G♯^6$ A^5 during measures 19 through 24. (Observe how the bass line ascends chromatically from F♯ to A on the downbeats of measures 19, 21, 23, and 24, followed by a restoration of F♯ at 24_3.[12] The G-B-D chord in measure 21 does not assert itself as a harmony.) Note also that the structural C of the broad descending fourth occurs in measure 24, not measure 19. Just as upper thirds occur in measures 1 and 3, so also the A<B<C ascent in measures 20 through 24 (forming parallel tenths with the bass) is enhanced by upper thirds: C down to A, D down to B, and E down to C, each filled in by step. The ^C_A

third spanned by this sequential initiative is a member both of the A chord at 24_{1-2} and of the D^7 chord at 24_3. (As mentioned above, the B and D at 24_3 displace chord members A and C.)

> Though Meyer and I interpret the span from A down to D in different ways during A_1, our D>C>B>A fourths during the B section converge. (Compare Meyer's example 22, graph 1a, and my **9.3**.) Yet his Roman-numeral analysis (in the same example) reflects a notion that I reject: namely, that all the chordal activity within the B section is derived from harmonic thinking.[13] As noted above, I instead interpret a large portion of the B section as a sequential progression, whose interior G-B-D chord (measures 21 and 22) consequently serves neither as I in G nor as IV in D. (Meyer proposes both of those harmonic interpretations.) Though normally a D<A connection via ascending 5–6 sequence would engage a total of nine chords, here Mozart takes advantage of the fact that the first (D^5) and sixth ($F\sharp^6$) elements of the sequence utilize the same pitch classes, thereby permitting a short-cut version of the ascent, engaging only four chords. Whereas Meyer regards the soprano C at 19_3 as a "provisional" statement of the deep C that will emerge during measure 24, I instead regard it as a local voice-leading phenomenon, enhancing the dominant-emulating character that pervades the 6-phase chords within the sequence. In addition, Meyer's willingness to entertain the possibility that a C<D<E ascent in the flute line during measures 19 through 23 continues with F♯<G in measure 36 (as proposed in his example 27, graph 3a, on p. 739) seems misguided to me. At 24_3 a hierarchically deeper D displaces the E. Consequently E is not available to serve as the basis for a continuing ascent through F♯ to G.[14]
>
> Also troubling are the parentheses that Meyer places around the V numeral at 24_3, corresponding to bass F♯. (See his example 22.) I interpret this F♯ as a reinstatement of the F♯ from 19_1, thereby establishing a continuity within the dominant prolongation that began in measure 14. Whereas I surmise that Meyer's concern relates to the chord's occurrence on a weak beat, I assert that it serves as the culmination of a broad prolongation of the dominant via an excursion to its upper-fifth chord and back. Consequently its structural weight far exceeds what its brevity and metrical position might imply.[15] Meyer's parentheses reinforce, rather than counteract, such implications, which I think need to be countered in this case.

Mozart: Symphony No. 40 in G Minor (K. 550), movement 3, Trio

Example 9.4 Analysis of Mozart: Symphony in G Minor (K. 550), mvmt. 3, Trio, mm. 27–42.

The A₂ section

Whereas the A_1 section is responsible both for establishing the key of G Major and for securing the dominant key, D Major, the A_2 section remains in G Major throughout. Nevertheless its sixteen measures are a suitable complement to the eighteen-measure A_1. Because there is less to accomplish, Mozart is careful not to dole out too much too quickly. The first phrase (26_3 through 32_2) is not as highly developed harmonically as was that which opened the A_1 section. Mozart reserves the tonic 6-phase chord and the supertonic from that opening phrase for the A_2 section's second phrase, which also incorporates features from A_1's second phrase while remaining squarely in the tonic key. The tonic 6-phase chord arrives (at 36_2) in a location comparable with that formerly occupied by the tonic's upper-third chord (at 12_2). (Compare **9.2** and **9.4**.) In that this chord is a fourth higher than that of A_1, the continuation confirms the tonic key rather than the dominant. Because of their location late within the movement, after the prolongation of background $\hat{2}$ during the A_1 and B sections, the B>A>G melodic lines within A_2 hook up with the background structure at their endpoints (G) rather than, as in A_1, at their initiation points (B). During this process the register again shifts an octave upwards (indicated by arrows in **9.4**). The cadence of measure 38, projecting the upper-register G as melodic goal, offers an opportunity for a final register transfer, this time a descending G>G arpeggiation. Note that the first violin D at 38_2, the equivalent of the A at 14_2 (which there articulates the arrival of background $\hat{2}$), is subsumed within this descending octave. Despite the seeming competition between lower and upper registers throughout the Trio, the ending amounts to a truce: the D>B>G portion of the octave descent sounds in both registers (in the first violin and flute lines) during the final measures.

I have proposed above that among the Trio melody's first five pitches (G<B<D>C>A), B and A form the deepest link, with C serving as B's incomplete upper neighbor. The D plays a subordinate role. Mozart provides further opportunities to observe the interactions among the pitches B, D, and C, allowing us to deepen our understanding of his construct. At 25_3 the D is placed in an explicitly dissonant context. Its resolution to C restores stability. In measure 27 the first horn does not mimic the B<D ascent, thereby confirming the preeminence of B. Finally, yet another dissonant context for D emerges at 34_1. Though the horns here mimic the sort of ascent that was presented by the oboes during 6_3 through 8_1, in this latter instance the entry of the bassoons makes even more imperative the descent of a second from the line's apex: here D to C. (Though the D is consonant, it works along with B, which clashes with the emerging D–F♯–A arpeggiation in the bassoon lines. Thus D's "resolution" is to the dissonant chordal seventh, C.)

Meyer's assessment of the harmonic progression within A_2, presented in his example 1, is straightforward. Though his symbols differ to some extent from mine, and though they convey less of the hierarchical richness of the passage than I attempt to achieve in my Roman numeral usage, his analysis conforms to standard literalist practice.[16] I find the array of lines presented in his example 30 (p. 744) more troublesome. The assertion of an upward trajectory for the C of 29_{1-2} in his graphs 3 and 4b seems to me problematic if the tonic of measure 30 in fact resolves the dissonance of measure 29. Meyer's reading is especially curious in that he accepts D, a pitch (at 33_1) that resides within a B<B octave, as C's successor. My disappointment in Meyer's reading rests in part on its abundance of conflicting ideas. (Note that C *does* descend to B in graphs 1, 2b, and 4a, but not in graphs 3 and 4b.) From my perspective the Trio projects one central idea to which all others conform: the transfer of the structural melodic pitches of a $\hat{3}$–$\hat{2}$–$\hat{1}$ descent between two registers. I propose a B<B connection in measures 1 through 8, an A>A connection in measures 14 through 26, a B<B connection in

measures 33 through 36 (accomplished during B's neighbor C), and a G>G connection in measures 38 through 42. It seems to me that despite Meyer's painstaking rigor and mindboggling detail, he never glimpsed the essence of the structure. The lines that matter to me, as displayed in my four graphs, are few and conventional. The lines that matter to Meyer are many, and some of them are eccentric.[17]

10 | Haydn: Symphony No. 96 in D Major ("Miracle"), movement 1

*in response to Warren Darcy, James Hepokoski,
and Lauri Suurpää*

One of the most profound changes in musical thought at the dawning of the new millennium has been the emergence of what James Hepokoski and Warren Darcy call Sonata Theory. We have made good use of some aspects of this perspective already in chapters 2, 4, and elsewhere within this volume. Their *Elements of Sonata Theory* is an inexhaustible resource, filled with commentary on a wide range of works by Haydn and Mozart, among others. In this chapter I focus on their interpretation of the first movement from Haydn's "Miracle" Symphony.[1] Though they selected this movement to elucidate the continuous exposition, the conjoining of their perspective on form and my perspective on harmony has led me to reject that interpretation. I will demonstrate below how the "Miracle" exposition in fact possesses a functional MC and thus is organized as a two-part structure. Concerned that limiting my focus to the exposition alone (as they do) might result in the loss of pertinent data, I address the entire movement. Indeed, the structure of the recapitulation does shed light on the organization of the exposition. Another analyst, Lauri Suurpää, likewise has used the Hepokoski/Darcy reading in formulating a perspective on Haydn's application of the continuous exposition.[2] Consequently I will assess his interpretation of the exposition as well.

The introduction (measures 1–17)

The characteristic harmonic trajectory proceeding from the tonic to the dominant is pursued during the introduction – twice (measures 1 through 6, and 7 through 17, as displayed in **10.1**). Such a reiteration has both local and broad repercussions: the musical surface of the introduction displays alternative possibilities for the traversal of the I–V expanse, while the notion of repetition resurfaces during the exposition's first part (P plus TR) and resonates with a dramatic moment of compositional transformation during S (at measure 57), as we shall see later. The D–F♯ expanse that announces the *Kopfton* in measures 1 and 2 is expressed melodically not in the

Example 10.1 Analysis of Haydn: Symphony No. 96 in D Major ("Miracle"), mvmt. 1, mm. 1–17.

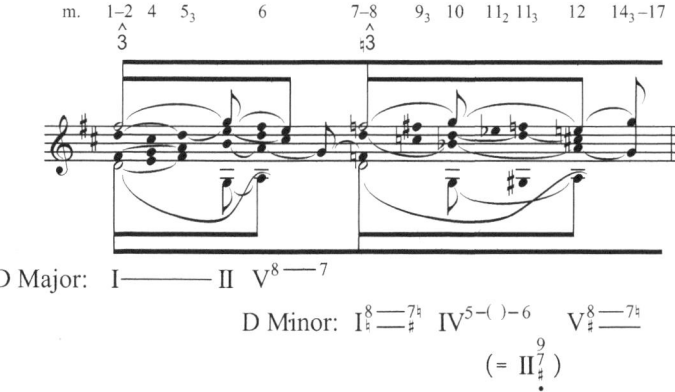

conventional shape D<F♯, but instead inverted, as D>F♯. Its arpeggiated realization (D>A>F♯) will be echoed by other significant arpeggiations, such as A<D<F♯ in measures 18 through 20.

The first statement of I–V begins with an unhurried tonic prolongation, leading from root position to first inversion. (Note that the stepwise E<F♯ connection in the bass is presented as E<D>C♯>B>A>G>F♯ in measures 4 and 5, in the context of a parallel progression of $^6_3$ chords, part of which will recur during TR.) Though accented, the II that heralds the dominant is squeezed into a mere eighth-note slot at the end of measure 5. Once the dominant falls into place (after downbeat embellishment), its cadential effect dissipates through the emergence of a dissonant minor seventh at the end of measure 6. The second introductory I–V progression begins at 7_1.

The latter phrase's character is somber, resulting from the conversion to the parallel minor key and the more intense chromaticism.[3] This phrase's internal harmonic progression contrasts that of the first phrase. Measures 8 and 9 display a flurry of activity: the F♯<G<A span that is gently pursued in the second violin line during measures 3 through 5 is accomplished (in its minor-mode equivalent, F♮<G<A) more quickly, via reaching-over (F♮ descends to E, G reaches over E, etc.[4]); and ultimately the minor tonic is converted into a dominant-emulating major chord with minor seventh. Consequently the principal harmonic event between I and V♯ during this phrase is IV. Its extension – a 5–6 shift during measure 11 – is clarified in 10.1. Here the 6-phase chord is highly evolved, with dominant-emulating G♯-(B♭)-D-F♮ replacing diatonic G-B♭-E.[5] Yet before that 6-phase chord arrives, IV's fifth, D, is embellished by chromatic upper neighbor E♭, with an

unfurling into $^5_3$ position.[6] Whereas the V at measure 6 is brief, that of measure 12 extends through measure 17. Note that whereas the dominant's seventh, G, in measure 6 works along with a major ninth B, in the second phase G is capped by the minor-mode ninth B♭ during 17_1.

> I propose that the double I–V introduction will be matched by a double I–V P–TR complex as the exposition proceeds. Consequently the neglect of this conspicuous feature of the introduction will leave one ill-equipped to deal with what otherwise may seem a strange series of events later. In fact, Hepokoski and Darcy do falter on this point, arguing against a medial caesura on V at measure 49 with the claim that "the I: HC option *had already been used up* earlier in m. 31" (1997, p. 135; 2006, p. 55; italics added). I counter that upon hearing the expanse from I to V *twice* between measures 18 and 49 (to be discussed in detail below, in conjunction with **10.2**), that V's MC potential is *enhanced*. Following the lead of Hepokoski and Darcy, Suurpää likewise does not investigate the introduction.

The exposition's primary-theme zone and transition (P and TR, measures 18–49)

Whereas our study of major-key sonata expositions by Haydn in chapter 2 focused on movements in which a medial caesura occurs on II♯ (Hepokoski and Darcy's V:HC MC), a common alternative structure instead leads to a medial caesura on the tonic key's dominant (I:HC MC). In the "Miracle" Symphony exposition, measure 18 through the midpoint of measure 31 aptly display how this option may be realized: a conventional tonic presentation during P (through 25_1) dovetails with a TR that leads via II in measure 30 to a half cadence on V. In a conventional continuation, caesura silence during the remainder of measure 31 might lead to S in the tonicized dominant key, A Major, beginning at 32_1.[7] The B>A>G (the dominant's ninth to seventh) that sounds instead during the remainder of measure 31 unexpectedly directs the progression back to the tonic for a repetition of all that has occurred since the introduction. From the perspective of how expositions tend to work, this is an oddity. Yet for this particular exposition it makes extraordinary sense, since we heard exactly this turn of events earlier – during the introduction, which even features an identical B>A>G ninth-to-seventh motion during measure 6! Though the second presentation of P and TR exhibits some minor alterations (less extreme than those

Example 10.2 Analysis of Haydn: Symphony No. 96 in D Major ("Miracle"), mvmt. 1, mm. 18–49.

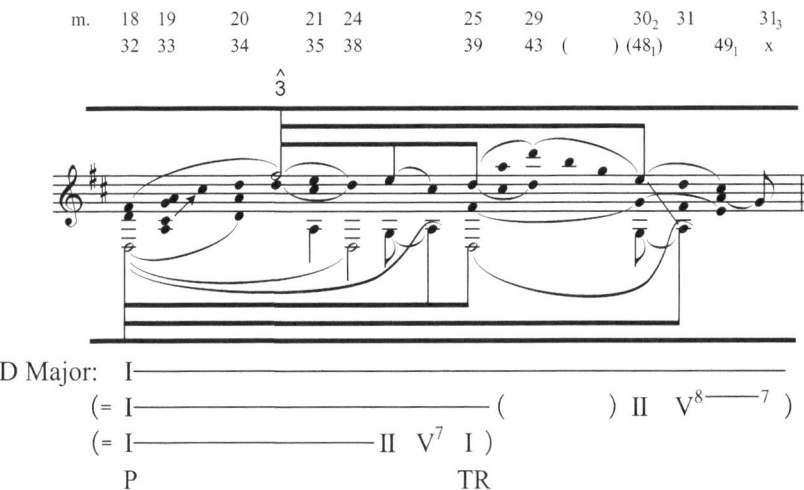

of the introduction's repetition), the structure is sufficiently similar to the initial statement that the same graph may serve as analysis for both. (See **10.2**.)

The presentation of tonic D Major within P is shaped as a long tonic expansion, through 24_1 (38_1), during which a foreground F♯>E>D third transpires, followed by a quick II–V^7–I cadential gesture, supporting a somewhat deeper descent from the *Kopfton* F♯ through E to D. TR opens with an extension of I-space, followed by a downward cascade to $\hat{2}$ (reminiscent of the introduction's cascade down to *Kopfton* $\hat{3}$) during measures 29 and 30 and then the HC on V. During the repetition this downward cascade is modified. Though B, G, and E sound prominently during measures 44 through 46, in their new context these pitches are subservient to the tonic. In fact, the content of measure 46 through the downbeat of measure 47 restates (more slowly) the approach to the first-inversion tonic from measure 5 (the second through fifth chords). Consequently the arrival of II is delayed until 48_1. (The parentheses around that measure number in **10.2** acknowledge that a substitution has occurred: the first violins sound B instead of E. Compare with measure 30, where B (as well as G) sounds *in addition* to E before the D>C♯ move to the cadence in measure 31.[8] The abbreviation as B>D>C♯ leaves the E fresh for presentation during S, which follows immediately after the C♯.) Despite these variants, the dominant that arrives at 49_1 – now without a succeeding B>A>G gesture and thus fully invested in its MC role – heralds the onset of S.

Whereas I propose that the HC moment is redundantly stated in measures 31 and 49, Hepokoski and Darcy, acknowledging that an "attempt" at an MC in the vicinity of measure 49 is "aborted" (1997, p. 135; 2006, p. 55), place that event instead at 57_1. (The type of MC has thereby shifted from their I:HC MC to their V:HC MC.) Because no suitable S follows after the latter point, they suggest that Haydn has employed a "bait-and-switch" tactic: leading listeners to suppose that a two-part exposition is in progress, but converting midstream to a continuous exposition.

Hepokoski and Darcy never precisely spell out their reading of measures 18 through 49. In **10.2** I propose that essentially the same structure occurs twice in succession. Consequently the V of 49_1 is a reiteration of the V of 31_{1-2}. This idiosyncratic structure, which perpetuates a repetitive urge already in play during the introduction, may offset the Hepokoski/Darcy dictum that "as a general principle, each MC option is normally accessible only one time during an exposition. This may be considered the nonredundancy feature of medial caesura practice" (2006, p. 40). I accept this V goal as a I:HC MC^9 and will show below how what follows its second statement conforms to the conventional structure of S, in the tonicized key of A Major.

Suurpää is concurrently closer to and further from my reading than are Hepokoski and Darcy. On the negative side, though he acknowledges the occurrence of "two extended phrases" during measures 18 through 49, he does not agree that the cadence on the dominant may serve as the exposition's MC. He argues against that interpretation on p. 180, suggesting that caesura fill by the woodwinds obscures the boundary. I interpret that woodwind activity as the onset of S: the E (= $\hat{2}$, *Kopfton* $\hat{3}$'s successor) is sounded in three registers by various woodwind instruments during the second half of 49_1. (This is the open-notehead E of my **10.3**.) On the positive side, he analyzes the A major chord of measure 51 as I in tonicized A Major, a necessary condition for my interpretation of the phrase that begins at the second eighth note of measure 49 as the onset of S (p. 178). Nevertheless his graph of the exposition (his example 1 on p. 179) destroys any potential for an interpretation of that A chord as a structurally deep moment: its soprano E is designated not as the arrival of background $\hat{2}$ (in accord with **10.3**) but instead as a passing note. The chord is interpreted curiously as an interior moment within a $^{F\sharp}_D X^{D\sharp}_{F\sharp}$ chromaticized voice exchange, despite its designation as a tonic.

The exposition's secondary-theme and closing zones (S and C, measures 49|50–83)

I make two simple yet controversial assertions about what happens following the HC at 49₁: (1) from 49|50 through the downbeat of measure 57, an eight-measure phrase transpires; and (2) this phrase resides squarely in the key of A Major, proceeding in accordance with one of tonal music's most normative harmonic progressions, I$^{5-6}$ II♯ V.

Look back for a moment at Haydn's writing in measures 28|29 through 31. The expanse from I through II to V in D Major is expressed there in a rather flamboyant manner, as follows:

	C♯↗D	A♯↗B	F♯↗G	D♯↗E	A
D Major:	I	(		) II	V

(In this discussion I employ the slanted arrow symbol to connect leading tones to their resolutions.) A circular progression descending in thirds links the governing harmonic progression's I and II. Transposing that trajectory into the dominant key, A Major, yields the following:

	G♯↗A	E♯↗F♯	C♯↗D	A♯↗B	E
A Major:	I	(		) II	V

For use in measures 49|50 through 57, Haydn takes advantage of the close bond between the fourth and seventh chords (both rooted on F♯), allowing for an abbreviated statement that proceeds directly from the F♯ to the B chord, thereby converting the circular progression connecting I and II into a connection from I$^{5-6}$ to II♯:

	G♯↗A	E♯↗F♯	B	E
A Major:	I^5——————6		II$^9_{7\sharp}$	V

The only irregularity within the phrase is the indecisiveness exhibited in measure 52: at first Haydn seems intent upon reiterating the G♯↗A succession (perhaps in reference to the reiterations of C♯↗D during measures 24 through 29), but he decides belatedly to proceed straightaway to the next point along his trajectory, F♯. The reiteration of G♯ offers more support to

Example 10.3 Analysis of Haydn: Symphony No. 96 in D Major ("Miracle"), mvmt. 1, mm. 49–71.

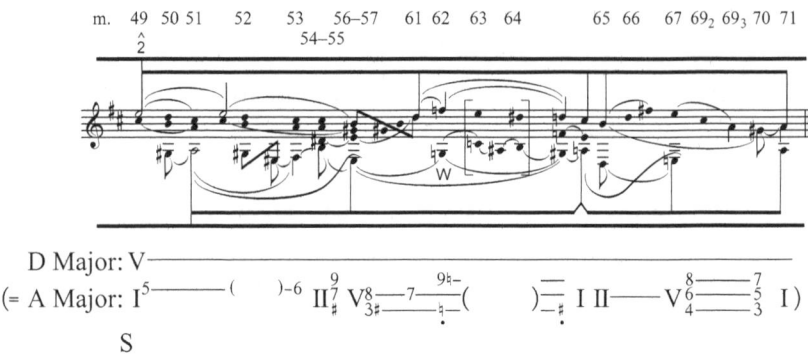

the establishment of the A tonic, whereas the shift to E♮ confirms that the phrase has a full agenda and establishes a pattern in which two measures will be spent on each of four events: the tonic's 5 phase, its 6 phase, the evolved supertonic, and the dominant.

Haydn masterfully changes gears upon arriving at the dominant in measures 56 and 57. An eight-measure phrase that proceeds from I to V, supporting an E>D>C♯>B melodic trajectory, projects the notion of antecedent, concluding with an interruption. The most likely continuation would be to repeat the phrase with suitable modifications so that, within the next eight measures, the reiterated melodic line will extend all the way down to tonic A, in conjunction with a PAC. However, this exposition has by now already presented *five* motions to a half cadence on $\hat{2}$ (the first four in the tonic key, D Major, as shown in **10.1** and **10.2**; the fifth in the dominant key, as shown in **10.3**, measures 49|50 through 57).[10] To proceed with a conventional consequent, incorporating yet another repetition of previously presented material, here might seem gratingly conventional and tedious. Rather than pursuing that predictable route, Haydn resuscitates the dominant of measure 57, transforming it into a viable V→, achieved through the incorporation of its seventh (measure 61) and minor ninth (measures 62 through 64$_2$).[11] Whereas the soprano B of measure 56 initially projects the sense that it will be the deepest B within the S region, in retrospect it takes on the role of an inner voice. A hierarchically deeper D emerges in measure 61, setting into motion the S region's broad E>D>C♯>B>A trajectory, supported by a double bass arpeggiation (A–E–A–E–A). As **10.3** indicates, the midpoint A major tonic chord arrives at the end of measure 64. The soprano B that is prolonged (via stepwise descent to G♯) during measures 65 through 70 – not the B of measure 56 – participates in the broad fifth-progression that shapes the S region.

The dominant's ninth often sounds in the vicinity of its seventh. (We have already noted several instances of this juxtaposition: the major ninth in measures 6 and 31 and the minor ninth in measure 17.) Haydn's gradual rebuilding of the dominant chord from the ground up, starting in measure 57, proceeds from root through third and fifth to seventh, at which point (measure 61) we may suspect that the initiative has run its course, since the rhythmic vitality comes to a halt.[12] Yet the ever creative (and playful) Haydn surprises us by pushing upwards one more notch, to F♮ (emboldened by a *forzando* presentation). Whereas G♯-B-D-F♮ would be an appropriate though routine chordal support for the ninth, Haydn instead allows G♯ to wobble to G♮, reserving G♯-B-D-F♮ for 64_2, immediately preceding the normative resolution to the A tonic. The chordal play here is quite subtle. On the one hand, G♮-B-D-F♮ stands in for the dominant E chord (as a variant of its upper-third chord). As such, we may expect that the G♮ wobble will revert to diatonic G♯, as does soon happen (as indicated by the slur connecting G♮ and G♯ in **10.3**).[13] On the other hand, the G♮ chord possesses an alternative potential meaning: not only as a mutant representative of E→, but also as a dynamic G♮→. Will that latter potentiality be held in check, confirming the potent E→ focus of the preceding six measures? Or will G♮ assert itself as a root? The latter option prevails. We experience G♮→C♮ and F♯→B usurpations of the intended dominant-tonic succession before a restored dominant E→ (represented by G♯-D-F♮ at 64_2) definitively moves to tonic A.[14] I interpret the C♮, F♯, and B chords as components of a parenthetical passage. Though the G♮ chord of measures 62 could revert directly to the E→ chord of 64_2, an alternative trajectory that has nothing to do with how the phrase ultimately proceeds is traversed over the course of four beats, before the reconstituted E→ sets things aright. ("No! The goal is not C♮, and not B, but instead what we expected all along: A!") During this passage the soprano descends chromatically from ninth F♮ to seventh D (the F♮ is restored in the chordal interior at 64_2), recalling the ninth-to-seventh descents (in the context of D Major's dominant) during measures 6, 17, and 31.

The arrival of the EEC at 71_1 coincides with the onset of the closing zone (C). The A pedal point, the broad A>G♯<A neighboring motions, and the melodic emphasis on E are reminiscent of the prolongational techniques – in the context of tonic D – employed during measures 25 through 29. The final climb to the minor seventh G♮ (measures 79 through 81, repeated in

measures 81 through 83) is a no-nonsense variant of the filled-in seventh E to D in measures 57 through 61. Its purpose here, of course, is to negate the stability of A Major as a tonicized key, in preparation for the restoration of D Major for the repeat of the exposition or for the more daring trajectory that will ensue during the development.

> Hepokoski and Darcy propose that "if TR produces a notable HC that is immediately followed by an 'acceptable' new theme in the proper subordinate key, that HC may be interpreted as a medial caesura" (2006, p. 30). Consequently I have endeavored to demonstrate above that what transpires beginning at measures 49|50 in fact represents such an S theme. Were they concerned that the theme's initial downbeat is not an A Major tonic chord? Apparently not, since in their section on "Troubleshooting MC Identifications" they advise: "the problem with the subsequent S might be only apparent. Is it an S governed by the new dominant key but one that happens to begin off-tonic (or off the tonic chord)?" (2006, p. 48). It appears to me that they have erred here. This analysis was created rather early within the extraordinary period of development that led to *Elements of Sonata Theory*. Given the enormous quantity of material they were juggling, the "Miracle" exposition did not receive the reconsideration that I suggest was warranted. Consequently much of what they have to say about it is off the mark, in my view.[15] The sort of harmonic-structural perspective that I advocate offers a worthwhile complement to Hepokoski and Darcy's Sonata Theory. As this case demonstrates, proceeding in formal analysis without fully and accurately assessing a work's harmonic dimension may easily lead to misreadings.[16]
>
> Suurpää's analysis conforms to that of Hepokoski and Darcy. Consequently our readings (his examples 1 and 2 and my **10.3**) have very little in common, despite the considerable overlap of pitch content in our graphs. My most urgent suggestion is that his acceptance of the A major chord of measure 51 as I in the tonicized dominant key should coincide with the onset of background $\hat{2}$. Though his foreground harmonic analysis reads "A: I," soprano E is designated as a passing note ("P") within an F♯>D♯ third, in my view a dubious interpretation. My second most urgent suggestion is that the E dominant chord that arrives in measure 56 be understood as extending until resolution to the tonic at 64_3, concluding the first of the two A–E–A bass arpeggiations that support first the upper, then the lower third of the E̠>A fifth-progression in the soprano.[17] (Consequently I am further along on that path by this

point than is Suurpää.) My concern extends not only to whether Suurpää's notation suitably represents what occurs in Haydn's score, but also to whether the notation represents a viable Schenkerian structure in and of itself.

The development (measures 84–153)

The movement's exposition and development both conclude with D Major's dominant harmony. The development's essence is prolongation, here achieved through the assertion of IV, which leads to a restored dominant and consequently deepens the listener's engagement with the harmony that was already in place at the onset of the exposition's S. (See **10.4**.) Whereas IV–V is syntactically apposite, V–IV is not. Consequently Haydn introduces this IV in a roundabout way: when it first sounds, we have good reason to interpret it as an internal element of an ascending sequential progression. Yet based on what follows we understand retrospectively that it asserts itself as IV.

As was also the case within both the introduction and the exposition, repetition plays an important role in the development's trajectory. Two broadly paced ascending 5–6 sequences are initiated within the development. Comparing **10.5** and **10.6**, note the correlation between measures 84 and 113, 86–91 and 114, and 99 and 132. The attainment of A Major's lowered mediant (C♮) in measure 104 provides the precedent that gives the G major region beginning in measure 132 a → thrust towards C♮.[18] What ensues thereafter (G to A – *not* C♮ – via G's upper-fifth chord, which, during a brief tonicization in measures 140 through 143, provides consonant support for the melody's passing F♯[19]) resonates instead as a conventional IV–V succession. The IV harmony that we eventually realize has emerged in measure 132 has no direct *harmonic* predecessor. Unexpectedly we find ourselves deposited at a location within tonal space from which a fresh approach to V may appropriately ensue.

Both sequential progressions contain quirks. In a more straightforward ascent the 5-phase B minor chord of measure 86 might lead directly to the 6-phase chord of measure 99. (See **10.5**.) Yet Haydn inserts a whimsical B→E alternative that eventually gives way to that 6-phase chord. (Note that the sequential ascent is diatonic in neither D Major nor A Major. The C♮ of measure 104 – a wobble – holds out through measure 112. This idiosyncratic sequential trajectory provides the groundwork for what Haydn plans to do later: because C♮ – *not* C♯ – is its goal, the G major chord that in measure 132

242 Harmony in Haydn and Mozart

Example 10.4 Analysis of Haydn: Symphony No. 96 in D Major ("Miracle"), mvmt. 1, mm. 18–172.

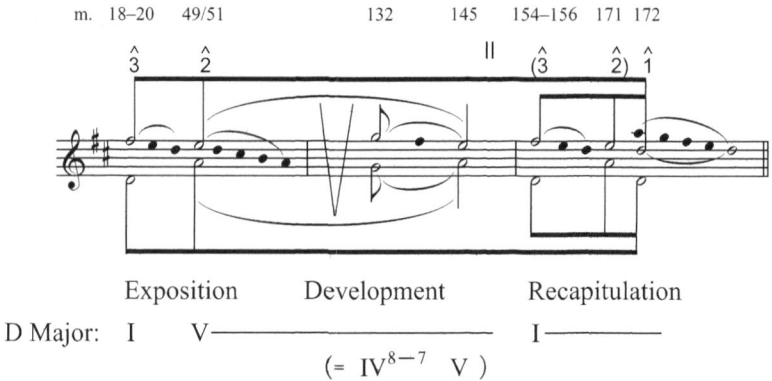

Example 10.5 Analysis of Haydn: Symphony No. 96 in D Major ("Miracle"), mvmt. 1, mm. 49–112.

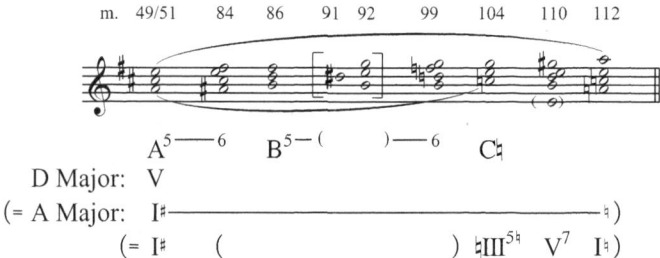

Example 10.6 Analysis of Haydn: Symphony No. 96 in D Major ("Miracle"), mvmt. 1, mm. 49–145.

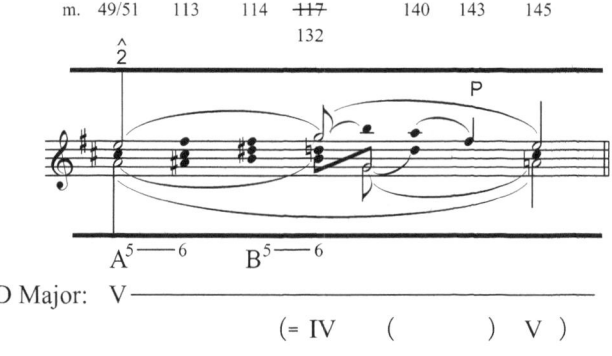

will assert itself as IV is introduced in measure 99.[20]) In the second sequence (shown in **10.6**) listeners likely will assume that B's 6-phase chord has arrived already at measure 117. Only as the broader progression unfolds does one comprehend that, instead, B is tonicized by means of a harmonic progression to its dominant (B Minor: I$^{5-6}_{\sharp 3-\natural 3}$ II⇒ V♯ during measures 114 through 129). That local dominant (F♯ major) and B's 6-phase chord (G major) are boldly juxtaposed in measures 129 through 132.

Any interpretation of a musical entity as complex as a Haydn development section is especially dependent upon judgments for which justification may not easily be provided. Though I propose that the structures displayed in **10.5** and **10.6** are coherent and innovative means of extending the A dominant through to the end of the development, a willingness to agree that a close correlation exists between these models and Haydn's score requires the acceptance of numerous interpretive decisions regarding hierarchical relationships among chords and regions, an acceptance that is sometimes challenged by how boldly Haydn presents materials that are not given much structural weight in these models. Whereas an exposition's tonal plan generally corresponds to one of just a few basic models, the internal workings of development sections vary widely.[21] Consequently most musicians who think about such things likely find development sections more enigmatic than most other entities within tonal practice. Though models such as those that I provide might offer insights, a hesitancy to accept their neat and tidy explanations certainly is a reasonable response.

My interpretation calls upon performers to counteract certain tendencies that might seem inherent in Haydn's score. First, the B➔E connection during measures 91 and 92 should not come across as a decisive departure from B. The E chord may in fact represent an unfurled $^6_4$ embellishment of the preceding minor $^5_3$ (measures 86 through 90), delaying the 6-phase chord of measures 99 through 103. The brackets that I place around this region in **10.5** suggest a hierarchical relationship that a literalist analysis may fail to diagnose. Second, the G chord of measures 117ff. should be interpreted within the broader context of a B-to-F♯ expanse (between measures 114 and 123). Though the B chord is of major quality, its D♯ may be interpreted as a wobble. With the arrival of bass G, B *Minor*'s 6-phase chord is utilized. The minor mode is further reinforced by the "augmented sixth" supertonic that emerges in measure 122. Just as the earlier B (measure 86) seemingly proceeding to E ultimately does not disrupt the emergence of B's 6-phase chord (measure 99), so also the progression from B (measure 114) to its local dominant F♯ (measure 123) does not disrupt the emergence of its 6-phase chord (measure 132).

The recapitulation (measures 154–203)

Both tonal and thematic parameters align for the onset of the recapitulation at measure 154. P's presentation here is similar to that from the exposition, though now with additional reinforcement from the woodwinds. The double statement of the P–TR complex that characterized the exposition is now absent. A single thrust to the dominant (again a I:HC MC) occurs between measures 161 and 171. This TR is freshly composed, incorporating features from both of the exposition statements: the D>B>G>E descent of measures 29 and 30 is now more broadly traversed (one descending third every two measures), while the G<G♯<A approach to the dominant root in measures 170 and 171 stems from measures 48 and 49.

One advantage in the choice of the I:HC MC as the goal of TR is that *the same* trajectory may be traversed in both the exposition and the recapitulation. (In contrast, the V:HC MC, which we explored in chapter 2, concludes with II♯. Since that harmony is not suitable as predecessor of an S in the home key during the recapitulation, the TR trajectory must be adjusted so as to conclude up a fourth or down a fifth, on V.) Yet in this particular exposition another factor relating to the opening of this specific S has offered Haydn an uncommon and delicious opportunity. Look again at measures 49 through 51. The exposition's MC occurs at 49_1 on A (V in the key of D Major). The following two measures proceed as E→A, reinforcing I in the tonicized key of A Major that will prevail during S. The exposition's

$$A \quad ' \quad E \rightarrow A$$

will be revised for the recapitulation (due to the tonic presentation of S) into

$$A \quad ' \quad A \rightarrow D$$

Haydn takes the bold step of merging those two A chords into the same moment, in measure 171. Consequently the MC and the onset of S collide. Whereas in measure 49 most of the orchestra observes the silence that is characteristic of an MC, in measure 171 the sixteenth-note pattern that in the exposition comes one measure later (measure 50) invades that silence. Confirming this early onset of S, measure 172 corresponds to measure 51, and – wonder of wonders – measure 173 restores the original intention of measure 52 (where G♯ was prevented from fulfilling its leading-tone tendency by the imposition of competing *forzando* E♯). Now, rather than the prompt succession to the tonic's 6-phase chord, the tonic D itself is boldly presented thrice: in measures 172, 174, and 176, while the II♯ that occupied two measures during the exposition's S (measures 54 and 55) now occupies, in drastically reduced form (with only the chord members G♯ and D sounding), the last beat of measure 176, before the dominant arrival on the following downbeat.

Haydn pursues the entire phrase above an A pedal point (though note the timpani D during the third sounding of the tonic in measure 176). In part because this phrase is based upon one from the exposition in which the local tonic is clearly projected in its second full measure, I accept the $^6_4$ chords of measures 172, 174, and 176 as the D Major tonic. Yet I am sympathetic to the alternative view that the dominant persists until 181_3. One might in that case regard the D>C♯<D>C♯<D of measures 25 through 29 to have been transformed into C♯<D>C♯<D>C♯<D>C♯, with the decisive C♯<D postponed until 181_{2-3}.[22]

The second "half" of S (corresponding to the second A–E–A bass arpeggiation in **10.3**), which in the exposition transpires between 64_3 and 71_1, is condensed in the recapitulation into a mere five beats (181_3 through 183_1). Whereas the F♯>E>D third-progression of P remains intact (hooking up to the fundamental structure at background $\hat{1}$ in its recapitulation context at 161_1), the A>G>F♯>E>D fifth-progression of S is less overtly realized. Perhaps because A serves duty as a pedal point at the bottom of the texture, it is not prominently stated in the upper register during the tonic chords that open S (measures 172 through 176), though it is boldly announced at 177_1,[23] after which the dominant's seventh G leads to F♯ – not in the soprano, as is conventional and as occurred during the exposition, but instead in the bass (at 181_3). The concluding E>D is presented only by the horns, leading to a robust PAC (= ESC) at 183_1.

The various alterations over the course of the recapitulation's P, TR, and S regions (especially the non-repetition of the P–TR complex) have led to savings of twenty-four measures, compared with the equivalent sector of the exposition. Haydn spends part of those savings on an expanded C to close the movement. A descending chromatic line inaugurates a progression that concludes with a II–V–I cadence in measures 186 and 187, followed immediately by a reciprocal ascending chromatic line that ignites the cadential process over again, though this time V lingers for several measures before a *minor* tonic emerges in measure 194 (perhaps as a nod to the second phrase of the introduction). Taking advantage of the presence of D and F♮, Haydn builds the supertonic that follows as G♯-B♭-D-F♮, within a progression that spans measures 194 through 198, as follows:

D Major: I♮   II⇛   V$^{8-7}$ I   II   V   I

The latter part of this progression is reiterated during five additional measures (at first II–V–I, then simply V–I), terminating at 203_1.

> When analyzing an especially novel passage, it is useful to assess how the composer deals with it in other contexts (if others are present). In a sonata movement, the recapitulation offers a rich source of content that may offer fresh insights regarding the workings of the exposition. In this movement it is helpful for the analyst to know that the P–TR complex, which Haydn repeats during the exposition, occurs only once during the recapitulation. That fact encourages one to interpret measures 32 through 49 as content that does not move the structure forward at all: that, in a deformation of the standard shape of a sonata exposition, we have a second chance to tap *the same* MC potentiality that is first offered at 31_2. Nothing stated in their work leads me to believe that Hepokoski and Darcy or Suurpää made good use of this data from the recapitulation.
>
> One especially problematic feature of Suurpää's example 1b is the relationship he proposes between the C major chord at 63_1 and the A major chord at 64_3. Though I am in general sympathetic to the 5–6 voice-leading technique, I do not think that it applies in this case. Instead, the A chord is hierarchically deeper than the C chord.[24] In my view Haydn offers a confirmation of that interpretation by retaining the D Major equivalent of the A chord (at 181_3), whereas the equivalent of the C chord, along with the entire parenthetical passage in which it resides, is absent from the recapitulation.

Notes

1 Harmonic practice in the late eighteenth century: twelve excerpts from string quartets by Haydn and Mozart

1. In *The Language of Music* (Oxford University Press, 1959), Deryck Cooke describes $\hat{5}<\hat{1}<(\hat{2}<)\hat{3}$ in a major key as "expressive of an outgoing emotion of joy" (p. 119).
2. The meaningful engagement of the tonic chord's pitches is broadly realized during a harmonic progression. Here the melodic line descends from F♯ to D during measures 3 through 8, while the foundational harmonic progression engages the roots D (measure 1), A (measure 4), and D (measure 8). In *FC* Schenker refers to a bass arpeggiation such as D–A–D as a "sacred triangle."
3. The pitch D is placed within parentheses in **1.1d** because it does not sound until the downbeat of measure 4 in the first violin melody (though it occurs in the viola line during 3_2). As displayed in the graph, and omitting the chromatic G♯, the passage's derivation from the second species of counterpoint may be perceived. In free composition the passing note D may shift to the accented downbeat location.
4. Just as the initial D-F♯-A tonic is embellished by C♯, E, and G in measure 1 (supporting ascending passing note E), the A-C♯-E dominant is embellished by G♯, B, and D (supporting descending passing note B) in measure 4. This procedure will be explored in the next section of this chapter. (See **1.2b**, Models 1 and 3.)
5. The fuller agenda of the consequent phrase often results in the omission of elements from the antecedent phrase. Here the first violin's low A of 4_2, which appealingly restores the A from the upbeat to measure 1, is sacrificed. (Note the complementary slurs – A<D<F♯ and E>C♯>A in **1.1d**.) During the consequent phrase Haydn extends the D>C♯ second that begins measure 4 into a full beat, so that the leading tone immediately precedes the arrival of $\hat{1}$.
6. I restate a question that has been pondered for centuries: see *TAH*, **5.4**.
7. Compare with *Schubert*, **3.1** and **3.2**.
8. Haydn employs a similar construction in his Symphony No. 82 in C Major ("The Bear"), mvmt. 4, mm. 9–11, where a G, equivalent to the F appoggiatura at 4_1, fills an entire measure.

9. A symbol such as (I) or "I" is sometimes encountered in analyses as a label for such a linear chord. I regard that practice as misleading and inelegant. My rows of Roman numerals, for example those placed within parentheses in **1.2c**, are free of such distractions, enhancing the focus on the *harmonic* trajectory.
10. See *Schubert*, p. 6.
11. See *TAH*, **2.7**, for an example from around 1861 in which the process of stacking thirds as a step in completing the harmonic analysis is vividly presented. Lobe's analysis using Arabic numerals and dots is equivalent to the modern analysis of E♭ Major: V^7 I V^7 I.
12. The dutiful but misguided labeling of chords within parallel progressions, as in I II III IV V VI VII I in the model proposed, has nothing to do with the workings of harmony.
13. I espouse the view that context is a vital component in the determination of a chord's function. Without knowing what *follows* the G-B♭-E♭ chord, one could not with such conviction assert, as I do, that it does not function as ♭II. What if, instead, the last chord of measure 84 were an A-C♯-E♮ dominant resolving to tonic at 85_1? In *that* context, G-B♭-E♭ indeed might be interpreted as ♭II. For a more extended discussion of this issue, see *Schubert*, pp. 14–15.
14. Whereas **1.4c** displays soprano B during the second half of measure 152 as the lower third of D (thus replicating the situation of measures 147 and 148, shown in **1.4b**), had A been achieved in measure 153, then this B would function as $\hat{2}$ in a structure akin to that displayed in **1.2c**, mm. 11–12. This excerpt is from the movement's recapitulation, in which the passage after the IAC is extended and intensified beyond what occurs during the exposition (where the theme is presented in the dominant key, E Major).
15. The belated arrival of a structural pitch is encountered frequently in Haydn's music. Within this excerpt the *Kopfton* $\hat{5}$ arrives during the tonic's transition to its 6 phase (measure 146), and the local passing note C♯ is withheld in the first violin line until the second half of measure 152. (See **1.4b** and **1.4c**.)
16. Several other wedge-shaped progressions of this sort are displayed in my "Schenker, Schubert, and the Subtonic Chord," in *A Music-Theoretical Matrix: Essays in Honor of Allen Forte (Part II)*, ed. D. C. Berry, *Gamut: Online Journal of the Music Theory Society of the Mid-Atlantic* 3 (2010), p. 156, fig. 13.
17. I assess such sequences in detail in my "Schubert, Chromaticism, and the Ascending 5–6 Sequence," *Journal of Music Theory* 50 (2006), pp. 253–275.
18. In *TAH* (pp. 185–190), my expression of concern regarding the means by which modern analysts deal with such chords was accompanied by pessimism about implementing any improvements. Now I am aggressively promoting a scale-degree approach, as was practiced by a range of authors from the eighteenth and nineteenth centuries. (See especially *TAH*, **1.6**, **1.11b**, **7.3b**, **7.4**, **7.18a**, and **7.18c**.)
19. The most common connector between a D and a B♭ chord would be an embellishing chord like that displayed in **1.2b**, Model 1: either D's embellishing

chord A-C(♯)-E or B♭'s embellishing chord F-A-C. A minor seventh may be included as well.
20. Compare with *FC*, fig. 43, ex. b4.
21. In some musical passages alternative chordal hierarchies may vie for acceptance. In this case the structural depth of the inverted, surging E♭ chord of measure 18 comes into question. Is it a reinstatement of the tonic (warranting a connection between measures 12 and 18) or is it a local embellishment of an A♭ chord (warranting a connection between the last chord of measure 17 and the chord of measure 19)? The fact that the tonic returns in measure 20 is a strong factor in my acceptance of the first of these readings, in which the bass A♭ of measure 19 serves as a neighbor to the tonic's third.
22. This graph's D♭ (measure 18) is placed within parentheses because D♭ does not sound in the first violin line at that point. (It is delayed until the following downbeat.) However, D♭ does occur within the chord – in the viola. A comparison with the first violin melody of measure 16 (which ends with the minor seventh pitch, F) further justifies placing the minor seventh pitch D♭ within measure 18.
23. A similar progression is addressed in my review of *Beethoven's* Tempest *Sonata: Perspectives of Analysis and Performance* (ed. Pieter Bergé), in *Music Theory Online* 16/2 (June 2010), paragraph 8, where I challenge James Hepokoski's assertion that the work's first-movement exposition closes on the tonic.
24. The *Kopfton* G ($\hat{3}$) sounds during the tonic's 6 phase at 15_2 and an octave higher during the following measure (in the midst of a embellishing-chord expansion of that 6-phase chord). During the opening measures of the movement, a progression similar to that of measures 12 through 15 – but ending on the tonic – occurs. Consequently the *Kopfton* G has already been established in a tonic context before its restatement during this 6-phase chord.
25. The excursion up a fifth from $\hat{2}$ and then back down again in measure 23 is reminiscent of the similar (though less animated) excursion from $\hat{2}$ in Haydn's Quartet in D Major [**1.1a**, m. 3].
26. Compare with Schubert's use of upper-third chords, discussed in my "Schenker, Schubert, and the Subtonic Chord" (2010), pp. 140–141.
27. Gretchen A. Wheelock is troubled by the juxtaposition of the leading tone A♯ (member of B Minor's major dominant) and the pitch A♮ that persists in the cello during measures 3–4 and 7–8. See her *Haydn's Ingenious Jesting with Art: Contexts of Musical Wit and Humor* (New York: Schirmer, 1992), pp. 103–106. Her perspective echoes that of Charles Rosen, who similarly pointed out the A♯/A♮ juxtaposition in *The Classical Style: Haydn, Mozart, Beethoven* (New York: Norton, 1971), pp. 115–116. In my more hierarchically oriented perspective, the A♯ is clearly the controlling pitch. A♮ is an embellishment, not a chord member. For a similar juxtaposition by Schubert, see his Piano Sonata in A Minor (D. 784), mvmt. 2, mm. 45 and 48, which I discuss in *Schubert*, p. 182.

28. The D to which I refer is the third pitch of the first violin line in measure 12. The downbeat D functions as a neighbor to C♯.
29. Haydn's *lizenza* annotation in measure 3 refers to the E♮<F parallel octaves. T. Enselein (*Der Kontrapunkt in Instrumentalwerk von Joseph Haydn*, Cologne: Dohr, 2008, p. 27) comments: "Auch hier betont Haydn in äußerst selbstbewußter Weise die Freiheit der Kunst gegenüber einer allzu rigorosen Regelauslegung." (Here as well Haydn emphasizes in a most self-assured manner the freedom of art compared with a too rigorous adherence to the rules.)
30. An alternative reading worthy of consideration is that D<$\underline{F}$ is unfolded during I and E♭>C during IV$^{5-6}$, followed by $\frac{(D)}{B\flat}$ at the cadential $^6_4$, a C>A unfolding and finally a unison B♭. That structure corresponds to the last model in *FC*, fig. 16, ex. 5. My analysis in **1.10c** does not exactly match any of Schenker's models in fig. 16, but instead corresponds to the second model in fig. 67, ex. 4b.
31. The nineteenth-century analysts Ernst Friedrich Richter and Johann Christian Lobe discuss a segment of this passage, transposed into C Major. See *TAH*, **5.8**.
32. The embellishing-chord resolution into a C major chord in measures 37 and 38 is sufficient grounds for the assertion of that C chord as ♮III$^{5♮}$. Yet to retain a sense of the hierarchical priority of I, in **1.11g** that Roman-numeral label is placed within parentheses below the symbols corresponding to **1.11f**.
33. Tonic A Major's diatonic upper-third chord is C♯-E-G♯. Its first through third chromatic variants are C♯-E♮-G♯, C♮-E-G♮, and C♮-E♭-G♮, respectively. Terminology for third-related chords is introduced in *Schubert*, pp. 56–60.
34. This topic emerges frequently in *Schubert*. Consult "modulo 7 vs. modulo 12" in its index (p. 320).
35. Because progressions in modulo 12 must be conveyed using music notation that was designed for modulo 7 compositions, chordal spellings often are arbitrary. The pitch that Haydn spells upon arrival as D♭ (44_1) becomes C♯ upon departure (46_2).
36. In his *Joseph Haydn and the String Quartet* (New York: Schirmer, 1974), Reginald Barrett-Ayres seems unaware of just how extraordinary this passage is. The extent of his commentary is as follows: "The music turns in a circle from G major, through B♭, and back to G major once again. [A reduction of the score, mm. 34–39] illustrates . . . the transition from G to B♭; the same progression, transposed up a minor third, serves as a transition from B♭ to D♭. [A reduction of the score, mm. 44–47] illustrates the transition back to G" (p. 234).
37. Observe that the noteheads D♭ and C♯ are juxtaposed in both **1.12b** and **1.12c**. When Haydn enters the domain of modulo 12, the tonal bias of seven diatonic pitch classes per octave is temporarily suspended. None of the twelve pitch classes (except perhaps the tonic itself) is of higher rank than any of the others. In a numerical notational system (with C = 0), the trajectory of measures 34 through 44 might be represented as 7<10<1. When Haydn transfers back into modulo 7 tonal space, "1" is represented by D♭ (which resonates with the tonal presumption of ascending two minor thirds). I propose that, in terms of what

follows, "1" functions not as the lowered fifth scale degree, but instead as the raised fourth scale degree: C♯. Because composers must employ notation that is designed to accommodate music with seven diatonic pitch classes, such enharmonic shifts are a common occurrence.

38. Examples of seismic composition are discussed in *TAH*, p. 236, and *Schubert*, pp. 137, 173–174, 284, and 291.

2 Anatomy of the I–II♯–V two-part exposition: twelve keyboard sonatas by Haydn

1. My use of the terms "supertonic" and "dominant" reflects a broad view of the sonata's tonal trajectory. Most analysts take a more local approach, interpreting II♯ as V in the tonicized dominant key.

2. James Hepokoski and Warren Darcy, *Elements of Sonata Theory: Norms, Types, and Deformations in the Late-Eighteenth-Century Sonata* (Oxford University Press, 2006), pp. 1–194. This work is cited often in my study and is the focus of chapter 10.

3. Whereas the excerpts discussed in chapter 1 were selected from a vast array of possibilities, allowing me to emphasize contexts for which my analytical perspective is especially well suited, the works discussed in chapters 2 through 4 appear because they fall within certain classes: a two-part exposition in a major key, an aria in the key of G Minor, or a sonata-rondo movement in D Major. Consequently I cannot be accused of hand-picking examples that favor my system while shoving less propitious contenders under the rug.

4. In his *Music in the Galant Style* (Oxford University Press, 2007, p. 141), Robert O. Gjerdingen describes this ascending motion as conventionally cadential: "The prototypical, standard clausula in galant music had a bass that rose from ③ to ④ to ⑤ before falling to ①." I assess Gjerdingen's perspective in detail in chapter 6.

5. An often-tapped property of the diatonic ascending 5–6 sequence is that its sixth chord restores the pitch classes of the initial chord, a convenient strategy for prolonging a single harmony. See my "Schubert, Chromaticism, and the Ascending 5–6 Sequence" (2006), pp. 258–261. Note that the 5–6 on A♭ in measure 3 (unfurled so that F sounds in the bass) serves as a conventional link between IV and V, but that the 5–6 on A♭ in measures 7 and 8 resides within a broader linear trajectory. The B♭-D-(F) chord in the second half of measure 8 is *not* the dominant arrival. Though some analysts would deploy Roman numerals (IV II V III VI IV) to explicate the inner workings of this sequential progression, I propose instead that a single harmony – IV – holds sway throughout. Without the prior presentation of the antecedent phrase, it would be difficult to justify regarding the A♭-C of measure 7 as an assertion of IV: instead the sequence would be understood as a connection between I-space and the IV of measure 10. However, only the analysis of I IV *followed by* a sequential extension of IV supports the upper-third unfolding A♭<C, as displayed in **2.5c**.

6. Though bass D could initiate a move away from the tonic (compare with bass A at 14_2 in $\boxed{35}$), in this case D is a temporary displacement of C, which is restored immediately in the upper register and during 9_2 in the interior register. A misguided notion of "deceptive cadence" might induce an inflation of this event's impact. The essential consideration instead should be that the root-position tonic chord of 5_1 is prolonged through measure 9, where it takes on a minor seventh (thus evolving into I→) en route to IV, the phrase's second structural harmony. The embellishing chord that often comes between tonic 5- and 6-phase chords is *not* a dominant that one would expect to participate in a cadence. Carl Schachter understands this: in his "*Che Inganno!* The Analysis of Deceptive Cadences," in *Essays from the Third International Schenker Symposium*, ed. A. Cadwallader (Hildesheim: Olms, 2006), pp. 279–298, he clearly distinguishes between such a "lower-level prefix to the VI" and "a structural dominant" (p. 281, referring to his Example 1c). I question even bringing up such a context in an article devoted to the deceptive cadence. In my notation, the progression of his example is I^{5-6} II→ V I. The initiating I-space is not a viable location for any cadence, deceptive or otherwise. Though the harmonic progression in the Haydn exposition is instead I^{5-6-5}→ IV^{5-6} V I, the embellishing chord between the 5 and 6 phases of I is likewise not a viable location for a cadence. However, as mentioned in the analytical discussion, the P section of this exposition is unusual in that content that plays a harmonic role during the first phrase performs a local embellishing-chord role during the second phrase.

7. These upper thirds may be understood as components of a subsidiary line that emerges from and then returns to the interior of the texture: F (end of measure 8), E♭ (measure 9), D<D (transferred to the upper register during measure 10), C (second pitch of measure 11), B♭>B♭ (restoration of the lower register during the second half of measure 11), and A (at the cadence in measure 12). A similar interior line is displayed in **2.1e**.

8. Compare with the situation at 7_1, where structural G<A♭ coordinates the upper-third line B♭<C. In this case, IV undergoes a 5–6 expansion, which accounts for the F at the end of 7_2.

9. As was also the case in $\boxed{23}$ (see footnote 7), these upper thirds are components of a subsidiary line that straddles two registers between measures 5 and 8. Observe that C emerges (via chromaticism) in the lower register at 7_1 before being hoisted above the A♭, which has structural priority due to its role as neighbor to the *Kopfton*.

10. The linear $\begin{smallmatrix}A♭>G>\ F\\C>\ B♭>A♭\end{smallmatrix}$ during measure 11 relates to $\begin{smallmatrix}C>\ B♭>A♭\\A♭>G>\ F\end{smallmatrix}$ during 7_{1-2}.

11. I explore a similar dramatic descent from a high point in Schubert's Impromptu in E♭ Major (D. 899, no. 2). See *Schubert*, p. 214.

12. Though the antecedent/consequent phrase structure is maintained during the restatement, some details of placement are altered. For example, the opening

D<E<F♯ is expanded from three to five beats, and yet the IV chord occurs on schedule both at 3_2 and at 13_2. (Observe that during the restatement soprano B appears *instead of* rather than *above* incomplete neighbor G.) In the varied consequent phrase IV arrives a measure earlier than in the initial consequent (18_1 versus 9_1), preceded now by a surging I→.

13. F♯'s upper third is presented as a lower sixth during 6_2. The resolution of F♯ is neglected. On the second try, F♯<A (in which the A sounds as both an upper tenth and upper third, during 7_4 and 8_2) is succeeded by G♯>E.

14. My determination of the *Kopfton* and interpretation of the theme's structure in general conflict with an early graph by Schenker, presented in his *Der Tonwille: Pamphlets in Witness of the Immutable Laws of Music, Offered to a New Generation of Youth*, ed. W. Drabkin, trans. I. Bent *et al.*, Oxford University Press, 2004–2005), vol. 1, pp. 153–155. On the other hand, we are in agreement that measure 16 – not measure 20 – is a dividing point in the structure.

15. For a similar perspective on the structure of P, see Kofi Agawu's "Haydn's Tonal Models: The First Movement of the Piano Sonata in E-flat Major, Hob. XVI: 52", in *Convention in Eighteenth- and Nineteenth-Century Music: Essays in Honor of Leonard G. Ratner*, ed. W. J. Allanbrook, J. M. Levy, and W. P. Mahrt (Stuyvesant, NY: Pendragon, 1992), pp. 3–22. Note that Agawu processes the melodic content of this passage as a linear ninth, whereas I process it as an octave (as shown in **2.9**) followed by a second. There is a sense of restoration and completion at 8_2 that is absent from Agawu's account.

16. In "Theorizing the Comic Surface," in *Music in the Mirror: Reflections on the History of Music Theory and Literature for the 21st Century*, ed. A. Giger and T. J. Mathiesen (Lincoln: University of Nebraska Press, 2002), pp. 195–216, here p. 205, Wye J. Allanbrook goes so far as to call the downbeat of measure 6 a deceptive cadence.

17. Compare with *FC*, fig. 19a and fig. 20, exs. 1–3.

18. William Rothstein offers an abundance of analytical observations concerning this exposition in *Phrase Rhythm in Tonal Music* (New York: Schirmer, 1989), pp. 132–141. Our readings diverge somewhat during S, where Rothstein proposes a third-progression (G>F>E♭) in tonicized E♭ Major, contrasting my fifth-progression descending from B♭ (= $\hat{2}$).

19. Marion A. Guck devotes lavish attention to the appoggiatura F of measure 1 in "Analysis as Interpretation: Interaction, Intentionality, Invention," *Music Theory Spectrum* 28 (2006), pp. 191–209, here pp. 204–206. I regard that pitch as a local manifestation of the same impulse that results in an embellishing-chord expansion of the tonic. Here G and B♭ serve as lower neighbors to the tonic's root and third. F similarly embellishes its fifth, from above and at the sub-chordal level. What seems wondrous to me (but goes unnoted by Guck) is how various potentialities from measure 1 and the first half of measure 2 are elevated to a more explicitly harmonic context in measure 5 and the first half of measure 6: the A♭<F>E♭>D♭>C melodic contour shifts to

become A♭>F>E♭>D♭>C, with the F receiving the harmonic support of IV and the pitches that in measure 1 form an embellishing chord asserted as a structural dominant in measure 5.

20. Sixteenth-note F sounds against D♭ and F at the end of 5_2, temporarily displacing the tonic's E♭ (= $\hat{5}$) with the support of IV. The context for a similar F during 7_4 lacks the lower D♭ and F. (Though the performer has by now released them, the C and E♭ quarter notes from 7_1 may be understood to persist.) Consequently the entire measure prolongs the tonic harmony. This latter F serves as a local passing note.

21. The F of 6_3 continues from E♭ in the first phrase, reaching the upper E♭ at 7_3 and reverting to the lower E♭ at 8_1. These arpeggiations are filled in by step.

22. These two structures are among Schenker's basic descending-fifth prototypes: see the second and third models in *FC*, fig. 16, ex. 5. Compare with the second model in *FC*, fig. 67, ex. 4b.

23. From my harmonic perspective the tonic's 5- and 6-phase chords are closely allied. Consequently the opening measures of TR in $\boxed{30}$ and in $\boxed{25}$ seem to me to be pursuing similar strategies: in the former, the opening of the P theme in the tonic key – *followed by* the 6-phase chord – inaugurates TR, whereas in the latter the opening of the P theme – *supported by* the 6-phase chord – inaugurates TR. Given that I^{5-6} is the conventional route to TR's goal II♯, in $\boxed{25}$ Haydn simply has moved forward in the tonal trajectory a bit sooner. In "Die 'Überleitung' im klassischen Stil: Hauptwege und Seitenwege in der Sonataexposition bei Haydn, Mozart und Beethoven," in *Passagen: Theorien des Übergangs in Musik und anderen Kunstformen*, ed. C. Utz and M. Zenck (Saarbrücken: Pfau, 2009), pp. 113–149, here, p. 126, Hans-Ulrich Fuß fails to comprehend the logic of Haydn's structure here, describing the "c-Moll-Insel" (C Minor island) as a "Fremdkörper" (foreign body).

24. Whereas I take care not to lose sight of the fact that B♭ Major functions as V in E♭ Major at the background level, here the tonicization of B♭ is strongly indicated during the concluding measures of TR. Note especially that the G♭-B♭-E♮ "augmented sixth" embellishing chord at 23_3 enhances the dominant character of the F chord to which it resolves (with soprano F, the expected resolution of the preceding E♮, elided to make way for minor seventh E♭, which likewise is a dominant trait).

25. The passage resides at the borderline between embellishment and harmonic progression. Though in an early draft of this note I argued against a harmonic interpretation, I now acknowledge a local tonicization, F Major: I→ IV♭ $V^{9♭}_{7}$ I. This progression contains a dominant-functioning chord, an element missing from the related passage in $\boxed{31}$.

26. Roger Kamien and Naphtali Wagner, who explore transition sections in "Bridge Themes within a Chromaticized Voice Exchange in Mozart Expositions," *Music Theory Spectrum* 19 (1997), pp. 1–12, likewise conclude that the structural V generally does not arrive until after the transition. Though their notation and

terminology differ from mine, one may correlate their augmented 6th with my evolved tonic 6-phase chord and their V/V with my II♯.

27. My practice of labeling the chord that concludes TR as II♯ in the movement's tonic key emphasizes the primary role of TR as predecessor of V. I intentionally distance myself somewhat from the Hepokoski/Darcy label V:HC MC, mentioned above.

28. Schenker's graph in *Tonwille* (2004–2005, vol. 1, p. 154) displays Roman numerals in the context of G Major beginning in measure 20. In the early 1920s Schenker had not yet penetrated to the background structure, and consequently there is no attempt to integrate the G>F>E>D>C of P and the D>C>B>A>G of S. If E serves as the movement's *Kopfton*, as I propose, a deep connection emerges between the E (= $\hat{3}$) of P and the D (= $\hat{2}$) of S.

29. Hepokoski and Darcy (*Elements of Sonata Theory*, 2006, p. 131) concur: "The implicit drama involved in producing the first satisfactory linear fifth-descent in the new key (a task of central importance to the sonata as a whole) is often the whole point of S – its implied difficulty in fulfilling its mission, the production of the EEC."

30. Note the similarity between the bass lines of measures 39–41 and 57–58, both supporting the ascending fifth-progression.

31. In his *Classical Form: A Theory of Formal Functions for the Instrumental Music of Haydn, Mozart, and Beethoven* (Oxford University Press, 1998, p. 105), William E. Caplin misreads the IV harmony at 42_1 as an inverted II. In my view, G-B-D♯ at the end of measure 41 is engaged in a surge: I→ pointing towards IV. Though IV's fifth is omitted at 42_1, certainly G is the appropriate note to imagine. The G♯ that follows is a chromatic passing note connecting this imagined 5-phase G and the 6-phase A on beat 2. As an aside, I need to register strong disapproval of Caplin's harmonic interpretation of measures 46 through 48 as V IV III II I. Though there are historical precedents for such a reading (see *TAH*, **3.4a**), there are also historical precedents for regarding such a reading as misguided (see *TAH*, **3.4b–c**).

32. IV's 5 phase occurs only during measure 42. In the later cadences a D>B unfolding during the tonic expansion ((45_2)/48_2, (50_2)/58_{1-2}, 60_1–60_2) is succeeded by a C>A or A<C unfolding supported by IV⁶. This C migrates to the tenor register in measures 59 and 61, where the structural line's continuation is presented.

33. My conception of S in $\boxed{25}$ contrasts that of Hepokoski and Darcy. They invoke their notion of trimodular blocks, proposing a division at measure 18. (See their *Elements of Sonata Theory* (2006), p. 177.)

34. The supertonic is prolonged via neighboring motions: $\begin{smallmatrix} C & <D(\flat)> & C \\ E\natural & <F> & E\natural \end{smallmatrix}$. The first set of neighboring notes is itself embellished by neighboring notes: $\begin{smallmatrix} D & <E\flat> & D \\ F & <G> & F \end{smallmatrix}$ at 20_1, resulting in the sounding of E♭ during the prolongation of a harmony that contains an E♮!

35. My reading of measure 26 is necessarily speculative, since these chords contain only two pitch classes each. I am influenced by the previous I^{5-6} II succession. Note that G and B♭ are joined by D at 26_3.

36. In $\boxed{25}$ a grace note confirms an assumed third scale degree. Here the upper note in the trill performs that function.
37. The assertion of E♮ during 31_3 is a debatable point. In that the same turn figure has occurred in the preceding two measures, perhaps F persists here as a pedal point lodged in the soprano. Yet I propose that this third time the E♮ and G, against G and two B♭s in the immediate context, take on the role of chord members, with the first F serving as a passing note and the second F as an anticipation. The unequivocal assertion of E♮ during 36_3 supports this reading.
38. Note how the A♮ and B♭ from measures 33–34 recur in measures 42–43. It is the dissonance of this A♮ against the preceding E♭ that allows me to propose that, of all the sixteenth notes in measure 43, it is the D that picks up the thread from the preceding segment of the line. After this D, the line continues downwards to C during the II chord at 44_1.
39. At 26_1 the C Major tonic's root position is attained, but in the melody we encounter a brief D>C delay (echoing that of 25_1). At 27_1 the soprano issue has been rectified, but the bass is delayed. Only at 30_3 do all the cadential features transpire optimally. The attainment of cadential closure and the close alliance between measures 17–18 and 29–30 are decisive factors in perceiving a continuation of S through 30_3, rather than regarding the content of measure 27 as the onset of C.
40. In both measures 32–33 and 37–38, the prototype that Haydn is deforming would proceed as a descending third to the leading tone: B>A>G♯. Haydn concludes that line only in the accompanimental figuration (A>G♯), while in the melody grace note C♯ reaches over the A to restore B prior to the tonic resolution. Compare with $\boxed{29}$, measures 17 and 18, where leading tone B does not sound even in an inner voice.
41. The dramatic C>D♮ seventh will return – without stepwise filling-in – during the exposition's closing zone (measures 37 and 38).
42. Though the C is attained in the Middle C register, it eventually soars to a high perch at 30_1. A two-octave drop of B♭ in measures 30 and 31 complements that upward transfer during measures 28 through 30. The G of the tonic resolution likewise shifts two octaves upwards in measures 32 and 33 (and 35 and 36).
43. The A♭-C-F chord in the second half of measure 24 does not assert itself as II. It instead functions as an embellishing chord. Not only is soprano F a neighbor: A♭ and C are also.
44. A subtle distinction should be made between the content of measures 30 and 35. In the former, the preceding emphasis upon C♯ (measures 27 and 29) supports a reading of the bass as a filled-in arpeggiation: E>C♯>A, projecting I^{5-6} II. In the latter, Haydn instead is nearing the end of a gradual descending register transfer of B: B (33_1), G♯ (34_1), E (35_1), after which we might expect B at 36_1. The B♮ at the end of measure 35 not only offers an early completion of the octave descent, but also projects a surge: the augmented E-G♯-B♮ chord is I➔ pressing towards

IV, which arrives at 36_1. Note that an ascending register transfer in measures 42 through 46 (G♯<B<E<G♯) complements this descending register transfer.
45. The notion of "incidental" and "essential" dissonances was introduced by Kirnberger. See *TAH*, pp. 18–19 and 37–39.
46. Unfolded thirds (some filled in by a passing note) pervade the passage: E♭>C during 26_4 followed by B♭<D (the D arriving "late") and then C>A during 27_{1-2}. These two lines converge on B♭ at the cadence.
47. The line proceeds as follows: from incomplete neighbor E♭ (first half of measure 40) through passing D (second half of measure 40 and all of measure 41) to C (first half of measure 42), with cadence on B♭ at 42_3. (The measure numbers in **2.26** indicate conceptual arrival points, not the extent of the prolongations.) The abundant figuration masks what beneath the surface amounts to a sloweddown repetition of 26_4 through 27_3.
48. I explore the subtonic chord in detail in "Schenker, Schubert, and the Subtonic Chord," *Gamut* 3 (2010). Concerning the interpretation of G-B♮-D-F at 51_3 as an evolved IV➔, compare with *Schubert*, **1.7**.
49. Whereas incomplete neighbor E♭ proceeds directly through passing note D to the dominant's C during the structure's first traversal (measures 38 through 41), an upward excursion (E♭<E♮<F) transpires during measures 52 through 58 before the line from E♭ continues downwards through D to C.
50. The D's arrival is so delayed that the local passing note C within a D>C>B♮ motion to the inner register occurs "late," after 6-phase G arrives in measure 34. Compare with C>B♭>A♮ in measures 35 and 36. Because the C is not so dramatically delayed, there is time for passing note B♭ to sound in its rightful position before the bar line (though A♮ is delayed until 36_2).
51. This neighbor is an unharmonized local embellishment, part of an embellishing chord like that displayed in **1.2b**, Model 2. The upper neighbor within the **2.20f** prototype, which resides deeper within the structure, is harmonized.
52. Note also that the retrograde of F<G♭<A♮<B♭ (measure 15) helps shape the bass line of measures 31 and 32.
53. Whereas the model of **2.29** shows the second scale degree arriving over the dominant, in this case that pitch (C in B♭ Major) arrives against bass E♮ near the end of measure 28, after which a local C>F stepwise motion to the interior of the texture transpires, prolonging the C into the dominant domain.
54. I interpret the high F as a cover tone. The melody projects D>B♭ A♮<C B♭.

3 Composition in a minor key: six arias in G Minor from operas by Mozart

1. I have excluded the Queen of the Night's aria, "Zum Leiden bin ich auserkoren" from *Die Zauberflöte*, which I interpret to be in B♭ Major despite its G Minor opening section (following a recitative in B♭ Major). That, the six arias explored in this chapter, and three additional arias in G Minor are assessed in Steven Jan's

Aspects of Mozart's Music in G Minor: Toward the Identification of Common Structural and Compositional Characteristics (New York: Garland, 1995), chapter 3. Jan proposes that "keys hold personal, private subjective associations for individual composers, such that a specific key is selected – compositional factors permitting – for the musical setting of texts articulating a specific concept" (pp. 53–54).

2. In *A History of Key Characteristics in the Eighteenth and Early Nineteenth Centuries*, 2nd edn. (University of Rochester Press, 2002, pp. 273–276), Rita Steblin assembles characteristics imputed to G Minor by twenty-three authors writing from 1691 through 1843. Whereas some views are closely aligned with Mozart's arias ("sadness," "discontent," "agitation"), others are contrasting ("sweet," "meek," "apathy").

3. The vocal melody of measure 27 is especially poignant, in that it bridges the sixth between the upper G and the passing B♭ that connects C (neighbor of the *Kopfton* $\hat{3}$) and A ($\hat{2}$). That passing B♭ is hoisted to the top of the texture by the first violins.

4. When the mediant leads to the dominant via an ascending sequence, the $\hat{2}$ of the fundamental line often will sound beneath the fifth scale degree. Compare with FC, fig. 26a.

5. In his *Aspects of Mozart's Music in G Minor* (1995), p. 73, Jan offers two graphs for this passage. Only the second posits root D for measure 40.

6. It is common for melodies to descend to the interior of chordal structures during the dominant. In **3.1b**, measure 19, A♮ appears in the soprano, though the vocal melody has by that point descended to F♯. Similarly in **3.4**, measure 29, C appears in the soprano, though the vocal melody has descended to A. (Note that the C sounds during varied reiterations of the dominant arrival in measures 31 and 33.)

7. The D-F-A chords at 77_1 and 78_1 are unfurled $^6_4$ embellishments of the A chord. The resolution of A➔ is instead the dominant-emulating D major supertonic of measure 80, as shown in **3.6**.

8. That one of these thirds is minor and the other major is of no consequence. What is important is that G Minor's diatonic third and sixth scale degrees are engaged.

9. One general principle that seems to hold true in most music by Haydn and Mozart is that a movement's initiating I-space will be confirmed by means of a broad stepwise filling-in (usually descending) of one of the intervals of its chord. A melody like Zaide's in measures 3 through 15, in which many arpeggiations occur, offers a challenge to holders of that notion. I proceeded very cautiously in analyzing this passage, eventually formulating **3.7a**. My pillars were D (at 3_1), B♭ (at 10_1), and G (at 15_1). Where is C? Where is A? Fortunately $V^{(7)}_{\sharp}$, which inevitably comes between two tonics within any substantial harmonic progression, offers a suitable venue for either C or A. Note that I did not select one of the C pitches sung by Zaide. Instead, I regard C as arriving during the II of measure

8, where C sounds briefly in the first violin but is absent from the vocal line. That C persists through the following dominant, prolonged by the local C>B♭>A motion. In the continuation, the A between B♭ and G is not concealed, though some readers may be concerned that I regard an internal pitch within a long arpeggiation (F♯>D>C>A>F♯) as a component of the structural descent. That interpretation is logical if B♭ and G pillars surround the arpeggiation: A is the pitch that the ear will embrace as a connector.

10. The path from V to I in measures 35 through 39 resembles a model presented by Louis and Thuille in their *Harmonielehre* [1907]. See *TAH*, **5.2c**.

11. If the G major chord *had* led to C Minor, then it could be regarded as the unfurled and chromaticized 6 phase of the preceding tonicized mediant B♭, within a G<B♭<C<D trajectory connecting the tonic and the dominant. (Compare with the G→C that occurs in **3.5**.) What transpires instead suggests that the B♭ region resides within a broad prolongation of I-space in G Minor. In any event, the situation is more nuanced than one would suspect from Charles Rosen's description of measure 62 as "the dominant of C minor": *Sonata Forms* (New York: Norton, 1980), p. 66.

12. Experienced Schenkerian analysts may notice that the structure I propose does not occur among Schenker's models in *FC*, fig. 16. (A similar passage occurs in **3.14**, later in this chapter.) William Rothstein explores alternatives to Schenker's orthodox structures in his "Transformations of Cadential Formulae in the Music of Corelli and His Successors," in *Essays from the Third International Schenker Symposium*, ed. A. Cadwallader (Hildesheim: Georg Olms, 2006), pp. 245–278. Schenker shows the span from $\hat{5}$ to $\hat{2}$ supported by the dominant in the context of a descent from $\hat{8}$ to $\hat{1}$ in his analysis of the Largo from Bach's Sonata No. 3 for Solo Violin in *Das Meisterwerk in der Musik: Ein Jahrbuch*, 3 vols. (Munich: Drei Masken, 1925, 1926, 1930); as *The Masterwork in Music*, ed. W. Drabkin, trans. I. Bent et al., 3 vols. (Cambridge University Press, 1994–1997), vol. 1, pp. 31–38. See also *FC*, fig. 119, ex. 17.

13. The IV harmony that arrives in measures 108–109 eventually undergoes a 5–6 shift, wherein the 6-phase chord C-E♭-A sounds in its dominant-emulating evolved state C♯-E♮-G-B♭ (measure 116). In that the pitch G occurs in both phases, Mozart is able to undertake a local embellishment: G<A♭>G. This A♭ is *not* the arrival of the 6 phase, nor is it the root of an asserted ♭II harmony. It is merely a chromatic upper neighbor to the IV harmony's fifth, G.

14. Here the mediant performs a mediating role between the tonic and the dominant. The fact that the mediant is tonicized but the dominant is not does not alter the basic ascending-fifth tonal trajectory during the A₁ section, characteristic of the first half of a binary structure. In a ternary structure the completion of that fifth (from III to V♯) often occurs during the B section.

15. B♭, the goal of the descending third, occurs at 10_1 and 13_1. During the first statement of "voi foste" the internal II^7 chord (C-E♭-G-A) is weakly presented:

G descends to leading tone F♯ after a single eighth note (during 8₁). During the second statement (measure 11) the supertonic more robustly evolves into dominant-emulating C♯-E♮-G-A, leading to a V♯–I cadence.

16. In the connection of chords such as G and C via an ascending 5–6 sequence, composers often take advantage of the fact that the third 6-phase chord reinstates the pitch classes of the first 5-phase chord (here the initial G-B♭-D is transformed into B♮-D-F-G). The hierarchical relationship between the third 5-phase and 6-phase chords may be ambiguous. Is the essence of the progression a stepwise ascent (here G<A<B♭<C), or instead a prolongation of the initial G until the arrival of C? Whereas **3.10a** acknowledges the inherent ambiguity, in **3.10b** the latter interpretation is wholeheartedly embraced.

17. Timothy Cutler presents other examples of this phenomenon in "On Voice Exchanges," *Journal of Music Theory* 53 (2009), pp. 191–226.

18. Compare with the III ( ) V♯ connections in other arias we have explored: **3.2** (measures 36–40) and **3.5**.

19. A stepwise descent is part of what gives a PAC its sense of closure. Because such lines are predictable and overused, Mozart sometimes avoids sounding those notes in his melodies, calling upon the listener's familiarity with the routine as he supplies a creative variant of the well-worn path. This aria's descending sixth D>F♯ in measure 18 (from upper third of B♭ to lower third of A) is frequently encountered. In my view it remains a variant, not the norm. Here the viola provides the missing links within the structural line.

20. The connection of the mediant and the subdominant via a 5–6 shift is a potentially ambiguous moment. Because the mediant's 6-phase chord contains the pitches of the tonic (perhaps in an evolved state, such as B♮ in place of diatonic B♭ at the end of measure 15), it may represent a restoration of that tonic, in which case the mediant would reside within a broader tonic prolongation. In **3.13a** I display the G of measure 14 as an extension of III, not as a restoration of I. (The parenthetical I below III⁶ is not on the same plane as the III. It indicates only that the 6 phase of III has the *local* effect of a tonic leading to IV.) This is a delicate and sometimes irresolvable issue within the analysis of music.

21. Steven Jan's analysis of "Ach ich fühl's" in his "The Evolution of a 'Memeplex' in Late Mozart: Replicated Structures in Pamina's 'Ach ich fühl's'," *Journal of the Royal Musical Association* 128 (2003), pp. 330–370, offers an interesting contrast to mine. For example, whereas I propose an asserted harmonic function for the last chord in measure 2, Jan describes it as "a grating ♯7–♮7–6–4–2 on G" (p. 333), analyzing the opening harmonic progression as a motion from the tonic to the subdominant and back.

22. Whereas the major dominant's diatonic upper-third chord is of diminished quality (e.g., A-C-E♭ in relation to F-A-C-E♭), composers often modify the chord to attain major quality (either A-C♯-E♮ or A♭-C-E♭). See *Schubert*, **1.8**, and my "Schenker, Schubert, and the Subtonic Chord" (2010). See also *FC*, fig. 111.

23. I^{5-6} II is awkward in a minor key for two reasons: (1) the tonic's diatonic 6-phase chord is dominant-emulating in the direction of ♭II, not diatonic II; and (2) the diatonic II chord's quality is diminished, preventing a dominant-emulating evolution of the preceding 6-phase chord (i.e., G♯-B♮-E♮ to A-C-E♭ will never occur).

24. My reading contrasts that which Felix Salzer presents in *Structural Hearing: Tonal Coherence in Music*, 2 vols. (New York: Boni, 1952; reprint edn., New York: Dover, 1962), ex. 483. Whereas I regard the movement as shaped by an interruption, he maintains *Kopfton* $\hat{5}$ until at least measure 26. (It is curious that he does not display the C of 26_1 as an open notehead with upward stem, as he does that of 32_1.)

25. Perhaps I am shirking my analytical duty – though perhaps I am instead resonating with Pamina's indecisiveness – by juxtaposing incompatible hierarchical relationships in my analysis of this passage. The diagram on p. 115 and **3.16a** display I in measure 25 as hierarchically deeper than the V of measure 26 (leading readers to suppose that the beams in **3.16a** will reach their goal Gs in the phrase that follows), whereas **3.16b** proposes an extension of V until measure 30. Whereas the I of measure 25 initially seems to inaugurate the final tonic prolongation, ultimately it fails to overpower the background V♯, which (as we later come to understand) persists until near the end of measure 30.

26. The A-C-E♭ diminished triad does triple duty within this aria: it serves as the fifth, seventh, and ninth of G Minor's dominant (at 37_2); as third, fifth, and seventh of B♭ Major's dominant (at 15_2); and as root, third, and fifth of the subdominant's 6-phase chord or the supertonic (at 3_2 and 26_1).

4 The happy ending: three sonata-rondos in D Major from piano concertos by Haydn and Mozart

1. This chapter's discussion of form derives from Hepokoski and Darcy, as articulated in chapter 18 ("Rondos and the Type 4 Sonata") of their *Elements of Sonata Theory* (2006). Their discussion of the sonata-rondo, which they call the Type 4 sonata, appears on pages 404 through 429.

2. For an extended discussion of my notion of "peculiar juxtaposition," see *Schubert*, pp. 26–31.

3. Haydn's modifications within TR during the recapitulatory rotation, explored below, support this reading.

4. Hepokoski and Darcy comment on the curious situation of the ESC in a sonata-rondo movement. Whereas the sonata ESC occurs at the close of the recapitulation's S (before the coda), that of a normative rondo occurs during the final refrain, which in a sonata-rondo movement occurs *after* S. (See their intriguing discussion and diagram in *Elements of Sonata Theory*, pp. 428–429.) In H. XVIII: 11 Haydn skirts this issue by bypassing S during the recapitulatory rotation.

5. Those who may have questioned my choice of F♯ rather than A as the *Kopfton* find here further evidence favoring that reading.
6. Mozart later makes up for his omission of the E: see measures 123, 233, and 334.
7. In light of what follows, I interpret D>C♯>B>A during 36_2 not as the filling-in of a D>A fourth, but instead as a D-to-B third followed by another third to the downbeat G♯. (Compare with the similar gestures in measures 38, 40, and 42.) Consequently the progression begins with a shift to the tonic's 6-phase chord, from which a B–E–A–D–... circular continuation ensues.
8. In chapter 10 I will elaborate upon my rejection of Hepokoski and Darcy's assertion that, once an HC alternative has been denied, it will not recur. As in the symphony movement that I analyze there, repetition plays an important role throughout this movement. Thus a reiteration of the TR structure becomes part of the composer's plan.
9. As we saw above, Haydn employs a similar sequential structure during the recapitulatory rotation's TR in H. XVIII: 11 (measures 288–291). Just as the D major chord at 289_1 there is not the dominant's resolution, so also in K. 451 the A major chord at 45_1 is not the dominant-emulating supertonic's resolution.
10. As mentioned on page 251, note 5, above, it is common for the first six chords of such a sequence (here E^{5-6} $F♯^{5-6}$ $G♯^{5-6}$) to be abbreviated to a single chord, since the first and sixth chords are constructed using the same pitch classes.
11. The juxtaposition of chords in measures 58 through 61, seemingly engaging the succession from V to IV, is similar to that which we encountered in H. XVIII: 11, measures 170 through 180. In both cases the structurally deep dominant arrives after the IV.
12. Initially the lower-strand notes occur on the beats while the upper-strand notes occur off the beats. That relationship is reversed in the expanded repetition that begins at 82_2.
13. Dissonant seventh G♮ works together with ninth B. Whereas G♮ resolves to *Kopfton* F♯, the B prepares the upper-third A. This can be observed most clearly at the juncture between the expositional and developmental rotations, measures 103 and 104: downward arpeggiation B>G>E (over mentally retained dominant root A) is answered by upward arpeggiation D<F♯<A.
14. My reading of the development offers an alternative to that of L. Poundie Burstein, presented in his "Mozart's Harmonic Experiments of 1784," in *A Composition as a Problem III: Proceedings of the 3rd International Conference on Music Theory, Tallinn, March 9–10, 2001*, ed. M. Humal (Tallinn: Eesti Muusikaakadeemia and Scripta Musicalia, 2003), pp. 15–26, ex. 5 (pp. 21–22). Whereas I interpret the melodic G in the vicinity of measures 172 through 184 as internal to an F♯<A third, it is for him internal to an A>E fourth; and whereas I regard the mediant of measure 200 as an intermediate goal, he places its soprano A within a stepwise ascent from E in measure 184 to B♮ in measure 201. We both unfold a bass third (C♯>A̲) at the development's close.

15. Note in **4.11** that I interpret the melodic E>D>C♯>B from the second half of measure 142 as a double-note descending unfolding of $\substack{E>D \\ C\sharp>B}$, answered by the ascending unfolding of $\substack{C\sharp \\ A\sharp}$ at the dominant arrival point. Compare with *FC*, fig. 43, ex. b4.
16. This elision matches that which occurs in the double-arpeggiation progression during S. See **4.9**, measures 85 and 86.
17. Note that the expositional rotation's I V alternative is not tonic-pointing. It would instead have been followed by a tonicization of V for the presentation of S. The recapitulational rotation's I V *is* tonic-pointing: V plays the role that II♮ played during the earlier transition.
18. The harmonic trajectories are distinct though equivalent: I II➔ V in the expositional rotation versus I IV$^{5-6}$ (= II➔) V in the recapitulatory rotation.
19. Hepokoski and Darcy (*Elements of Sonata Theory*, 2006, pp. 425–427) regard Mozart's frequent presentation of a new tonic-key theme at the outset of a sonata-rondo finale's TR as the borrowing of a feature from his concerto first movements (the Type 5 sonata).
20. A contrasting reading of this passage is offered by Joel Galand in "The Large-Scale Formal Role of the Solo Entry Theme in the Eighteenth-Century Concerto," *Journal of Music Theory* 44 (2000), pp. 381–450, here p. 433. Whereas I regard the stepwise D>D octave of 53$_2$ through 54$_1$ as a filling-in of a D>A>F♯>D arpeggiation, a context in which the downbeat G functions as a passing note, he interprets that G as a member of a line from the A at 53$_1$ to the F♯ and E at the half cadence. (Full disclosure: Galand was my student as an undergraduate.)
21. Some readers may be disappointed that I resist the Hepokoski/Darcy harmonic analysis of the juncture between TR and S as V I in the tonicized dominant key. (Though figure 2.1 on page 17 of their *Elements of Sonata Theory* proposes that the exposition's Part 1 – P plus TR, through the MC – is in the "Tonic key," in practice they begin the dominant tonicization before the MC.) Sentences such as the one that this note annotates demonstrate one advantage to maintaining a broad tonic-key focus throughout. I agree, of course, that the dominant is tonicized during S and thus becomes a local I.
22. Though initially I considered projecting descending fifths from E throughout, I found that analysis forced. I could not make a good case for the absence of the pitch D in the vicinity of measures 95–96 and 99–100. I prefer the reading in which the opening tonic is extended through a pair of voice exchanges: $\substack{C\sharp \\ A}X\substack{A \\ C\sharp}X\substack{C\sharp \\ A}$ in measures 89 through 92 (with the final C♯ much delayed) and 93 through 96, and $\substack{C\sharp \\ A}X\substack{A \\ C\sharp}X\substack{C\sharp \\ A}$ in measures 97 through 100 and 101 through 104. From this perspective the keyboard E that arrives just after C♯ during 104$_1$ is a surprise, a last-minute realization of something we may well have given up hope of attaining.
23. Because this sequence is diatonic rather than obstinate, the return of the tonic at its endpoint is not in question. Note, however, that Mozart elides two chords. A normative tonic-to-tonic sequence of this type would have proceeded as

A^5 $G\sharp^6$ $F\sharp^5$ E^6 D^5 $C\sharp^6$ B^5 A^6 $G\sharp^5$ $F\sharp^6$ E^5 D^6 $C\sharp^5$ B^6 A^5

Mozart substitutes a first-inversion A major chord for C♯⁵, thereby bringing the progression to a close two chords earlier than anticipated.

24. The symbols of music analysis are a communicative tool that should work efficiently and unambiguously in conveying the wide range of events that an analyst may wish to explore. When one writes A Major: ♭II⁵♮ V, one is acknowledging that the supertonic's root B♭ is a wobbly note. Diatonic B♮ will be restored during the dominant harmony that follows, while the F♮'s downward lean has the dominant's root E as its goal. The situation in measures 130 and 131 offers an extraordinary notational challenge, since the supertonic switches quickly from one sort of evolution to a highly contrasting one. Here the B♭ wobble is negated not by the dominant's B♮, but instead by the manifestation of II→ (D♯-F♯-A-C♮), whose unsounded root is B♮. In this context ♭II is not an appealing analytical symbol, because there is no way to track the resolution of the wobble *during* the supertonic prolongation. I regard placing "♭–♮•" to the *right* of the Roman numeral as the most effective means of conveying what occurs here. (Schenker's occasional juxtaposition of ♭II and ♮II fails to convey how a single harmonic function persists between the two chords. See, for example, his *Harmonielehre: Neue musikalische Theorien und Phantasien I* (Stuttgart: Cotta, 1906); as *Harmony*, ed. O. Jonas, abridged trans. E. M. Borghese (University of Chicago Press, 1954), pp. 72 and 74.)

25. D Major's diatonic 6-phase chord is D-F♯-B, as occurs (unfurled) in measure 65. The first chromatic variant is D♯-F♯-B, the second is D-F♮-B♭, and the third is D♭-F♮-B♭. This terminology is introduced in *Schubert*, pp. 56–60, and displayed in music notation there as **2.17**.

26. The bass B♭>A♭>F♯ in measures 197 through 200 is one of the strangest I have encountered in Mozart. I offer two thoughts on the matter. In order to make the re-emergence of the D Major tonic all the more astonishing, Mozart might have been intending a feint, pretending to inaugurate a chromatic ascending 5–6 sequence whose first three chords would be B♭ (measure 197), G♭ (measure 200, here with a $^6_4$ embellishment that is not given the opportunity to resolve), and then presumably C♭. In this context, the bass would more appropriately be spelled as B♭>A♭>G♭, a conventional major-third traversal. Yet by measure 202 it is apparent that F♯ really is F♯ – not G♭. In that context measures 200 and 201 might best be interpreted as D⁶, rather than as G♭$^6_4$. If that is so, then measures 198 and 199 may be interpreted as an embellishing chord of D (that which is often called a "common-tone diminished seventh": root D with E♯ lower neighbor of F♯, G♯ lower neighbor of A, and B upper neighbor of A). In that interpretation, the bass jumps from the lower-third chord's B♭ to a G♯ [A♭] neighbor to A, which would be a 5-phase restoration after the 6-phase B♭

(within a broad $D^{5-6\flat-5}$). Instead of resolving to that A, however, the line jumps downwards to the D chord's third, F♯. The A is withheld for two additional measures.

27. Whereas in measures 71 and 72 the A major chord does *not* assert itself as a harmony (it instead might be described as a grandiose anticipation of the $^6_4$ that embellishes D Major's supertonic in measure 73), the equivalent chord in the transposition of the recapitulatory rotation – D major in tonicized G Major in measure 219 – does assert itself as a local dominant.

5 Haydn: Symphony No. 45 in F♯ Minor ("Farewell"), movement 2

1. James Webster, *Haydn's "Farewell" Symphony and the Idea of Classical Style: Through-Composition and Cyclic Integration in His Instrumental Music* (Cambridge University Press, 1991). Webster's analysis of the second movement appears on pages 57 through 64.
2. Later, on p. 62, Webster describes the new theme that begins in measure 17 as "incipiently transitional."
3. The principal reason why I favor the upper register during S is that it will persist during C and throughout the development. The lower register is restored at the outset of the recapitulation.
4. C♮ and A♯ rarely occur in such close proximity. (But see *TAH*, **7.19b** and **7.20b**.) Perhaps in response to the melodic diminished third of measure 35, Haydn embellishes resolution pitch B with upper whole step C♯ in measure 36.
5. A<A♯<B reprises the bass motion in the concluding measures of TR. Compare with **5.2**.
6. Webster clearly places the divide before 46_3 in that example, though he uses the measure number 47 for this spot in his example 2.10 and on page 63 refers to a "poignant, minor-colored paragraph mm. 47–69." Not a trifling upbeat, 46_3 both restates the paragraph's opening tonic harmony and reinstates the melody pitch B. At 47_1 the progression has already proceeded beyond the tonic: the violin's B there serves as a suspension displacement of A. Granted, if this phrase had followed the model of the earlier one (beginning at 29_1) more closely, it would have begun at 47_1.
7. In his textual commentary Webster refers to a "diatonic resolution onto I^6 (mm. 66–69)" (p. 62). This appears to contradict his example 2.10, which displays a B (dominant) prolongation extending from measure 50 until resolution in measure 71. In my view, if there is to be only one bass B in that example to convey the foundational structure, it should be the B of measure 70.
8. The unfolding of an A̲>F♯ third (filled in by G♯ or G♮) occurs twice during measures 47 through 50. A is reinstated at 53_3 and, after an upper-third excursion, descends to G♯ in measure 56. The broad role of A is apparent in **5.3**. Webster's G♯ is not a participant in this structure.

9. In the context of a circle of fifths, diatonic G♯-B-D will lead to a chord rooted on C♯ rather than on A. (The latter outcome would require the assertion of root E.) Consequently the evolved version *does* project the diminished G♯ chord's normative tendency.
10. By comparing Haydn's spelling of the II→ chords in measures 60–61 and 166–167, one discovers that the second violin's B♯ in the latter passage is an enharmonic respelling of what would have appeared as C♮ in a simple transposition. That C♮ is restored in measure 174. Haydn's B♯ spelling facilitates normative-looking chordal constructs during the interior of the voice exchange (e.g., G♯-B♯-D♯-F♯ rather than G♯-C♮-D♯-F♯), but at the endpoints certainly it is to be understood as the supertonic's downward-tending ninth, C♮.
11. The long horizontal line connecting the two V Roman numerals in Webster's Example 2.12c is an explicit articulation of that analytical interpretation.

6 Haydn: String Quartet in G Minor (op. 20, no. 3), movement 3

1. Gjerdingen, *Music in the Galant Style* (2007). In addition, Gjerdingen edited and contributed to a special *Journal of Music Theory* issue devoted to *partimenti* (vol. 51, no. 1, 2007).
2. See *Music in the Galant Style*, chapter 2.
3. See *Music in the Galant Style*, chapter 3, noting how the harmonic contexts of the Prinners in Gjerdingen's exs. 3.14, 3.16, 3.18, and 3.22 differ from those of the other examples and also from one another.
4. A few samples:

    - Ex. 10.4, Var. II: I would place the number ❸ at 54_1, not 53_2. (Compare with *FC*, fig. 43, ex. b4.) The G that Gjerdingen selects is conceptually an inner-strand note that "belongs" under the downbeat B.
    - Ex. 11.13: I would reverse the hierarchical relationship between the sixth and seventh treble clef noteheads of measure 18. (The ❹ is an incomplete neighbor to the initial ❸, followed by a passing note leading to ❷. Gjerdingen's analysis makes the second ❸ appear to be a reinstatement of the earlier one.)
    - Ex. 25.19: I would place the number ❼ above the A♮ that occurs during 5_2, not above that during 5_1. (The first A♮ functions as a lower neighbor, not as an anticipation.) And I would finish the job at hand: the A♮>E♭ augmented fourth during beat 2 resolves to D<B♭ during beats 3 and 4. Thus the final notehead of measure 5 deserves a ❶.

5. Gjerdingen's analysis of this movement appears on pages 369 through 397 of *Music in the Galant Style*.
6. Letter from Leopold Mozart to his son Wolfgang, 4 December 1780, in *Mozart Briefe und Aufzeichnungen: Gesamtausgabe*, vol. 3, edited by W. A. Bauer and O. E. Deutsch (Kassel: Bärenreiter, 1963), p. 45. In his *Haydn, Mozart and the Viennese School* (New York: Norton, 1995), Daniel Heartz remarks: "The

symphonies in C and D in this group (Nos. 22 and 23) are particularly showy and lacking in much original content. The Italian overture relied mostly on stock figures and harmonic-rhythmic clichés, in keeping with the speed of composition that was usually imposed, rather than on novel ideas and their working out. We can assume that Mozart at home wrote under no such time constraints; he simply preferred the Italian style for the time being" (p. 568).

7. I chart the early development of harmonic analysis in *TAH*. (See especially chapter 1.) At first, Arabic numbers rather than Roman numerals were used. Trydell's practice was widely disseminated through its presentation in the "Music" article of the *Encyclopaedia Britannica*, published in 1771 – one year before Haydn's quartet was written. The indifference of Italians to harmonic analysis, a trait that Gjerdingen perpetuates, is evident through their almost total absence from *TAH*. The Milanese composer Bonifazio Asioli's *Trattato d'armonia e d'accompagnamento*, published around 1813, is exceptional. (Gjerdingen, on p. 427, praises Asioli as a "maestro" with a "copious musical knowledge" without mentioning that he advocated a rather sophisticated practice of scale-step harmonic analysis, described in *TAH*, p. 246. An uncharacteristically simple example appears there as **4.5a**. In the accompanying commentary, my remark that "the analyses employ frequent shifts of tonal center, though these shifts are not announced" applies also to Gjerdingen's practice. Yet note an important distinction: Asioli is dealing with progressions of roots, whereas Gjerdingen restricts himself to pitches, in keeping with his conviction that harmony does not emerge as an important factor in music until the nineteenth century.)

8. In this variant, the presentation of a P TR ' S / C cycle is shared by a development and a tonal resolution, as will be explained below. Chapter 17 of Hepokoski and Darcy's *Elements of Sonata Theory* (2006) is devoted to the Type 2 sonata.

9. Gjerdingen's analysis appears in his ex. 27.7 on pp. 386ff.

10. Though the scope of my historical investigations contrasts Gjerdingen's, *TAH* and my earlier *Music Theory from Zarlino to Schenker* (Stuyvesant, NY: Pendragon, 1990) offer ample evidence that my musical sensibilities, like his, have been shaped by a careful consideration of analytical procedures from past centuries.

11. By unfolding the third from C to A, the C remains a viable chord member of the V that emerges with the A. (Thus my label in **6.1** is V^7.) The C is touched on again during the sixteenth-note descent of beat 3 but does not sound at the end of the measure.

12. All the pitches of TR's thirds are unfolded in the first violin melody: G<B (3_3 to 13_1), A>F♯ (14_1 to 16_1), and E<G (17_1 to 17_2).

13. As with the B at 7_2 (discussed above), Haydn moves the D into an accented position. I have asserted the analyst's prerogative to move that passing note back to the location corresponding to its contrapuntal origin. (Species counterpoint is, of course, one of the cornerstones of eighteenth-century music.

Though my project centers on harmony, my voice-leading graphs are rich in associations with the contrapuntal training that was as pervasive during the eighteenth century as was the study of *partimenti* upon which Gjerdingen focuses.)

14. In his ex. 27.7 Gjerdingen provides a keyboard reduction of the score along with Haydn's sketch, which contains four measures that were later deleted. Since these deleted measures are included in the count, all subsequent measure numbers are four higher than those of the published score. Readers who are using Gjerdingen's score might wish to write in the lower set of numbers, starting with 19 at Gjerdingen's 23.

15. The double voice exchange (^E_GX^G_EX^E_G) and contrasting contour of the cello line in measure 17 suggest that the initiative begun in measure 13 is concluded.

16. This progression likewise was a factor in my critique of James Webster's analysis of a movement by Haydn in chapter 5, above, and in my critique of Richard L. Cohn's analysis of a movement by Schubert in *Schubert*, chapter 12.

17. Compare with measure 96, the equivalent passage during the tonal resolution, where a transposition of the pitch that I place within parentheses during the exposition actually occurs.

18. To maximize the surprise, Haydn maintains the A<B whole step in the bass between measures 25 and 26. A more characteristic approach to II (in A Major) would have been achieved by filling in that second as A<A♯<B, allowing the tonic's evolved 6-phase chord A♯-C♯-E-G to sound before the arrival of II. The C♯ and A♯ within the second violin figuration during 26_{1-2} serve as partial compensation for that omission.

19. My reading of measures 30 through 37 as an expansion of the D tonic appears to conflict with that of William Drabkin, *A Reader's Guide to Haydn's Early String Quartets* (Westport, CT: Greenwood Press, 2000), p. 120, who suggests that "the submediant [m. 31] ... allows the harmony to pass smoothly from the resumption of D major [m. 30] to a subdominant (G) [m. 32 or mm. 38–40?] stretched over ten bars."

20. The G♯ that occurs near the beginning of the Monte Principale's fourth measure (numbered 22 by Gjerdingen) "belongs" with the E and D at the end of the preceding measure. The similarity between the two halves of the phrase (D D$^{7♯}$ G followed by E E$^7_{3♯}$ A) invites the implementation of my notion of Peculiar Juxtaposition (see p. 122, above). In the first segment the initiating chord is hierarchically the deepest, whereas in the second, the concluding chord is. (See also *Schubert*, pp. 26–31.)

21. The earliest examples in *TAH* to show the analysis of a single event in multiple keys are **6.1** and **6.3b** (Lampe, 1737), **6.9** (Holden, 1770), and **6.15b** (Vogler, 1802). See also the commentary regarding Vogler (1776) on p. 173.

22. There is a curious equal sign between the staves of measure 26 (his measure 30) in Gjerdingen's ex. 27.7. Does it refer to a key shift? I have assumed that the ② below the staff corresponds to the pitch E ($\hat{2}$ in D Major). Yet perhaps there is a

typographical error here: Gjerdingen may have wanted to convey that for the first two beats of its dotted-half value, bass B functions as ⑥ in D Major, but that at beat 3 it is reinterpreted as ② in A Major. (If that is the case, the notation should read ⑥ = ②, and the ② should be in horizontal alignment with the ⑥.) Though the "D Major:" and "A Major:" notation that precedes my Roman numerals may seem stodgy, it is a reliable means of assuring that the tonal context of my analysis is not in doubt.

23. A similar close occurs in Schubert's "Die junge Nonne," mm. 60–61 and 82–83. See *Schubert*, chapter 9. Section headings within Gjerdingen's chapter 11 propose that ⑦–① is "characteristic of the soprano," while ②–① is "characteristic of the tenor."

24. The first violin's E at 63_3 is an astonishing note. Had Haydn wanted to match the contour of measure 60, he would have placed a passing note D♮ there instead. Though its sounding against F♮ and D♯ is an extreme clash, the E may be interpreted as an anticipation of measure 64's E.

25. Compare with *Schubert*, **4.6**. Here the relationship between A and C is being negotiated by their E and G dominants.

26. While A descends to G♯ in the second violin, the melodic E>C third leads to B<D, which in turn proceeds to $\frac{C}{A}$.

27. Johann Kirnberger, *Die Kunst des reinen Satzes in der Musik*, vol. 1 (Berlin: Decker & Hartung, 1771), pp. 110–111 (note); as *The Art of Strict Musical Composition*, trans. David Beach and Jurgen Thym (New Haven, CT: Yale University Press, 1982), pp. 128–129 (note).

28. Kirnberger's assessment of direct and distant key relationships, published in 1771, is presented in *TAH*, pp. 210–211. His ranked order of direct relationships to G Major is D, e, b, C, and a.

29. See especially his remarks on pp. 415–416 of *Music in the Galant Style* (2007).

30. Gjerdingen proposes, "the real art of composition lay in guiding their patron's and audience's moment-to-moment experiences" (*Music in the Galant Style*, 2007, p. 424).

31. Carl Dahlhaus, *Neues Handbuch der Musikwissenschaft*, vol. 6: *Die Musik des 19. Jahrhunderts* (Wiesbaden: Akademische Verlagsgesellschaft Athenaion, 1980), p. 215.

7 Mozart: String Quintet in C Major (K. 515), movement 1

1. Agawu's analysis is found in his *Playing with Signs: A Semiotic Interpretation of Classic Music* (Princeton University Press, 1991), pp. 80–99; Spitzer's is found in the essay "A Metaphoric Model of Sonata for Two Expositions by Mozart," in *Communication in Eighteenth-Century Music*, ed. D. Mirka and K. Agawu (Cambridge University Press, 2008), pp. 189–229. For a contrasting perspective, see the analysis by Henry Burnett and Roy Nitzberg in their *Composition, Chromaticism and the Developmental Process: A New Theory of Tonality* (Aldershot: Ashgate, 2007), pp. 217–225.

2. Schubert utilizes the same construction in a passage from his Piano Sonata in A Minor (D. 537), mvmt. 3, which I discuss in detail in *Schubert*, pp. 3–8. I find Danuta Mirka's analysis of a similar passage from Haydn's String Quartet in D Major (op. 50, no. 6, mvmt. 3, mm. 32|33–35) unconvincing because she does not invoke the notion of collision: two consecutive syntactic elements occupying the same musical moment. She instead invokes words such as "unclear," "mysterious," "eccentric" (twice), "misleads," and "contradictory." From tonic $^{F\sharp}_D$ the lower strings descend in parallel thirds to a downbeat ^B_G, which I regard as a premature arrival of the supertonic third and fifth, colliding with B-D♯-A, the D tonic's dominant-emulating 6-phase chord, which syntactically should precede the supertonic. My assessment of the phrase's harmonic progression working mostly in two-measure chunks certainly has implications for Mirka's endeavor to come to terms with the meter:

m.	33	34	35	36	37	38	39	40	41	42	43	44
	$\hat{5}$		$\hat{4}$				$\hat{3}$				$(\hat{2})$	
D Major:	I^5——	⌐6	II——	( )		V^7——	I^5——		—6——		II♮	V
			(= VI→)									

See her *Metric Manipulations in Haydn and Mozart: Chamber Music for Strings, 1787–1791* (Oxford University Press, 2009), pp. 54–55.

3. Note also that in measures 16 and 17 of the quintet, the outer lines fill in the spans C>G and E<G diatonically, whereas in measures (44)/46 through 55 they span E<G and A>G (substitute for C>G) chromatically.

4. Though Agawu mentions the occurrence of IV (at 16_4, I presume), he is silent about the harmonic implication of his graph's two adjacent ^D_F intervals (at 15_3 and 18_1). As **7.1c** shows, I regard these as two *separate* instances of II. Clearly the supertonic falls within Agawu's harmonic system: he employs the numeral ii in several analyses elsewhere in his book. Consequently I do not think that he is referring to either of my II chords in his assertion of "a I–IV–V progression" (p. 93). Curiously, though his use of Roman numerals is meager and mine is luxuriant, Agawu's IV is not one that I employ: I do not perceive that F, A, and C during 16_4 coordinate to form an asserted harmony. Instead bass F is a passing note within a broad, seventeen-measure arpeggiation of the tonic triad, echoing the local C<E<G from 1_1 to 2_1. G-C-E at 17_1 is a second-inversion tonic, not a cadential $^6_4$.

5. The dominant's unconventional minor third, B♭, prepares the imminent dominant-emulating tonic's 7♭. (In other words, B♮ is elided.) One might propose that when a tonic chord is dominant-emulating, the preceding dominant may emulate the supertonic: the G–C–F progression will sound like II V^7 I in F Major. I refrain from fully endorsing that perspective because I regard the C (I$^{7\flat}$) chord, an extension of that of 57_3, to be the hierarchically deepest of these three chords.

6. Compare with **1.10d**.
7. To emphasize C would be equivalent to Agawu's emphasis on G at 39_1 during the E>E descending octave within P's consequent phrase.
8. For me, "harmonic" and "sequence" are mutually exclusive notions, though I acknowledge that for most analysts the notions mingle. Few analysts distinguish between what I call sequential and circular progressions.
9. The E>C>A contour is echoed by the cello during 93_{3-4}.
10. Whereas the unfoldings in measure 85 resemble those presented by Schenker in FC, fig. 43, ex. f1, measure 87 is closer in spirit to fig. 43, ex. f2: inner-strand C>B>A comes between E and its D>C continuation.
11. Using Kirnberger's terminology introduced on p. 78, the G is an essential dissonance, which must await the dominant arrival before resolution, whereas the B is an incidental dissonance, since it could resolve during the evolved II chord (as 9–8), though in this instance it does not.
12. Though initially I was pleased to note that Spitzer proposes (p. 209) the Roman numeral IV^7 for measure 106 – a point of agreement with my analysis in **7.3b** – upon careful study of his ex. 7.11b (p. 211) I realized that he proposes a B>B octave followed by C at 106_3, a conception that is at odds with my G>E>C bass descent in thirds.
13. The voice leading here is subtle. I propose that the second violin F♯ at 101_2 joins with the C that follows directly thereafter in the first violin to form a diminished fifth, whose resolution $\genfrac{}{}{0pt}{}{B}{G}$ falls on beat 3 before E is introduced. Had Mozart instead intended a stepwise descent in thirds, likely he would have written D rather than D♯ at 101_4, G rather than G♯ at 102_4, etc. Consequently the B and D at 106_2 are not part of an asserted I harmony, but instead serve as neighbors to the C and E of IV.
14. This technique is a feature of tonality that François-Joseph Fétis regarded as the hallmark of his *ordre pluritonique*, whose inauguration he attributes to Mozart. See *TAH*, p. 174.
15. Compare with *TAH*, **3.9b**.
16. Though subtle, another relationship with S is operative beginning at measure 182. The prominent D<E>D>C>B line (coordinating with inner-voice B<C>B>A>G) that is repeated several times during measures 86 through 98 (as displayed in **7.3a**) is matched by the development's G<A♭>G>F>E♭ (coordinating with inner-voice E♭<F>E♭>D>C) during measures 182 through 191 (as displayed in **7.5b**).
17. Compare with *FC*, fig. 111a and fig. 113, ex. 3. See also *Schubert*, **1.8**. My "Schenker, Schubert, and the Subtonic Chord" (2010) offers an extensive exploration of the subtonic/dominant relationship.
18. The sequence contains some variation within the local figuration. During the C➔ phase, the first violin connects the chordal root and third as C<C♯<D<E, whereas during the D➔ phase the equivalent third is filled in as D<D♯<E<F<F♯. The final third is preceded by a lower neighbor (D♯ at 249_3) and proceeds as E<F♯<G♯.

19. G<C>B during measures 322 through 324 recalls the initial first violin utterance of measures 4 and 5.
20. Compare with measures 128 through 131 in **7.4** (in the tonicized key of G Major).

8 Mozart: *Don Giovanni* (K. 527), Act I, Scene 13: Donna Anna's recitative and aria

1. My review of Schachter's *Unfoldings: Essays in Schenkerian Theory and Analysis* (1999) appears in *Music Theory Online* 5.3 (October 1999).
2. In preparation for the creation of the second through fourth editions of Schachter's *Harmony and Voice Leading* (co-authored with Edward Aldwell), the publisher (currently Schirmer, also the publisher of my textbooks) commissioned me to write a candid review of the previous edition for in-house use. The most recent one was submitted in July 2008, as *Schubert* was nearing completion.
3. Schachter's analysis was presented at the Second International Schenker Symposium at the Mannes College of Music in New York, held in March 1992. I was in the audience. A revised version, "The Adventures of an F♯: Tonal Narration and Exhortation in Donna Anna's First-Act Recitative and Aria," appeared in *Theory and Practice* 16 (1991), pp. 5–20, and is reprinted in Schachter's essay collection, *Unfoldings: Essays in Schenkerian Theory and Analysis*, edited by Joseph N. Straus (Oxford University Press, 1999), pp. 221–235. I use the page numbers from *Unfoldings* in my citations.
4. Schachter joined Matt Hughes and Lawrence Moss for a symposium on Schubert's Moment musical in C Major, *Journal of Music Theory* 12 (1968), pp. 184–239.
5. Another example is Schubert's "Ganymed," analyzed in *Schubert*, chapter 5.
6. As is the case in "Ganymed" as well, the transfer of tonal center is not played out by the competing tonics (C and D) themselves, but instead by their respective dominants (G and A). See *Schubert*, **5.6**.
7. I discuss the notion of seismic shift in *TAH* (p. 236), in *Schubert* (pp. 137 and 173–174), in my review of *Beethoven's Tempest Sonata* (2010), and on p. 40, above.
8. The distinctive ♯$\hat{4}$ < $\hat{5}$ motive was introduced during measures 11 through 14 of the opera's overture.
9. Consequently Donna Anna's F in measures 4 and 5 is a neighbor to E♭, not a passing note from G. (E♭ ascends directly to F in two instruments, and indirectly in two others, during measure 3 and 4.) Just as *Kopfton* E♭ coordinates with upper-third G, Donna Anna eventually extends to F's upper-third A♭ (measures 7 and 8).
10. It is interesting that in his analysis of the ensuing aria (his example 9.7), Schachter instead proposes $\hat{3}$ (F♯) as the *Kopfton*, with a prominent upper-

third A in measures 75, 83, and 95. My analysis projects a consistent relationship between the tonic's third and fifth (C Minor: E♭<G and D Major: F♯<A) shared by the recitative and the aria.

11. Though the arrow notation is less precise (for example, it does not distinguish between chords traditionally labeled as V^7/V and vii^{o7}/V), I find it useful especially in the contexts of a written commentary and classroom instruction.
12. For comparison, consider the situation in which a composer ascends three half steps only twice – not four times – in modulo 12: for example, 7 10 1. (We touched upon this issue in chapter 1. See **1.12b**.) The attainment of 1 is easily accomplished in modulo 12. But if this 1 is then shoved back into modulo 7 tonal space, the composer must come to terms with how to proceed from a chord that is alien to the contextual diatonic environment. (The 1 chord is in fact 7's antipode.) I discuss how Schubert deals with this situation in my analysis of his "Die Einsiedelei" (*Schubert*, pp. 113–116), where I also refer to cases by Beethoven and Liszt. There are many other references to modulo 12 tonal space within *Schubert*.
13. The exposition of Mozart's Piano Sonata in C Major (K. 545), movement 1, analyzed by Schenker in *FC*, fig. 47, ex. 1, fig. 88c, and fig. 124, ex. 5a, presents a similar situation. Note that Schenker labels the chord equivalent to that of the recitative's measure 24 as a *Teiler* (divider), indicative of a non-modulatory stance. Even though the dominant root G is preceded by F♯, at the most fundamental level the sonata remains in C Major. (In my terminology the evolved II chord is not actually a dominant; it instead is dominant-emulating.) The G chord that launches S (measure 14) is V in C Major, tonicized as I in G Major in the context of the local progression. Schenker employs *both* of those numerals.
14. Consider briefly the mechanics of the circular progression leading up to the G major arrival. The most direct connection of two chords whose roots are separated by four half steps would be, for example, G-B♭-D (minor) to E♭-G-B♭ (major). (I offer charts of descending and ascending third-relationships in *Schubert*, **2.17** and **2.20**.) The latter is replaced by E♭-G♭-B♭ (minor) in measure 25 because it serves as the initiator of the next downward cycle. Though we might expect to hear E♭-G♭-B♭ to C♭-E♭-G♭ [B-D♯-F♯] (major), its minor equivalent occurs instead in measure 31, for the same reason. The final cycle succeeds in going where one expects it will – B-D-F♯ (minor) to G-B-D (major) – since the G chord does not serve as the base for an extension of the cycle.
15. Of course, errors may inadvertently creep in during any complex undertaking. I write this note as I near completion of the final pre-submission proofreading of the *Harmony in Haydn and Mozart* manuscript, and admit that I have uncovered dozens of minor blemishes akin to Schachter's flat. Though one might hope that any such errors that make it into print would be corrected during a reprinting (as in Schachter's *Unfoldings* compilation), publishers are not always accommodating. For example, though I was aware of a few small errors in the

hardback edition of *TAH*, the paperback edition that followed was printed without corrections, in accordance with the contract that I signed with the Press.
16. This state of affairs matches that which we encountered in our analysis of P and S in Haydn's Piano Sonata in E♭ Major (H. XVI: 52) in chapter 2.
17. The foundation for this ascending 5–6 sequence is as follows: F^5 $F\sharp^6$ G^5 $G\sharp^6$ A^5. In its realization the 6-phase chords are further evolved, while the 5-phase chord on G is elided. (For another example of a 5-phase elision, see *TAH*, p. 81.)
18. Edward Aldwell and Carl Schachter with Allen Cadwallader, *Harmony and Voice Leading*, 4th edn. (Boston, MA: Schirmer, 2011), pp. 602–605.
19. Donna Anna's melody is built from three unfolded thirds during this passage (77_2 through 79_3): G>E F♯>D E>C♯. The second violin line reinforces the principal strand.
20. The D and F♯ at the downbeats of measures 80 through 83 function as accented passing notes within the dominant prolongation: E | F♯ G and E | D (C♯) thirds are projected melodically, even if in measures 81 and 82 only the viola line presents the D>C♯ while Donna Anna or the line of the lower strings leaps away from the D. Note especially that Mozart places the stepwise ascending A<G seventh under a single slur every time that it occurs. That is a potent indication that he did not intend for the internal F♯ to represent the third of a resolving tonic chord. The dominant – *not* the tonic – is being prolonged during these measures.
21. Notes such as Donna Anna's E during 79_2 are analytically pesky, with something of a wild-card character: sometimes they are mere incomplete neighbors embellishing the notes that precede them (Schachter's view here), while at other times they are anticipations of the following chord (my view here).
22. Compare with *FC*, fig. 23a.
23. Analysts might reasonably disagree regarding whether the initial D Minor tonic is reasserted at 96_1. I decided against that reading (noting especially Mozart's slurs that do *not* lead to D in the lower strings during measures 95 and 96), interpreting the D chord instead as internal to a connection via descending thirds between the tonic's upper-third extension and its unfurled 6-phase chord.
24. Yet recall the "Mozartean fifths" introduced in *TAH*, **7.17**.
25. I also reject the dotted slurs that Schachter twice employs to connect Fs between measures 90 and 94. I regard the internal F (in two octaves) as a passing note between G at 91_4 (shown in my graph but not in Schachter's) and E at 93_1. This G>F♮>E third prolongs the C♯ chord.

9 Mozart: Symphony in G Minor (K. 550), movement 3, Trio

1. Leonard B. Meyer, "Grammatical Simplicity and Relational Richness: The Trio of Mozart's G Minor Symphony," *Critical Inquiry* 2 (1975–1976), pp. 693–761

(including an appendix containing the score). In note 17 I will briefly assess analyses of the Trio by Heinrich Schenker and by Robert O. Gjerdingen.

2. Already a graduate student in organ performance at the Eastman School of Music, I entered the Ph.D. program in music theory there in fall 1976. Within a year I had begun the study of the history of music theory (with David Russell Williams), of Schenkerian analysis (with John Rothgeb), and of chromatic harmony (with Douglass Green) that are integrated within my Cambridge harmony project. After completing the organ degree, I resigned from the theory program and continued my Ph.D. studies at Yale University.

3. Walter Piston, *Harmony* (New York: Norton, 3rd edn., 1962).

4. The D at 1_2 launches an upward trajectory that is held in check until measure 7, where it succeeds in bringing about the transfer of *Kopfton* B to the upper register.

5. Consequently I propose a revision in the perspective displayed in Meyer's example 17, graph 1a (p. 715). That line should be interpreted not as a mere ascending arpeggiation of a tenth (G<B<D<G<B), but instead as the attainment of *Kopfton* B in the lower register (G<B̲) followed by an ascending register transfer (B̲<D<G<B).

6. Consequently the representation of this passage in Meyer's example 5, graph 2b, seems to me to be wrongheaded. I cannot imagine how a performer could concurrently project the perspectives of graphs 2b and 4.

7. Compare with *Schubert*, **3.1**, mm. 1–5.

8. I wonder why the second ii is not followed by a 7. Certainly the viola G on the first beat of measure 5 is prolonged, via passing motion to interior chord member E during beat 2, until resolution on F♯ at beat 3. (The situation is similar to that explored in *TAH*, **5.1**.) Meyer's literalist symbol makes it appear that this dissonance is rescinded rather than resolved. I also wonder why no 7 appears beside the V of measure 3.

9. Though a high B occurs at 8_1, by that point the trajectory towards the upper-third chord has already begun. I interpret this B as a suspension above an imagined bass A (which sounds in the flute line two beats later). In **9.2** I have taken the liberty of imaginatively placing the completion of the ascending arpeggiation to B within the tonic context of measure 7, displaying a normative structure that Mozart here deforms through the "late" arrival of the B.

10. Though I propose a background connection between the A of measures 14 through 26 and the G of measures 32 and 38, the interruption structure allows an approach to the G from above, as B>A>G̲. This latter A is an interior component of this final tonic prolongation and consequently is not available for meaningful connection to the A from the preceding tonicized dominant.

11. See also **3.14**, measures 87 through 95.

12. This structure closely parallels what we observed in measures 7 through 13: G<A<A♯<B>G.

13. Despite the full array of Roman numerals in his example 1, Meyer also refers to measures 22 through 25 as a "sequential progression" (p. 695). I suggest that he has in mind the wrong linear initiative (he proposes a descending circle of fifths rather than an ascending 5–6 sequence) and that he applies it in the wrong location. A close examination of his example 1, measures 18|19 through 25, reveals the oddity of his interpretation. Mozart employs three successive ascending arpeggiations in quarter notes in the lower strings, each connected via a slur: D–F♯–A–D, D–G–B–D, E–G♯–B–E. That sequential ascent terminates with the arrival of the A-C-E chord at 24_{1-2}. Meyer's circle begins in the middle of that initiative, with the third of these arpeggiations, and then continues through two measures of half-note followed by quarter-note motion in the bass. My sequence, in contrast, coincides with the presentation of those arpeggiations and concludes at the precise moment when the arpeggiations give way to the half and quarter notes. Meyer's "E–A–D–G–(C)" circle is for me the concluding 6–5 of the sequential ascent to D's upper-fifth chord (E–A, with the E chord (= G♯^{6}) unfurled into $^5_3$ position and chromaticized), the restoration of the previously stated dominant (A–D), the motion from this dominant to the tonic-asserting $^6_4$ passing chord (D–G), and finally a progression from G back to dominant D, via C. These extraordinarily varied motivations within an intensely hierarchical context are flatted out by Meyer into a one-dimensional circular progression.

14. F♯ emerges first in the lower register at 34_1, as G's lower neighbor. It soon is transferred to higher registers, peaking with the flute F♯ at 36_1 before returning to G. The voice leading is G>F♯<G, not E<F♯<G (as Meyer proposes).

15. This passage is an example of what I refer to as a "peculiar juxtaposition." (See p. 122, above, and *Schubert*, pp. 26–31.) Though on the surface it may seem that the G♯→A and F♯→G seconds would mandate that A and G be regarded as the hierarchically deeper pitches (a notion that Meyer's parentheses reinforce, as does his discussion of "uniform processes" on p. 735), the broader context suggests that F♯ and its chord instead help define the extent of V-space.

16. As would many other analysts, Meyer refers to the arrival of E-G-B at 36_2 as a "deceptive cadence" (p. 746). I reserve the word cadence for an event that occurs where one expects a phrase ending, which is not the case here. Whereas one might reasonably analyze measures 3 and 4 (using Meyer's notation) as V^7 proceeding to I, followed by vi, in measures 35 and 36 the stable I is elided. Consequently the V^7 proceeds directly to vi. Chromatic passing note D♯ assists in the redirection of the progression. One might even regard D♯ as evidence of a 6-phase chord, often deployed in the connection of two harmonies related by step: thus V^{5-6} VI (using my notation), wherein the 6-phase D-F♯-B has evolved into dominant-emulating D♯-F♯-A-C. As **9.4** shows, this chord is internal to a broad I^{5-6}–II–V^7–I progression, whose only cadence – a PAC – occurs at 38_1.

17. Anticipating my criticism, Meyer defends himself in his footnote 92 (p. 753). Two other analytical contributions should be assessed briefly. Schenker offers

an analysis of the entire symphony in the second volume of *Das Meisterwerk in der Musik* (1925–1930/1994–1997). His commentary on and detailed three-level graph of the Trio appear on pages 88 through 91 of the English version. Comparing that reading with the model in *FC*, fig. 23, I suspect that Schenker might have reconsidered his choice of $\hat{5}$ as the *Kopfton* had he analyzed the Trio near the end of his life. I interpret the C of measures 34 [Schenker's 76] through 36 [78] as a neighbor to B, not a passing note from D. (The B<D>C motive of measure 1 shifts metrically to become B< | D>C in measures 33 and 34.) I doubt his imputation of an imagined root D in measure 8 [50]. Instead the bass moves without hindrance from the tonic root G to the B minor chord of measure 12 [54], which I regard as the principal event between the tonic's 5- and 6-phase chords. (Whereas Schenker's bass slurring – minus the imagined D – coordinates with that interpretation, his soprano melody sails past that moment.) Though the section's goal D major harmony is interpreted as V in his graph a, the preceding A➔ chord is nowhere interpreted as II♯. Again, in his more mature *FC* there are numerous instances of such chords being labeled as II♯, or of a chord such as C♯-E-G-B♭ being labeled as ♯IV (which I interpret as an evolved II♯ with absent root). The middle section's ascending line, A<B<C, is displayed in an exemplary fashion, but the parallel line below it, F♯<G<G♯<A, is curiously broken into two segments. Based on the frequent filling in of octave-related pitches within the Trio, I give greater weight to soprano A in measure 26 [68] as a lower-octave reinstatement of the $\hat{2}$ from measure 14 [56]. A similar concern pertains to the closing measures, where a G>G octave prevails.

Gjerdingen offers an appraisal of the opening section of the Trio in his *Music in the Galant Style* (2007), pp. 437–438. In two important respects his analysis is closer to Schenker's reading from 1926 than is mine. First, note that both Schenker and Gjerdingen shift to D Major beginning in measure 7 [49]. In my view the issue of tonicization does not surface until after the cadence. It is only the D–A–D motions in measures 14 through 18 that trigger a tonicization. The C♯ in measure 13 does not warrant that analytical action. (This is not a post-Schenkerian notion, but instead a post-1926 Schenkerian notion. Compare with the similar $\hat{3}$–$\hat{2}$‖ spans in *FC*, fig. 23; fig. 40, ex. 1; fig. 40, ex. 4; fig. 46, ex. 1; and fig. 76, ex. 2. Only in fig. 114, ex. 2, does he complement the principal II♯ analysis with a supplemental analysis as V in the tonicized dominant key.) Second, both Schenker and Gjerdingen trace a blithe stepwise descent of a sixth (B to D) over the course of the section. I instead perceive greater hierarchical richness. As **9.2** displays, the B>A>G>F♯ fourth serves to prolong the initial B. (B remains a chord member when the F♯ sounds in measure 12.) The A and G of measure 13 shape a second descent from B. (Again, B remains a chord member when the G sounds.) Only at 13_3 [55_3] do Schenker and Gjerdingen part company. As is also the case in my reading, Schenker proposes an imagined A there as the successor of the long-prolonged B.

10 Haydn: Symphony No. 96 in D Major ("Miracle"), movement 1

1. Hepokoski and Darcy's analysis of the "Miracle" exposition first appeared in "The Medial Caesura and Its Role in the Eighteenth-Century Sonata Exposition," *Music Theory Spectrum* 19 (1997), pp. 135–137. That commentary was incorporated, without substantive alteration, in their *Elements of Sonata Theory* (2006), pp. 55–58.
2. Suurpää's analysis appears in his "Continuous Exposition and Tonal Structure in Three Late Haydn Works," *Music Theory Spectrum* 21 (1999), pp. 178–181.
3. In his String Quintet in C Major (analyzed in chapter 7, above), Mozart juxtaposes major and minor keys in consecutive phrases of P. Yet his writing there lacks Haydn's potency in this regard, since Mozart quickly restores the major mode. Haydn persists with the minor hue to the end of the introduction. (The F♯ at 9_3 is a chromatic pitch within D Minor, *not* the restoration of diatonic F♯ after an F♮ wobble in D Major.) Consequently the D Major restoration at measure 18 imbues P with an especially jovial character.
4. Compare with *FC*, fig. 41, ex. a4.
5. I am comfortable imagining B♭ (rather than B♮) here due to the local reiteration of this succession – *with* B♭ – from 12_3 through 13_2.
6. Granted, many readers may want to deploy a ♭II Roman numeral for this chord. Yet IV's 6 phase derives from an unsounded E, not from E♭. To better understand my resistance to a ♭II analysis in this context, see Sechter's interpretation (published in 1853–1854) of a similar passage, which I explore in *TAH*, pp. 200–203.
7. Hepokoski and Darcy did not invent this analytical notion. See, for example, Schenker's application of this structure in the context of Mozart's Piano Sonata in C Major (K. 545) in *FC*, fig. 47, ex. 1. Note that the outer-voice pitches G and D in measure 14 (*not* measure 12) are connected to the background beams. Measures 1 through 12 of Schenker's graph correspond to my **10.2** (where the A and E in the vicinity of measures 30–31 and 48–49 are displayed as *filled-in* noteheads); measures 14 through 28 of Schenker's graph correspond to my **10.3**, which displays a middleground fifth-progression descending from background E.
8. Compare how the pitch D is harmonized in various locations: D sounds against G♯ at the end of measure 11 and also against A at the beginning of measure 12. The latter (only) prevails at 31_1; the former (only) prevails at 48_3.
9. Between the HC moment and the MC an optional extension of the dominant may occur (what Hepokoski and Darcy call "dominant-lock"), and between the MC and S optional "caesura-fill" (CF) may occur. In my view, neither of these prolongational strategies is operative here. Hepokoski and Darcy instead regard what occurs in the measures after the potential "I:HC MC point" at 49_1 as CF that soon veers off unacceptably (measure 52), thereby voiding the viability of the half cadence on A as an MC herald of S. I instead regard that supposed CF as

the onset of S. Exemplifying Haydn's penchant for thematic unity, both P and S open with a series of thirds descending in stepwise motion: staccato in the strings in measure 18, legato in the woodwinds in measure 49, while the D–A–D bass of measures 18 through 20 is matched by its dominant-key equivalent A–E(G♯)–A in measures 49 through 51. In addition, the "ta ta ta | ta" rhythm of 18_2–19_1 pervades the opening phrase of S.

10. It is in the nature of an introduction and of a TR (of the I:HC MC type) to end on a dangling dominant. Thus the first four cadences require no consequent. During S, however, a PAC in the dominant key (the EEC) is the expected goal.

11. Compare this situation with the revitalized dominant in Haydn's String Quartet in G Minor, displayed in **6.3** and discussed on p. 174.

12. One may get a clear picture of what Haydn regarded as essential versus the extraordinary elaboration that his creativity generated during this passage by comparing how he proceeds once the dominant's seventh arrives during the exposition and during the recapitulation. In the latter (in the restored key of D Major), the passage from 61_2 through 64_1 is absent. That is, *two beats* after the dominant's seventh arrives, the resolution to the tonic occurs (measure 181). Note that in measure 64 the resolution is to a root-position tonic A (outer voices resolving inwards: $\frac{D}{G\sharp}$ to $\frac{C\sharp}{A}$) whereas in measure 181 the resolution is to a first-inversion tonic D (outer voices resolving outwards: $\frac{C\sharp}{G}$ to $\frac{D}{F\sharp}$).

13. I explore the relationship between the dominant and subtonic chords (including a detailed assessment of Schenker's comments and examples on the topic) in my "Schenker, Schubert, and the Subtonic Chord" (2010).

14. The B chord at 64_1 "should" be of minor quality, but the melody's E>D second is subdivided into E>D♯>D, with the D arrival delayed until the following chord. The juxtaposition of three stepwise-related dominant-to-tonic candidates is reminiscent of a passage that I explore in *Schubert*, pp. 97–99.

15. Since it is my policy not to correspond with authors while I am engaged in formulating my analyses in conjunction with theirs, I did not ask Hepokoski or Darcy whether, during the nine years between the appearance of the article and of the book, anyone had kindly suggested to them that they should reconsider their interpretation. (Though Hepokoski was my colleague at the University of Minnesota when the article appeared, I was at that time immersed in *TAH* and was not following his work closely.) It appears that at least one of Hepokoski's students looked carefully at this movement while under his influence, since a University of Minnesota Music Library copy of the score (M1001.H4 L3 1951 11, viewed on June 21, 2010) is marked with Sonata Theory terms not all derivable from the published analysis, as follows: m. 18: "P as grand antecedent"; m. 25: "false TR"; m. 32: "TR as dissolving consequent"; m. 39: "TR"; m. 52: "evaded" (erased); m. 57: a long comment including the words "HC rejected," "FS" (= *Fortspinnung*), and "caesura fill to PAC" (all erased). Because the library staff is aggressive in erasing markings from scores, it is

not possible to determine whether the erasures represent the student's change of mind or instead a subsequent cleansing.

16. In my review of *Beethoven's* Tempest *Sonata* (2010), paragraph 8, I question another of Hepokoski's readings on similar grounds.
17. My reading of a bass resolution on A at 64_3 is confirmed by Haydn's treatment of this passage during the recapitulation, as explained in note 12. Suurpää's reading of an auxiliary cadence, which treats that A chord as an appendage of the C♮ mediant, has no counterpart during the recapitulation. Haydn's deletion of the C♮ chord – but not the A chord – in that latter context suggests that the hierarchical relationship between those two chords during the exposition is the opposite of what Suurpää proposes.
18. Recall also the potent G♮→C♮ succession within the exposition (measures 62–63).
19. I propose that 140_1 corresponds to consonant (D)-F♯-A, before the 6-phase B-D♯-F♯-A chord emerges later in the measure.
20. In the context of A Major, the sequence might more typically have proceeded from B♮-D♯-F♯-G♯ to C♯-E-G♯. D Major's diatonic B-D-G to C♯-E-G, though functional, lacks dominant-emulating thrust. Note that Haydn substitutes the evolved chord A♯-C♯-E-G for the A♯-C♯-F♯ shown in **10.6**, measure 113, and that a wobble (D♯) emerges in measure 114.
21. Edward Laufer's "Voice-Leading Procedures in Development Sections," *Studies in Music from The University of Western Ontario* 13 (1991), pp. 69–120, provides an exemplary overview of this topic. After presenting a set of concise general models, he offers numerous detailed analyses of individual development sections. My reading in **10.4** and **10.6** corresponds approximately to his fig. iii-b.
22. Peter H. Smith offers an interesting perspective on similar thorny issues in his "Structural Tonic or Apparent Tonic?: Parametric Conflict, Temporal Perspective, and a Continuum of Articulative Possibilities," *Journal of Music Theory* 39 (1995), pp. 245–283. Consider the familiar diagram that might represent either an ornate vase or facing profiles, depending on which part is regarded as solid. A musical equivalent of this sort of ambiguity results from an alternation between the pitches A-C♯-E and A-D-F♯. Do the D and F♯ serve as upper neighbors to C♯ and E, respectively, or does the A chord resolve to the D chord (in second inversion)? Usually what follows the A-D-F♯ chord will help the listener in confirming one or the other of these interpretations. Yet one situation – the presentation of these two chords in alternation over several measures (as occurs in measures 171ff.) – can lead to the mystifying situation in which listeners might not be able to discern which of two viable interpretations is being projected, as in the vase/profiles quandary. (I discuss a similar quandary regarding a passage from a mazurka by Chopin in *TAH*, pp. 157–160.) Given Haydn's mischievous streak, I suspect that he has purposefully placed a haze of ambiguity over this segment of his composition. The foundation for Haydn's ruse resides in measures 50ff. Clear

hierarchical relationships reside within unambiguous two-measure units during an eight-measure phrase:

```
              G♯↗ A    E♯↗  F♯   B ─────→  E ─────
               •  •    •    •    •    •    •    •
A Major:      I⁵ ──────── 6 ────     II♯ ──── V ────
```

Transferring that orientation to measures 171ff. results in the following:

```
              C♯↗ D    C♯↗  D    C♯↗  D  E → A
               •  •    •    •    •    •    •
D Major:      I ────────────────────────── II♯ V
```

Note that the thematic content of measures 171 and 172 fully supports this reading: ascending sixteenth notes to the chordal seventh transpire during the first measure, followed by descending eighth notes during the second measure, as in measures 50 and 51. Yet this reading depends upon the assumption that a measure has been deleted during the recapitulation, where one finds no equivalent for measure 49. (That is, measures 49 and 50 merge into measure 171, a possibility that emerges due to the changed tonal circumstances of the recapitulation, as explained above.) Also note the oddity that, whereas the phrase that begins in measure 50 is a normative eight measures in length, the one that begins in measure 171 is only seven. Consequently an alternative interpretation emerges, one in which the nature of the embellishment changes. In **1.2b**, Model 1, we saw how lower neighbors to a chordal root and third may perform an embellishing role. This possibility corresponds to the relationship between measures 50 and 51. Model 2, in contrast, employs upper neighbors to a chordal third and fifth in the embellishing role. This possibility might correspond to the relationship of measures 172 and 173. Consequently a competing interpretation of this latter region emerges, as follows (now beginning one measure later, in measure 172):

```
                   D  to  C♯     D  to  C♯      D   E → A
                   •    •        •    •         •    •
D Major:           V ─────────────────────────
(= A Major:        I ─────────────────────────  IV  V⁷. I )
```

In this reading only the third D (which is reinforced by the timpani) asserts a harmonic role, as IV within tonicized A Major.

23. Though a considerable departure from the structure of the exposition, one productive way of interpreting the melody of measures 172 through 177 would be as an *ascent* to A: F♯<G♯<A. Compare with *FC*, fig. 38d.
24. Hepokoski and Darcy concur: they refer to the C chord as "♮III of the anticipated A major" (1997, p. 137; 2006, p. 55).

List of references to music examples

1.1a	8	3.1b	96, 258
1.1c	10, 33	3.2	97, 98, 101, 103, 260, 118
1.1d	16, 21, 31, 32, 121	3.3	101
1.2	82	3.4	99, 102, 103
1.2a	13, 33	3.5	99, 102, 259, 260, 116
1.2b	247, 24, 27, 35, 248, 211, 281	3.6	103
1.2c	13, 16, 248, 19, 153	3.7b	105
1.3c	19, 33	3.7c	103
1.4a	19	3.8	227
1.4c	19	3.10d	113, 116
1.4d	19, 21, 185	3.11	113
1.5b	22, 103	3.14	259, 275
1.6b	27	4.1	128, 149
1.7b	92	4.13	147
1.10d	271	4.14	149
1.11g	38	4.9	263
1.12b	38	5.2	265
2.1	67	6.3	279
2.12	70	7.1d	200
2.13	133, 188	7.2a	200
2.14	143	7.3a	271
2.14b	188	7.4	272
2.17	264	7.6a	186
3.1a	96, 101,	9.2	229

Select bibliography

Agawu, V. K., *Playing with Signs: A Semiotic Interpretation of Classic Music*, Princeton University Press, 1991
"Haydn's Tonal Models: The First Movement of the Piano Sonata in E-flat Major, Hob. XVI: 52," in *Convention in Eighteenth- and Nineteenth-Century Music: Essays in Honor of Leonard G. Ratner*, ed. W. J. Allanbrook, J. M. Levy, and W. P. Mahrt, Stuyvesant, NY: Pendragon, 1992, pp. 3–22
"Prospects for a Theory-based Analysis of [Mozart's] Instrumental Music," in *Wolfgang Amadè Mozart: Essays on His Life and His Music*, ed. S. Sadie, Oxford: Clarendon Press, 1996, pp. 121–131
Alegant, B., "A-Major Events," in *Keys to the Drama: Nine Perspectives on Sonata Form*, Farnham: Ashgate, 2009, pp. 199–224
Allanbrook, W. J., *Rhythmic Gesture in Mozart:* Le Nozze di Figaro *and* Don Giovanni, University of Chicago Press, 1983
"Two Threads through the Labyrinth: Topic and Process in the First Movements of K. 332 and K. 333," in *Convention in Eighteenth- and Nineteenth-Century Music: Essays in Honor of Leonard G. Ratner*, ed. W. J. Allanbrook, J. Levy, and W. P. Mahrt, Stuyvesant, NY: Pendragon, 1992, pp. 125–171
"Theorizing the Comic Surface," in *Music in the Mirror: Reflections on the History of Music Theory and Literature for the 21st Century*, ed. A. Giger and T. J. Mathiesen, Lincoln: University of Nebraska Press, 2002, pp. 195–216
"Mozart's K331, First Movement: Once More, with Feeling," in *Communication in Eighteenth-Century Music*, ed. D. Mirka and K. Agawu, Cambridge University Press, 2008, pp. 254–282
Almén, B., *A Theory of Musical Narrative*, Bloomington: Indiana University Press, 2008
Amon, R., *Lexikon der Harmonielehre*, Munich: Doblinger, 2005
Andrews, H. L., "The Submediant in Haydn's Development Sections," in *Haydn Studies: Proceedings of the International Haydn Conference, Washington, D.C., 1975*, ed. J. P. Larsen, H. Serwer, and J. Webster, New York: Norton, 1981, pp. 465–471
Anson-Cartwright, M., "The Development Section in Haydn's Late Instrumental Works," Ph.D. diss., The City University of New York, 1998
"Chromatic Features of E♭-Major Works of the Classical Period," *Music Theory Spectrum* 22 (2000), pp. 177–204
"Tonal Conflicts in Haydn's Development Sections: The Role of C Major in Symphonies No. 93 and 102," in *Structure and Meaning in Tonal Music:*

Festschrift in Honor of Carl Schachter, ed. L. P. Burstein and D. Gagné, Hillsdale, NY: Pendragon, 2006, pp. 227–235

Baker, J. M., "Chromaticism in Classical Music," in *Music Theory and the Exploration of the Past*, ed. C. Hatch and D. W. Bernstein, University of Chicago Press, 1993, pp. 233–307

"Chromaticism, Form, and Expression in Haydn's String Quartet op. 76, no. 6," *Journal of Music Theory* 47 (2003), pp. 41–101

Beach, D., "A Recurring Pattern in Mozart's Music," *Journal of Music Theory* 27 (1983), pp. 1–29

"Motive and Structure in the *Andante* Movement of Mozart's Piano Sonata K. 545," *Music Analysis* 3 (1984), pp. 227–241

"The First Movement of Mozart's Piano Sonata in A Minor, K. 310: Some Thoughts on Structure and Performance," *Journal of Musicological Research* 7 (1986–1988), pp. 157–186

"The Initial Movements of Mozart's Piano Sonatas K.280 and K.332: Some Striking Similarities," *Integral* 8 (1994), pp. 125–146

"Motivic Enlargement and Phrase Expansion: Illustrations from Two Works by Mozart," *Journal of Schenkerian Studies* 3 (2008), pp. 1–17

Beghin, T., "Haydn as Orator: A Rhetorical Analysis of His Keyboard Sonata in D Major, Hob. XVI: 42," in *Haydn and His World*, ed. E. Sisman, Princeton University Press, 1997, 201–254

Beghin, T., and Goldberg, S. M., eds., *Haydn and the Performance of Rhetoric*, University of Chicago Press, 2007

Bribitzer-Stull, M., "The Cadenza as Parenthesis: An Analytic Approach," *Journal of Music Theory* 50 (2006), pp. 211–251

Budday, W., *Harmonielehre Wiener Klassik: Theorie – Satztechnik – Werkanalyse*, Stuttgart: Berthold & Schwerdtner, 2002

Burnett, H., and Nitzberg, R., *Composition, Chromaticism and the Developmental Process: A New Theory of Tonality*, Aldershot: Ashgate, 2007

Burnett, H., and O'Donnell, S., "Linear Ordering of the Chromatic Aggregate in Classical Symphonic Music," *Music Theory Spectrum* 18 (1996), pp. 22–50

Burnham, S., "Haydn and Humor," in *The Cambridge Companion to Haydn*, ed. C. Clark, Cambridge University Press, 2005, pp. 61–76

Burstein, L. P., "Surprising Returns: The VII♯ in Beethoven's Op. 18 No. 3, and Its Antecedents in Haydn," *Music Analysis* 17 (1998), pp. 295–312

"Comedy and Structure in Haydn's Symphonies," in *Schenker Studies 2*, ed. C. Schachter and H. Siegel, Cambridge University Press, 1999, pp. 67–81

"Mozart's Harmonic Experiments of 1784," in *A Composition as a Problem III: Proceedings of the 3rd International Conference on Music Theory, Tallinn, March 9–10, 2001*, ed. M. Humal, Tallinn: Eesti Muusikaakadeemia and Scripta Musicalia, 2003, pp. 15–26

"Mozart's Recomposed Bifocal Transition Sections," in *A Composition as a Problem V: Proceedings of the Fifth International Conference on Music*

Theory, Tallinn, September 28–30, 2006, ed. M. Humal, Tallinn: Eesti Muusika- ja Teatriakadeemia, 2008, pp. 25–36

"Mid-Section Cadences in Haydn's Sonata-Form Movements," in *Haydn 2009: A Bicentenary Conference*, ed. P. Halász, *Studia musicologica: An International Journal of Musicology of the Hungarian Academy of Sciences*, 51/1–2 (2010), pp. 91–107

"Echt oder Falsch? Zur tonalen Rolle der 'falschen Reprise' in Haydns Sinfonie Nr. 41," trans. F. Diergarten, in *Joseph Haydn (1732–1809)*, ed. S. Urmoneit, Berlin: Weidler, 2009, pp. 95–127; expanded version in English, as "True or False? Reassessing the Voice-Leading Role of Haydn's So-Called 'False Recapitulations,'" *Journal of Schenkerian Studies* 5 (2011), pp. 1–37.

Byros, V., "Foundations of Tonality as Situated Cognition, 1730–1830: An Enquiry into the Culture and Cognition of Eighteenth-Century Tonality, with Beethoven's *Eroica* Symphony as a Case Study," Ph.D. diss., Yale University, 2009

"Towards an 'Archaeology' of Hearing: Schemata and Eighteenth-Century Consciousness," *Musica Humana* 1 (2009), pp. 235–306

Caplin, W. E., "The 'Expanded Cadential Progression': A Category for the Analysis of Classical Form," *Journal of Musicological Research* 7 (1986–1988), pp. 215–257

Classical Form: A Theory of Formal Functions for the Instrumental Music of Haydn, Mozart, and Beethoven, Oxford University Press, 1998

"Harmonic Variants of the *Expanded Cadential Progression*," in *A Composition as Problem II: Proceedings of the Second Conference on Music Theory, Tallinn, April 17–18, 1998*, ed. M. Humal, Tallinn: Eesti Muusikaakadeemia and Scripta Musicalia, 1999, pp. 49–71

"The Classical Cadence: Conceptions and Misconceptions," *Journal of the American Musicological Society* 57 (2004), pp. 51–117

"Zur Klassifizierung harmonischer Fortschreitungen," in *Musiktheorie zwischen Historie und Systematik, 1. Kongreß der Deutschen Gesellschaft für Musiktheorie, Dresden 2001*, ed. L. Holtmeier, M. Polth, and F. Diergarten, Augsburg: Wißner, 2004, pp. 245–253

"Schoenberg's 'Second Melody', or, 'Meyer-ed' in the Bass," in *Communication in Eighteenth-Century Music*, ed. D. Mirka and K. Agawu, Cambridge University Press, 2008, pp. 160–186

Caplin, W. E., Humal, M., and Wintle, C., "Analytical Symposium on the Second Movement (*Andante*) from W. A. Mozart's Symphony in G Minor (K. 550)," in *A Composition as a Problem II: Proceedings of the Second Conference on Music Theory, Tallinn, April 17–18, 1998*, ed. M. Humal, Tallinn: Eesti Muusikaakadeemia and Scripta Musicalia, 1999, pp. 153–181

Churgin, B., "Harmonic and Tonal Instability in the Second Key Area of Classic Sonata Form," in *Convention in Eighteenth- and Nineteenth-Century Music: Essays in Honor of Leonard G. Ratner*, ed. W. J. Allanbrook, J. Levy, and W. P. Mahrt, Stuyvesant, NY: Pendragon, 1992, pp. 23–57

Cole, M., "Haydn's Symphonic Rondo Finales: Their Structural and Stylistic Evolution," in *Haydn Yearbook XIII 1982*, ed. H. C. Robbins Landon, I. M. Bruce, and D. W. Jones, University College Cardiff Press, 1983, pp. 113–142

Cooke, D., *The Language of Music*, Oxford University Press, 1959

Cube, F.-E. von, *The Book of the Musical Artwork: An Interpretation of the Musical Theory of Heinrich Schenker*, trans. D. Neumeyer, G. R. Boyd, and S. Harris, Lewiston, NY: Edwin Mellen Press, 1988

Damschroder, D., "Schubert, Chromaticism, and the Ascending 5–6 Sequence," *Journal of Music Theory* 50 (2006), pp. 253–275

  Thinking About Harmony: Historical Perspectives on Analysis, Cambridge University Press, 2008

  Harmony in Schubert, Cambridge University Press, 2010

  Review of *Beethoven's Tempest Sonata: Perspectives of Analysis and Performance* (ed. P. Bergé), *Music Theory Online* 16/2 (June 2010)

  "Schenker, Schubert, and the Subtonic Chord," in *A Music-Theoretical Matrix: Essays in Honor of Allen Forte (Part II)*, ed. D. C. Berry, *Gamut: Online Journal of the Music Theory Society of the Mid-Atlantic* 3 (2010), pp. 127–166

Drabkin, W., "An Interpretation of Musical Dreams: Towards a Theory of the Mozart Piano Concerto Cadenza," in *Wolfgang Amadè Mozart: Essays on His Life and His Music*, ed. S. Sadie, Oxford: Clarendon Press, 1996, pp. 161–177

  A Reader's Guide to Haydn's Early String Quartets, Westport, CT: Greenwood Press, 2000

Dudeque, N., *Music Theory and Analysis in the Writings of Arnold Schoenberg (1874–1951)*, Aldershot: Ashgate, 2005

Ellis, M., *A Chord in Time: The Evolution of the Augmented Sixth from Monteverdi to Mahler*, Farnham: Ashgate, 2010

Enselein, T., *Der Kontrapunkt im Instrumentalwerk von Joseph Haydn*, Cologne: Dohr, 2008

Eybl, M., "Archäologie der Tonkunst: Mozart-Analysen Heinrich Schenkers," in *Mozartanalyse im 19. und frühen 20. Jahrhundert: Bericht über die Tagung Salzburg 1996*, ed. G. Gruber and S. Mauser, Laaber-Verlag, 1999, pp. 133–145

Federhofer, H., and Mann, A., *Barbara Ployers und Franz Jakob Freystädtlers Theorie- und Kompositionsstudien bei Mozart*, Kassel: Bärenreiter, 1989 [*Wolfgang Amadeus Mozart: Neue Ausgabe sämtlicher Werke X/30/2*]

Forte, A., "Generative Chromaticism in Mozart's Music: The Rondo in A Minor, K. 511," *The Musical Quarterly* 66 (1980), pp. 459–483

Fuß, H.-U., "Die 'Überleitung' im klassischen Stil: Hauptwege und Seitenwege in der Sonataexposition bei Haydn, Mozart und Beethoven," in *Passagen: Theorien des Übergangs in Musik und anderen Kunstformen*, ed. C. Utz and M. Zenck, Saarbrücken: Pfau, 2009, pp. 113–149

Gagné, D., "'Symphonic Breadth': Structural Style in Mozart's Symphonies," in *Schenker Studies 2*, ed. C. Schachter and H. Siegel, Cambridge University Press, 1999, pp. 82–108

Galand, J., "Form, Genre, and Style in the Eighteenth-Century Rondo," *Music Theory Spectrum* 17 (1995), pp. 27–52
 "The Large-Scale Formal Role of the Solo Entry Theme in the Eighteenth-Century Concerto," *Journal of Music Theory* 44 (2000), pp. 381–450
Gersthofer, W., "Thema und harmonischer Proceß: Analytische Überlegungen zum Kopfsatz des 'Hoffmeister'-Quartetts KV 499," in *Mozart Studien*, ed. M. H. Schmid, vol. 3, Tutzing: Schneider, 1993, pp. 191–207
Gjerdingen, R. O., *A Classic Turn of Phrase: Music and the Psychology of Convention*, Philadelphia: University of Pennsylvania Press, 1988
 "Courtly Behaviors," *Music Perception* 13 (1995–1996), pp. 365–382
 Music in the Galant Style, Oxford University Press, 2007
Goldenberg, Y., *Prolongation of Seventh Chords in Tonal Music*, 2 vols., Lewiston, NY: Mellen, 2008
Grandjean, W., *Mozart als Theoretiker der Harmonielehre, mit Abdruck der Generalbasslehren von Albrechtsberger und "Mozart,"* Hildesheim: Olms, 2006
Grave, F., "Recuperation, Transformation and the Transcendence of Major over Minor in the Finale of Haydn's String Quartet Op. 76 No. 1," *Eighteenth-Century Music* 5 (2008), pp. 27–50
 "Galant Style, Enlightenment, and the Paths from Minor to Major in Late Instrumental Works by Haydn," *Ad Parnassum* 7/13 (2009), pp. 9–41
Grayson, D., *Mozart: Piano Concertos No. 20 in D Minor, K. 466, and No. 21 in C Major, K. 467*, Cambridge University Press, 1998
Guck, M. A., "Analysis as Interpretation: Interaction, Intentionality, Invention," *Music Theory Spectrum* 28 (2006), pp. 191–209
Haimo, E., "Parallel Minor as a Destabilizing Force in the Abstract Music of Haydn, Mozart, and Beethoven," *Dutch Journal of Music Theory* 10 (2005), www.djmt.nl/vol10/nr02/art03
Harutunian, J. M., *Haydn's and Mozart's Sonata Styles: A Comparison*, Lewiston, NY: Edwin Mellen Press, 2005
Hatten, R., *Interpreting Musical Gestures, Topics, and Tropes: Mozart, Beethoven, Schubert*, Bloomington: Indiana University Press, 1994
Heartz, D., "The Great Quartet in Mozart's *Idomeneo*," *The Music Forum* 5 (1980), pp. 233–256
Hepokoski, J., and Darcy, W., "The Medial Caesura and Its Role in the Eighteenth-Century Sonata Form Exposition," *Music Theory Spectrum* 19 (1997), pp. 115–154
 Elements of Sonata Theory: Norms, Types, and Deformations in the Late-Eighteenth-Century Sonata, Oxford University Press, 2006
Hertzmann, E., Oldman, C. B., Heartz, D., and Mann, A., eds., *Thomas Attwoods Theorie- und Kompositionsstudien bei Mozart*, Kassel: Bärenreiter, 1965 [*Wolfgang Amadeus Mozart: Neue Ausgabe sämtlicher Werke* X/30/1]
Humal, M., "Tonal Strategies in Two Slow Sonata-form Movements by Mozart (K. 279 and K. 333)," in *A Composition as a Problem V: Proceedings of the Fifth*

International Conference on Music Theory, Tallinn, September 28–30, 2006, ed. M. Humal, Tallinn: Eesti Muusika-ja Teatriakadeemia, 2008, pp. 69–85

Jan, S. B., "X Marks the Spot: Schenkerian Perspectives on the Minor-Key Classical Development Section," *Music Analysis* 11 (1992), pp. 37–53

Aspects of Mozart's Music in G Minor: Toward the Identification of Common Structural and Compositional Characteristics, New York: Garland, 1995

"The Evolution of a 'Memeplex' in Late Mozart: Replicated Structures in Pamina's 'Ach ich fühl's,'" *Journal of the Royal Musical Association* 128 (2003), pp. 330–370

The Memetics of Music: A Neo-Darwinian View of Musical Structure and Culture, Aldershot: Ashgate, 2007

Kaiser, U., *Die Notenbücher der Mozarts als Grundlage der Analyse von W. A. Mozarts Kompositionen 1761–1767*, Kassel: Bärenreiter, 2007

Kamien, R., "Aspects of Motivic Elaboration in the Opening Movement of Haydn's Piano Sonata in C♯ Minor," in *Aspects of Schenkerian Theory*, ed. D. Beach, New Haven, CT: Yale University Press, 1983, pp. 77–93

"Aspects of the Neapolitan Sixth Chord in Mozart's Music," in *Schenker Studies*, ed. H. Siegel, Cambridge University Press, 1990, pp. 94–106

Kamien, R., and Wagner, N., "Bridge Themes within a Chromaticized Voice Exchange in Mozart Expositions," *Music Theory Spectrum* 19 (1997), pp. 1–12

Kotta, K., "On the Unprepared Tonic at the Beginning of the Recapitulation in Some of Mozart's Early Piano Sonatas," in *A Composition as a Problem V: Proceedings of the Fifth International Conference on Music Theory, Tallinn, September 28–30, 2006*, ed. M. Humal, Tallinn: Eesti Muusika-ja Teatriakadeemia, 2008, pp. 57–68

Kramer, L., "Haydn's Chaos, Schenker's Order; or, Hermeneutics and Musical Analysis: Can They Mix?" *19th-Century Music* 16 (1992–1993), pp. 3–17

Larson, S., "Recapitulation Recomposition in the Sonata-Form First Movements of Haydn's String Quartets: Style Change and Compositional Technique," *Music Analysis* 22 (2003), pp. 139–177

LaRue, J., "Bifocal Tonality in Haydn Symphonies," in *Convention in Eighteenth- and Nineteenth-Century Music: Essays in Honor of Leonard G. Ratner*, ed. W. J. Allanbrook, J. Levy, and W. P. Mahrt, Stuyvesant, NY: Pendragon, 1992, pp. 59–73

Laufer, E., "Voice-Leading Procedures in Development Sections," *Studies in Music from The University of Western Ontario* 13 (1991), pp. 69–120

"Revised Sketch of Mozart, K. 545/I and Commentary," *Journal of Music Theory* 45 (2001), pp. 144–146

Lerdahl, F., "Calculating Tonal Tension," *Music Perception* 13 (1995–1996), pp. 319–363

Tonal Pitch Space, Oxford University Press, 2001

Lowe, M., *Pleasure and Meaning in the Classical Symphony*, Bloomington: Indiana University Press, 2007

McClary, S., "A Musical Dialectic from the Enlightenment: Mozart's Piano Concerto in G Major, K. 453, Movement 2," *Cultural Critique* 4 (1986), pp. 129–169

"Narratives of Bourgeois Subjectivity in Mozart's *Prague* Symphony," in *Understanding Narrative*, ed. J. Phelan and P. J. Rabinowitz, Columbus: Ohio State University Press, 1994, pp. 65–98

Meyer, L. B., "Grammatical Simplicity and Relational Richness: The Trio of Mozart's G Minor Symphony," *Critical Inquiry* 2 (1975–1976), pp. 693–761

"Commentary [on Mozart's Sonata K. 282]," *Music Perception* 13 (1995–1996), pp. 455–483

Minturn, N., "Reading Mozart's Piano Sonata in D Major (K. 311) First Movement," in *Keys to the Drama: Nine Perspectives on Sonata Form*, ed. G. Sly, Farnham: Ashgate, 2009, pp. 101–127

Mirka, D., *Metric Manipulations in Haydn and Mozart: Chamber Music for Strings, 1787–1791*, Oxford University Press, 2009

Miyake, J., "Another Recurring Pattern in Mozart's Music: Obligatory Register in Two Mozart Expositions," in *Essays from the Fourth International Schenker Symposium*, vol. 1, ed. A. Cadwallader, Hildesheim: Olms, 2008, pp. 129–143

Moreno, J., "Subjectivity, Interpretation, and Irony in Gottfried Weber's Analysis of Mozart's 'Dissonance' Quartet," *Music Theory Spectrum* 25 (2003), pp. 99–120

Narmour, E., "Analyzing Form and Measuring Perceptual Content in Mozart's Sonata K. 282: A New Theory of Parametric Analogues," *Music Perception* 13 (1995–1996), pp. 265–318

Neumann, F., "Zur harmonischen Typik des Durchführungsteiles bei Mozart und Beethoven," in *Beethoven-Almanach 1970*, Vienna: Lafite, 1970, pp. 151–155

Oster, E., "Analysis Symposium: W. A. Mozart, Menuetto in D Major for Piano (K. 355)," *Journal of Music Theory* 10 (1966), pp. 32–52; reprinted in *Readings in Schenker Analysis and Other Approaches*, ed. M. Yeston, New Haven, CT: Yale University Press, 1977, pp. 121–140.

Phipps, G. H., "A Fantasy on Modal Identity: Implications and Explications in Mozart's K. 475 through Fundamental-Bass Strategies," in *A Composition as a Problem V: Proceedings of the Fifth International Conference on Music Theory, Tallinn, September 28–30, 2006*, ed. M. Humal, Tallinn: Eesti Muusika-ja Teatriakadeemia, 2008, pp. 102–117

Polth, M., "In den Freiräumen der Schenkerschen Tonalität Harmonische Effekte durch Tonfelder in der Prager Sinfonie," *Dutch Journal of Music Theory* 11 (2006), www.djmt.nl/vol11/nr03/art01

"Singularität und strukturelle Beziehungen: Analytische Bemerkungen zu Haydns Klaviersonaten," in *Joseph Haydn (1732–1809)*, ed. S. Urmoneit, Berlin: Weidler, 2009, pp. 267–304

Rasch, R., "Circular Sequences in Mozart's Piano Sonatas," *Dutch Journal of Music Theory* 11 (2006), www.djmt.nl/vol11/nr03/art03

Ratner, L. G., *Classic Music: Expression, Form, and Style*, New York: Schirmer, 1980

Riley, M., "Hermeneutics and the New *Formenlehre*: An Interpretation of Haydn's 'Oxford' Symphony, First Movement," *Eighteenth-Century Music* 7/2 (2010), pp. 199–219

Rosen, C., *The Classical Style: Haydn, Mozart, Beethoven*, New York: Norton, 1971
  Sonata Forms, New York: Norton, 1980

Rothstein, W., *Phrase Rhythm in Tonal Music*, New York: Schirmer, 1989

Salzer, F., *Structural Hearing: Tonal Coherence in Music*, 2 vols., New York: Boni, 1952; reprint edn., New York: Dover, 1962
  "Haydn's Fantasia from the String Quartet, Opus 76, No. 6," *The Music Forum* 4 (1976), pp. 161–194
  "The Variation Movement of Mozart's Divertimento K. 563," *The Music Forum* 5 (1980), pp. 257–315

Schachter, C., "The Adventures of an F♯: Tonal Narration and Exhortation in Donna Anna's First-Act Recitative and Aria," *Theory and Practice* 16 (1991), pp. 5–20; reprinted in Schachter, C., *Unfoldings: Essays in Schenkerian Theory and Analysis*, ed. J. N. Straus, Oxford University Press, 1999, pp. 221–235
  "Mozart's Last and Beethoven's First: Echoes of K. 551 in the First Movement of Opus 21," in *Mozart Studies*, ed. C. Eisen, Oxford University Press, 1991, pp. 227–251
  "Idiosyncratic Features of Three Mozart Slow Movements: The Piano Concertos K. 449, K. 453, and K. 467," in *Mozart's Piano Concertos: Text, Context, Interpretation*, ed. N. Zaslaw, Ann Arbor: University of Michigan Press, 1996, pp. 315–333
  "Deception, Disguise, and Mistaken Identity in the Finale of Mozart's *Prague* Symphony," in *A Composition as a Problem III: Proceedings of the 3rd International Conference on Music Theory, Tallinn, March 9–10, 2001*, ed. M. Humal, Tallinn: Eesti Muusikaakadeemia and Scripta Musicalia, 2003, pp. 5–14.
  "*Che Inganno!* The Analysis of Deceptive Cadences," in *Essays from the Third International Schenker Symposium*, ed. A. Cadwallader, Hildesheim: Olms, 2006, pp. 279–298
  "E Pluribus Unum: Large-Scale Connections in the Opening Scenes of *Don Giovanni*," in *Essays from the Fourth International Schenker Symposium*, vol. 1, ed. A. Cadwallader, Hildesheim: Olms, 2008, pp. 3–22

Schenker, H., *Harmonielehre: Neue musikalische Theorien und Phantasien I*, Stuttgart: Cotta, 1906; as *Harmony*, ed. O. Jonas, abridged trans. E. M. Borgese, University of Chicago Press, 1954
  Der Tonwille: Flugblätter zum Zeugnis unwandelbarer Gesetze der Tonkunst, einer neuen Jugend dargebracht, 2 vols., Vienna: A. J. Gutmann, Leipzig: F. Hofmeister, 1921–1924; as *Der Tonwille: Pamphlets in Witness of the Immutable Laws of Music, Offered to a New Generation of Youth*, ed. W. Drabkin, trans. I. Bent *et al.*, Oxford University Press, 2004–2005

Das Meisterwerk in der Musik: Ein Jahrbuch, 3 vols., Munich: Drei Masken, 1925, 1926, 1930; as *The Masterwork in Music*, ed. W. Drabkin, trans. I. Bent et al., 3 vols., Cambridge University Press, 1994–1997

Der freie Satz: Neue musikalische Theorien und Phantasien III, Vienna: Universal, 1935; rev. edn., ed. O. Jonas, Vienna: Universal, 1956; as *Free Composition*, trans. and ed. E. Oster, New York: Longman, 1979; reprint trans. Stuyvesant, NY: Pendragon, 2001

Five Graphic Music Analyses, New York: Dover, 1969

The Art of Performance, ed. H. Esser, trans. I. S. Scott, Oxford University Press, 2000

Schmalfeldt, J., "Cadential Processes: The Evaded Cadence and the 'One More Time' Technique," *Journal of Musicological Research* 12 (1992), pp. 1–52

Sly, G., "Schubert's Innovations in Sonata Form: Compositional Logic and Structural Interpretation" (including an appendix by E. Laufer, "Revised Sketch of Mozart, K. 545/I and Commentary"), *Journal of Music Theory* 45 (2001), pp. 119–150

Smith, C. J., "The Functional Extravagance of Chromatic Chords," *Music Theory Spectrum* 8 (1986), pp. 94–139; response by D. Beach and reply by C. Smith in *Music Theory Spectrum* 9 (1987), pp. 173–194

"The Love of Fundamentals Is the Root of All Evil: Alternatives to Harmonic Fundamentalism," in *A Composition as a Problem V: Proceedings of the Fifth International Conference on Music Theory, Tallinn, September 28–30, 2006*, ed. M. Humal, Tallinn: Eesti Muusika-ja Teatriakadeemia, 2008, pp. 5–24

Smith, P. H., "Structural Tonic or Apparent Tonic? Parametric Conflict, Temporal Perspective, and a Continuum of Articulative Possibilities," *Journal of Music Theory* 39 (1995), pp. 245–283

Snyder, J. L., "Schenker and the First Movement of Mozart's Sonata, K. 545: An Uninterrupted Sonata-Form Movement?" *Theory and Practice* 16 (1991), pp. 51–78

Somfai, L., *The Keyboard Sonatas of Joseph Haydn: Instruments and Performance Practice, Genres, and Styles*, trans. C. Greenspan and L. Somfai, University of Chicago Press, 1995

Spitzer, M., "The Retransition as Sign: Listener-Orientated Approaches to Tonal Closure in Haydn's Sonata-Form Movements," *Journal of the Royal Musical Association* 121 (1996), pp. 11–45

"Haydn's Reversals: Style Change, Gesture and the Implication-Realization Model," in *Haydn Studies*, ed. W. D. Sutcliffe, Cambridge University Press, 1998, pp. 177–217

Metaphor and Musical Thought, University of Chicago Press, 2004

"A Metaphoric Model of Sonata Form: Two Expositions by Mozart," in *Communication in Eighteenth-Century Music*, ed. D. Mirka and K. Agawu, Cambridge University Press, 2008, pp. 189–229

Steblin, R., *A History of Key Characteristics in the Eighteenth and Early Nineteenth Centuries*, 2nd edn., University of Rochester Press, 2002

Stern, D., "Mozart's Adagio in B minor, KV 540," *Journal of Schenkerian Studies* 1 (2005), pp. 149–168

Stoffels, L., *Drama und Abschied: Mozart – die Musik der Wiener Jahre*, Zurich: Atlantis, 1998

Suurpää, L., "Continuous Exposition and Tonal Structure in Three Late Haydn Works," *Music Theory Spectrum* 21 (1999), pp. 174–199

"The First-Movement Exposition of Mozart's 'Prague' Symphony: Cadences, Form, and Voice-Leading Structure," *Dutch Journal of Music Theory* 11 (2006), www.djmt.nl/vol11/nr03/art02

"Form, Structure, and Musical Drama in Two Mozart Expositions," *Journal of Music Theory* 50 (2006), pp. 181–210

"Expression, Form and Voice-Leading Structure in Mozart's B-minor *Adagio*, K. 540," in *A Composition as a Problem V: Proceedings of the Fifth International Conference on Music Theory, Tallinn, September 28-30, 2006*, ed. M. Humal, Tallinn: Eesti Muusika-ja Teatriakadeemia, 2008, pp. 86–101

Webster, J., "The D-Major Interlude in the First Movement of Haydn's 'Farewell' Symphony," in *Studies in Musical Sources and Style: Essays in Honor of Jan LaRue*, ed. E. K. Wolf and E. H. Roesner, Madison, WI: A-R Editions, 1990, pp. 339–380

"The Analysis of Mozart's Arias," in *Mozart Studies*, ed. C. Eisen, Oxford University Press, 1991, pp. 101–199

Haydn's "Farewell" Symphony and the Idea of Classical Style: Through-Composition and Cyclic Integration in His Instrumental Music, Cambridge University Press, 1991

Wen, E., "A Disguised Reminiscence in the First Movement of Mozart's G Minor Symphony," *Music Analysis* 1 (1982), pp. 55–71

"The Andante from Mozart's Symphony No. 40, K. 550: The Opening Theme and Its Consequences," in *Structure and Meaning in Tonal Music: Festschrift in Honor of Carl Schachter*, ed. L. P. Burstein and D. Gagné, Hillsdale, NY: Pendragon, 2006, pp. 247–258

Wheelock, G. A., *Haydn's Ingenious Jesting with Art: Contexts of Musical Wit and Humor*, New York: Schirmer, 1992

Willner, C., "Chromaticism and the Mediant in Four Late Haydn Works," *Theory and Practice* 13 (1988), pp. 79–114

Winter, R. S., "The Bifocal Close and the Evolution of the Viennese Classical Style," *Journal of the American Musicological Society* 42 (1989), pp. 275–337

Zimpel, C., *Der kadenzielle Prozeß in den Durchführungen. Untersuchung der Kopfsätze von Joseph Haydns Streichquartetten*, Hildesheim: Olms, 2010.

Index of Haydn's works

Piano Concerto in D Major (H. XVIII: 11), 121–130, 262

Piano Sonata in A Major (H. XVI: 30), 49–50, 58–60, 78, 88

Piano Sonata in A♭ Major (H. XVI: 46), 53–55, 67, 76–77, 88

Piano Sonata in C Major (H. XVI: 35), 51–52, 66–67, 68–70, 88

Piano Sonata in D Major (H. XVI: 51), 50, 63, 76, 88

Piano Sonata in E Major (H. XVI: 31), 50–51, 61, 72–74, 88

Piano Sonata in E♭ Major (H. XVI: 25), 49, 60, 70–72, 88

Piano Sonata in E♭ Major (H. XVI: 28), 55–56, 65–66, 74–75, 88

Piano Sonata in E♭ Major (H. XVI: 45), 44–48, 66, 78–80, 87–88

Piano Sonata in E♭ Major (H. XVI: 49), 55, 61–62, 80–83, 88

Piano Sonata in E♭ Major (H. XVI: 52), 52–53, 62–63, 84–87, 88

Piano Sonata in F Major (H. XVI: 23), 48, 64–65, 83, 88

Piano Sonata in F Major (H. XVI: 29), 43–44, 63–64, 75–76, 88

String Quartet in A Major (op. 55, no. 1), 16–19, 185

String Quartet in B Minor (op. 33, no. 1), 27–30

String Quartet in D Major (op. 50, no. 6), 266

String Quartet in D Major (op. 71, no. 2), 35–38

String Quartet in D Major (op. 76, no. 5), 3–8, 249

String Quartet in D Minor (op. 42), 8–13

String Quartet in E♭ Major (op. 71, no. 3), 33–35

String Quartet in F Minor (op. 55, no. 2), 30–33

String Quartet in G Major (op. 54, no. 1), 38–40

String Quartet in G Minor (op. 20, no. 3), 166–182

Symphony No. 45 in F♯ Minor ("Farewell"), 153–165

Symphony No. 82 in C Major ("The Bear"), 247

Symphony No. 96 in D Major ("Miracle"), 232–246

Index of Mozart's works

Don Giovanni (K. 527), 205–220

Entführung aus dem Serail, Die (K. 384), 110–114

finta giardiniera, La (K. 196), 95–99

Idomeneo (K. 366), 105–110

Mitridate, re di Ponto (K. 87/74a), 89–95

Piano Concerto in D Major (K. 451), 130–140

Piano Concerto in D Major (K. 537), 140–150
Piano Sonata in C Major (K. 545), 273, 278

String Quartet in D Minor (K. 421), 13–16, 19–22
String Quartet in E♭ Major (K. 428), 22–27
String Quintet in C Major (K. 515), 183–204, 278
Symphony in G Minor (K. 550), 221–231

Zaide (K. 344/336b), 99–104
Zauberflöte, Die (K. 620), 115–119

Index of names and concepts

Agawu, V. K., 183, 186–188, 190–191, 193–194, 195–196, 199, 203–204, 253
Allanbrook, W. J., 253
antipode, 38, 40, 273
applied dominant, 6, 164, 175, 255, 273
Asioli, B., 267
assertion, 4, 6, 8, 11, 12, 13, 15, 16, 19, 22, 27, 32, 37, 73, 83, 93, 97, 100, 104, 141, 159, 164, 166, 185, 196, 197, 208, 223, 227, 241, 243, 250, 251, 254, 256, 259, 260, 265, 270, 271, 274, 276
augmented sixth chords, 19, 21, 102, 103, 158, 199, 209, 243, 255
auxiliary cadence, 280
auxiliary progression, 127

Barrett-Ayres, R., 250
Burnett, H., 269
Burstein, L. P., 262

caesura-fill, 278, 279
Caplin, W. E., 255
Chopin, F., 280
chordal evolution, 4, 5, 6, 7, 15, 19, 26, 30, 32, 35, 40, 57, 62, 64, 67, 71, 72, 73, 78, 82, 83, 92, 94, 103, 104, 106, 113, 125, 129, 144, 148, 158, 161, 164, 172, 175, 183, 186, 197, 209, 214, 216, 220, 233, 238, 255, 257, 259, 260, 261, 264, 266, 268, 271, 273, 274, 276, 277
circle of fifths, 38, 40, 102, 103, 106, 108, 109, 111, 127, 132, 135, 138, 145, 147, 148, 161, 162, 163, 187, 191, 197, 199, 202, 217, 262, 266, 276
circle of thirds, 27, 125, 208, 210, 237, 273
closing zone, 41, 68, 87–88, 123, 133, 135, 145, 160, 194–196, 237–241, 245, 256
coda half-rotation, 128–130, 150
coda rotation, 138–140
Cohn, R. L., 268
collision, 22, 162, 185, 186, 197, 207, 244, 270
common-tone diminished seventh chord, 24, 213, 264

continuous exposition, 232, 236
Cooke, D., 247
counterpoint, 3, 12, 171, 247, 267
Cutler, T., 260

Dahlhaus, C., 182
Darcy. *See* Hepokoski
developmental rotation, 123–128, 135–138
dissonance
  essential and incidental, 78, 257, 271
dominant emulation, 4, 7, 11, 15, 33, 38, 40, 41, 48, 56, 68, 77, 81, 82, 85, 87, 90, 92, 93, 94, 96, 102, 106, 125, 135, 136, 139, 147, 149, 158, 162, 164, 172, 175, 178, 179, 185, 187, 188, 197, 198, 209, 212, 214, 224, 226, 228, 233, 258, 259, 260, 261, 262, 270, 273, 276, 280
dominant-lock, 278
Drabkin, W., 268

elision, 32, 40, 62, 63, 67, 75, 77, 92, 104, 135, 137, 144, 158, 186, 197, 219, 254, 263, 270, 274, 276
embellishing chord, 8, 11, 24, 35, 37, 48, 54, 60, 62, 66, 82, 92, 109, 116, 118, 135, 213, 217, 219, 248, 249, 250, 252, 253, 254, 256, 257, 264
enharmonic equivalence, 114, 147, 197, 200, 210, 211, 213, 219, 250, 251, 264, 266
Enselein, T., 250
equal subdivisions of the octave, 38, 208
essential expositional closure, 41, 68, 70, 77, 78, 83, 87, 123, 133, 135, 144, 145, 158, 175, 192, 239, 255, 279
essential structural closure, 128, 130, 139, 150, 163, 204, 245, 261
expositional rotation, 121–123, 130–135, 140–145, 263

Fétis, F.-J., 271
Fuß, H.-U., 254

Index of names and concepts

Galand, J., 263
Gjerdingen, R. O., 166–168, 171, 173, 175–176, 180–182, 251, 267, 277
Guck, M. A., 253

Heartz, D., 266
Hepokoski, J., 41, 58, 120, 147, 168, 175, 176, 180, 208, 232, 234, 236–237, 240–241, 246, 249, 255, 261, 262, 263, 267
humor, 64, 78, 241, 280

interruption, 7, 11, 41, 68, 71, 72, 83, 90, 99, 108, 140, 141, 144, 145, 154, 183, 186, 192, 216, 217, 219, 226, 238, 261, 275

Jan, S., 257, 258, 260

Kamien, R., 254
Kirnberger, J. P., 180, 257, 269, 271

Laufer, E., 280
linear progression, 41, 53, 89, 102, 145, 174, 193
Lobe, J. C., 248, 250
Louis, R., 259
lower-third chord, 35, 264

medial caesura, 41, 58, 80, 106, 111, 122, 128, 131, 132, 133, 138, 139, 144, 147, 155, 172, 175, 176, 180, 190, 191, 206, 208, 210, 232, 234, 236, 240, 244, 246, 263, 278
Meyer, L. B., 221, 223, 225–226, 228, 231, 276
Mirka, D., 270
modal mixture, 37, 62, 102, 125, 144, 178, 185, 186, 198, 217, 233
modulo 7 vs. modulo 12, 38, 40, 208, 250, 273
Mozart, L., 167
musical topics, 183

Nitzberg, R., 269

obligatory register, 8
ordre pluritonique, 271

parallel fifths, 35, 218, 219, 274
parallel octaves, 195, 250
parallel progression, 13, 70, 141, 233, 248
parenthetical passage, 239, 246
partimenti, 166, 268
peculiar juxtaposition, 122, 133, 261, 268, 276
Piston, W., 221
primary-theme zone, 41, 43–58, 120, 121–122, 130–131, 140–141, 153–154, 167–171, 183–188, 234–237

reaching-over, 78, 133, 145, 183, 217, 221, 233
recapitulatory rotation, 125, 128–130, 138–140, 145–150, 261, 263
registral shift, 12, 16, 19, 44, 50, 53, 56, 59, 63, 96, 143, 155, 157, 158, 160, 164, 170, 174, 176, 186, 192, 226, 229, 230, 252, 256, 275, 276
Richter, E. F., 250
Rosen, C., 249, 259
Rothstein, W., 253, 259

Salzer, F., 261
Schachter, C., 205, 207–209, 210–211, 213–214, 216–217, 218, 219–220, 252
Schenker, H., 167, 205, 224, 247, 250, 253, 254, 255, 259, 264, 271, 273, 276–278
Schubert, F., 249, 252, 269, 270, 272, 273
Sechter, S., 278
secondary-theme zone, 41, 58, 67–87-, 123, 133–135, 144–145, 156–160, 173–176, 191–194, 237–241
seismic composition, 40, 206, 208, 211, 251, 272
sequence, 19, 21, 25, 40, 48, 71, 93, 97, 99, 100, 103, 105, 106, 116, 124, 125, 128, 129, 133, 136, 145, 162, 191, 197, 202, 212, 227, 228, 241, 243, 248, 251, 258, 260, 262, 263, 264, 271, 274, 276, 280
Smith, P. H., 280
solfeggi, 166
sonata-rondo. *See* Type 4 sonata
Spitzer, M., 183, 186–188, 194, 195–196
Steblin, R., 258
substitution, 29, 113, 185, 235
surge, 7, 11, 16, 32, 37, 73, 92, 103, 129, 135, 136, 138, 139, 143, 145, 147, 148, 158, 175, 178, 179, 188, 190, 197, 249, 253, 255, 256
Suurpää, L., 232, 234, 236–237, 240–241, 246

Thuille, L., 259
tonal resolution, 176, 180
tonicization, 62, 68, 93, 94, 96, 98, 99, 102, 105, 106, 111, 116, 121, 125, 126, 127, 135, 136, 144, 161, 173, 174, 176, 178, 180, 186, 187, 205, 206, 211, 212, 213, 224, 225, 236, 240, 241, 243, 244, 251, 254, 259, 263, 272, 275, 277
transition, 41, 58–67, 122, 131–133, 141–144, 155–156, 170–173, 187–191, 202, 208, 234–237, 261, 263
Trydell, J., 267
Type 1 sonata, 120, 147
Type 2 sonata, 168, 176, 180, 267

Type 3 sonata, 120, 123, 135, 140, 176
Type 4 sonata, 120, 123, 140, 261
Type 4^1 sonata, 120
Type $4^{1\text{-exp}}$ sonata, 147
Type 5 sonata, 263

unfolding, 3, 22, 24, 30, 32, 46, 79, 85, 96, 99, 100, 116, 119, 141, 168, 171, 174, 185, 192, 214, 218, 250, 251, 255, 262, 263, 267, 271, 274
unfurling, 8, 13, 21, 22, 24, 57, 61, 73, 78, 79, 97, 100, 104, 106, 111, 124, 125, 130, 135, 138, 159, 166, 179, 196, 203, 223, 227, 234, 243, 258, 259, 264, 274, 276
upper-fifth chord, 141, 227, 228, 241, 276
upper-third chord, 29, 35, 37, 92, 103, 106, 125, 126, 127, 136, 148, 190, 217, 224, 229, 239, 249, 250, 260, 275

voice exchange, 4, 19, 32, 44, 83, 87, 92, 100, 129, 131, 164, 170, 217, 237, 263, 266, 268

Wagner, N., 254
Webster, J., 153–154, 156, 159–160, 163, 164–165, 265, 266, 268
Wheelock, G. A., 249
wobbly note, 30, 32, 102, 109, 111, 116, 119, 125, 148, 149, 186, 239, 241, 243, 264, 278, 280

5–6 shift, 4, 5, 13, 21, 22, 32, 37, 38, 41, 46, 67, 127, 147, 158, 179, 246, 251, 252, 259, 260
I:HC MC, 122, 128, 132, 206, 208, 236, 244, 278, 279
V:HC MC, 122, 133, 208, 236, 244, 255
♭II, 15, 30, 32, 126, 187, 211, 248, 259, 261, 264, 278